The look of Catholics : portrayals in popular

The Look of Catholics

Portrayals in Popular Culture from the Great Depression to the Cold War

ANTHONY BURKE SMITH

UNIVERSITY PRESS OF KANSAS

Published by the University Press of Kansas (Lawrence, Kansas 66045), which was organized by the Kansas Board of Regents and is operated and funded by Emporia State University, Fort Hays State University, Kansas State University, Pittsburg State University, the University of Kansas, and Wichita State University

Portions of the Introduction and Chapter 3 were previously published in Anthony Burke Smith, "America's Favorite Priest: *Going My Way* (1944)," in *Catholics in the Movies*, ed. Colleen McDannell (New York: Oxford University Press, 2007), 107–126.

Smith, Anthony Burke.
The look of Catholics : portrayals in popular culture from the Great Depression to the Cold War / Anthony Burke Smith.
    p.   cm. — (CultureAmerica)
Includes bibliographical references and index.
ISBN 978-0-7006-1716-6 (cloth : alk. paper)
    1. Catholics—United States—History—20th century.
2. Popular culture—United States—History—20th century. 3. Mass media—Social aspects—United States—History—20th century. 4. Catholics in motion pictures—History—20th century.
5. Nationalism—United States—History—20th century. 6. Community life—United States—History—20th century. 7. United States—Social conditions—1933–1945. 8. United States—Social conditions—1945–1989. 9. Cultural pluralism—United States—History—20th century. 10. United States—Ethnic relations—History—20th century. I. Title.
E184.C3S65 2010
282.092—dc22   2010005705

British Library Cataloguing-in-Publication Data is available.

Printed in the United States of America
10 9 8 7 6 5 4 3 2 1

To my parents,
Marie Burke Smith and Eugene J. Smith

CONTENTS

ACKNOWLEDGMENTS

This book began a long time ago and was sustained by the patience, support, and enthusiasm of numerous people, too many to acknowledge fully here. However, I would like to give special recognition to several colleagues and mentors. In the American Studies Department of the University of Minnesota, David W. Noble, Lary May, and George Lipsitz introduced me to many of the key concepts and ideas that inform this book. I am especially grateful to David; I sense I am still only beginning to absorb all he taught me about American culture.

At the University of Dayton (UD), I could not have asked for a more receptive and supportive community of scholars and colleagues. Una Cadegan's persistence in clearing a space for serious intellectual work on Catholicism was essential for allowing me to pursue ideas and test arguments. Susan Trollinger shared her understanding of visual rhetoric with me at a crucial moment in the writing of this book, opening new insights into my subjects. Cecilia Moore has always been a fellow traveler in pursuing a different path for studying Catholics. William V. Trollinger provided enormous help in encouraging my inclinations and was a great conversational partner who kept me in mind of the bigger picture of twentieth-century American history as I focused on the history of Catholics within it. His excitement and smart advice about my project has been invaluable in seeing it through to completion. William Portier and Sandra Yocum were with me and this project even before I arrived at UD. Their encouragement and confidence in my work has been unflagging and has carried me through many moments of doubt. Their friendship has proven to be far more than mere "temporary bouts of joy."

Grants from the University of Dayton, both from the Graduate School and the Forum on the Catholic Intellectual Tradition Today, gave me the opportunity to conduct lengthy research into archives in Los Angeles and Washington, D.C. Many graduate assistants in the Department of Religious Studies at UD helped enormously in tracking down material in libraries; they include Damian Costello, Scott McDaniel, Justin Menno, Sue Sack, and Adam Sheridan.

Many other scholars and friends also provided enormous help. Christopher J. Kauffman, Margaret McGuinness, and Elizabeth McKeown all encouraged my thinking and writing at various stages of this project. I began conversations with Timothy J. Meagher about Irish Catholics and American politics immediately after graduate school and have never ceased to benefit from his insights and knowledge. Ever since I met David J. O'Brien, his generosity and support have been unfailing—I could not have asked for a better champion of my project. Colleen McDannell and the group of wildly talented scholars involved with the "Catholics in the Movies" project, particularly Judith Weisenfeld, Paula M. Kane, Tim Meagher, Darryl V. Caterine and Tom Ferraro, provided a wonderful and intensely stimulating weekend at the University of Notre Dame that benefited not only my thinking on Bing Crosby but also my whole project.

One person in particular—James T. Fisher—has been both an enthusiastic supporter and an exemplary scholar in American Catholic studies, and this book would not have been realized without his unflagging interest. Jim's superb, courageous work challenging boundaries, mixing up categories, and pursuing the hard questions has helped make my own efforts possible. His friendship and wise insights into Catholics, popular culture, and American studies have kept me going.

Father James Heft, SM, in good Marianist fashion offered generous hospitality for a lengthy stay in Los Angeles while I pursued research. Carrie Krasnow and Peter Canning cannot possibly realize how valuable the evenings spent sharing details of my research while drinking wine on their back patio in the hills of LA proved. Their willingness to put me up for two long trips to Southern California is a testimony to their deep friendship.

Good archivists, I am convinced, are secular saints—at least the ones with whom I had the luck to work. Above all, Barbara Hall at the Margaret Herrick Library at the Academy of Motion Picture Arts and Sciences was unstinting in her help during numerous research trips. Zoran Sinobad at the Library of Congress helped me navigate the library's rich collections. Joann Meyer at the Douglas County Historical Society, Omaha, Nebraska, responded wonderfully to my inquiries about press coverage of *Boys Town* in Omaha.

My editors at the University Press of Kansas, Nancy Scott Jackson, Kalyani Fernando, and Ranjit Arab, have been enormously patient and never gave up on this project, for which I am intensely grateful, and thanks, too, to Jennifer Dropkin for book production. In the final stages of copyediting, Joan Sherman provided wonderful assistance and understanding.

Finally, I cannot begin to thank my family adequately. My brother Mark has listened to me for so many years talk about Catholics, movies, and politics that I am sure he knows my book better than I do. His support has been expressed in every conceivable manner: as good ear, sounding board, probing questioner, smart counselor, and—not the least—financial assistant many years ago. My two sons, Colman and Noah, who have grown up watching old movies, have been more patient with me than any father has a right to expect. Their presence in my life has kept everything else in perspective, and I have learned the most valuable lessons from them. This project also could not have happened without my wife Maureen, who has had to bear the burden of the ups and downs of this entire journey for a long time. Her keen eye as a reader, her willingness to hear me work out ideas, and her unequivocal insistence on the value of this book are but the beginning of her contribution. More important has been her utter confidence and love, which has made all this work worthwhile. Finally, I want to thank the two people who always encouraged me to follow where my questions and enthusiasm led me—my mother, Marie Burke Smith, and my father, Eugene J. Smith. Their love, generosity, and fierce commitment to learning have taught me what really matters about Catholics in America.

PRIESTS, GANGSTERS, AND COWBOYS: CATHOLIC OUTSIDERS, AMERICAN INSIDERS, AND THE CONTEST OVER NATIONAL COMMUNITY

In 1946, a Michigan woman wrote to Eric Johnston, head of the Motion Picture Producers' Association, to complain about the spate of Catholic movies that Hollywood had recently released. "How much longer do we have to tolerate Catholic pictures? As much as we like to hear Bing Crosby, I, and many others have resolved *not* to see any more of his pictures—until he adopts a different theme. After all America is still a Protestant country, and the majority prefer non sectarian stories."[1]

Though clearly hostile to Catholicism, the woman had a point. Popular culture seemed to have gone Catholic crazy at midcentury. Not only the Bing Crosby hit about a New York City parish priest, *Going My Way* (1944), but also a whole host of other very successful films of the late 1930s and 1940s, including *Boys Town* (1938), *Angels with Dirty Faces* (1938), *The Fighting 69th* (1940), and *The Song of Bernadette* (1943), indicated a movie infatuation with Roman Catholicism.[2] Hollywood's star treatment of Catholics, however, proved only the tip of a cultural iceberg that constituted a veritable Catholization of the American imagination in the middle years of the twentieth century. Both on screen and behind the camera, Catholics had become major players. Ethnic Catholic film directors such as John Ford, Leo McCarey, and Frank Capra were responsible for some of the most popular and influential movies of the thirties and forties, including *Stagecoach* (1939), *The Grapes of Wrath* (1940), *The Awful Truth* (1937), and *It Happened One Night* (1934). Taken together, the representations of Catholics in motion pictures and films by Catholic directors constituted a remarkable moment in the Catholic ascendancy in modern American culture.[3]

Beyond movies, Catholicism enjoyed extensive treatment in photojournalism and television. *Life* magazine, the most spectacular jewel in Henry R. Luce's media empire, kept a steady bead on Catholics from its first issue in 1936 through the postwar years. In the process, Luce and *Life* turned Catholicism into a subject celebrating the American good life at home and global power abroad.[4] In the midfifties, Americans could also tune in to the prime-time television show *Life Is Worth Living* and catch the dramatic performances of Bishop Fulton J. Sheen, who presented himself as a moral guide for all Americans as they wrestled with the dilemmas of postwar life.[5]

This book examines the cultural work of Catholic images in a period of intense social and political change. I argue that representations of and by Catholics manifested the cultural struggle over national definition waged between the New Deal Americanism of the 1930s and the American Century of the postwar era. Catholic communalism and moral traditionalism proved enormously productive subjects within the mass media through which to imagine new conceptions of national community between the Depression and early Cold War. Catholics in popular culture were, in fact, always about more than Catholicism. The highly Americanized renderings of Catholics did more than simply turn Catholics into good citizens; they also provided a cultural space in which to elaborate new understandings of an American community that included Catholics. The range and duration of Catholic imagery in these decades demonstrated the extent to which Catholicism provided a "visual terrain" upon which competing understandings of a pluralist nation could be developed.[6]

By encouraging viewers to look at Catholics, Catholic representations directed Americans to imagine their society in particular ways. During the 1930s, representations of and by Catholics helped elaborate a new reformist, communitarian Americanism, articulating aspirations for social transformation in terms of the experiences of ethnic, religious minorities. The "foreign" character of Catholic communalism assumed new legitimacy in a popular culture privileging collective solutions to economic collapse. Americanizing Catholicism in the context of the Depression, Hollywood generated popular images of mutuality and interdependence.

But beginning in the 1940s and continuing into the postwar period, Catholic communalism within the mass media assumed dramatically different meanings. Ethnic, religious difference directed pluralism toward conservative social ends. The visually compelling, ritualistic character of Roman Catholicism provided a popular vehicle for developing consensual renditions of community. Rather than highlighting the conflict between the common good of an ethnically diverse people and the private interests of elites, Catholic representations of community served to legitimate a social order characterized by culturally attuned, practical leaders and traditional institutions of religion, home, and military capable of addressing the challenges of modern life. Tracing the changes in the popular image of Catholics over a thirty-year period allows us to understand not simply the Americanization of Catholicism but, even more, the dramatic cultural transformations in national community as the American Century triumphed over the reformist hopes of New Deal society after World War II.

The changing character of popular representations of and by Catholics therefore demonstrates the fierce contest over Americanism between the 1930s and 1950s that cultural historians have argued produced the Cold War consensus. Indeed, the work of Lary May, Michael Denning, Wendy Wall, and Lizbeth Cohen provides useful context for explaining why Catholics became so prevalent in the popular culture beginning in the 1930s.[7] Though by no means identical in their accounts of cultural change, these scholars collectively show that popular culture assumed a deeply political role in thirties America, providing a means by which ethnic and class identities transformed the definition of national community. They reveal that this new Americanism reflected the experiences and aspirations of its working-class, ethnic, and immigrant creators and audiences that challenged the traditional cultural order of the nation. Far from offering simple escapism from the Depression, therefore, popular culture in the thirties had appeal precisely because it represented a modern America that looked and sounded more like what audiences knew from their experiences than that of Anglo-American culture. Within this era of cultural and political ferment, Hollywood played a particularly crucial role. As May has argued, movies enjoyed their enormous popularity during the thirties because they fostered a new "multicultural republic" that combined an inclusive pluralism with demands for economic democracy.[8]

But World War II dramatically undermined the reformist voices of the Depression era within popular culture. The demands for national unity curtailed critiques of America's inequities and the expression of alternative values. Hollywood was at the center of these changes. As May has shown, movies helped Americans accept diminished social expectations through stories that offered conversion narratives in which heroes abandoned their earlier progressive commitments and embraced traditional institutions.[9] Citizenship in this new cultural context of consensus became equated with accepting existing conditions in the United States rather than advocating social change.

The Cold War consolidated this conservative redirection of Americanism. The public realm became identified as a dangerous sphere in need of ordering by authority figures. Movies, television, and popular magazines encouraged Americans to look instead to the private realm of material abundance, homes, and entertainment to satisfy their social aspirations and needs.[10] Within this postwar social order, ethnic outsiders played an important role. Once perceived as "foreigners," they now served as signs of this new American consensus so long as they left behind values and commitments that disrupted the imperatives of cultural unity.

This history of political conflict over Americanism in popular culture accounts for the pervasive role of Catholics in mass media beginning in the 1930s. As the religion of ethnic outsiders and working-class peoples as well as a faith that emphasized communal bonds over individual rights, Catholicism provided a popular subject through which new understandings of the nation could be imagined in an era of capitalist crisis. *The Look of Catholics: Portrayals in Popular Culture from the Great Depression to the Cold War* thus complements and extends work by historians on the role of popular culture in the struggle over modern American identity. This scholarship has illuminated the mass media as an arena for class, ethnic, and ideological conflict, yet considerations of religion have been remarkably lacking. But precisely because mass culture was a terrain of political conflict, the widespread presence of Catholics in popular culture deserves scrutiny. How did American images of Catholics as well as Catholic images of America relate to wider struggles involving class, ethnicity, social justice, and the nation that popular culture addressed? What cultural work did popular representations of Catholics do in the formation of Catholics and, more important, of American community and identity in a period of shifting boundaries between social mainstream and margin and between the United States and the world?

To understand why Catholic outsiders became so central to the cultural transformation in popular values beginning in the thirties, we need to recognize the pivotal role of anti-Catholicism in the long cultural history of American nationalism. Lyman Beecher, the nineteenth-century Protestant minister and father of the influential Beecher clan, including Harriet Beecher Stowe, provided a particularly useful expression of the imagined community of the Anglo-Protestant American nation.[11] In 1835, he wrote *A Plea for the West*, a text that demonstrated the mutual constitution of

American frontier democracy and anti-Catholicism within nineteenth-century nationalist discourse. The book was based on talks Beecher gave while in the East to raise funds for his school, the Lane Seminary in Cincinnati, Ohio. In fact, while in Boston, Beecher delivered an address condemning Catholicism a day before an infamous attack on an Ursuline convent by angry mobs in neighboring Charlestown.[12]

In *A Plea for the West,* Beecher proclaimed that the "conflict which is to decide the destiny of the West will be a conflict of institutions for the education of her sons, for purposes of superstition, or evangelical light, of despotism or liberty."[13] By emphasizing the West as the religious and redemptive locus of American identity, Beecher elaborated a dualism that characterized Anglo-American culture for the next century—tyranny versus freedom, hierarchy versus democracy, and, particularly important, the enclosed, restrictive structures of Old World Catholicism versus the new productive spaces of the American frontier.[14]

This trope of American openness and Catholic restraint informed the phenomenally successful anti-Catholic fantasy written by Maria Monk in 1836, which purportedly recounted the true-life horrors of a young woman who had escaped the confines of a Catholic convent where she had observed and been forced to participate in unspeakable degradation perpetuated by priests and nuns. *The Awful Disclosures* of Maria Monk demonstrated that American anxieties about Catholicism often found expression in depictions of Catholic space. Fears of Catholic power assumed cultural potency through spatial and architectural motifs. Catholic institutions such as convents and monasteries embodied physical entrapment and social stasis, and priests signified corporate tyranny that controlled medieval landscapes of submission and confinement.[15]

The cultural antithesis of American freedom and Catholic constraint that structured the nationalist imaginary persisted throughout the nineteenth and early twentieth centuries, as evidenced by repeated anti-Catholicism in the populist and progressive eras. In the late nineteenth century, the prominent reformer and nativist Josiah Strong made emphatically clear in his *Our Country: Its Possible Future and Its Present Crisis* (1885) that the true American nation had no room for Roman Catholics. The New Era of Calvin Coolidge and Warren Harding during the 1920s witnessed a flourishing of a very old Protestant nationalism, which resulted in celebrations of free markets, anti-immigration legislation directed largely at southern and eastern European Catholics and Jews, and the teetotaling morals crusade of Prohibition.[16] The defeat of Al Smith, the Irish

American Catholic who ran as the Democratic candidate for president in 1928, capped a decade of intense efforts to keep Catholics out of the sacred landscape of the Anglo-Protestant American nation.

But the Depression inaugurated a cultural crisis that challenged this symbolic configuration of the national imagination. The economic collapse discredited unregulated, individualistic capitalism as a threat to the public good. In its place, communal values, commitments, and aspirations now assumed new centrality. Taking widely disparate, even conflicting forms, cooperative beliefs nevertheless focused the social and political discourse of the nation.[17] The American people's search for alternatives to laissez-faire capitalism therefore opened new space for communal alternatives such as those offered by Catholicism.

Indeed, during the early 1930s, anti-Catholicism in America receded as the nation's turn to collective solutions gave the traditional Catholic emphasis on the common good over individual interests a new credibility. The Depression actually witnessed a flourishing of social Catholicism. The radio priest Father Charles Coughlin was perhaps the most famous example, but others such as John A. Ryan, Charles Owens Rice of Pittsburgh, and Bernard Sheil of Chicago, helped make Catholicism a prominent dimension of public culture in the thirties.[18]

But Catholic communalism had other sources as well, beyond the official social teaching of the church. The lived communitarianism of ethnic Catholicism that profoundly shaped American cities, particularly in the East and Midwest, embodied an urban vernacular that offered alternative cultural memories and practices for imagining a mutualist, interdependent vision of the common good.[19] As much an ethos of humility, sacrifice, and weakness as cultural equipment for survival, this popular Catholicism had little patience with the bromides of American success and individual achievement. It embodied the unofficial but deeply resonant Catholic local knowledge, riddled with contradictions and paid for in pain and struggle, that provided alternative ways of imagining collective life in the modern American city.[20]

Because of the Depression, Catholics found themselves at the center of the most pressing issues of the nation during the 1930s. As members of a largely urban, ethnic, working-class community suffering from a prolonged, society-wide economic calamity, their problems—jobs, wages, social security—became the nation's problems. The rise of an effective labor movement rested to a great degree on the participation of Catholic industrial workers. Similarly, the new national political coalition led by Franklin D. Roosevelt (FDR) during the 1930s and 1940s possessed a large Catholic constituency. Thus, as the nation turned to collective solutions to economic and social problems, Catholics assumed an unprecedented importance in America.

The shift in values that the Depression engendered became manifest in the premiere cultural institution of popular America—Hollywood— even before Roosevelt took office. As Lary May has shown, movies did not merely reflect New Deal sentiments; they also provided the symbolic language for the new America that the New Deal sought to realize in politics and social reform. In the early thirties, Hollywood cinema gave expression to the anger and discontent many Americans felt toward the existing social order through popular urban, ethnic gangster films such as *The Public Enemy* and *Little Caesar*. But movies went beyond critique to offer new, inclusive, reformist visions of America. By the midthirties, Hollywood films had developed new heroes and stories that combined the energy and dynamism of urban ethnic minorities with American values of social progress and democratic populism. The cultural margins and center merged in Hollywood movies to create a new Americanism predicated on popular commitments to civic participation, ethnic pluralism, and desire for the modern good life. Movies such as *It Happened One Night*, *The Thin Man* series, and *42nd Street* all expressed a new American community of social interdependence and class and ethnic difference.[21]

These changes in cultural values, I argue, also produced distinctly thirties-style Catholic films, such as *Boys Town*, *Stagecoach*, and *Ruggles of Red Gap*, that signified the new Americanism May has identified. Both movies explicitly including Catholics and movies made by Catholics such as John Ford revised conceptions of American society by denoting the common good through the inclusion of ethnic, religious minorities and cultural outsiders. Further, the films emphasized the centrality of public cooperation and mutuality for the success of the community.

Catholics on screen and behind the camera thus became prominent architects of popular New Deal Americanism. Their work helped elaborate alternative understandings of the national community predicated on reform and ethnic pluralism. At the center of this Catholic involvement in the new representation of American identity lay images and understandings of cooperative social community. The revolution in values and ideas of 1930s America created a cultural space for the "foreignness" of Catholic communitarianism to assume a role in rendering the American common good in cooperatist, interdependent terms. From *Boys Town* to *Stagecoach*, from popular priest to outlaw cowboys, representations of and by Catholic outsiders helped forge new definitions of national community in an age when economic crisis had delegitimized older assumptions about the virtues of American individualism and Anglo-Saxon dominance.

But this new reformist Americanism found itself under siege in the 1940s, and representations of and by Catholics changed as well. Efforts to contain and even oppose this alternative, critical vision of the nation gained momentum as demands for war mobilization and national unity displaced commitments to social reform. Business interests and conservative politicians as well as the shifting focus of the liberal state (famously expressed by Roosevelt that Dr. New Deal had to become Dr. Win-the-War) severely challenged the cultural priorities of the previous decade. After the war, conservative forces found renewed strength through a Cold War anticommunism that undermined earlier commitments to social reform.[22]

Precisely because of Catholicism's identity as a religion of urban, working, and ethnic peoples, counterreformist forces found in the religion an attractive subject with which to construct a more conservative nationalism. To accomplish this project, however, an Americanized Catholicism would have to be shorn of its reformist associations and the critical implications of the social consciousness of the 1930s. As a result, representations of Catholic community were scrubbed clean of any disruptive, oppositional meanings. Rather than marking cultural conflict, highlighting injustice, or encouraging social reform, Americanized images of and by Catholics in the 1940s and 1950s rendered community in terms of responsive, culturally attuned leaders and traditional social institutions such as church and family as sources of personal happiness, moral renewal, and national strength.

One of the most dramatic transformations in the representation of Catholicism occurred in the pages of the nation's most influential newsweekly, *Life*. In its initial years of the late 1930s, the photomagazine traded in stereotypes of Catholics as ethnic Others, visualizing Catholicism as a religion of hierarchical subservience and exotic rituals. Yet once the magazine gained its editorial and ideological voice through its editor, Henry R. Luce, and his vision of the American Century in the early forties, *Life* attributed new significance to Catholicism. The magazine found in Catholics a useful subject with which to culturally map both the United States and the world in terms of its own vision of American global leadership and national consensus.[23]

The photojournal's treatment of Catholicism revealed the intensely ideological debate about the nation that informed popular depictions of Catholics. The magazine was founded and run by Ivy League Anglo-Protestants who realized that in the middle of the twentieth century, Catholicism was too important a subject to be left to the New Deal coalition and the critics of capitalism. *Life*'s Catholics demonstrated that Luce's call for an American Century was more than a policy prescription for global power; it also encompassed a new cultural formation that wove together capitalist leadership, middle-class prosperity, internationalism, and religious minorities in order to challenge the reformist claims to represent the nation that had clustered around the New Deal in the thirties. Far from simply embodying a recycled version of Protestant America, the American Century was powerful precisely because it recognized the social realities of religious difference that had transformed the nation in the twentieth century. By granting Catholicism legitimacy within both the nation and the world envisioned in terms of American greatness, *Life* used Catholics to bury the critical, socially conscious Americanism of the thirties.

Luce's ideas regarding the twentieth century as the era of U.S. global leadership abroad and an expansive, capitalist democracy at home proved an influential ideological context for popular representations of Catholicism in American culture in the forties and fifties. One of the most successful movies of the 1940s, *Going My Way* (1944), about a young, hip Catholic priest who saves an urban parish from financial ruin, offered movie audiences a version of Luce's American Century of national consensus tailored for the home-front audiences during World War II. Other very popular movies such as *The Fighting 69th* (1940) and *The Song of Bernadette* (1943) also directed Catholicism away from the social reformism of the 1930s by aligning Catholics with the moral unity and spiritual commitment of a nation at war.

As a result, movie representations of Catholics during World War II manifested a larger conversion narrative from reform to consensus, which Lary May has argued characterized Hollywood productions during the forties.[24] This cultural shift extended beyond explicit images of Catholics to the ways in which ethnic Catholic filmmakers such as John Ford and Leo McCarey envisioned America. By imagining community as a story of united fronts against external enemies in such films as *My Darling Clementine* (1946) and *Fort Apache* (1948), Ford's social dramas helped articulate a vision of America that echoed the anticommunist militarism that Luce championed under the guise of the American Century.

The extent to which the American Century proved consequential for representations of Catholics in the postwar period is also demonstrated by Bishop Fulton J. Sheen's popular television show, *Life Is Worth Living*, from 1952 to 1957. In the 1930s, Sheen had enjoyed a reputation as the Catholic Church's leading apologist in the United States. After the war, the bishop, who had been responsible for Luce's wife, Clare Booth Luce, entering the Catholic Church, became a national religious figure. Manifesting the retreat from the public life and social reform of the postwar era, his television show encouraged viewers to look to the traditional, private institutions of American life—religion, home, and family—for solutions to their problems.

Representations of and by Catholics in the 1940s and 1950s therefore demonstrated the vital role Catholicism played in the elaboration of the American Century, which eroded reformist meanings of national identity. But these postwar representations also revealed how unstable and fragile this cultural project of the American Century was. As much as these expressions sanctioned a retreat from the alternative Americanism of the thirties, they also showed how difficult it was to suture Catholic traditions and memories to the national consensus after World War II. Indeed, only a few years after Bing Crosby taught American audiences that Catholics were safe for the nation, Fulton Sheen appeared weekly on television to remind viewers once again that Catholicism was a part of the American way of life. Similarly, no sooner had John Ford's postwar films turned community into an affirmation of the American nation than they anxiously reflected back on the limits and unfulfilled promises of American democracy that postwar culture tried to deny.

Consequently, this book examines a range of popular representations—both of Catholics in movies, television, and photojournalism and of cinematic portrayals of America by Catholic film directors—in order to illuminate the cultural work of Catholicism in the contest over imagining the modern American nation. The look of Catholics moved in multiple directions within popular culture during the mid-twentieth century, with the construction of Catholics through images of the American mass media and Catholic perspectives on the nation via popular representations of American symbols and myths. American culture portrayed Catholics even as Catholics imagined America. It is the complex interplay and mutual constitution of Catholic particularity and American commonality that is the subject of this book.

By making popular images the focus of an exploration of Catholics in public life, my study complicates understandings of Catholics and twentieth-century American culture. Ever since Will Herberg, many scholars have seen Catholic identification with the nation in terms of an American way of life characterized by individualism, material success, and capitalist democracy. Even when the value of Catholics' arrival in the mainstream after World War II has been questioned, this picture of the American community predominates.[25] Yet I argue that when Catholics identified with America in the 1940s and 1950s, they were participating in what historians such as May, David W. Noble, and others have shown was a wider, dramatic rejection of an alternative, reformist, public-oriented Americanism that had emerged during the thirties.[26] The ubiquity of Catholics in popular movies, television, and photojournalism testified to their role in the contest over American definition. Far from passively assimilating into the postwar nation, Catholics became actively involved in popular culture, demonstrating their agency in the cultural formation of modern American community.[27]

My study of Catholics and popular culture in the mid-twentieth century also differs from many accounts that stress the powerful Catholic pressure group known as the Legion of Decency and the church's successful efforts to censor American films.[28] There can be no doubt of the impact on Hollywood of the Catholic crusade to clean up the movies. Indeed, the Legion represents perhaps the most successful endeavor undertaken by the church to influence American culture. If the Legion explains a great deal about Catholicism's prominence in Hollywood, however, it can also explain too much. As Francis Couvares has argued, attention to the influence of the Legion on American movies often offers its own morality play, pitting small-minded, moralistic censors against movie artists fighting for creative freedom.[29]

But the power of the Legion cannot explain everything about Catholics in Hollywood movies. The Catholic influence on movie censorship may account for the privileged treatment of Catholicism in Hollywood's portrayal of religion, but it does not explain why such movies as *Boys Town* and *Going My Way* appealed to national, and not just Catholic, audiences. Furthermore, a focus on the Legion obfuscates the role of Catholics such as directors Ford and McCarey and actors Bing Crosby, James Cagney, and Irene Dunne in creating the multiethnic popular culture of modern American film.[30] Finally, Catholicism provided an intensely compelling subject beyond movies. Early television and photojournalism demonstrated that the new visual mass media found Catholics, with their elaborate churches, ritualistic religious practices, and exotic devotions, a particularly rich subject to exploit in the elaboration of their own claims on the collective imagination. A focus on the Legion of Decency therefore does not adequately recognize the importance of Catholicism within a wider twentieth-century American culture remade by visual images.

Other treatments of Catholics in popular culture have begun to correct this narrow focus on the Legion. Some have argued for a distinctly sacramental vision expressed in films by Catholic directors such as Ford.[31] More recently, scholars have recognized that movies did not simply reflect but also actively constructed Catholicism in America.[32] Others have looked beyond movies and belatedly recognized the importance of Sheen and his television show in postwar American culture.[33]

However, even though studies have increasingly attended to aspects of the Catholic presence in American popular culture, none have connected the disparate parts or taken stock of what it means that Catholics were involved in so many dimensions of American mass media. Nor have they adequately situated these numerous cultural expressions in the broader historical context of American society between the Depression and the Cold War. The result is not so much a lack of awareness but rather only a partial understanding of Catholic participation within twentieth-century American culture.

By explaining the widespread representation of Catholics as evidence of their role in the cultural formation of Cold War consensus, I bring Catholics into the center of popular culture and politics of the mid-twentieth century. Images of and by Catholics told powerful narratives about the meanings of American citizenship and belonging, about the kinds of national community in which Catholics lived and the organization of American society that allowed them to practice their religion.[34] I am particularly interested in examining how, by constructing new images of Catholicism, these popular expressions imagined the American community during a period of intense political and social contest. I am less concerned with whether or not these images reflected some authentic Catholic identity and more curious as to how and why popular media repeatedly turned to Catholicism to address wider social concerns of economic justice and reform, cultural difference, national unity, international realities, anticommunism, and even the question of culture itself.

I examine popular texts for their use of Catholic imagery in signifying social values, and beyond that, I consider Catholic films in the context of other movies of their era that addressed similar preoccupations in order to identify the particular work of Catholic visual representation. In addition to analyzing the visual texts as expressions of social values and beliefs, I also examine extratextual material, including reviews, newspaper accounts, publicity campaigns, and studio press books, to indicate the public significance that Catholic representations assumed within American culture at that time.

Because I argue the Catholic role in the cultural struggle over Americanism extended beyond explicitly Catholic content in mass culture, as in *Going My Way*, I also examine the films of John Ford and Leo McCarey. But unlike other studies that acknowledge Catholicism as a major influence on Catholic filmmakers such as Ford, I focus less on the sacramental character of their films and more upon how the movies manifest a "textually submerged" ethnic Catholicism.[35] Thus, even though Catholicism may not have been explicitly represented, I locate a Catholic presence in the ethnic cultural memories of the Catholic minority struggle in America that haunted and structured their films' highly Americanized subject matter. This ethnic Catholicism materialized as recurrent preoccupations in these films with cultural conflict between elites and social margins, boundaries and their permeability, comic displacements and geographic mobility. In this context, therefore, I interpret westerns and screwball comedies not as the triumph of a "universal" American identity over ethnic Catholic particularity but as evidence of the deeply ethnic constitution of even the most Americanized of cultural forms of expression.[36]

To demonstrate the centrality of Catholics in the cultural struggle over American national definition during the mid-twentieth century, I first examine public Catholicism of the 1930s in Chapter 1. Religious philosophy, social thought, and cultural practice combined to forge a "Catholic front" that was both comparable to and a response to the Popular Front of secular leftists during the Depression. The Legion of Decency was but the most successful effort of this wider Catholic initiative to influence American culture, which also included the Catholic Youth Organization (CYO), Catholic radio, and religious rituals in the streets of urban America. The result was that Catholics assumed a highly visible role in America during the 1930s, which the producers of the nation's mass culture could not help but notice.

Chapter 2 examines Hollywood's appropriation of Catholicism during the 1930s and early 1940s as the expression of the cultural changes in national identity precipitated by the Depression. I explore the transformation in the depiction of Catholics from *Boys Town* in the midthirties to *The*

Song of Bernadette during the war as symbolizing the rise and then the displacement of reformist conceptions of American community in the popular imagination. Chapter 3 examines the most famous and success-ful Catholic priest film of the era, *Going My Way*, as an early expression of the American Century. Rejecting the socially conscious, public values of depictions of Catholics in the 1930s, the Crosby film utilized Catholicism to imagine instead an expansive privatized American society of church, entertainment, and high culture.

Chapter 4 then turns to look directly at how Henry Luce's ideological vision of America rendered Catholics by examining the representation of Catholicism in *Life* magazine from its inception in 1936 until 1960. If Crosby and *Going My Way* indicated how Catholics seized the cultural spaces opened by popular media to present Catholicism to their fellow citizens, *Life* revealed the deep investment that one of the most influential journals of twentieth-century America made in Catholicism to elaborate its own very partial but powerful construction of the nation and the world. Chapter 5 extends an analysis of the role of Catholics in imagining the American Century by exploring Fulton J. Sheen's television series, *Life Is Worth Living*, from 1952 to 1957. Sheen's show demonstrated that the new social arrangements of the Cold War consensus gained legitimacy by drawing upon and reworking the cultural memory of alternative ethnic traditions such as Catholicism.

The final two chapters of the book shift the focus to offer a close, in-depth analysis of the work of two Catholic filmmakers, Leo McCarey and John Ford, in order to consider how the cultural transformation in popu-lar Americanism involved Catholics beyond their explicit representation in popular media. Chapter 6 examines McCarey's films as expressions of ethnic imagination, and Chapter 7 explores the representations of religion in the films of John Ford. These two directors demonstrate the extent to which Catholic sensibility both shaped and was shaped by the symbolic restructuring of American community between the New Deal and postwar periods.

Beginning in the thirties, therefore, Catholics in mass culture chal-lenged the long history of Protestant nationalism and anti-Catholicism in the United States—one thoroughly textualized and semiotic—to de-ploy Catholic difference for new understandings of the nation. Initially, these portraits articulated Catholic communalism in terms of a socially reformist vision of America. Hollywood films in particular translated Ca-tholicism into the popular religion of New Deal America—ethnic, urban, communitarian, and skeptical of Puritan pieties. But Catholicism also proved useful for the more conservative visions of the nation that emerged in the 1940s to counter the reformist impulses of the New Deal. In the cultural context of war and the postwar era, images of Catholic community and authority helped legitimate an American society in which reform was no longer perceived as urgent. Popular representation of Catholicism encouraged assimilation rather than social transformation. This use of Catholic tradition, however, led to the creation not of continuity with the past but of new forms of American identity. As conventional or sentimental as Crosby's Father O'Malley or Bishop Sheen or Ford's patriotic Irish Catholic westerns may have appeared, their real significance lay in forging a new postwar world of the American Century. In the process of severing the nation from its Anglo-Protestant heritage, these representations of the forties and fifties also abetted the diminution of the alternative values of reform and social justice; in their encouragement of pluralist unity, they narrowed the possibilities for social critique; in their privileging of Irish American Catholics as cultural brokers between insiders and outsiders, they often occluded the voices of other minorities.[37]

Popular representations of and by Catholics thus demonstrated the importance of Catholics in the cultural struggle between reformist and consensual visions of American community between the 1930s and 1950s. Catholics both benefited from and exacerbated the decline of Protestant cultural authority in the twentieth century. The years from the New Deal to the early Cold War provided an extended Catholic moment in the country's collective psyche, as demonstrated by popular culture's extensive investment in Catholicism. But their rise to prominence as signs of a new America ultimately turned Catholics into accomplices of a postwar nation defined by anticommunist righteousness, political conservatism, and a corporate social order. The long journey of Catholics from margin to center in the United States traversed the contested grounds of popular culture. In the process, Catholics helped forge the pluralist identity of the American community. Whether they prove as important to the nation's self-understanding again can only be imagined.

THE CATHOLIC FRONT: RELIGION, REFORM, AND CULTURE IN DEPRESSION-ERA AMERICA

In a letter to *Commonweal* magazine in January 1935, Agnes K. Maxwell described a successful project of Catholic street activism in Albany, New York, in which women from the local chapter of the National Council of Catholic Women (NCCW) petitioned newsstands in the heart of the city's downtown to carry Catholic periodicals. Targeting the heavily trafficked business district, the women got the city's vendors to carry prominent Catholic journals such as the Jesuit weekly, *America,* and the diocesan newspaper, the *Evangelist,* as well as *Commonweal* itself. Maxwell noted the women realized that simply offering Catholic literature was not enough. A conscious campaign of encouraging Catholic patronage was necessary. "Though wishing to reach non-Catholics as well," she wrote, "we could not depend upon their patronage, especially in the beginning, and the dealers would not continue to carry the magazines unless there was a call for them." Therefore, the NCCW women orchestrated a campaign to reach out to "business women employed in office buildings and stores" near the newsstands. Individual women assumed responsibility for "watching and encouraging the work of the newsstand in or near their building and reporting on conditions."[1]

The Catholic women in Albany were not alone during the thirties in promoting Catholicism in the streets of urban America. In cities such as Boston and Detroit, Catholics viewed newsstands as vital in the promotion and dissemination of Catholic ideas to the urban populace.[2] But Maxwell's description of NCCW efforts in Albany provides a particularly detailed account of Catholic cultural politics in the city streets of Depression-era America. Pursing a strategy of boring from within, Maxwell and her colleagues utilized the public identity of the Catholic women who worked in the buildings, businesses, and stores of Albany's downtown to cultivate cells of active surveillance and solidarity that would promote Catholic popular journalism.

The 1930s, in fact, witnessed a flourishing of Catholic cultural initiatives intended to both consolidate Catholicism in America and insert Catholic voices into the broader American society. As the Albany women demonstrated, much of this project was aimed directly at modern urban culture and the mass media. Historians of American Catholicism in the early twentieth century have stressed the distinctive cultural world that Catholics inhabited, ranging from schools to devotional practices to neighborhoods.[3] The extensive and comprehensive character of this unique culture has often been construed as an indication of Catholic separation from the wider currents of twentieth-century America. Although much of Catholic life *did* take place in separate institutions and practices, the Depression had a profound impact in reorienting this Catholicism. The economic crisis sharpened Catholicism into an assertive culture determined to imprint itself upon the nation as a whole.

Much like Michael Denning's characterization of the Popular Front as a wide-ranging "cultural front" that attempted to win allegiance to a secular leftist vision through popular culture, Catholic culture responded energetically to the collapse of capitalism, interpreting the economic calamity as a moment of moral and cultural possibility.[4] It promoted a robust discussion of social issues and also led to widespread efforts to construct a Catholic way of life. As part of this project, attempts were made to insert Catholic perspectives into the public arena of Depression-era America. From theater to sports, street parades to radio, Catholic leaders and activists took advantage of the crisis in cultural authority precipitated by economic collapse to advocate their own alternative vision of the nation. Indeed, Catholicism in the thirties became a religious-cultural front in its own right, utilizing urban, mass culture to promote Catholic values as the solution to the problems facing the American people.

Catholicism, the Depression, and the End of American Laissez-Faire Innocence

By the early 1930s, Catholic life in the United States was framed by a set of distinctive institutions and practices that constituted what John McGreevy has identified as a world of "parish boundaries." Particularly in the cities of America, Catholics organized themselves around the local parish, producing a culture intensely local in character, in which neighborhood and religion reinforced each other. Religious worship, schooling for children, social life, and even urban space converged to provide Catholics a dense, lived communitarianism.[5]

But in addition to the local character of the Catholic experience, Catholicism also increasingly assumed a national, panethnic dimension after World War I. The Catholic bishops, for instance, established their own National Catholic Welfare Conference in 1919, an institutional vehicle intended to offer the American hierarchy a collective voice on issues of national importance. Among the most prominent features of this organization was its Social Action Department, headed by the Reverend John A. Ryan, the noted Catholic social reformer who had written the Bishops' Program of Social Reconstruction of 1919, an early and far-sighted call for social reforms, including a living wage, the right of workers to organize, and a form of Social Security.[6]

The nationalization of Catholicism in the 1920s occurred not only within the leadership of the church but also in its intellectual life. *Commonweal* magazine, a weekly journal founded and edited by lay Catholics, was an important forum for Catholic views on culture, politics, and society. More academically, the American Catholic Philosophical Society, founded in 1926, offered an organization for the promotion of Catholic neo-Thomist philosophy. And *Thought*, a quarterly devoted to cultivating the Catholic intellectual tradition, emerged in the 1920s as well. Much of this Catholic intellectual life arose to counter new developments in social thought, particularly historical materialism, pragmatism, and psychology. Catholic thinkers saw themselves as protecting transcendent, metaphysical truth and the spiritual foundation of culture against the corrosive effects of a skeptical, disenchanted, modern world.[7]

As a result, an extensive Catholic cultural infrastructure opposed to secular modernism had emerged after World War I. Equally vital during the 1920s, this subculture served to protect immigrant and ethnic Catholics from a resurgent nativism in America during the twenties. With hostility to immigration reaching a crest and the Ku Klux Klan on the march again, the church provided Catholics a needed buffer against cultural attack.[8]

But the events of the 1930s gave a new direction to the subculture, expanding its focus from creating a protective environment for Catholics to asserting the value of Catholicism for the wider nation. The Depression appeared to Catholics to vindicate their opposition to traditional liberalism. A nation prostrate because of industrial capitalism looked to a number of Catholics like evidence that they had been correct all along about the bankruptcy of modernity.

Many Catholics construed the Depression as more than an economic catastrophe; they saw it as a moral and cultural indictment of individualism and free markets as well. Archbishop John T. McNicholas of Cincinnati asserted in a 1931 radio address, "Capitalism may not realize it, but it is on trial before the world today. It can only reform itself according to Christian justice."[9] The editors of the Jesuit weekly, *America,* claimed that "the laissez-faire policy, with its exaggerated respect for 'individualism,' has brought the country to the verge of ruin. For at least three-quarters of a century, in our desire to conserve a proper degree of individualism, we gave too free a hand to the great industrial and financial powers, and they violated every principle of justice, humanity, and even of common decency, for private gain."[10] Another editorial in September 1933 asserted, "Steel, coal and oil have grown rich and powerful on blood and brutality. Until 1933, that policy has been to them in every respect a most admirable policy."[11] Similarly, George Stuart Brady, writing in the *Sign,* claimed that capitalism before the New Deal "was anarchistic in its business economy and was without moral obligation in its relation to labor. . . . Men who in private life were charitable and kind were frequently unscrupulous and hard in ordinary business dealings. Such was the 'American Individualism' advocated and practiced during the prosperity era."[12]

As the nation sank deeper into the Depression, Catholics turned readily to their own alternative tradition of social thought as embodied by Pope Leo XIII and his encyclical, *Rerum Novarum* (On the Condition of Labor) of 1891; Pope Pius XI's *Quadragesimo Anno* (On the Reconstruction of Social Order) of 1931; and the American Bishops' Program of Social Reconstruction of 1919. These documents all recognized the rights of workers to organize unions and the legitimate role of the state in securing the common good in modern society. Pius XI's encyclical in particular proposed a far-reaching reform of the industrial order, calling for a reconstruction of society into guildlike councils composed of businesspeople, labor representatives, and consumers to establish fair wages, conditions, and prices.[13] As McNicholas asserted in articulating Catholic social teaching, "Capital and Labor need each other. They must be brought together as never before to work for the common good, recognizing that they sit at the council table as equals in the dignity of human nature. A new understanding must be arrived at; their mutual dependence must be recognized."[14]

This mutualist, interdependent vision of society informed many Catholics' highly favorable perception of Franklin Roosevelt. It did not hurt, of course, that in the final days of the 1932 presidential campaign, during a speech in Detroit, Roosevelt himself quoted from Pius's *Quadragesimo*

Anno.[15] A number of Catholics interpreted Roosevelt's presidency in highly religious terms, and *Commonweal* portrayed FDR as a fearless man of faith giving hope to a people traumatized by the Depression. Commenting on Roosevelt's inaugural address, the magazine noted that "religious people know that all their President's qualifications to deal with the crisis which confronts his nation rest upon and are strengthened and supported by his true and faithful trust in God." The editorial interpreted the new president's words of encouragement as meaning that "we have but to stretch forth our hands—not to grasp each man for selfish sake—but in human co-operation for the human weal of all," signaling a new turn to collective solutions to the country's crisis.[16] Later, after Roosevelt had announced his New Deal, the magazine claimed that social justice had found its "practical leader" in the new president and that it was "truly a reformation of the spirit" that he led.[17]

Roosevelt's New Deal and particularly the National Recovery Administration (NRA), which established industry groups to set wages, prices, and hours of work, were initially greeted enthusiastically by many Catholic commentators and thinkers. In fact, Catholics interpreted the NRA as an expression of the principles of Catholic social teaching. *America*'s editors wrote, "The Recovery Act [establishing the NRA], it is true, stops short of the ideals of perfection shown to the world by Leo XIII and Pius XI. But it recognizes the excellence of these ideals, and it proposes to bring some elements of justice and charity into fields that have long been ruled by rapine and hatred."[18] Indeed, commentators and writers described the New Deal in the language of Catholic social teaching, emphasizing the ethos of the common good and social justice that Roosevelt's reforms embodied. Thus, *America* also praised the New Deal by claiming, "The civil authority is at last realizing that there are rights more sacred than the right to hold property, and that the primary function of government is to exercise due control of all the agencies in society to do justice to all, and to show favor in particular to the needy."[19] The leading Catholic social reformer, John A. Ryan, claimed, "Never before in our history have government policies been so deliberately, formally and consciously based upon conceptions and convictions of moral right and social justice."[20] The Jesuit Wilfrid Parsons described the "revolution" of the New Deal as the death knell for the era of "struggle for mastery between individuals." And he added that "the new concept of social justice had taken its place. The day of the pioneer was over, though his sons had hardly realized it; and the era of cooperative enterprise had dawned."[21] Many Catholics greeted the arrival of Roosevelt and the New Deal with the hope that they could turn the nation's economy around and that the country itself would regain its bearings through an infusion of Catholic corporatist values.

Over time, however, a number of Catholics would break from Roosevelt and the New Deal. Father Charles Coughlin, the enormously popular radio priest of the early 1930s who originally gave hearty support to the president, eventually became a fierce critic.[22] Coughlin devolved into delivering anti-Semitic tirades against Roosevelt, claiming he was beholden to Jewish bankers and communists, and other Catholics also parted company with the administration particularly by middecade. After the Supreme Court ruled the NRA represented an unconstitutional delegation of congressional authority to the president, the focus for much of the Catholic support for the New Deal evaporated. In addition, the perception that there was a leftist slant among Roosevelt's advisers together with his "court-packing" attempt to expand the Supreme Court with friendlier justices and the growing assertiveness of the labor movement made some Catholics anxious about the direction of the nation's public life. In early 1938, for example, *America* magazine expressed frustration with the administration's failure to end the Depression and encouraged more favorable treatment of business. And the *Catholic World* delighted in the defeat of many Democrats in the midterm elections of 1938, interpreting it as a rebuke of Roosevelt. Its editor, James Gillis, was so opposed to the president's policies that he even boasted of his own "American individualism."[23]

Other Catholics looked for radical change beyond the New Deal, refusing to pin their hopes on an expanded state. Dorothy Day and Peter Maurin founded the Catholic Worker movement in the depths of the Depression in 1933 as witness to the radical call of voluntary poverty and personalism they and those attracted to the Catholic Worker project believed authentic Christianity demanded. Similarly, Paul Hanley Furfey, a Catholic sociologist and a colleague of Ryan's at Catholic University of America (CUA), eschewed Ryan's social reformism in favor of envisioning a just society predicated on a conversion to corporate works of mercy.[24]

Still, many Catholics continued to actively champion social justice in the public arena through the thirties. During the 1936 presidential campaign, Ryan took to the airwaves to counter Coughlin's denunciation of Roosevelt and gave a full-throated defense of the New Deal. Cardinal George Mundelein of Chicago, another Catholic ally of Roosevelt's, told the annual convention of the Holy Name Society, a Catholic men's devotional organization:

The trouble with us in the past has been that we were too often allied or drawn into an alliance with the wrong side. Selfish employers of labor have flattered the Church by calling it the great conservative force, and then called upon it to act as a police force while they paid but a pittance of wage to those who worked for them. I hope that day is gone by. Our place is beside the poor, behind the working man.[25]

In a speech at the National Catholic Social Action Conference in 1938, Archbishop Edward Mooney of Detroit continued to critique individualism as a reactionary political philosophy: "Individualism's favorite defense is to raise the cry *Americanism,* and to point to the spectre of government absolutism as the looming alternative. . . . This defense is not valid against the program for a Christian social order which . . . stands for the protection of private property and the uplift of the proletariat through a more just distribution of that property."[26] At the same conference, Rev. Raymond A. McGowan, a protégé of John A. Ryan's, offered a robust defense of government in securing social justice. "In Catholic social teaching," he asserted, "there is no trace of anti-government. Government is the sovereign protector and promoter of justice and the common temporal good." The role of government, he argued, was first "to regulate property, income and work [so] that all people will have work and all have a good livelihood." Second, the government "must, as far as possible, protect, foster, rely on and guide the people's own organizations in industry, farming, trade and the professions so they themselves will be establishing justice and promoting the general good."[27] So although some Catholics had turned their backs on reform or looked elsewhere for spiritual renewal, many others remained committed to a Catholic vision of social justice.

Catholics' response to the Depression in the 1930s indicated that many believed the country had reached a pivotal moment in its history. As Americans searched for recovery from economic crisis and for societal reform, many Catholics imagined the Protestant past of the nation being left behind for a more Catholic present and future. Ryan, in fact, attributed the ethical bankruptcy of capitalism that led to the Depression to a Protestant failure "to apply the moral law to industrial relations."[28] With the coming of Roosevelt and the New Deal, a number of Catholics envisioned a new dispensation in American life. Corporate values would replace individualism. Organization and coordination would triumph over anarchic freedom and license.

The Depression thus generated an intense confidence among many

Catholics regarding the importance of their own values and beliefs for the nation. Even the appeal of communism among some Americans seemed to vindicate their animosity toward liberal individualism. In an essay entitled "Thunder on the Left," Catholic literary critic Francis X. Connolly noted that the appeal of Marxism was rooted in its comprehensive account of humanity, which liberalism could not offer. He stated, "The very obvious fact that man cannot live intelligently without attempting to achieve something which is beyond himself seemed to elude the liberal. Marxist criticism on the other hand recognized man's incompleteness. . . . The real strength of the Marxist position flows from its essential humility." Connolly confessed that "the Marxist gains seem to me to be extraordinarily optimistic signs," for Catholic critics would find "in the Marxist an opponent with principles sufficiently clear and hard to provide a point at issue." He was confident, however, that Catholicism would ultimately win the day against Marxism: "When the modern world is forced to examine the Marxist discipline, and finds that it is after all a patterned disorder, mathematical inaccuracy, we shall progress toward the dynamic equation of Thomas Aquinas."[29]

Connolly's literary criticism, like the Albany women of the NCCW, demonstrated that Catholic confidence during the Depression extended beyond social and political thought into broader areas of culture. Indeed, the cultural sphere became a key means through which Catholics promoted themselves in American life. Amid social breakdown and the rise of radical proposals, Catholics advanced their own ideas, beliefs, and practices as a redemptive possibility for America. The tumultuous character of the 1930s not only consolidated the Catholic subculture in America but also forged it into a cultural front offering an alternative both to a discredited liberalism and to more dramatic alternatives such as Marxism. Like the cultural front of secular radicals that Michael Denning has illuminated, Catholic cultural activists embraced America's urban and mass culture in an effort to promote their beliefs for a nation struggling for direction.

The Catholic Spaces of Thirties America

One area in which Catholic culture attempted to duplicate and respond to leftist efforts was the sphere of popular theater. During the Depression, a small but vocal group of Catholics actively sought to cultivate a Catholic theater. William J. O'Neil, Alfred Barett, Rev. M. Helfen, Urban Nagle, Mary Fabyan Windeatt, and particularly the journalist, playwright, and later Hollywood writer Emmet Lavery all argued publicly for the value of an organized Catholic theater movement. Explicitly taking a page from the cultural advances of the leftists, these Catholics called for a parallel Catholic theater that would help promote Catholic culture in America.

O'Neil, for instance, proposed a "planned theater" that would offer a popular drama based on "Christian standards" to challenge the reigning entertainments on Broadway. He believed such a project, though not a Catholic theater, would be "predominantly Catholic in executive personnel."[30] Windeatt bemoaned that "the voice of the Church is all but missing from the American stage. The WPA theater project is using federal funds to finance a program which is shot through with Communism." She placed her hopes in amateur groups, calling such organizations "genuine fields for the new, as the Communists have already discovered."[31] The Reverend M. Helfen, founder and president of the Catholic Drama Movement, also pursued a strategy of cultivating a Catholic theater movement, calling upon "young Catholic actors" and "their pioneer spirit for Catholic Action on the Catholic stage." His call appeared to work because he was able to report that many young actors came to the headquarters of the Catholic Drama Movement in Oconomowoc, Wisconsin, and developed several plays that won engagements in Milwaukee and Chicago.[32]

But the effort that gained the most attention was one spearheaded by Lavery and his National Catholic Theater Conference. Consciously taking a cue from the New Theater movement of the Left, Lavery advocated a "right-wing" theater. Showing how such terms could have fluid meanings in the thirties, Lavery was both an ardent champion of the Catholic front in American theater and a defender of the Federal Theater Project against charges of communist propaganda. Lavery would eventually settle in Hollywood as a screenwriter working with such noted directors as Douglas Sirk, who filmed Lavery's novel about the Jesuits, and Edward Dymtryk, one of the "Hollywood 10" brought before the House Un-American Activities Committee (HUAC) in the late forties.

Writing in *Commonweal* to champion the National Catholic Theater Conference, Lavery pointed to the success of the Left in the theater: "From being a mere voice of protest in the theater, a small but aggressive minority, our brothers on the Left by dint of hard work and courageous propaganda have raised themselves to a dominant position." He continued, "They are good salesmen and shrewd showmen. And they have so colored our theatre perspective by their persistent energy that they have nearly won the day." Identifying what was at stake in the theater, Lavery wrote that "the Left Wing has a culture to sell." But when he looked at Catholics, he only saw "laggards." He asserted that "there are Catholics in pictures and in the theatre today who are loath to admit their lively interest in Catholic culture." He therefore argued for the "value of collective action" and a "special point of view." He claimed there was a "great need for a Right Wing theater, even among people who are not Catholic. . . . And once we unite our efforts, we project a theatre on a scale more vast than any the Left Wing can ever hope to achieve."[33]

Lavery called for coordinating existing Catholic parish and college theaters into a national conference "devoted to common standards, the interchange of experience with the world's best drama and the creation of additional theater units." Like other Catholics such as Windeatt and Helfen, he looked beyond Broadway for creating a Catholic theater movement. Hoping to take advantage of the existing infrastructure of parishes and colleges among Catholics, Lavery envisioned an alternative social base for theater. He also believed that a national Catholic theater could serve as a vehicle for creating a truly popular Catholic culture. He envisioned the stage as fostering "the Catholic way of life opened up to the masses who may never join the Catholic Book Club or identify themselves with the Catholic Poetry Society."[34]

Lavery's hopes were at least partially realized when the Loyola Community Theater of Chicago took up his proposal and offered to host a national convention of Catholic dramatists. The Dominican priest Urban Nagle, who headed the Blackfriar's Guild in Washington, D.C., also championed the project. In June 1937, the National Catholic Theater Conference was founded. Announcing the plans for the formation of the conference, Lavery rhapsodized in *America* that "once we unite, we do give collective emphasis both to the theaters and to the works of our dramatists. We do something more, too. We give new heart to the dramatists who would cherish the Catholic tradition and we create new dramatists."[35] In August, the conference held a second national meeting in Washington hosted by Nagle's Blackfriar's Guild and established a national office at Catholic University of America.[36] Thus, by the late 1930s, Lavery could point to a Catholic alternative to left-wing theater in America. Although never achieving the grandiose dreams he hoped for it, the Catholic theater movement nevertheless proved that in the thirties, some Catholics were determined to seize the cultural terrain to promote a distinctly Catholic vision for America.

Newspapers provided another popular arena for Catholics' attempts to insert themselves into the wider urban culture of America during the Depression. The membership of the Albany chapter of the National Council of Catholic Women was but one element in an extensive discourse that considered the effective use of news media to publicize Catholicism. Some of this discussion critiqued the secular press for unfair or biased treatment of Catholics. But Catholic commentary also imagined more constructive possibilities. Some Catholics believed that the time was right for a Catholic daily.[37] Others advocated developing better relationships with the existing papers' city editors. Indeed, this discourse on the news often contained an implicit critique of church practices regarding the media and the reticence to engage newspapers.

In a lead editorial entitled "Let Catholics Take Warning!" Michael Williams, the founder and editor of *Commonweal*, issued a call to arms to Catholics to make more effective use of modern news media both to advance Catholic principles and to protect Catholic interests. Concerned that the media overlooked the persecution of Catholics in Mexico, Spain, and the Soviet Union, Williams told his readers that Catholics "should organize for real action." The action Williams called for involved mobilization on the cultural front. He believed that Catholics lacked the "instruments" to promote Catholic principles and positions in the modern mass culture. He worried that they were "woefully unorganized for the purposes of legitimate propaganda, for the education of public opinion, and for cooperation with other groups willing and able to promote or to defend all human rights." Recognizing the new mass media as a "missing link in the chain of Catholic social action," Williams encouraged Catholics to think more broadly about how to effectively harness newspapers and publicity to educate America on the contribution Catholicism could make in addressing the world's ills. He believed that his own magazine, *Commonweal*, played a crucial role in this effort, but he encouraged Catholics to expand their fields of operation, including by cooperating with secular organizations.[38]

William's editorial helped spawn a wide-ranging discussion in *Commonweal* over Catholic use of the news media. Stuart D. Goulding launched a blistering attack on the reticence of Catholic diocesan and parish clergy to engage the press. Their silence, Goulding believed, only hurt the church in America. Without informed, intelligent news coverage, most non-Catholic Americans could only be mystified by the church and its distinctive practices. Like Williams, Goulding, a newspaperman himself, realized the great opportunity the new world of mass media offered Catholics for promoting themselves in modern America. In an almost breathless manner, Goulding described the insatiable demand papers had for news: "Wireless, cable, telephone, wire ticker, teletype, telegraph, news letters, minute by minute bring the latest news to the papers for rapid transmission to the public." He encouraged Catholics to plunge into this world of constant news. Realizing that the urban news media was transforming public consciousness, he called Catholics to become actively engaged in shaping how their image was perceived by their fellow citizens.[39]

On a more practical level, Joseph Healey argued for the development of diocesan news bureaus under the leadership of newspeople who understood the newspaper trade.[40] Likewise, Murray Powers, a news editor in Canton, Ohio, argued that diocesan officials needed to be more proactive in publicizing newsworthy Catholic events.[41] He suggested that Catholic leaders take more seriously the traditional Saturday religion page in city papers and feed editors the news of Catholic life. "All feast days . . . the Forty Hours Devotions, missions, the crowning of Mary in the month of May—such subjects, handled intelligently and cooperatively, will bring untold publicity and worthwhile publicity too."[42]

Clem Lane, a Chicago newspaper reporter, extended the potential cooperation between the church and news media beyond ordinary Catholic parish life to the role of the Catholicism in the life of cities. He cited examples from his own coverage in Chicago on a "two-fisted barrel-chested Franciscan priest, who started a 'hotel' for unemployed youths . . . the archdiocesan school system with its 200,000 pupils . . . the social justice program of the National Catholic Alumni Federation; features about the St. Jude League, Catholic policemen's organization." Lane's list actually reflected much of the public Catholicism that characterized urban America. Like Healey, Lane believed dioceses could take more effective advantage of the new media by hiring priests who understood both the work of the church and the newspaper business to publicize Catholic life in the urban centers of America.[43]

Such men as Goulding, Lane, and Healy realized the crucial role the news media played within modern urban culture. In their efforts to encourage Catholics to assume an active relationship with news and publicity, they functioned as cultural workers on the Catholic front, straddling the worlds of urban news reporting and the Catholic subculture. They simultaneously offered criticism of Catholic isolation from secular newspapers and advocated the role of the news media in cultivating a larger Catholic presence on the urban landscape of modern America.

The Catholic front, however, extended beyond the urban dailies and mass publications. It was also involved with the new electronic media of radio, indicating additional efforts to insert Catholicism into the new, mass culture of urban, industrial America. In March 1930, the National Council of Catholic Men (NCCM) began a radio program, the *Catholic Hour*, that was broadcast on Sunday evenings on NBC Radio. The genesis of the show lay in the anti-Catholic politics of the 1928 presidential election between Al Smith and Herbert Hoover. Responding to the bigotry against Catholics that influenced the presidential campaign, the NCCM sponsored a radio program that would explain Catholicism to popular audiences. Edward J. Heffron, the executive director of the organization, explained that the primary goal of the show was "to set before the radio audience, in their true light, the teachings and practices of the Catholic Church, hoping only that this will create better understanding and overcome prejudice."[44] NBC agreed to broadcast the hourly show on Sunday evenings but shortened it to thirty minutes in the early 1930s; the program nonetheless kept its original title. Originally, the *Catholic Hour* was broadcast on 22 stations in 17 states. Ten years later, the show had expanded to 94 stations in 41 states.[45] Heffron claimed that over its first ten years, the radio program had increased its listener mail from 12,000 pieces (in 1930) to 175,000 (in 1940), with 20 percent of the mail coming from non-Catholics.[46] Strong audience interest led the NCCW to publish the speakers' talks. In its first decade, the *Catholic Hour* published 1.25 million pamphlets of the radio addresses and prayer books associated with the show.[47]

The show's format combined explications of Catholic teachings and practices with musical performances. As a broadcast intended to explain Catholic beliefs, it became a vehicle by which numerous prominent Catholics could reach mass audiences. Among them were John Ryan, who spoke on Catholic social teaching and the industrial order, and Daniel Lord, addressing the appeal of Christianity.[48] The most successful speaker, however, turned out to be Fulton J. Sheen, moral theologian at Catholic University of America, who combined his authority as a neo-Thomist philosopher with a flair for drama. Sheen spoke on a range of issues, including Catholic devotionalism, family life, communism, and social justice. The *Catholic Hour* actually offered Sheen his initial entrance into the world of mass media, a move that would culminate during the 1950s with his popular television show *Life Is Worth Living*.

One of the most successful and long-lasting cultural projects of the Catholic front of the 1930s involved the Catholic Youth Organization founded and run by Bishop Bernard Sheil of Chicago. The CYO became widely known for its programs that aided poor and homeless youth, particularly its popular boxing tournaments. Combining Catholicism, Sheil's commitment to social justice, and the popular culture of sports, the CYO epitomized the mix of religion, reform, and culture that characterized much of the Catholic front in the thirties. Created in 1930, when Sheil was the chaplain at the Cook County jail and was seeking ways of helping young men avoid the dead end of prison, the CYO specialized in offering recreation and leisure activities to urban youth. From its roots in Chicago, the CYO spread throughout the United States to major cities such as New York and San Francisco. By the mid-1930s, the CYO was serving 200,000 in Chicago alone. Although clearly Catholic in nature—Sheil was quoted as asserting the "objective in every phrase of work among our Catholic youth must be 'all things for Christ and Christ alone'"—the CYO's leaders, including Sheil, prided themselves on having an organization that was open to any youth in need, regardless of religion.[49] The group's efforts ranged from securing medical and dental care for young people to providing arts exhibits, hotels for girls, vocational education classes, and numerous sports activities. CYO boxing leagues and tournaments became widely covered sporting events. The finals of the Chicago boxing leagues were held each year in Chicago Stadium, and the annual Chicago–New York CYO boxing matches were additional highpoints of the organization's sporting events.[50] Sheil's success in turning CYO boxing contests into newsworthy events indicated his astute understanding of popular currents in urban America. Combining religion, youth, sports, and urban journalism, he forged a highly visible, popular form of social Catholicism at the center of the industrial popular culture of America in the 1930s.

The CYO's boxing tournaments became popular rituals in urban America. But Catholicism ritualized the streets and space of the nation's cities in many other ways as well. The devotional and liturgical character of Catholicism generated highly public expressions of Catholic community during the 1930s. Gatherings in urban stadiums and street parades that drew large crowds, noteworthy citizens, and ecclesiastical authorities turned cityscapes into celebrations of Catholic strength and prominence. In 1931, 105,000 people gathered at Los Angeles's Olympic Stadium to celebrate the sesquicentennial anniversary of Catholicism in the city. Cincinnati's Holy Name Society procession of 1934 involved 45,000 men marching through city streets to Crosley Field, the new home of the Cincinnati Reds. There, the crowds were greeted by the papal delegate,

Archbishop Amleto Giovanni Cigognani, as well as Alfred Smith, the Democratic presidential candidate of 1928 and former governor of New York, and Archbishop John McNicholas. Similarly, in Detroit's public park, Belle Park Island, Catholics celebrated an Assumption Day rally honoring Mary that "reportedly [drew] 15,000 people in 1939."[51]

Marian devotions could assume dramatic public expression in American cities. In Chicago, a devotion to the Sorrowful Mother at Our Lady of Sorrows Church drew "nearly 70,000 people a week by 1938." The same devotion in Detroit attracted a smaller but still quite respectable crowd of 4,000 people a week in a single church by 1939.[52]

One of the most dramatic instances of the Catholization of urban spaces, however, occurred in September 1935 with the National Eucharistic Congress held in Cleveland, Ohio. For three days, hundreds of thousands of Catholics from across the country descended on the city to celebrate the Eucharist in a series of Masses and benedictions that culminated with a spectacular display of pageantry involving hundreds of bishops, priests, Catholic laypeople, and schoolchildren on the field of Cleveland's Municipal Stadium. The cardinal and archbishop of New York, Patrick Hayes, served as papal representative for the occasion. Al Smith and the U.S. postmaster and representative for President Roosevelt, James Farley, gave talks to gatherings of 100,000. Fulton J. Sheen spoke to the crowds as well. The candidates of that year's mayoral race all agreed to refrain from campaigning during the period of the congress. All appeared at the reception for the papal delegation.[53]

In addition to using the city's Municipal Stadium to hold its large public celebrations, the congress laid claim to the streets of Cleveland. On his arrival, Cardinal Hayes was greeted by 20,000 people at the city's train terminal. A dozen bands of Catholic fraternal and social organizations escorted the cardinal to Cleveland's Cathedral of St. John the Evangelist.[54] A front-page story in the *New York Times* vividly conveyed the religious spectacle as the cardinal and other priests entered the cathedral: "Franciscans in coarse brown robes and sandals, Benedictines in black, Dominicans in white and the white and black clad members of the Order of the Precious Blood came next as the members of the religious orders filed past. They were followed by diocesan clergy in cassocks, surplices and birettas. Four hundred Monsignori came next. . . . Forty-four Bishops and fifteen Archbishops followed."[55] Finally, Bishop Joseph Schremb of Cleveland, Archbishop John McNicholas of Cincinnati, and Cardinal Hayes, the papal legate, concluded the procession.

Other events of the congress included a large reception for Cardinal Hayes at the city's Public Hall, with 15,000 people in attendance. An official letter of welcome from Franklin Roosevelt, read by James Farley, ensured that Catholics realized the New Deal president acknowledged their celebration. An evening crowd of 43,000 at Municipal Stadium, with 25,000 more listening to speakers outside, heard Al Smith harangue communism and Fulton J. Sheen speak on the Mystical Body of Christ.[56]

The following and final day of the congress witnessed the most dramatic display of Catholicism in the city, involving 250,000 people. A group of 22,000 Catholic marchers paraded through downtown to the stadium, which was holding 100,000 attendees for the closing ceremony of a final benediction of the Eucharist. Some 125,000 people lined the streets to watch the parade, and another 25,000 congregated outside the packed stadium. As the marchers entered the stadium, they formed a human version of a monstrance, the vessel that holds the Eucharist for display in Catholic devotions. Those participating in creating the monstrance included bishops, priests, academicians, laypeople, members of the Knights of Columbus, representatives of fourteen national groups dressed in native clothing, and schoolchildren.[57] As the culmination of three days of devotion and ceremony, the living monstrance offered the citizens of Cleveland as well as the entire nation a spectacle of popular Catholicism. Piety, politics, and urban celebration converged in a major sporting venue to communicate the distinctive Catholic presence in American culture during the Depression years.

The most successful effort of the Catholic front, however, proved to be the church's crusade to clean up the movies in the early 1930s. The story of the Catholic Church's involvement in Hollywood censorship is well known.[58] But its influence in regulating movies has often been isolated from the larger project Catholics pursued in using mass culture to promote their values and beliefs in America. At the time, many Catholics perceived reform of American culture as equal to the transformation of a bankrupt economy. Movies actually offered an important instance in which the modern industrial character of America and cultural renewal converged for Catholics. Tellingly, when the popular devotional magazine *Ave Maria* critiqued the movies for insulting the moral character of the American moviegoing public, it condemned "the industrialists of Hollywood," linking films with a term of derision reserved during the Depression for capitalist elites.[59]

Motion pictures had been a target of moral crusades throughout the previous decade, particularly by Protestant groups. Yet such efforts were only sporadically effective. Censors had trouble agreeing with each other, which undermined their efforts to win concessions from Hollywood. Given the diffuse, local character of censorship, however, the movie studios also found themselves in a costly, never-ending dilemma of reediting their movies to appease state and city review boards.

Catholic leaders had also been concerned about immorality in movies, and in 1930, sensing an opening in the effort to reform movies, they took action. Two Catholics, the Jesuit priest Father Daniel Lord and Martin Quigley, the publisher of the movie theater trade paper *Exhibitor's Herald*, proposed a production code for the studios to follow in their treatment of subject matter. Because Quigley was an insider to the industry, he had no interest in shutting down movies. Instead, he and Lord offered a more effective and less costly means of censoring immorality than cutting movies after they were produced to meet the myriad demands of state and local censors. By offering a code of production as a guideline in the making of movies, the Lord Quigley proposal provided the studios with a surer means of avoiding the wrath of moral crusaders.[60]

The code itself addressed the role of movies as a major new influence in popular conceptions of morality and argued that filmmakers therefore had a responsibility to inculcate respect for traditional moral authority and treat marriage, family, the law, and religion with deference. "Religion is lowered," it stated, "in the minds of the audience because of the lowering of the audience's respect for a minister."[61] The code also addressed the treatment of sensitive subjects such as crime, sexuality, and dress, demanding that illicit and immoral behavior not be treated in an attractive manner.

The studios accepted the code in 1930. However, they also continued to produce movies that ignored it. Indeed, as the Depression worsened and movie attendance plummeted, the studios realized that the films audiences were most attracted to were the kind the code condemned.

By 1933, Catholic attitudes toward Hollywood hardened, as many believed their trust in the film industry had been betrayed. In April, *America* magazine complained of "the recent trend to more and more smut" in Hollywood films.[62] In June, the Jesuit magazine became more proactive. Indicative of the Catholic front's intertwining of social and cultural reform, its lead editorial of June 24 asserted:

So the time has come for society to resume control over this industry [the motion picture industry], just as it is doing over banking, investment houses and industry itself. . . . What form will it take? The Catholic Church, when it acts in united fashion under its constituted heads, can be a very powerful fact in public life. If our Bishops, as we hope they will, take the lead by pointing out to our people that they are forbidden by natural law to view spectacles that flout morality as set forth in the Code, then we will make a great stride forward in a social control that will be effective.[63]

Immediately following this call for united Catholic action against immoral movies, the magazine included a second editorial, "The New Deal," offering a robust defense of Roosevelt's economic policies.[64]

By late 1933, movie studio violations of the code led Catholic leaders to conclude that Hollywood could no longer be trusted. Catholic bishops did not support state intervention against Hollywood, but they did believe the church needed to take more direct action against the motion picture industry. At the November 1933 meeting of the American Catholic hierarchy, the bishops created a subcommittee on the motion picture problem, headed by John T. McNicholas, the archbishop of Cincinnati who also championed papal social teaching. This committee formulated the Legion of Decency, intended to send a clear signal to Hollywood that Catholics would not accept morally offensive films. The Legion asked Catholics to pledge not to attend "salacious and immoral pictures."[65] The group grew quickly, particularly in many eastern urban dioceses where there were many Catholics and movie houses.

The film studios, fearing the growth of the Legion and the possibility of a Catholic boycott of their products, agreed to strengthen self-censorship in June 1934. The large number of Catholics in the eastern cities where the studios had some of their most prominent movie theaters, coupled with the public prominence of the bishops among Catholics, made filmmakers attentive to Catholic sensitivities. Furthermore, the hierarchical leadership of the Catholic Church proved attractive to the movie studios, whose management believed it would be easier to work with a single organized pressure group led by the bishops than to constantly wage expensive and time-consuming battles with numerous state and local censor boards.

The major studios agreed to a powerful new industry entity, the Production Code Administration (PCA), headed by Joseph Breen, an Irish

Catholic from Philadelphia. The major film producers agreed to submit all scripts to the PCA and gain approval from the office before producing a movie. Further, no film would be released in the major studios' theaters without a PCA seal of approval. Studio violation of this rule would result in a $25,000 penalty. Equally important, the appeal process regarding censors' decisions on scripts and films was taken out of the studios' hands in Hollywood and given to the board of directors of the Motion Picture Producers' Association in New York. This meant that overturning Breen's evaluations of a film script would prove difficult. Filmmakers also agreed that theater owners could refuse to show any film released before July 15, 1934, the date the new PCA went into effect, for moral reasons.[66]

Hollywood's willingness to give the Production Code real teeth represented a remarkable victory for the Catholic Church. Yet the PCA represented more than the capitulation of the movie studios to Catholic power. The debate about movies in the early thirties had as much to do with the struggle over cultural authority in America as it did with issues of artistic freedom. Hollywood found in the Catholic Church a useful partner in its effort to ward off more costly or draconian measures of government censorship. Correspondingly, Catholics used the movies to push Protestants aside as representatives of traditional morality. As Jonathan Munby points out, "Increased Catholic involvement in policing American morality . . . corresponded to the declining fortunes of nativism and Protestantism."[67] Catholic leaders believed that cleaning up the movies provided them with a new role as guardians of what one Catholic figure called "the moral happiness of America." In an essay entitled "Catholic Action's Big Opportunity," Owen McGrath, a Paulist priest in New York, asserted the Legion was well positioned to take advantage of the cultural crisis in America and reshape the nation:

> It is not a question of a Catholic party in politics; it is now an urgent matter of sincere Catholics injecting Christian principles into American life, into business, government and education. If Catholics will not do this, who will? Paganism and Protestantism have failed in their erroneous attempts to influence or regulate our national life peacefully or honorably; they have brought about a lamentable degeneration of national character, resulting in the present condition of open indecency, depraved business relations and ruinous educational institutions. Now, it appears, Catholics have stood forth to do battle.[68]

And doing battle is just what the Legion and many Catholics chose. The new regulatory regime of Hollywood films represented the most prominent example of Catholic involvement in American life during the 1930s. For the next three decades, the Legion and the Production Code Administration it helped spawn would cast a profound influence on the content and character of Hollywood cinema.

Far from remaining isolated in a separate world, therefore, Catholics utilized the crisis and uncertainties generated by the Depression to insert themselves in the major cultural debates of the nation. Not surprisingly, by 1938 the *New Republic* was wondering if the country suffered from a "Catholic problem." The magazine's anxiety, as John McGreevy has argued, reflected a widespread unease among many liberals in the late 1930s about Catholic assertiveness.[69] Already quite distinctive because of their religious practices and rituals, Catholics became even more visible on the national scene as they took advantage of urban culture and mass media to advance their claims, much to the chagrin of some other Americans. Only by becoming a cultural front, however, could Catholics have made themselves into a problem for the intellectual guardians of the nation's well-being.

A Catholic Tendency in America

With its sports leagues and youth organizations, its devotional spectacles and massive religious parades, its newspaperpeople and radio programs, its theater groups and morals crusades, Catholicism became popular culture in 1930s America. The Depression inspired many Catholics to literally and figuratively take to the streets and proclaim the value of their faith and church for the nation. That much of this Catholic confidence rested on ambiguous foundations did not seem as vital at the time as its ability to inspire mobilization. But the hope that the nation's search for alternatives to laissez-faire capitalism would lead Americans to Catholic social teaching proved wishful thinking. The country was not quite ready to follow the popes in the reconstruction of the social order. In reality, Catholic boasts of the national importance of their own beliefs betrayed as much anxiety as self-assurance. The devotional ethos of redemptive suffering that Catholics such as Fulton Sheen preached on the *Catholic Hour* not only encouraged the spiritual practices of the faith but also expressed the church's fear about its place in an indifferent modern world.[70]

Yet because Catholics took urban, mass culture seriously, the nation's popular culture industry also took Catholics seriously. Jack Warner, at

Warner Bros. studio, and Henry Luce, creator of *Life* magazine, found Catholics too attractive a subject to be ignored. But as they focused on them, the representation of Catholicism also dramatically changed. It became detached from its original context of the Catholic subculture and rearticulated within larger debates over American identity, assuming a whole new set of cultural meanings. In the hands of the professionals in Hollywood, at *Life* magazine, and eventually even in television, Catholicism served not simply to showcase the religious diversity of America but also to help reimagine the national community itself during a period of intense cultural conflict. In fact, the fate of the New Deal nation can be traced through the fortunes of Hollywood's most unlikely hero—the urban Catholic priest. How that happened is the subject of the following chapter.

CHAPTER TWO

A NEW DEAL IN MOVIE RELIGION:

THE PUBLIC SPHERE OF

CATHOLIC FILMS

In June 1952, the nondenominational Protestant magazine *Christian Herald* published an article by Spyros P. Skouras, the president of Twentieth Century–Fox Film Corporation, entitled "Religion and the Movies."[1] Skouras wanted to assure readers that Hollywood understood "its tremendous responsibilities to the cause of religion." Writing at the height of the Cold War, he believed that movies were an important medium that, by promoting religion, served the fight against America's enemies. "Church and screen," he asserted, "are joined together in the defense of the spiritual heritage of Western civilization against the threats of a pagan philosophy." The Twentieth Century–Fox president pointed to the biblical epics *Samson and Delilah, David and Bathsheba,* and *Quo Vadis* as examples of the movie industry's commitment to religious films. Readers of the *Christian Herald* were particularly familiar with the latter two pictures. They had voted *David and Bathsheba* the best film of 1951 in a poll sponsored by the magazine and *Quo Vadis* the best picture of the month for January 1952, later honoring it as the best film for all of 1952.[2]

Skouras also acknowledged Protestant concerns about the prevalence of Catholicism in movies, stating, "We of the motion picture industry have received many complaints from various Protestant denominations that our pictures do not sufficiently cover Protestant subjects. It is true that the majority of purely religious pictures have been Catholic subjects, but circumstances are responsible for this rather than intention." Skouras explained that "there are some Catholic writers and producers in our industry who like to undertake subjects of this kind." Conversely, he believed Protestants were not "promoting material by outstanding Protestant writers that is adaptable to the screen."[3]

The studio head concluded his article by returning to the struggle against communism. This, Skouras pronounced, was "the great crusade of modern times." Both Protestants and Catholics, he said, had a valuable role to play in encouraging Hollywood to produce religious movies that would "combat the godless common enemy, communism."[4]

Skouras's article illustrated the ties between religion, movies, and anticommunism that characterized Hollywood cinema after World War II.[5] But his admission that Catholics had until recently dominated the movies touched on another dimension to the cultural politics of religion and film, one that led back to an earlier era—the 1930s, when Catholicism emerged as the religion of popular America in Hollywood film. The reasons for this development were numerous, but particularly critical was the ability of Catholic imagery to signify the new Americanism that Lary May argues characterized movies in the thirties.[6] During the Depression, Hollywood constructed a compelling new character in the figure of the urban, ethnic Catholic priest who battled for social justice. The popular films *San Francisco* (1936), *Boys Town* (1938), and *Angels with Dirty Faces* (1938) offered audiences a representation of religion that was urban, vigorous, and aligned with the marginal people and forgotten youth of industrial America. Many other films also located the priest on the same imagined terrain as Hollywood's ethnic gangster. In fact, as I argue in this chapter, movies created the Catholic priest as the cultural twin rather than the foil of the famed ethnic mobster. Whereas the gangster voiced anger and discontent toward a bankrupt Anglo-American social order, the priest symbolized the possibilities of another, different America predicated on ethnic pluralism and social reform. The visually distinctive look of Catholicism provided a cinematically attractive means by which to express what historian Robert S. McElvaine has called the new "moral economics" of American culture during the Depression, in which communal values of cooperation and shared effort displaced the rugged individualism of the twenties.[7] In Hollywood, Catholicism became the religious expression of New Deal America.

The City of God in the City of Angels

Most accounts of Catholics in Hollywood film during the thirties and forties emphasize the Catholic pressure group known as the Legion of Decency together with movie censorship.[8] To be sure, the Legion's influence in establishing the regulatory regime of classical American cinema after 1934 cannot be denied. Yet concentrating on the Legion risks obscuring the larger cultural importance of movies as an arena for the emergence of new understandings of American identity during the 1930s. As Lary May has argued, movies functioned as a new public sphere, where traditional

Anglo-American conceptions of national community were contested and new American identities rooted in ethnic and class experiences forged. However, precisely because movies assumed a reformist, even radical role in American culture, during the 1940s they became subject to conservative pressures to promote national unity and social harmony.[9]

Examining the representation of Catholics in movies during this period underscores May's argument about the politics of Hollywood cinema, for film depictions of Catholics during the thirties contributed to the cultural transformation of national identity by associating Americanized images of religious minorities with social justice. This reformist character of Catholic imagery, however, would not last into the forties. As Hollywood jettisoned progressive politics for national consensus, movie Catholicism also changed, abandoning its social consciousness for the spiritual mobilization of the home front. By the midforties, *The Song of Bernadette*, a pious story of a young female saint, had displaced the public ethos of *Boys Town* and *Angels with Dirty Faces*. Film representations of Catholics in the 1930s and 1940s consequently provide a case study of wider cultural changes in the United States, revealing the deeply contested character of national definition between the New Deal and World War II eras.

Despite this, Hollywood's treatment of Catholics has received relatively little attention compared to the gangster films and comedies of the period.[10] When Catholic representations are recognized at all, their role in the construction of modern American identity has been overlooked. Thus, Les and Barbara Keyser have considered movie images of Catholics in the context of the Catholic experience in America.[11] And Charles Morris has read the popularity of these movies as evidence of the church's ability to assert itself in mass culture rather than as a sign of broader transformations in American cultural identity.[12]

Yet recent scholarship in religion and movies has underscored the value of studying the representation of Catholics in popular movies as important cultural documents.[13] No longer preoccupied with assessing the religious or theological quality of films, religious studies scholars now approach movie depictions as themselves constitutive of religious identity. Such work also reveals the role of religious imagery in movies in the articulation of other key social identities, such as ethnicity, race, and gender.

Therefore, in considering Catholics in 1930s and 1940s movies, this chapter shifts the focus from the Legion, which was treated in the last chapter, to films themselves and their reception, thereby highlighting the cultural work performed by Catholic representations in the creation and decline of reformist Americanism in the popular imagination. But before examining the depiction of Catholics, it is first necessary to consider the cultural role of movies in the 1920s and early 1930s and the fate of Protestant America on screen.

Culture, Politics, and Religion in Early Twentieth-Century American Film

With deep roots in ethnic and working-class neighborhoods, first as nickelodeons and later as multireel entertainments, movies emerged as a cultural expression of immigrant and marginal urban groups that were excluded from social power and respectability. Yet as Lary May has shown, by the second decade of the twentieth century, movies had assumed a prominent role in the remaking of the middle class. As members of the white-collar middle class increasingly lost control of their work lives within corporate and bureaucratic structures, a new leisure culture offered freedom in the private realm. Movies helped facilitate this cultural transformation by modeling a new consumerist ethic. They showed how the private realm could be reimagined as a place of personal expression, desire, and emotional fulfillment. Movie houses themselves were patterned on architectural styles derived from Old World Europe or exotic cultures, wrapping moviegoers in a physical environment of fantasy divorced from the larger public realm and social life.[14]

As movies helped revitalize the modern middle class, they were also effectively detached from their working-class and ethnic origins. Consequently, much of the new commercial culture of the 1920s assumed a respectable Anglo-American character. Indeed, the middle-class transformation of traditionally ethnic and working-class leisure practices paralleled Prohibition and immigration restrictions in attempting to contain the growing presence of Jews and Catholics in urban America. But the New Era consumerism and the new middle-class culture it fostered experienced a legitimation crisis with the crash of 1929.

The Depression placed into doubt the affluence that was celebrated in movies of the previous decade. Indeed, Hollywood itself was not immune to the economic collapse. Studios faced a sizable decline in profits in the early thirties, in part because people had less money to spend on entertainment, including movies. However, as May and Thomas Doherty have shown, the industry also suffered because the film formulas that had worked in the twenties were unable to sustain popular interest in the subsequent decade.[15] Audiences were no longer content with stories that reflected the prosperity and confidence of the 1920s.

Films that did succeed in the early thirties were those that broke from existing conventions.[16] These movies gave expression to the despair and frustration that many Americans felt as the Depression worsened, anguish that no one, particularly Herbert Hoover, seemed capable of addressing. Many films portrayed the existing social order as bankrupt or irrelevant. Social problem films, women's melodramas, and horror films all registered the people's frustration and discontent with traditional cultural authority.[17]

No genre better conveyed the cultural transformation that Hollywood cinema embodied than the new gangster films of the early thirties, such as *Little Caesar* (1930) and *The Public Enemy* (1931). Not only did they privilege characters who operated outside established authority, they also focused attention on the ethnic character of urban America. As portrayed by the Jewish American Edward G. Robinson and the Irish American James Cagney, the gangster was particularly appealing because he literally and figuratively gave voice to ethnic minorities who had been considered un-American.[18]

Collectively, these movies represented a pervasive challenge to the cultural status quo.[19] The established Anglo-American middle class, associated with an exclusionary Americanism of the twenties, became the focus of discontent. Traditional institutions such as the law, business, and marriage were all portrayed as deeply flawed. Religion itself did not escape the searing cultural critique of early thirties cinema.

The Representation of Protestants in Early Thirties Cinema

Movies at the beginning of the 1930s, often dubbed "pre-Code" cinema because they were made before the enforcement of the Production Code, have generated particular interest among film scholars because of their liberal treatment of subjects that became taboo later in the decade.[20] Although "sin in soft focus" may have been portrayed quite frankly, the seemingly staid subject of religion also received attention on screen. Reflecting the wider cultural pattern of social discontent of early thirties cinema, however, film depictions of religion were often quite critical. Notably, the religion in question was Protestant. Frank Capra, for instance, made two movies about religion in the early 1930s, *The Miracle Woman* (1931) and *The Bitter Tea of General Yen* (1933). Both films cast a jaundiced eye upon America's dominant religious tradition.

The Miracle Woman was loosely based on the life of evangelist Aimee Semple McPherson. It chronicled the rise of Florence Fallon (played by Barbara Stanwyck) as a popular preacher who used fraudulent miracles to win a following among unsuspecting believers. The film opens with a scathing portrait of mainline Christianity as Florence, the daughter of a minister, enters the pulpit of a respectable church one Sunday morning to announce to the congregation that her father has just died. Florence proceeds to berate the people in the pews for their coldness in firing her father as their minister, which she claims led him to die of a broken heart. When one member asks her to stop her tirade and remember she is in a house of God, she retorts, "What God? Whose God? This isn't a house of God. It's a meeting place of hypocrites." She goes on to condemn members of the congregation for their greed and selfishness, asking them, "Who of you are poor in spirit? Which of you are poor? Which of you is merciful?" The people all leave their pews and exit the church while Florence continues to pour out her emotions. One man, named only Hornsby, remains. He is impressed with Florence's public performance and suggests that she take her talents on the road as a preacher so that they can both make a fortune preying on people's hopes and faith. He tells Florence, "Religion is like everything else. It's great if you sell it. No good if you give it away."

Florence agrees to Hornsby's offer, and together they create the hugely successful and popular evangelist Sister Fallon, who even has a radio program, *How to Have Faith*. In her Temple of Happiness, Florence performs nightly miracles, staged with the help of hired shills who pretend to suffer from a variety of illnesses. She brings in the money but soon becomes uncomfortable with the fraud she is perpetuating. Eventually, on her final night at the temple, she confesses to the assembly of believers. But as she stands on stage and admits the truth to her followers, a fire accidentally breaks out and consumes the building. Florence barely escapes with her life. The film ends with Hornsby pursuing a new angle as a boxing promoter and Florence returning to honest religious work as a member of the Salvation Army.

In its portrayal of religion, *The Miracle Woman* expresses a kind of social anger at religion similar to the anger directed toward the legal system in many gangster films. Its hostility toward mainline religion is palpable in Florence's unrelenting torrent of criticism hurled at respectable Christians as hypocritical and greedy. Its equation of evangelism with salesmanship conveys a stringent critique of popular faith as a product of charlatans and ignorance.

The Bitter Tea of General Yen, made two years later, also cast Protestantism in a negative light. Set during the civil war in China, the film opens among the Christian missionary community in Shanghai. As a torrential rainstorm pours down and Chinese citizens of the city flee the encroaching warlords, the white American Christians are preparing to celebrate the marriage of Dr. Bob Strike (Gavin Gordon), a young missionary, and his childhood sweetheart, Megan Davis (Barbara Stanwyck), whom a guest describes as being from "one of the finest old Puritan families in New England." Megan has decided to come to China not only to marry Bob but also to help with his mission to the Chinese.

But ultimately, she becomes a convert to the enigmatic, powerful warlord General Yen (Nils Asther). In one dramatic scene, she has shed her Western clothes and is dressed in traditional Chinese robes; she kneels at the feet of Yen and tells him that she will never leave him. Megan's "conversion" to Yen suggests both the psychic release from her New England Puritan background and the cultural impotency of respectable middle-class Protestant America in the face of ethnic Others. Her willing submission to Yen actually underscores a comment made earlier in the film by another character, the Bishop Harkness, who despaired at the inability of Christians to make greater progress among the Chinese. *The Bitter Tea of General Yen* thus portrays Protestant Americans as a culturally and emotionally exhausted group of individuals who are no longer able to affect the world or even retain the allegiance of their own kind.

To be sure, some films offered a more favorable treatment of Protestantism. Yet even a film that accorded respect to it, such as *The Man Who Played God* (1932), failed to generate much excitement. The *Hollywood Reporter* labeled that particular film "Clean, Wholesome, and Dull."[21] The movie's main character is Montgomery Royale (George Arliss), an elderly, wealthy bachelor and successful pianist who tours the Continent performing for royalty. When described by a high-society woman as "religious," Monty demurs, "I don't think I'm what you call religious. But I've always regarded my mother and God as my two best friends." When an anarchist explodes a bomb during one of his recitals for a European king, Monty loses his hearing. Cut off from his music, he sinks into a depression and abandons his faith in God. He retreats into his private apartment on Fifth Avenue, high above Central Park. After learning how to read lips, Monty spends his days looking down on the poor people in the park, visually "eavesdropping" on their plights. Reveling in his newfound ability to secretly learn of the lives of unsuspecting park-bench dwellers, he soon realizes that he can perform acts of charity by helping the people he spies upon. With the aid of his manservant, Monty arranges to give money to people in distress and in the process regains his faith in God.

An affirmation of religious belief, Montgomery Royale is the polar opposite of the gangsters who were burning up the screen when *The Man Who Played God* was released. Indeed, the image of Monty on the roof of his Fifth Avenue penthouse apartment as he peers down through his binoculars at the citizens of Depression-era New York, proud of his goodwill and faith, offers a striking juxtaposition to the criminal gangsters and savvy women who strutted the metropolitan streets, secular, aggressive, and sexual. It is no wonder, then, that the *Hollywood Reporter* dismissed the movie as dull.

Another religious film, *The Sign of the Cross*, raised problems of a different sort. Boring it was not. Religious groups roundly condemned the film as an assault on morality. The director, Cecil B. DeMille, was surprised by the objections to his film.[22] He should not have been. Nudity, orgies, lesbianism, and titillating costumes were packed into a film ostensibly celebrating the virtues of early Christian martyrs. DeMille may have professed respect for Christianity, but viewers who construed the film as being more interested in earthly desires than spiritual concerns could not be blamed for misreading the movie.

Taken together, depictions of religion in the early thirties manifested the cultural transformation in values precipitated by the Depression. Movies that captured the energy of marginal subcultures, such as *Scarface* and *The Public Enemy*, consigned religion to a minor significance at best. Films that directly addressed Christianity oscillated between Hollywood spectacle and portrayals of religious hypocrisy and cultural exhaustion. Even appreciative portraits of Protestantism underscored its genteel distance from the tumultuous realities of Depression-era America.

Hollywood's Catholic Priest and New Deal America

Unfriendly depictions of religious authority were one of the major concerns of moral crusades against Hollywood in the late 1920s and early 1930s. Although the Catholic Legion of Decency may not have had the interests of Protestant churches at heart, it did worry that films undercut respect, particularly among children, for social and moral order. By 1934, the movie industry had agreed to abide by the Production Code Administration, led by the Irish Catholic Joseph Breen, in order to police itself. No longer would movies treat social institutions irreverently or allow criminals to escape punishment.

As a result, the portrayals of Catholics, particularly priests, that emerged in the middle and late thirties arose in the context of the new regulatory regime in Hollywood cinema embodied by the PCA. With Breen at the helm of the PCA and the Catholic bishops orchestrating a yearly pledge on the part of Catholics to refrain from attending immoral movies, it is not surprising that Catholics enjoyed highly favorable treatment in films of this period. Critics who later accused the industry of indulging Catholic tastes had plenty of evidence on screen to support their claims.

Nevertheless, the midthirties witnessed the start of a remarkable run of films about Catholics that would extend into the next decade. More was at work than Hollywood's effort to placate the church. Many of the movies proved enormously successful, both commercially and critically, among them: San Francisco (1936); Boys Town (1938), which won Spencer Tracy an Academy Award for best actor; Angels with Dirty Faces (1938); The Fighting 69th (1940); Knute Rockne (1940); The Keys of the Kingdom (1943); God Is My Co-pilot (1943); The Fighting Sullivans (1943); and The Song of Bernadette (1943).[23]

Collectively, these movies marked a Catholic moment in American cinema and popular imagination. The late 1930s and early 1940s saw a concentration of Catholic-marked movies, but significant differences in emphasis and theme emerged over time. Tracing the changes within these films from the thirties to the forties illuminates the eclipse of social consciousness in popular imagination that occurred by World War II. When the cycle of Catholic movies began in the 1930s, they presented a decidedly reformist view of Catholics, aligning the nation's largest religious minority with the values of social cooperation and interdependence that characterized Depression-era culture.

The construction of Catholicism as a symbol of American social justice in these thirties reform films, particularly San Francisco, Boys Town, and Angels with Dirty Faces, rested heavily upon presenting the priest as a champion of marginal people and forgotten youth. Movies worked hard to locate the Catholic cleric on the same imagined cultural terrain as the gangster, traversing the similar gritty landscape as Hollywood's most attractive figure from the early thirties. This strategy reflected, in part, the industry's needs and imperatives, for incorporating the Catholic priest into the gangster movie allowed a variation on a theme that genres depended upon for success. By the midthirties, gangster movies had already enjoyed a lengthy run at the box office. The priest character gave a new twist that kept crime dramas fresh.

Even more important, the use of the priest character reflected the changed regulatory landscape of Hollywood in the middle and late thirties. Indeed, the Catholic cleric helped represent the "moral landscape" of post-Code films that contrasted dramatically with the films of the early thirties, as Thomas Doherty has shown.[24] Inclusion of the priest allowed studios to continue to produce crime films within the censorship framework established by the PCA, which insisted that crime be defeated by the forces of proper social authority.

But the presence of the priest figure also indicated that in order to succeed, the visual regime of classical Hollywood cinema still had to win the allegiance of moviegoers by producing films that spoke to their interests and desires. The use of the Catholic priest therefore privileged a moral authority commensurate with and expressive of the very urban, ethnic world of the street-savvy criminal who appealed to movie audiences. If the gangster represented social destruction, the Catholic priest signified social affirmation. But in the 1930s, that affirmative vision was tied explicitly to social reform of the existing order. The priest therefore did not so much obviate the gangster as culturally echo him in a more constructive communitarian direction. As much an expression of New Deal reformist culture as an effect of the PCA, Hollywood's Catholic priest represented the revolution in social values that gangster films helped inaugurate and that movies such as *Angels with Dirty Faces* and *Boys Town* extended.

The cycle of Catholic reform films began in 1936, the year of Roosevelt's landslide reelection victory, with *San Francisco* (1936). The Metro-Goldwyn-Mayer (MGM) epic about the San Francisco earthquake of 1906 has Spencer Tracy playing a tough Father Tim Mullin, who both helps the city's poor and holds his own inside a boxing ring. Father Mullin provides the moral anchor for the film's two leading characters, Blackie Norton (Clark Gable), the owner of a casino and dance hall who leads the civic efforts to reform the commercial district, and Mary Blake (Jeanette MacDonald), a country parson's daughter and singer in Blackie's club with whom Blackie has fallen in love. The film ends with Father Mullin, Blackie, and Mary accompanying the citizens of San Francisco in a march through the city; they sing "The Battle Hymn of the Republic" in a demonstration of collective public resilience after the devastating earthquake.

Even more explicit in linking the priest and the urban underworld together was *Angels with Dirty Faces* (1938), which also proved to be popular with moviegoers. The crane shot that traverses a crowded street of a multiethnic neighborhood to open the film establishes the urban, working-class world in which its two main characters, Rocky Sullivan (James Cagney) and Jerry Connolly (Pat O'Brien), play out their lives together. Rocky grows up to be a mobster, moving in and out of prison while rising up the ladder of organized crime. Jerry sticks to the straight and narrow and becomes a priest, whose parish is the very one that he and Rocky belonged to as kids. Father Jerry is not so much the gangster's opposite as his cultural brother, cut from the same urban, ethnic, working-class cloth. A scene where Rocky returns to the old neighborhood after his release from prison and visits Jerry at their old parish church vividly conveys their shared identity. Their recounting of all their youthful misadventures demonstrates that even though they may have taken different paths as adults, their common roots in the ethnic neighborhood run deep.

Initially, Rocky even helps Jerry with the boys' club the priest has created as an alternative to the criminal culture of the streets. But Cagney as a gangster is a terrible character to waste, and as Rocky attempts to reassert his place within the mob syndicate, he and Jerry part company. As the criminal domination of the city becomes evident, the priest tells Rocky he is determined to destroy the mob's influence in order to save the kids of the city, even if that means bringing down his old friend.

Angels portrays Jerry as a very publicly oriented priest. The cleric meets with newspaper reporters to enlist support for his crusade. He offers a radio talk calling for public action. Newspaper headlines blare, PRIEST DECLARES WAR ON UNDERWORLD VICE. A camera zooms in to highlight the words FATHER CONNELLY SAYS HE WILL LEAD A REAL REFORM MOVEMENT. A poster announces a "mass meeting" with the priest. The use of newspaper headlines, radios, and posters all align Father Jerry with the public world of the city. Assigning a very civic role to the priest, *Angels* utilizes the moral authority of the Catholic cleric to symbolize social reform. One mobster even complains that the priest has unleashed a "tidal wave" of reform that threatens the entire gangster operation, further underscoring the public identity of Father Jerry.

Although the movie's image of the cleric as reformer suggested the Protestant, middle-class crusades for good government of the progressive era, Father Jerry also resonated with more immediate associations of 1930s social reform. His use of the radio clearly referenced Father Coughlin's popular broadcasts critiquing capitalists. But the Depression also had other vocal priests, such as Bernard Sheil in Chicago and Charles Owen Rice in Pittsburgh, who championed social action on behalf of workers and the downtrodden.[25] Their presence in the public sphere gave the priest of *Angels with Dirty Faces* additional cultural resonance. In addition, mobsters (or the criminal "organization," as one newspaperman calls the gangsters in the film) often served as an indirect sign of industrial capitalism within Hollywood movies. Father Jerry's tidal wave of reform therefore suggested not simply clean government but also a social movement challenging the modern corporate interests undermining the common good of society.

Both the reform theme and the doubling trope that structures Rocky and Jerry's relationship culminate in the film's climax, in which the priest asks the gangster to act "yellow" as he faces the electric chair. Hoping that his friend will realize the street boys will emulate Rocky's criminal life if they believe the mobster died heroically, Jerry wants Rocky to sacrifice his dignity for the sake of others. At first, Rocky refuses, determined to maintain his pride in the face of death. But as he is strapped into the chair, viewers hear and indirectly see Rocky's frantic pleas to be saved from electrocution. The effect of this ignominious death upon Father Jerry's boys is just as the priest had hoped. The final scene has the cleric leading the kids up the stairs of the clubhouse to the church to pray for Rocky's soul. The movie leaves ambiguously open the ultimate reason for Rocky's final actions. But the possibility that he did feign cowardice suggests the mobster proved to be the most significant reformer of all in the entire film, serving the priest's own public goals but in the gritty, life-and-death terms of the streets.[26]

In 1938, the year in which *Angels with Dirty Faces* was released, MGM returned to the winning formula of the crusading priest of its earlier hit *San Francisco* with the enormously popular *Boys Town*. This film, based on the true story of Father Edward J. Flanagan of Omaha, Nebraska, and his reformatory for unwanted boys, won high praise from critics. The *Film Daily* raved, "The film is compelling in its human qualities, so much so that an audience can readily live the struggles of Father Flanagan."[27] The *Motion Picture Herald* was even more laudatory, "Cold, black type alone cannot begin to describe the dramatic power of 'Boys Town.' . . . While the screen has had many stories concerned with juvenile regeneration, it never has had one like 'Boys Town.'"[28] *Newsweek* was not quite as enthusiastic but nevertheless praised the film as "heart-warming." *Time* also applauded its "commendable simplicity" and highlighted the "most impressive scenes," including those involving "the working of student government" depicted by the boys of Father Flanagan's reform town.[29]

Boys Town opens with Father Flanagan hearing the death-row confession of a prisoner who attributes his criminal life to his early years, when

Hollywood's Catholic priest of the 1930s as depicted in Boys Town *(1938): occupying the same cultural landscape as the tough guys and gangsters from crime dramas, Father Flanagan (Spencer Tracy) battles against social injustice. Courtesy of Photofest.*

he was a "lonely starving kid" who slept in a "flophouse with a bunch of drunks, tramps and hoboes." The prison-house setting and the criminal's confession immediately tie Father Flanagan to the world of urban crime and punishment that was a staple of Hollywood's gangster films. The man's story of being dropped by the state into reform schools that only hardened him into a criminal leads Flanagan to propose a new solution to teenage delinquency. He decides to create an alternative institution, not a reformatory in the traditional sense but a town for boys that would reach out to the city's most neglected members and transform them into public-minded citizens. Flanagan's project of according respect and dignity to abandoned boys and allowing them to assume responsibility for running a new community of their own making epitomizes the cooperative, compassionate values that Robert McElvaine argues characterized American culture in the Depression.[30]

Boys Town, in fact, turns the Catholic priest and his institution into models of reformist America. The film depicts Flanagan's crusade as a challenge to reigning social authorities, as demonstrated by the priest's unsuccessful attempt to gain the support of the city's powerful newspaper publisher, Hargraves. When Flanagan asks the news baron why he is so hostile to his project, Hargraves responds, "There is a feeling in official circles that you are setting up a tacit criticism of things as they are." When Flanagan persists, the publisher retorts, "You know, you're flying in the face of the very best of public opinion." The priest's activities on behalf of the dispossessed therefore are presented as an implicitly political challenge to the status quo rather than simple charity. *Boys Town's* Catholicism does offer an affirmative vision of society, in keeping with Hollywood's regulatory regime, but it is one associated with the active reform of injustice and the creation of new forms of inclusive, cooperative community.

The actual construction of Boys Town further underscores the reformist, public character of Father Flanagan's dream. Through a montage of shots of the teenage boys digging trenches, laying bricks, and physically building the reform city, the movie visually imagines the enterprise as practically a WPA project. These shots are rendered from a variety of angles, capturing the energy of collective work, and they culminate with an image of the new Boys Town, a modern building that proudly sits upon the heartland prairie, the creation of the boys themselves.

In addition to depicting the physical labor of the boys as an exercise in New Deal public works building, the movie also stresses Boys Town as a democratic institution run by its members. All the boys take responsibility for the maintenance and running of their city. Indeed, the film's story revolves around one teenager, Whitey Marsh (Mickey Rooney), who arrives at Boys Town committed to an individualistic ethic—"I ain't helping nobody"—only to come to appreciate the value of the institution and its virtues of collaboration by the end of the movie.

The movie devotes a great deal of attention to the election of the mayor of Boys Town, chosen from among the boys themselves. Campaign signs, speeches, and collective assemblies of the community all associate Father Flanagan's experiment in reform with civic virtues of public participation. The film even ends not in church or in Father Flanagan's office but in the assembly hall, with the boys having chosen a repentant Whitey as mayor of their community.

Democracy extends even to the handling of religion. A lunch scene after the arrival of Whitey stresses that Father Flanagan's institution is a place of religious tolerance. Before the boys start eating, they say grace. A series of shots that show the boys praying to themselves, including a Jewish boy reciting a prayer in Hebrew, offers a portrait of religious pluralism. A boy sitting next to Whitey explains, "At Boys Town, every boy worships as they please, think the way they want to. If you are a Catholic or a Protestant you can go on being one."

The film's identification with the New Deal is made particularly transparent by Flanagan's response to one of the boys running for mayor, Tony Ponessa. Tony, who happens to be running on the "progressive" ticket as his campaign sign declares, has a bad leg and walks with a limp. When he gets discouraged about running for election, Flanagan tells him about another person who was "ill for a long time but had the courage to get well. People began to cheer him for lots of things and he became president of the United States." The identification of Roosevelt with the ethnic, "progressive" Tony Ponessa serves to condense the film's larger equivalence of Boys Town with the public energy and social reformism of the New Deal. Father Flanagan is even a deficit spender, as is made clear in the numerous scenes in which he waves off concerns that he has dug Boys Town deep into debt to pay for his expansive plans to care for more destitute boys.

Boys Town therefore used Catholic imagery to advance a social reformist narrative of America during the 1930s. Its expression of civic renewal through social consciousness and mutual cooperation captured the cultural mood of New Deal America and made it one of the most successful films of 1938. But the profitability of the film represented only one measure of its success, for not only did Father Flanagan's city for boys offer a story of public revitalization but the movie itself became the source of communal spirit off screen as well.

The world premiere of the film in Omaha, Nebraska, home of the actual Boys Town, revealed the film's ability to organize the new pluralist civic identity of thirties America. In preparation for the film's opening, the mayor of Omaha proclaimed the date of the premiere as Boys Town Day and turned over city offices to the boy officials elected at the real Boys Town. Catholic, Protestant, and Jewish leaders were contacted and promised to cooperate in promoting the film. Then, on the night of September 7, 1938, 30,000 people gathered outside the Omaha Theater to celebrate the world premiere of *Boys Town*. The film's stars, Tracy and Rooney, and Father Flanagan himself greeted the crowd. The mayor of Omaha described the enormous gathering outside the theater as a "recognition of and tribute to a great humanitarian, Father Flanagan." Other local and state dignitaries included the president of the Omaha Chamber of Commerce, the governor of Nebraska, and Bishop James Ryan of Omaha, each of whom spoke to the crowd. Their words were carried over 107 radio stations from a live hookup by the Mutual Broadcasting System. Inside the theater, a crowd of 2,000, among them the president of B'nai B'rith, heard brief talks from the stars and many of the same officials, such as Bishop Ryan.[31]

The ability of *Boys Town* to encourage a shared, pluralist public culture extended beyond Omaha. Across the country, the movie generated enthusiastic responses from public officials and civic groups alike. In Superior, Wisconsin, the mayor turned over city offices to boys chosen by the local schools and Boys Scouts as part of the opening of the film in that community.[32] In Syracuse, New York, one movie theater turned itself into a Boys Town for a day and hosted winners of a high school election to serve as city officials. The "elected officials" were treated to a lunch at a downtown restaurant and a showing of the movie. The local newspaper published a review of the film by a "boy critic" who was part of the special screening of the movie.[33] In Fall River, Massachusetts, the local *Herald-News* placed a quote from Father Flanagan—I HAVE NEVER REALLY FOUND A BOY WHO WANTED TO BE BAD—above its masthead on the front page as part of its support for the film.[34] Fall River also saw the election of local boys to run the city for a day as part of a broad campaign to publicize the film. The theater owner responsible for the promotion claimed such cooperation was a first for local theaters.[35] Similarly, in Queens, New York, the borough president, district attorney, police inspector, supreme court justice, city editor of the *Daily Star*, and manager of the Loew's Triboro theater agreed to turn over their jobs for a day to honor students chosen from local public schools. Catholic schools declared a half-day holiday, with the "entire student body marching to theaters on opening day."[36]

Father Flanagan himself received star treatment and even wrote a piece for the popular fan magazine *Photoplay* about the institution he founded.[37] He also wrote, "I Meet Spencer Tracy," for *Liberty* magazine (reprinted in *Catholic Digest*), in which he proclaimed, "All Hollywood seems to participate in a growing social consciousness which is abroad the land. In such pictures as *Winterset* and *Dead End* the motion-picture industry has demonstrated its power along these lines. *Boys Town* will, I believe, be its first attempt at a social-service theme developed upon actual fact and living figures."[38]

Not surprisingly, many Catholics applauded *Boys Town*. Referring to the movie's complimentary treatment of Father Flanagan, *Commonweal*'s reviewer asserted, "When the films do crash through with an exposition of the fine work of a member of our faith, they should be encouraged."[39] Leonard A. McMahon, writing in *Sign*, the magazine of the Passionist Fathers, claimed, "Here is a picture . . . about a strictly Catholic theme that will be seen by about 50,000,000 that 'go' for a good picture."[40]

Boys Town therefore generated enormous enthusiasm both in and out of movie theaters, turning a film about a Catholic priest's reform of wayward youth into an occasion for identification with the civic realm. The film demonstrated how popular representation of Catholics linked social consciousness, ethnic pluralism, and civic life together during the thirties. By rearticulating the figure of the priest from a strictly Catholic context into a more extensive social landscape of class, economic, and ethnic differences, movies utilized Catholicism to narrate a new reformist identity for Depression-era America. As the success of *Boys Town* as well as *Angels with Dirty Faces* and *San Francisco* indicated, by the late thirties movies had made Catholics into the nation's favored religious minority by identifying them with a new public realm of pluralism and social justice.

The New Convention of Catholicism in Thirties Cinema

The Spencer Tracy and Pat O'Brien/James Cagney movies proved commercial hits that helped create a new reform-minded image of Catholicism in popular culture, but these films were quite exceptional in the acclaim they received. Moviegoers were just as apt to encounter Catholic imagery in numerous other films that presented the priest in minor roles, among them *Over the Wall* (1937), *We Who Are about to Die* (1938), *You Only Live Once* (1938), *The Devil's Party* (1938), and *Castle on the Hudson* (1940). Significantly, these movies were all crime and social problem films, indicative of how intertwined the criminal and the priest, the underworld and the church had become in Hollywood's portrayals of contemporary American society.

It was from such numerous, prosaic films that the image of the compassionate prison chaplain or the priest of the ethnic neighborhood became conventionalized in the popular imagination. For example, in William Dieterle's *The Great O'Malley* (1937), the evocation of working-class, immigrant life in New York City includes a priest, Father Patrick, who is a friend of the cop, James Aloysius O'Malley, and the neighborhood counselor. Similarly, *Off the Record* (1939), a film starring Pat O'Brien (in a nonclerical role) about a young boy who takes to the street after the death of his mother, briefly utilizes the figure of the Catholic priest in the opening scenes to suggest both the working-class Catholic milieu in which the plot unfolds and the Catholic priest as a mediator between the poor and the social welfare system. Father Jerry in *The Devil's Party* counsels hope that everything will work out. Father Connor in *Over the Wall* encourages a wrongfully condemned prisoner to remember that his "tomorrows" can lead to a better day. In all these films, the priest is a minor figure but nevertheless helps to elaborate the urban, working-class world Hollywood found audiences craved.[41]

San Francisco Docks (1940) is a particularly illuminating example of this conventional representation of the Catholic priest. The *Hollywood Reporter* review described the character of the movie's priest as "time worn," and indeed it did incorporate many of the features identified with the Catholic priest in 1930s and 1940s films.[42] The movie tells the story of a young longshoreman, Johnny Barnes (Burgess Meredith), wrongfully convicted of murdering a waterfront politician whom he saw pawing his girlfriend, Kitty; the cast of characters includes a two-fisted priest, Father Cameron (Robert Armstrong).

Cameron is actually a friend of Johnny's, and he champions the worker's plight when the young man is accused of murder. The circumstantial evidence points to Johnny's guilt, and when he is arrested, Father Cameron pleads Johnny's case to the district attorney. The lawyer, though convinced of the young man's guilt, asks the priest what he would do in his shoes. Father Cameron replies, "I'm a priest and you are a prosecuting attorney and they're just about the opposite ends of the pole but I'd let Johnny Barnes go and find the real criminal." As Cameron's response suggests, crime functions as an indirect signifier of working-class injustice, and *San Francisco Docks* utilizes the figure of the Catholic priest to represent a public voice defending the cause of the working man.

Father Cameron (Robert Armstrong) and his wharf-rat friend (Barry Fitzgerald) tracking down a killer in San Francisco Docks *(1940), one of a number of films in the 1930s and early 1940s that aligned the priest with the modern, working-class city and its people. Courtesy of Photofest.*

Eventually, Father Cameron and Kitty locate the real killer, Monte March, holed up in an apartment. When the killer refuses the priest's demand that he surrender, the cleric kicks in the door of the apartment in a blaze of gunfire from March. March escapes out the window with Cameron in pursuit. Observing Father Cameron chase March into the alleys, longshoremen in the street follow the priest, and the hunt for the real killer becomes a collective effort of the workingmen of the docks led by the Catholic priest. Cameron and the longshoremen corner March, and when March attacks him, the priest hits the killer with a right hook that levels the criminal. With the murderer apprehended, Johnny is released and returns to the docks, where a welcome home party is waiting for him at Kitty's father's saloon.

San Francisco Docks contained numerous conventions that informed Hollywood's rendition of the priest of the thirties. He was virile, good with his fists but compassionate, identified with the working-class milieu of the modern city, and an advocate of justice. But in the thirties, those conventions carried potent ideological significance. Class and economic concerns had created a new public sphere in American life, epitomized by the popular support for New Deal initiatives. From Father Cameron to Father Flanagan, from B movies to major studio productions, from *San Francisco Docks* to *Boys Town,* Hollywood turned Catholicism into a sign of a reformist nation. The Americanization of Catholics represented not merely the inclusion of religious minorities but also a transformation in the terms of national belonging. In the figure of the Hollywood priest, religious difference and social consciousness converged to forge a new popular Americanism.

Soldiers, Saints, and the Counterreformation of Forties Cinema

The reform-mindedness of America in the 1930s would not survive the following decade.[43] The growing threat of fascism and war diverted many people's attention to the tragedies unfolding in Europe; this was particularly true among political leaders and intellectuals. The military buildup demanded by Roosevelt starting in the late thirties also had a marked impact on the fortunes of the economy and brought the nation out of the Depression.

The 1940s nevertheless witnessed a continuing fascination with Catholicism in Hollywood. Although the movie priest of the urban neighborhood remained a fixture of popular imagination, Catholic films in "the shadow of war" also expressed wider cultural shifts that were reshaping notions of American identity.[44] Among the most popular Catholic movies of the decade were *The Fighting 69th* (1940), which told the story of the fabled Irish army brigade, the 69th Regiment of New York, and its famous Catholic chaplain, Father Francis Duffy, during World War I, and *The Song of Bernadette* (1943), a film about Bernadette Soubirous, the young nineteenth-century French saint and the miraculous shrine at Lourdes.

It would be a mistake, though, to read Catholic movies of this era, such as *The Song of Bernadette,* as simply religious sentimentality divorced from broader social currents. Indeed, they reflected the eclipse of progressive change that characterized much of American culture in the forties.[45] These movies broke dramatically in theme and content from the previous decade's productions, which had aligned Catholicism with progressive social change. Rather than highlighting inequities in existing society and focusing religious representation around issues of social justice, the films of the forties fostered cultural unity and identification with the private sphere. Like many other films of the era, such as those in the war platoon genre, Catholic movies encouraged Americans to abandon their doubts about the nation and spiritually rearm themselves for the country's defense. The decade began with a movie that foreshadowed the growing conservatism in Hollywood's treatment of Catholics—a film that once again teamed James Cagney and Pat O'Brien, now no longer battling on the urban streets of America but confronting one another in the cause of war. Shifting the focus from the ethnic neighborhood to the military regiment, *The Fighting 69th* rearticulated Catholicism from matters of reform to issues of national consensus.

The premiere of the film in New York City was greeted with much fanfare by members of the 165th Regiment (as the old 69th Regiment was called by the 1930s) and by movie fans as well. Veterans of the regiment gathered at the Waldorf-Astoria for a twenty-second anniversary reunion and a preview of the film. The event was broadcast to gatherings of veterans of the division in forty other cities. Among the speakers addressing the reunion were Governor Herbert H. Lehman of New York; William Donovan, the commander of the "Fighting 69th"; and General Douglas MacArthur, who spoke by radio. Bishop John F. O'Hara, former president of Notre Dame and the supervisor of Catholic chaplains in the U.S. Army, was also in attendance, along with numerous other military officials. The *New York Times* reported that Lehman commemorated Father Duffy as a "'brave and kindly priest who placed duty to God and man above all else'" and praised the film's message that "'from all races and creeds and from all walks of life comes equally the willingness to serve and to sacrifice in a just cause.'"[46]

Publicity played up both the martial and the religious dimensions of the film. Advertisements promoted the movie as an action adventure. In some ads, Father Duffy was portrayed as but one member of the military brigade. The *Motion Picture Herald* reported that some exhibitors utilized the American Legion as part of promotional events.[47] Other efforts encouraged Catholic identification. In addition to the presence of Bishop O'Hara at the premiere festivities, for instance, a Catholic priest in Danville, Illinois, spoke of Duffy at Mass in advance of the local opening of the film.[48] Further, five weeks after the premiere in New York, Fulton J. Sheen spoke at a communion breakfast to veterans of the 69th, condemning the loss of respect for authority in the United States.[49]

The film itself offered a narrative of social reconciliation through the story of army chaplain Father Duffy (O'Brien) and a recalcitrant new recruit, Jerry Plunkett (Cagney). The young man has signed up for the chance to gain glory in the war in Europe. Long before the brigade ships out, however, Plunkett alienates everyone in the 69th except Father Duffy. Cagney's character symbolizes the residual, unmelted ethnic, urban culture intruding upon the nation-state's project of war making. But Duffy goes the extra mile to help Plunkett overcome his selfishness and cowardice. By the end of the film, Plunkett repents, returns to his Catholic faith, and is transformed from an angry malcontent into a self-sacrificing soldier.

The celebratory story of Father Duffy and the 69th helped revise the image of World War I, which, as Thomas Doherty has pointed out, remained a deeply troubling memory in the popular imagination for much of the 1930s.[50] War in *The Fighting 69th*'s rendering was no longer a failed cause but a valiant effort to preserve American ideals. In the same fashion, the army was rehabilitated into an admirable feature of American society. Rather than a bankrupt purveyor of death and destruction, the army became an institution that welcomed ethnic and religious outsiders such as Plunkett, a Jewish soldier named Moscowitz, and the Catholic Father Duffy himself.

In fact, the film not only gave a new affirmative meaning to the military, it also reworked the image of an Americanized Catholicism. Through the character of Father Duffy, *The Fighting 69th* detached Catholicism from its public role in thirties films and turned it into a sign of the melting-pot nation. Social unity now became imagined through identification with traditional institutions such as the army. Whereas Father Flanagan allowed Jews, Catholics, and Protestants to find commonality in the shared project of building a new, civic enterprise such as Boys Town, Father Duffy signified that religious outsiders could find a home in America by subordinating themselves to the demands of war and the military state.

The Fighting 69th therefore introduced a new institution in which Hollywood placed the Catholic priest. The old ethnic neighborhood had been replaced by boot camp and battlefield. The Catholic cleric gave voice to assimilationist allegiances rather than demands for social change. In shifting the context and character of Hollywood's favorite religious character, the film demonstrated that the emergent consensus culture of the 1940s and 1950s entailed a rearticulation in the representation of ethnic and religious minorities away from a public sphere of reform and experimentation.

Made prior to U.S. involvement in World War II, *The Fighting 69th* actually anticipated the platoon movies of that war such as *Air Force,* which acknowledged ethnic diversity in order to subordinate it to demands of the nation-state.[51] These films used war to imagine an escape from the New Deal era, echoing Roosevelt's own admission that Dr. New Deal had become Dr. Win-the-War. No film, however, better demonstrated the ways the fight against fascism encouraged Americans to transcend their social conflicts than the popular *Song of Bernadette,* an account of Bernadette Soubirous, a nineteenth-century French peasant girl who claimed to have visions of a "lady" believed to be the Virgin Mary. Even more than *The Fighting 69th,* this film broke from the thirties reform films and directed moviegoers' attention to traditional virtues of religious belief and faith in God.

One might have thought that a film about a young, French Catholic saint responsible for a shrine assumed to have miraculous healing powers would have only a narrow appeal among American moviegoers in the midst of World War II. But *The Song of Bernadette* adeptly tailored Catholic particularity to mass audiences by translating saintliness into a symbol of spiritual courage and commitment. The French girl of nineteenth-century Lourdes functioned as a surrogate for a generalized faith in the face of opposition from government bureaucrats and secular skeptics. Bernadette offered audiences a religion shorn of reformist priests and ecclesial indictments of social injustice in favor of individual belief. The result was a film that utilized Catholic devotion to narrate private reasons for the political obligations of war.[52]

The movie tapped into a long history involving Bernadette and the shrine at Lourdes, one with which many American Catholics would have been familiar. It originated in events surrounding a poor, sickly peasant girl who in 1858 claimed to have had a series of visions of a young woman dressed in white at a grotto outside Lourdes.[53] Bernadette asserted that the woman identified herself as the Immaculate Conception, the understanding of the Virgin Mary as conceived without sin that only a few years before had been promulgated as dogma by the papacy. Equally significant, at the apparition's request, Bernadette had dug a hole in the ground at the base of the grotto. Out of this hole emerged waters that would become the famous source for healing that has drawn millions of pilgrims to Lourdes ever since.

Although Bernadette and Lourdes were European, they functioned as rich, polyvalent symbols within American Catholic devotional life in the twentieth century. The Holy Cross order of priests who founded the University of Notre Dame, for example, became actively engaged in promoting Lourdes by distributing its miraculous water in the United States and building a replica of the shrine on their campus in South Bend, Indiana.[54] Other Catholics also built numerous Lourdes grottoes, making tangible, as John McGreevy argues, the transnational connections that bound American Catholics to their European brethren.[55]

Yet what brought Bernadette and Lourdes to the attention of many non-Catholics in 1942 was a book by a Jewish refugee fleeing the Nazis, *The Song of Bernadette*. Franz Werfel's story became a commercial best seller, and Twentieth Century–Fox quickly bought the movie rights. Werfel's own dramatic escape from the Nazis by way of Lourdes, France, and a visit to the famous shrine added both an ecumenical character and a wartime currency to the story of Bernadette for popular audiences in the midforties.[56]

Werfel's popular account of Bernadette and the apparitions at Lourdes entered into a complex set of existing discourses and practices among American Catholics involving pilgrimage, healing and illness, the miraculous, sanctity and sainthood, science, and even war and peace.[57] Yet when the film arrived in theaters, it was associated with decidedly American referents. The studio, Twentieth Century–Fox, commissioned Norman Rockwell to paint a portrait of Jennifer Jones as Bernadette, which was widely used in the film's ad campaigns. Patrons at the Rivoli in New York as well as the Exeter Theater in Toledo, Ohio, were given free color reproductions of the Rockwell painting.[58] Huge billboard cutouts of Rockwell's rendition of Bernadette, underscoring her individuality, fronted movie theater marquees and lobbies in New York, Milwaukee, New Haven, and Atlanta.[59]

An ad in the Protestant *Christian Herald* detached Bernadette from her devotional context by using the Rockwell portrait. At Bernadette's feet, a crowd of people were clustered, but there was no indication of the shrine or grotto or even the church in the ad. Above her head was the copy, "A motion picture so deep in its understanding . . . so powerful in its emotional sweep . . . that for one immortal moment you touch the eternal truth . . . the final fulfillment . . . of everything you are . . . or ever hope to be."[60] The *Motion Picture Daily* went even further in generalizing the appeal of the film, praising the movie as "a picture about plain people, their problems and their pains, their prides and their prejudices, their living and their dying, their hearts and their souls."[61]

The Song of Bernadette was promoted and received within a context of the nation's wartime struggles. Thus, Twentieth Century–Fox highlighted a quote by the film's scriptwriter, George Seaton, in one piece of promotional material: "If the picturization of this story of Bernadette Soubirous, who so fearlessly faced a world filled with doubt and hatred succeeds in giving someone courage to remain steadfast against the forces that are intent upon destroying all faith and hope, then I shall feel that I have, in part, fulfilled my obligation."[62] Similarly, *Variety* noted that Bernadette offered "a strong and inspirational religious theme, particularly strengthening in these troublous [sic] times when people are turning to God."[63] Terry Ramsaye editorialized in the *Motion Picture Herald* that *Song of Bernadette* was a "picture of faith born of faith under ordeals," referring to the plight of Franz Werfel. He claimed the film "is not for those who expect to be lulled into salvation, but it will be a stirring experience for the many who are willing to accept the disappointments of the Now as part of the path to a better Tomorrow."[64]

The filmmakers' choice of Catholicism as the sign of spiritual commitment for wartime America understandably excited Catholic critics and moviegoers alike. *Commonweal's* movie reviewer wrote that the film "is a hymn sung in praise of the girl who was chosen to be visited by Our Lady."[65] The *Sign* dubbed *Song of Bernadette* "the most important production of the cinema year. . . . Amid the amoral chaos of the hour it stands as a shining guidepost to the only true and lasting solution to our problems."[66] Movie theater owners writing in the "What the Picture Did for Me" column in the *Motion Picture Herald* noted the Catholic audience for *Bernadette*. One exhibitor in North Vernon, Indiana, asserted, "If you have a lot of Catholics in your community, play it. They came out in spite of the $1.10 price which isn't justified by the picture. My regular customers stayed away."[67] G. H. Maxon, exhibitor of the Strand in Jewell, Iowa, wrote, "This is strictly a religious offering and will appeal to your Catholic customers."[68] A movie house operator in Middlebury, Vermont, stated, "We had the preview showing in the state of Vermont and all the priests in our community recommended that their parishioners see this feature without fail. Patrons came for miles to see it and declared it was absolutely wonderful."[69]

As both a story of so-called ordinary people and an account of a Catholic saint, *The Song of Bernadette* managed to appeal to diverse audiences. The film was an enormous commercial success in the winter and spring of 1944 even as the film's studio kept prices for the movie high throughout the year in an effort to maintain its prestige value.[70] The film also garnered five Academy Awards, including the best actress award for Jennifer Jones's portrayal of Bernadette.

The film reflected the cultural work Catholic representations during the 1940s performed in directing moviegoers to identify with a privatized world of religion, faith, and piety. Though ostensibly about the travails of an innocent girl in nineteenth-century France, *The Song of Bernadette* spoke deeply and directly to the American home front. Rendering sanctity as a conflict between individual belief and arrogant, God-denying state officials, the movie turned Catholic devotion into a cultural justification for the righteousness of the country's fight against totalitarianism.[71] In the tumultuous war years, Hollywood showed how even Old World Catholicism could be harnessed to American identity. Thanks to the movies, the young saint from Lourdes took her place right alongside Betty Grable and Rita Hayworth as an icon of a nation at war.

The Song of Bernadette exemplified a wider pattern of forties cinema that Lary May has identified as the World War II conversion narrative, in which characters abandoned their prior allegiances to reformist and critical values in favor of cultural consensus.[72] In such films as *Air Force,* individuals learned the virtues of commitment to a larger cause than themselves only after initial skepticism. However, *Bernadette* offered a variant of this cultural narrative of conversion by privileging a main character who remained steadfast in her faith and ultimately triumphed over the forces of elite doubt.

The film is structured around a series of resistances to Bernadette's belief that she experienced an apparition of "the Lady." Initially, her parents tell her to quit believing in her visions; then, the town officials are shocked and disturbed that such "religious fanaticism" has persisted in the nineteenth century. The nun at Bernadette's school is one of her harshest critics, assuming the girl is attempting to call attention to herself. The head priest of Lourdes also wants nothing to do with Bernadette's story. The local bishop is particularly dubious and distances himself from the girl's claims.

The opposition to Bernadette helped make her unwavering commitment to her belief appear heroic. At a time when Americans were engaged in a war to protect religious liberty as one of the four basic freedoms for all people, the innocent French girl offered moviegoers a clear symbol of the right of religious choice, a right for which the nation was fighting. But the movie's attention to the forces of opposition arrayed against

Bernadette did more than simply heighten dramatic tension. The film also highlighted resistance to Bernadette's faith in order to portray its eventual defeat. First, her mother and father come to believe their daughter's story. In addition, the priest slowly realizes that Bernadette may be a "vessel of grace." The school nun repents of her cruel treatment of the girl and dedicates herself to helping Bernadette in her final years. Even the town's public officials ultimately abandon their opposition.

One of the film's most effective devices in narrating its story of conversion from skepticism to commitment involves the recurrent scenes of officials commenting on the events surrounding the grotto. In the process, moviegoers watch skeptics turn into believers. Initially, the public officials look down upon the poor peasants enthralled by "religious superstition." Their isolation from the streets—signified by walls and the windows and doorways through which they observe the action—increases their separation from the ordinary people who are aligned with Bernadette. But through the course of the film, many of these men embrace the "miracle" of Bernadette. Their own transformation underscores the notion that the peoples' faith is ultimately more powerful than the elitist beliefs of godless state officials.

The most dramatic instance of conversion involves Imperial Prosecutor Dutour (Vincent Price), an intensely antireligious skeptic who is Bernadette's most dedicated opponent. Throughout the film, he is relentless in his efforts to prevent the spread of the girl's story and is determined to deny the pilgrims the benefits of the grotto's healing waters. Dutour epitomizes arrogant state bureaucracy opposed to the religious faith of the people. Even his title, imperial prosecutor, repeatedly invoked through the film, implies the malevolence of state power. But in the end, even he is converted, as dramatized in a scene in which he wanders through the crowd at the shrine and kneels before the gates at the grotto asking Bernadette to pray for him in his own time of illness.

As a movie about the life of a nineteenth-century French saint, *The Song of Bernadette* may appear to have had little connection with the cultural politics of the 1940s. Yet considered within the context of Hollywood's efforts during the war to distance itself from the critical reformism of the previous decade, *Bernadette* assumed significance as a narrative of cultural conversion from public to private realms. Public life, personified by the town officials and particularly Dutour, was associated with elitism, hostility to religion, and opposition to the freedom of worship. In the world of this film, the public sphere was antidemocratic, identified with godless state bureaucracy. It was in the realm of personal faith that *Bernadette* identified with traditional American values of individualism and freedom of religious expression. Bernadette's heroic commitment to her beliefs made a private realm of individual faith and perseverance a focus of collective identification.

The Song of Bernadette therefore demonstrated the cultural impact that the popular mobilization for war had on the symbolic terms of American identity. Hollywood found in the story of nineteenth-century European Catholicism a powerful subject through which to represent the commitments and ideals of a wartime nation. But this achievement came with a price. Lourdes focused attention on the virtues of the spirit itself, encouraging moviegoers to forget the material concerns and social hopes that had informed films of the previous decade. Next to Bernadette's grotto, Father Flanagan could not hold a candle.

Thus, by the midforties, Catholicism found itself in a remarkable, unexpected position. Thanks to Hollywood, it had become the popular religion of modern America. That development rested upon a wider cultural transformation of national identity that had begun during the 1930s. Catholicism proved a useful subject with which to elaborate the social and cultural changes of a modern America remade by urbanization, industrialization, and ethnic, religious pluralism. Until the thirties, however, those social realities remained only partially incorporated into the national imaginary.[73] The Depression undermined traditional conceptions of American community that had privileged Anglo-Protestantism and allowed alternative voices and perspectives new legitimacy. The very foreignness of Catholics became a strong stance from which to reimagine the nation along urban, ethnic, and communal terms. The Depression and movies therefore not only Americanized Catholicism but also created Catholic representations that elaborated a reformist vision of society. Because Hollywood had established Catholics as signs of a new public, pluralist Americanism in the thirties, Catholicism also proved useful in redirecting national allegiance along more private lines, as evidenced by films such as *The Song of Bernadette*, when events pushed social concerns to the side. Images of Catholics found new relevancy in the changing cultural context of wartime America.

Yet not everyone was happy with the idea of Catholics as emblems of national community. Indeed, a number of Protestants wrote to Eric Johnston, the head of the Motion Picture Producers' Association, complaining of the prominence of Catholic themes in the movies. The Michigan woman mentioned earlier who was concerned about Bing Crosby was not alone in worrying about the collapse of Protestant cultural authority that movies suggested. For instance, one filmgoer from Toledo, Ohio, wrote Johnston, "I as a movie patron and a Protestant make a protest over the flood of Catholic films that are being thrust on the movie public . . . I am tired of paying, through the purchase of show tickets, for Catholic propaganda." A woman from Cedartown, Georgia, chastised Johnston for confusing Catholicism with Christianity in America: "Why does Hollywood seem to think that a priest or nun symbolizes religion for the movie going public. Such is not predominantly the case, I assure you." Another writer charged that Hollywood had confused Catholic spectacle for authentic religion. She wrote Johnston, "Most religions have something substantial and inspirational to offer; perhaps not as much ceremony and ritual as the Catholic faith—*but* do these two features really *make* a religion? . . . Just drop in on the Baptists, Methodists, Christian Scientists, and Lutherans, etc. and you'll have an idea of how they turn to God for daily bread."[74]

These letter writers sensed the cultural significance of popular Catholic films in the 1930s and 1940s. Operating within older traditional assumptions that equated Protestantism with true Americanism, they saw the film industry's focus on Catholicism as a conscious effort to ruin the nation. Yet even though movie producers were sensitive to the possibility of a church-led boycott, the success of *Angels with Dirty Faces* and *The Fighting 69th* indicated that many moviegoers liked Hollywood's Catholics. And one film in particular would take the Catholic representation of America to a whole new level of popular appeal, critical acclaim, and cultural impact. That film, more than any other, marked a dramatic rejection of the social reformism that earlier Catholic movies such as *Boys Town* signified. Unlike *The Song of Bernadette*, it targeted the very urban ethnic landscape that had aligned Catholics with the social ethos of the 1930s. Little did moviegoers realize at the time that *Going My Way*, a movie about a young and modern priest who saves a Catholic parish, would have such import for American culture. But the magic of Bing Crosby proved irresistible to audiences eager to exchange the struggles of the past for the comforts of an untroubled future. I now turn to this film and the next phase in the Catholic moment in American popular culture.

CHAPTER THREE

COOL CATHOLICS IN THE HOT
AMERICAN MELTING POT:
GOING MY WAY, BING CROSBY,
AND HOLLYWOOD'S NEW FAITH
IN CONSENSUS

In the Academy Award contest for the best picture of 1944, *Going My Way* faced stiff competition from Billy Wilder's crime drama *Double Indemnity*. The two films could hardly have been more different. One starred Bing Crosby as a young, easygoing Catholic priest who saves a New York City parish from foreclosure. The other offered a powerful story of illicit love turned murderous as Fred McMurray played a Southern California insurance salesman, Walter Neff, who falls for the wife (Barbara Stanwyck) of a client. Together, they plot to kill the husband to gain the insurance payout. But once the deadly act is committed, they turn upon each other. What starts out as romance ends up fatal even for the couple, with Neff left to bleed to death on the floor of his corporate office from a gunshot fired by his lover.

Going My Way wound up winning the best picture award and sweeping the Oscars, earning not only the top prize but also awards for best director, best actor, best supporting actor (Barry Fitzgerald), best story (Leo McCarey), best screenplay (Frank Butler and Frank Cavett), and best song (Johnny Burke and James Van Heusen). The seven awards the film won capped a remarkable run for *Going My Way*. The academy's judgment proved to be in sync with popular tastes as the movie enjoyed phenomenal box office success. Bing Crosby, dressed in clerical garb, was an easier sell than McMurray and Stanwyck conspiring to murder in the aisles of a suburban grocery store.

The contrast between these two films from 1944 is instructive in illuminating the larger contours of American culture during the 1940s. *Double Indemnity* and *Going My Way* represented alternative visions of America and pointed to two contrasting futures of the postwar nation—

a noirish world of corruption, confusion, and anxiety versus a hopeful, affirmative vision of existing social arrangements. One would inspire a postwar counterculture; the other would culminate with John F. Kennedy, another cool, young, confident, and secularized Catholic who also captured the American imagination.[1]

Going My Way has usually been read as symbolic of the growing Americanization of Catholics in the mid-twentieth century. Much analysis therefore is preoccupied with the extent to which the movie accurately reflected Catholic life at the time. Yet a movie that enjoyed the popular impact that the McCarey film did is certainly of more significance than simply as a reflection of Catholic assimilation.[2] The picture resonated far beyond the Catholic enclave and therefore needs to be situated within a broader cultural context of the forties in which Catholic imagery helped to shift the coordinates of American community away from the social allegiances and hopes of the previous decade.

In this chapter, I argue that Going My Way actually represented an early and enormously popular expression of Henry Luce's American Century, a vision of the nation that would triumph in the postwar years. Drawing upon and revising already familiar images of Americanized priests, the film used Catholicism to construct an appealing vision of modern society shorn of conflict and disruptive memories of struggle. The nation was in quite good shape, the movie implied, once people could be shown the opportunities America offered rather than dwelling on its problems. Father O'Malley served as genial guide to this project, encouraging filmgoers to leave behind their fears and doubts and embrace the good times to be enjoyed inside the contemporary social order.

But O'Malley was not simply reminding Americans of what they already knew about their nation. By affirming American society, this highly assimilated priest, in fact, represented a repudiation of the reformist values of the New Deal era. Community, in the hands of O'Malley and Going My Way, no longer centered on the common good of ordinary citizens, ethnics, and outsiders against the private interests of elites and the culturally privileged. Instead, this film narrowed the focus of community to practical, culturally attuned leaders who turned traditional social institutions into attractive alternatives to the public world of the modern city. Going My Way's deployment of Catholic imagery helped reconfigure the symbolic landscape of modern America, erasing from both the critical and communitarian values that had characterized their representations in thirties cinema. By offering a compelling new look to established authority, the figure of Father O'Malley signified the larger transformation in popular Americanism that Lary May has shown characterized Hollywood cinema in the 1940s.[3] An expansive private realm displaced the public sphere; cultural style triumphed over collective action; cool, executive control took command over social challenge.

At the very moment when World War II had turned in the country's favor, therefore, American audiences encountered a confident, youthful Catholic priest who taught them how to imagine their society when the soldiers came home. In the process, the film replaced the cultural ethos of mutuality and interdependence of the Depression era with a moral economy of pragmatic leadership and responsive corporate institutions. Therein lay the larger significance of *Going My Way*—by constructing a new kind of Catholic parish for moviegoers, it buried the reformist culture of the thirties and helped lay the foundations for the postwar consensus.

A Catholic Moment at the Movies

A movie about a Catholic parish priest may have seemed an unlikely subject for a Hollywood hit in 1944. After all, this was not a film that simply included a priest character or involved Catholics on the gridiron, in an army unit, or in a reformatory. Nor was this about the miraculous. *Going My Way* offered audiences a lengthy, two-hour story about a young cleric's efforts to turn around a failing New York City church. The response to the picture was stunning, transforming the film into a cultural event.

The movie had its domestic premiere on May 3, 1944, at New York's Paramount Theater, where it would enjoy a record-breaking box office and tie for having the longest run in the house's history at ten weeks.[4] From major metropolitan centers to small towns, *Going My Way* struck a deep chord with audiences, leaving a lasting impression of Crosby's suave priest and upbeat Catholicism.[5] A survey of theater owner responses to the film demonstrated the impact it enjoyed across the country. Sid J. Dickler, manager of the Belmar Theater in Pittsburgh, proclaimed in October 1944, months after its release, "The film is unequalled in any respect by any film of this day or era. . . . This picture gave me the all-time house record for attendance and box office during its five-day run. Without a doubt it could have been easily held over for another two days and possibly more."[6] Likewise, movie theater manager Thomas di Lorenzo, catering to what he referred to as a "small-town" audience in New Paltz, New York, wrote, "We can't add anything which has not already been recorded about this picture. We billed it as 'the most popular picture of the year,' and this proved at our box office, at least, where it did top business for the year."[7] Finally, C. W. Ritenour, manager of the Milford Theater, in Milford, Illinois, with a rural patronage, acknowledged that *Going My Way* was "a prestige picture with good box-office appeal."[8] The Crosby picture would become the box office champion of 1944, towering over its competition, particularly during the summer months of its initial release.

Critics were similarly enthusiastic for the picture. *Newsweek* described the movie as "a warm, delightful comedy of a kind that is universal in its appeal and close to tops as entertainment."[9] *Life* called it "a fine, human movie" and "one of the few satisfying interpretations of the priesthood to emerge from Hollywood."[10] Even A. O. Dillenbeck, the movie reviewer for the mainline Protestant *Christian Herald,* asserted that the film "transcends all bounds of sect or creed in its human, wholesome handling of the politics and problems common to any Church of God."[11]

More sophisticated critics found themselves liking the movie almost against their skeptical instincts. Manny Farber, in the *New Republic,* wrote that "though *Going My Way* is continually jazzed up with obvious entertainments and too-fortuitous circumstances, there are a number of fine things done with the circumstances, the most commendable being the natural, informal way that the people are allowed to go about."[12] James Agee in *Time* wrote, "Strictly speaking this hardly has a right to pose as a religious film. There is no real contest with evil or with suffering. . . . Yet it has, inadvertently, a good deal of genuine religious quality, and is often a beautiful piece of entertainment."[13]

Catholics, as might be expected, found the movie particularly compelling. Philip Hartung in *Commonweal* described *Going My Way* as "steeped in practical Catholicism."[14] *Extension* magazine wrote that "so many of the clerical characters who trod the silver screen are priestly sticks—too solemn, too pompous or too superior to bear any resemblance to Father Tim whom we've known and loved all our lives." But about the priests of *Going My Way,* the magazine continued, "They're *real: they're the priests we've known all our lives.*"[15] It concluded its review by asserting, "*Going My Way* isn't just a funny picture! Underneath its frothy surface, it has managed to give a true picture of the Church and her priests. They're human—yes! They have their foibles and faults—but they're great guys."[16]

The movie even generated commentary and reflection beyond film critics. In an essay entitled "Is Catholicism 'Going My Way'?" a Methodist convert to Catholicism, John Clarence Petrie, explained to readers of the Protestant *Christian Century* magazine that the phenomenal success of the movie was due to the fact that "it humanized an institution that seems highly impersonal to the average man." Petrie suggested that the portrait of the clergy in the movie captured the "friendly relationships between people and priests" that was distinctive to American forms of Catholicism and not found in the church in Europe or Quebec. The essay appealed to Protestant sentiments by attributing the unique personable qualities of American priests to the fact that Catholics in the United States lived in a society where they faced "friendly competition" from Protestants.[17] Thus did the *Christian Century* turn Catholic success into Protestant virtue.

The impact of *Going My Way* extended as far as the federal government. The Office of Inter-American Affairs (OIAA), created by Franklin Delano Roosevelt during World War II to promote U.S.–Latin American relations through cultural exchange, had an eye on the film as well. Indeed, in the OIAA's efforts to promote a favorable image of the United States to Catholic countries in South America, some considered friendly to fascists, it assumed an active interest in Hollywood's depiction of Catholicism. Walter T. Prendergast, the office's point man on all things Catholic who reported directly to the agency's director, Nelson Rockefeller, suggested toning down the treatment of a young couple in *Going My Way* that might offend Latin American audiences.[18]

The widespread success of the movie among such different groups indicates that its highly Americanized priest represented more than Hollywood's effort to curry favor with Catholics. Indeed, O'Malley offered an intensely fluid, border-crossing image of cultural difference that allowed numerous and often contradictory identifications from film audiences. Catholics, Protestants, critics, and even government officials invested the movie's construction of an affable priest with their own significance.

Paramount Pictures encouraged this multifaceted image of O'Malley, as can be seen from the press books it sent to movie exhibitors. Realizing that a film about a Catholic priest might alienate Protestants and other non-Catholics, the studio offered theater owners opportunities to play down the Catholic angle in their advertising. On facing pages of one press book, for example, two nearly identical advertisements for the film showed O'Malley at a piano, surrounded by children, clearly attempting to attach Crosby's identity as a popular singer to the movie. The more interesting aspect of the ad related to the differences in O'Malley's clothing between the two images. One had him dressed in his baseball jacket and cap, the other had him in his clerical collar. The guidance from the studio to the exhibitors said, "Local conditions should dictate which of the treatments to use."[19]

But it was not only marketing that made the film appealing to diverse filmgoers. The moviemakers themselves, particularly director Leo McCarey and star Bing Crosby, created a portrait of Catholics that reflected their own more relaxed, West Coast religious experience. Elizabeth Armstrong's suggestive depiction of the Southern California art, jazz, and design scene emerging in the 1940s as a contrast to East Coast styles and favoring cooler, more detached forms aptly describes Going My Way's rendering of Father O'Malley as well.[20] In its laid-back, casual image of the priest, the film presented a decidedly West Coast construction of New York City Catholicism, which explains why Crosby's representation was such a novel figure for moviegoers in the 1940s. Although it is tempting to suggest that the new vibe emerging in Los Angeles drifted over from Central Avenue to the Paramount studio lot during production of Going My Way, it is just as likely that Crosby's performance emerged out of years of constructing his radio and singing persona *and* out of a West Coast Catholicism not quite as encumbered by the dense, tribal loyalties that shaped Catholic life in the Northeast.

Bing Crosby grew up in an Irish Catholic, Yankee household in Spokane, Washington. His father, a white-collar worker in a local brewing company, converted to Catholicism when he married Bing's mother. Crosby attended public schools for primary and secondary education, then spent high school at the nearby Jesuit-run Gonzaga High. His Catholic upbringing also included years as an altar boy and a college education with the Jesuits at Gonzaga University, which he left just shy of graduating to pursue a music career. Both Catholic and non-Catholic influences therefore shaped his early years, laying the foundation for a flexible, confident movement in and out of the Catholic world.[21]

Crosby was but one element in the West Coast backstory to Going My Way. Director Leo McCarey was another Catholic of mixed ethnicity, actually born and raised in Los Angeles. His father, Thomas Jefferson McCarey, was a famous boxing promoter in the early twentieth century, and his mother was a French immigrant. He attended both Catholic and public schools in the city and graduated from the University of Southern California (USC), which, according to Kevin Starr, was a "product of Anglo-American Los Angeles" and served "the desire for professional training and upward mobility" in the region.[22] At the same time, McCarey claimed that an aunt, a nun at the Immaculate Heart Convent in Hollywood, was a prominent influence on his life.[23] Perhaps even more than Crosby, McCarey was a Catholic deeply immersed in the world beyond the Catholic subculture.

A third Catholic involved in *Going My Way* was the songwriter Johnny Burke, who penned some of the film's top hits, including "Swinging on a Star." Burke, like Crosby and McCarey, was born on the West Coast. Originally from northern California, he attended the University of Wisconsin before making it big as a songsmith.[24]

Thus, when the makers of *Going My Way* constructed an easygoing Catholicism, their own experiences provided ample material to draw upon. Indeed, the very border-crossing character of Father O'Malley made some Catholics uncomfortable. For instance, a priest of the Holy Cross order, Patrick Duffy, wrote to Leo McCarey in September 1944, a few months after the release of *Going My Way*. Early in the letter, he stated that he had met McCarey and Crosby on the set of the movie during filming. But he wrote that he was now stationed on an island in the Pacific theater of war with the navy. Duffy applauded McCarey for a job well done but then chastised him for missing the real drama of the story of a priest:

> Leo, the Faith and the priesthood are *loaded* with drama. . . . Again, I ask you to tell the story of a priest's vocation. . . . You did your work admirably in Going My Way. But on the way back from the movie do you know what one gob asked his mate? He asked, "Did Bing lay that girl?" And the other guy said, "No ya, dumb b—. Priests don't do that stuff." And the other fellow said, "Aw; No?" . . . You see, Leo, you did a marvelous job— listen to the nation if you doubt me—but you didn't finish it. It can be done. What's the matter, are you a sissy—why don't you try it?[25]

Clearly, Father Duffy worried that McCarey had made O'Malley too worldly, but the Holy Cross priest's fulminations missed the extent to which *Going My Way* addressed larger concerns than just the character of the priesthood. The movie was actually very worldly, albeit in ways that Duffy failed to acknowledge. The film used Catholicism to imagine a very different kind of American community than had characterized Hollywood cinema in the 1930s. A story about a Catholic parish allowed a reassessment of communal values so central to Depression-era culture.[26] Father O'Malley served as avatar not simply of a new kind of modern priest but also of a consensual Americanism in which social reform became irrelevant.

In turning the priest into everyman, *Going My Way* rearticulated the meanings of the American citizen as well. The highly assimilated cleric offered an affirmative rather than critical vision of community, encouraging allegiance to traditional cultural authorities. At the heart of the film was an effort to reconcile communal values to Americanism by denying their alternative cultural and oppositional potential associated with the thirties' portraits of cooperative, interdependent social identity. That project resonated far beyond Protestant-Catholic tensions to address the core issues of national identity and purpose at midcentury. Social renewal, this wartime movie suggested, would emerge not from an alliance of the people demanding change but through the practical guidance of "progressives" such as O'Malley. By inviting Americans to see Catholics as modern and as ordinary as themselves, the film asked viewers to also abandon the memories of the thirties. *Going My Way*'s portrayal of urban Catholics jettisoned the social struggles and communal aspirations for justice of movies such as *Boys Town* and *Angels with Dirty Faces* and offered instead the promise of community organized around new, practical leaders and the safety of traditional social institutions.

Constructing the Catholic Parish, Remaking the American Community

At stake in *Going My Way* was nothing less than a symbolic cleansing of the streets of urban America, ridding them of all the critical, reformist energies that Hollywood had recognized in the 1930s. This explains why Father O'Malley's first appearance in the movie occurs in a scene set on the streets of New York. By introducing the hip, young cleric as he navigates a bustling city thoroughfare, the movie enacts a reversal of cultural authority established in earlier movies involving ethnics—O'Malley owns the urban landscape, the city does not produce the priest. Within the film's first several minutes, therefore, its reorientation of modern American community is declared.

In this introductory scene, movie viewers first *hear* the voice of Crosby before they even see Father O'Malley. In this way, the filmmakers take advantage of the audiences' knowledge of Crosby as a popular singer and radio host, which they brought with them to the movie houses. The first, high-angle shot of O'Malley presents a striking image of the priest in tailored clerical suit; the white sidewalk he stands upon highlights the contrast with his dark clothing. A straw boater hat, however, sits jauntily upon O'Malley's head, immediately signaling his difference from the traditional images of priests. The movie's first shot of O'Malley thus sets the stage for the rest of the film: here is a youthful, modern priest who will not only occupy but also serve as focus of the modern city.

When one of the kids playing stickball in the street asks O'Malley to take his place, the priest joins the game, thereby demonstrating his man-in-the-street character as well as his identification with the masculine world of sports. But another boy hits the ball into a neighbor's window, leaving O'Malley to deal with the irate man. The obstinate, unfriendly response of the neighbor gives O'Malley an opportunity to display his temperate, self-possessed way of dealing with adversity. The camera follows him as he saunters up the stairs to calm the man down; the confident movement of O'Malley's body echoes the modern assurance symbolized by his straw boater. The scene ends with the priest retrieving the ball the angry man has thrown back onto the street. And when a passing water truck douses O'Malley, his ability to contain his frustration, signified by a slight gesture of a raised arm, demonstrates that he remains in control. The fact that he gets soaked brings the priest down to the earthly humiliations of everyday life; that he does not get angry indicates that he is one poised fellow. This early scene therefore plays a crucial role in establishing the character of O'Malley as a striking mixture of old and new. He is introduced as the cool emblem of the traditional Catholic Church, Roman collar and straw boater converging on the body of a self-possessed cleric, indicative of a new face of religious leadership in contemporary America.

The movie elaborates O'Malley's identity as an assured navigator of the American metropolis through his contrast with the pastor of St. Dominic's, Father Fitzgibbon, whom he supplants as leader of the parish. Elderly where O'Malley is youthful, cantankerous where O'Malley is mellow, rigid where the younger man is fluid, Fitzgibbon embodies the older generation of clerical leadership whose time has passed. Indeed, the film implies that Fitzgibbon's poor stewardship is responsible for St. Dominic's difficulties. Nowhere does it suggest the parish's financial straits may be tied to the economic plight of the working-class parishioners it serves.

If O'Malley's brand of traditional moral leadership is attractive because of his laid-back confidence, the film further diminishes the authority of older styles of leadership by infantilizing Fitzgibbon. When he attempts to leave St. Dominic's after learning that the bishop wants O'Malley to take control, he is returned to the rectory door by the neighborhood cop; he trails behind the policeman like a child reprimanded for his wayward antics. A subsequent scene in which Fitzgibbons has taken to bed because of a cold he incurred while running off in the rain extends the childlike character of the elderly priest. Tucked in bed, Fitzgibbon nods off as O'Malley sits by his bedside singing an Irish lullaby.

Unlike *The Jazz Singer,* an earlier film about intergenerational ethnic conflict, *Going My Way* does not need to kill its father figure, Fitzgibbon.

His complete emasculation means that he poses no threat to the son, O'Malley, and his Americanized cultural difference. In fact, by the end of the film, the elderly priest acknowledges the merits of the young man's practical ways and even agrees to accompany him on a round of golf. The growing friendship of the two priests suggests reconciliation between past and present, but in reality, O'Malley has clearly triumphed. The future, the movie implies, belongs to men like the youthful priest, individuals who are able to take advantage of the modern world around them to revitalize established institutions such as St. Dominic's.

In addition to defending himself against the initially suspicious Fitzgibbon, O'Malley works to turn a group of neighborhood street kids into a parish choir at St. Dominic's. At first, the kids are skeptical of O'Malley's efforts, associating them with a feminized religiosity. One boy, Herman, points out to his friends the flimsy white altar boy garments that hang in the church basement and shakes his head in disapproval. Yet O'Malley is able to persuade the boys to give his idea of forming a choir a try by making clear that he understands their concerns. "I like fun as much as anybody," he tells them. His mention of having worked with the St. Louis Browns baseball team ("my team," he declares) and his promise to take them to a game and buy them hotdogs further demonstrate that O'Malley is a regular guy. Though he may be a priest, he is painted in *Going My Way* as able to connect with modern kids by relating to their interest in sports and having fun. In fact, the first song O'Malley teaches the boys has nothing to do with sacred music but is the playful "Three Blind Mice." Only after he has alleviated their fears that he is a pious bore does he attempt to introduce a more serious music lesson. Popular culture is thus O'Malley's means through which to direct the kids into the church. A later scene showing the priest and the boys at a movie house underscores the tight connection between the priest and mass culture.

Associating O'Malley with popular culture is central to the film's construction of the priest as an authority figure. Religion, he suggests, is a part of modern America, not an out-of-date remnant of the past. But O'Malley of course offers a very respectable alternative to the world of the streets by encouraging the boys to join a choir. Indeed, his unorthodox style of appealing to their contemporary tastes in order to shepherd them into the parish demonstrates that he is a new kind of leader in a very traditional institution, one who can direct contemporary culture toward the renewal rather than the subversion of existing moral and social authority. *Going My Way* thereby presents the young priest as an attractive alternative to

While elderly, old-school Father Fitzgibbons (Barry Fitzgerald) rests, the smooth, young Father O'Malley (Bing Crosby) eases his way into command of St. Dominic's parish in Going My Way *(1944). Courtesy of Photofest.*

other kinds of street authority, left unrepresented by the film, and, beyond that, as an alternative to all the urban heroes of Hollywood cinema in the 1930s—from gangsters to newspaper reporters to detectives—who signify the worldly pleasures and aspirations of modern America.

O'Malley's dealings with another character, Carol James, an aspiring singer new to the city, extends the image of the priest as a religious authority adept at dealing with the contemporary world. His counseling of the young woman demonstrates that he is also wise to the ways of youthful love. When the neighborhood cop brings her to O'Malley on suspicion that she may be soliciting on the street, the priest offers a friendly ear while she explains her need to escape parental restraints back home. His ability to relate to her travails gives him credibility in her eyes as someone who understands romantic desire. It also does not hurt, of course, that he informs the would-be singer of his own earlier career as a jazz musician before becoming a priest. In stark contrast to O'Malley's youthful, culturally sensitive approach to Carol, Fitzgibbon shows up and tells her to go home and wait for a husband. The two men's very different responses to Carol's plight illustrate the contrasting styles of their clerical leadership and at the same time highlight O'Malley's calm and self-possessed approach to the challenges of modern life.

Even O'Malley's ability to turn around the fortunes of the parish connects a revitalized Catholicism with contemporary culture. Hoping to entice a group of record company executives to buy a song he wrote, O'Malley performs with the boys at the Metropolitan Opera House, accompanied by the orchestra led by Tomaso Bozanni, a clear reference to Arturo Toscanini, who was the conductor of the popular NBC Radio orchestra at the time. The executives initially turn O'Malley down. But another song he performs—a fun, upbeat favorite among the boys—wins over the executives, manifesting O'Malley's talent as a songsmith of contemporary tastes. The purchase of that song allows the parish debt to be paid. O'Malley arranges the payment in such a way that Father Fitzgibbon believes his homily at Sunday Mass has been responsible for the great increase in the Sunday collection. The scene in which even the record company executives are in the church pew placing a check in the collection plate offers another sign of the young Americanized priest's ability to have things "his way." The resolution of the parish's fortunes is an improbable scenario, to be sure, but the significance of this turn of events lies less in its realism than in its articulation of an alliance between the poised and contemporary priest, the traditional institution of the Catholic parish, and modern mass culture.

Going My Way's portrait of a new kind of religious leader also held major consequences for the understanding of social community suggested by the film. O'Malley's very modern identity encouraged moviegoers to shift their attention to changes at the top of communal institutions rather than challenges from below. Going My Way's story of generational succession implicitly framed social change in terms of a new leadership that was able to harness popular desires for the revitalization of traditional institutions.

Most American movies, of course, focus on heroic individuals who act as leaders of some kind. Significantly, however, O'Malley is a leader who never develops through the course of the film. He does not grow into his leadership role, nor does he emerge from someplace within the community he represents. Rather he is the change, a change from above, who revitalizes existing social arrangements. In his role as a new kind of culturally attuned leader of traditional institutions, O'Malley represents more than a Catholic priest; he is an emblem of a more restricted conceptualization of community as compared to that seen in many movies of the thirties such as *Boys Town,* in which leaders embodied the struggles and aspirations for social change of the people they represented. Beneath O'Malley's smooth, relaxed confidence lies the model corporate executive who would dominate the postwar age of consensus.

In the process of portraying Father O'Malley's effective leadership, the film also revised the portrayal of the rest of the community. In place of workers and citizens as the populace of the modern metropolis, *Going My Way* presented the parishioners and friends of Father O'Malley. The "people" were no longer imagined as the locus of social justice or as signs of cultural transformation but as beneficiaries of effective guidance as well as an audience for appealing, modern styles of leadership. Their resistance was directed not so much against social elites and injustice, as was the case in thirties' formulations, but rather, as manifested by the neighborhood boys of St. Dominic's, against old-fashioned forms of authority. They can, *Going My Way* implies, be realigned with traditional institutions if they can be persuaded by sensible leaders.

The film's appealing evocation of a new kind of priest consequently held more cultural significance than simply updating a portrait of Catholicism. *Going My Way* reoriented Catholic communalism away from the social struggles and economic populism of the 1930s and toward a depoliticized harmony by focusing collective identity upon a capable, youthful leader who coolly rehabilitates traditional institutional authority and tames popular culture for conservative ends.[27] Change, Father O'Malley suggested, comes from within traditional social arrangements and through the leaders themselves, not from new movements without. Precisely in its Americanization of Catholic religious authority, *Going My Way* turned a story of an urban parish into an allegory of cultural leadership for a wartime culture eager to get beyond the social conflicts of the New Deal era.

If O'Malley's portrait of a new kind of institutional leadership provided one means by which the film rejected 1930s' conceptions of community, its particular representation of space provided another. *Going My Way* utilized a narrative of a young priest to revise traditional associations of Catholic space as foreign places of danger. And by normalizing a particularly Catholic urban landscape, the film also displaced the public meanings of city space that informed many comedies, dramas, and gangster films in the 1930s.

Within the Gothic fantasies of nineteenth-century nativist imagination, Catholic architecture and space signified entrapment. The *Awful Disclosures* of Maria Monk, for instance, rested heavily upon the use of convents as scenes of moral, sexual, and social depravity. *Going My Way*, by contrast, invited viewers into the intimate spaces of the Catholic parish rectory, garden, and basement to reveal a familiar, reassuring world of respectability and propriety.[28]

With the rectory garden used as the setting for a number of scenes, the visual look of the clerical world subtly shifts. Far from signifying danger, the garden is an oasis of nature and light, contrasted with the busyness of the city streets that O'Malley seems constantly to be wandering. The gently gurgling fountain that Fitzgibbon shows O'Malley assumes a more prominent position within the camera shots of the garden than the statue of the Virgin Mary in the background. By placing the priests in this particular setting, *Going My Way* encourages moviegoers to revise their notions of the private realm of clerics as something alien and consider it instead as a place of peace, tranquility, and order.

This reform of Catholic space extends to the depiction of the rectory itself. Its interior design exudes cleanliness, propriety, and solidity, suggesting not Gothic isolation but Victorian middle-class respectability. In the dinner scene, early in the film, between O'Malley and Fitzgibbon, the two priests are surrounded with the trappings of traditional bourgeois living. A Tiffany-styled lamp hangs from the ceiling over a dining table covered with a white tablecloth. Oak doors, wainscoting, and wallpaper compose the background. Cut-crystal glassware and china set the table. As O'Malley gets up to answer the door, the camera tracks the young priest and pans across other rooms that feature well-upholstered furniture and vases of fresh-cut flowers.

The dinner sequence is immediately followed by a shot that epitomizes the movie's framing of its priests as paragons of respectability: O'Malley is seated at a piano, playing a traditional tune in the rectory parlor. Even the lace curtains on the windows behind Father Chuck convey gentility. Further in the background lies the garden, deepening the image of lightness and order.

But the film's effort to challenge traditional associations of Catholic space as dangerous is most dramatic in its portrayal of the church basement—the site in the nativist imaginary as the underground venue of Catholic political and sexual perversion. *Going My Way* stages the basement of St. Dominic's as the place for O'Malley's first singing lesson with the neighborhood street kids, led by the skeptical Tony Scaponi. A wide, long-distance shot incorporating low ceilings and sheets draped over furniture makes the basement appear like a large storage room rather than a labyrinth of hidden chambers and dark passageways. After a brief sequence in which some of the boys debate why the priest has asked to meet them, O'Malley appears, well lit within the mise-en-scène, clad in his St. Louis Browns jacket and baseball cap. It is here that he breaks down the kids' skepticism about forming a choir through humor and his self-deprecating manner. With Crosby at the helm, the basement becomes an audition room as the priest leads the boys in voice practice. In the background are a wheelbarrow, wooden boxes, and hay, making the basement once imagined by nativists as a place of bondage no more threatening than a well-used barn.

But even as *Going My Way* uses O'Malley to revise older cultural associations of Catholic space, it also is careful to locate the young priest in the wider world of the modern metropolis. He may be the new man inside the parish, but, the film also insists, he is also the hip denizen of the wider world. The city becomes a terrain for Father O'Malley's extensions into the numerous cultural spaces of contemporary America. The priest takes the neighborhood kids to the movies. We observe him assisting an ornery and destitute parishioner about to be thrown out of her apartment and onto the street. We see him playing a round of golf with Father Fitzgibbons and another young curate. We watch as he watches his old girlfriend perform *Carmen* at the Metropolitan Opera House. Finally, we observe O'Malley playing his music with the parish kids at the Met.

This all amounts to a continuous enactment of border crossings. The ease with which O'Malley passes from the world of the parish into the wider city is contrasted with the difficulty Father Fitzgibbon experiences even in leaving the rectory. He is rarely seen beyond the rectory, church, and garden, and when he does venture forward, he finds himself lost. Yet this is not so much Fitzgibbon's entrapment as a sign of an older, ethnic Catholicism's inability to negotiate modern, mass culture America. Put another way, Catholicism and cultural space are reimagined as generational symbols—Old World priest associated with the world of the parish and American priest signifying engagement with the modern world. *Going My Way* banishes antebellum Romanism by renarrating Catholicism as a story of acculturation in which ethnic parochialism gives way to mid-twentieth–century American pluralism.

But *Going My Way*'s rendering of Catholic and urban space holds even larger cultural significance. In pulling back the veil of the Catholic world to reveal a place of normalcy, the film's depictions of space lay siege to the progressive associations of the urban landscape that cultural historian Lary May has identified in Hollywood films of the 1930s. Numerous screwball comedies, dramas, and crime films in the Depression years had privileged a realm of nightclubs, restaurants, bars, backstages, theaters, and hotels as primary loci of identity. Within the imagined world of thirties cinema, these places provided the cultural arena where people often encountered each other, forged relationships, and even developed new shared allegiances. Indeed, the nightlife of the modern metropolis symbolized a new public world of social change. Similarly, the urban streets became the context of ethnic energy, social struggle, and communal renewal. Movies such as *The Thin Man, Ninotchka,* and *Angels with Dirty Faces* imbued the modern urban landscape with cultural and even spiritual vitality.[29]

This dynamic world of the modern commercial city is conspicuously absent in *Going My Way*. Privileging instead parish rectory, opera house, and golf course, it rejects the public realm in favor of safer, less threatening identifications. Religion, high culture, and leisure institutions offer social stability and personal security in place of the diversity and élan of the modern city imagined during the thirties.

In this way, O'Malley's wanderings through the streets of New York City signify his ability to successfully navigate the modern world, and beyond that, they point to an alternative mapping of an urban landscape devoid of social struggle and inequality. The priest's journeys beyond the parish, so crucial to differentiating his identity from that of Fitzgibbon (who remains completely within the parish), constitute a dramatic reworking of modern society, forging a symbolic alliance between church, Old World high culture, and American popular entertainment to displace the popular desires and identities that informed Hollywood's depiction of the city during the Depression years.

The representation of urban space in *Going My Way* consequently highlights the extent to which the very understanding of culture itself is ultimately at stake in the film's portrait of Catholicism. The movie's account of a young cleric elaborates what May argues was a narrative of conversion from past identifications with an expressive modern culture to the safety and security of traditional cultural authority in 1940s films.[30] O'Malley's appeal both to characters within the film and to movie viewers is a product of the ease with which this man of the cloth deals with contemporary society. But his worldliness, the film makes clear, rests upon his prior secular involvements, which he abandoned when he became a priest. O'Malley, for instance, makes reference to his earlier career as a jazz musician, indicating an earlier life that was deeply immersed in modern urban culture. But even more, the presence of his former girlfriend in the film demonstrates that O'Malley was a sexually experienced man of the world, challenging traditional assumptions about clergy as being out of touch, as embodied in Father Fitzgibbons.

But O'Malley's journey from jazzman to Catholic cleric traces a shift from the modern culture of experimentation to traditional institutions of enrichment and edification, resulting in the containment of the social and personal desires that popular film in the thirties helped articulate. In becoming a priest, he has rejected a secular past in favor of a religious future. His familiarity with music, movies, and sports provides him with a contemporary identity. But this priest's acquaintance with modern culture serves traditional ends. O'Malley's music, for example, is a dramatically tamed-down version of the jazz of the time. His "hit" song, "Swinging on a Star," which the record company executives agree to produce, is middle-of-the-road material. O'Malley's thoroughly modern priest in reality dissociates popular culture from its expressive, reformist, and critical associations of the thirties and rearticulates it as a subordinate element in the service of established social institutions. Going his way means abandoning the experiments of the past for the security of a refurbished corporate order.

O'Malley's alliance with popular culture therefore directs modern desires and their disruptive potential into safe, harmless entertainment.[31] The other cultural institutions *Going My Way* privileges further demonstrate the conservative meanings the movie has assigned to the social role of culture itself. The proposal that O'Malley offers the neighborhood kids as an alternative to the world of the streets is revealing—a church choir that brings them respectability. Similarly, the priest's ex-girlfriend epitomizes traditional high, rather than modern, culture. She is an opera singer whose performance of *Carmen* provides an opportunity for a lengthy scene of O'Malley watching her sing an aria. The site of his triumph in winning a record contract is the Metropolitan Opera House, where he and the boys are accompanied by the house orchestra. The choir, the Metropolitan Opera, and O'Malley's own identity as priest together elaborate an understanding of culture as a genteel project of enrichment and moral cultivation.

Intimations of the preclerical worldliness of Father O'Malley: his old girlfriend, Jenny (Risë Stevens), in a flirtatious moment with "Chuck" in Going My Way *(1944). Courtesy of Photofest.*

Going My Way's valorizing of traditional institutions such as religion and high culture represented a rejection of the modern notions about culture as transformation or critique that informed many thirties films. As May has shown, earlier movies (*Footlight Parade*, for instance) celebrated urban popular culture as a vehicle for creating new identities and transforming society into a more democratic community. Mass culture is often represented as more than simple entertainment; it was a challenge to traditional conceptions of culture and the possibility of fostering new modes of inhabiting the modern world.[32]

Even those movies from the thirties that acknowledged traditional culture approached it less as something to be schooled into and more as a resource to be reworked and opened to alternative perspectives and voices. Tradition in this conceptualization could be made to serve progressive goals. Will Rogers utilized small-town Americana to justify a politics of social reform, exemplifying the "radicalism of tradition." In similar

Culture as cultivation: Father O'Malley (Bing Crosby) singing at the Metropolitan Opera with kids from the neighborhood. Note Fortunio Bonanova on the far left as the conductor, a stand-in for the well-known opera conductor and symphonic leader Arturo Toscanini. Courtesy of Photofest.

fashion, *Young Mr. Lincoln* (1939) revised the national symbol of Abraham Lincoln as a great statesman into a story of a country lawyer defending poor folk against injustice and social elitism.[33]

Going My Way, however, countered these modern assumptions about culture embedded within many New Deal–era films. It imagined traditional culture as a bulwark of security amid the dangers of the contemporary world. Religion and opera signified cultural institutions of personal improvement and alternatives to the social experiments of the streets. Simultaneously, popular culture provided existing social institutions with new appeal and relevancy. But the consequence of this shift reduced mass culture to entertainment, erased of its critical edge. Tellingly, *Going My Way* never showed the young female singer that Father O'Malley coached actually singing in a nightclub. The parish rectory was about as far away from home as viewers got to see her perform.

The Difference Catholicism Makes

Bing Crosby and Leo McCarey created a potent cultural mix in 1944 that spoke deeply to American filmgoers during a period of intense social and cultural change. Religion, popular culture, and Americanism converged to construct a pleasing, affirmative portrait of contemporary society. But within its easygoing charm, *Going My Way* offered a powerful revision of American identity in which the character of social community and even culture itself were at stake. Precisely by articulating the difference that urban Catholicism signified in terms of mass culture and a story of generational succession, the film reoriented the symbolic coordinates of community in the popular imagination, undermining the reformist values of the previous decade.

Yet one may wonder why a film about Catholics provided such a popular alternative to the socially conscious, reform values of thirties communalism. If American culture in the 1940s sought safety by reclaiming traditional values, why did it look to Catholicism? Why did it not pursue a return to stories about American Protestants? A brief comparison with the representation of Protestantism in a popular film from the same period, *One Foot in Heaven* (1941), helps explain the importance of Catholic imagery in the transformation of Americanism during the 1940s.

One Foot in Heaven chronicled the life of a Methodist minister, William Spence, from his conversion experience at the turn of the century through his old age in the Depression era.[34] A number of prominent Protestant clergy, including Norman Vincent Peale and Daniel Poling, assisted in the production of the film, suggesting that Protestant leaders were trying to catch up to the Catholic Legion of Decency's influence in Hollywood, which was widely acknowledged. *One Foot in Heaven* depicted the stresses that ministerial life had on Spence's wife and children, the constant moves that characterized the career of a minister, and the awkward negotiations that ministers had to pursue with difficult and powerful members of their congregations.

Yet much of the film takes place in the early years of the twentieth century and in rural, small-town settings, giving the movie an intensely retrospective view of religion in America. When Spence does become pastor of a large church in Denver, the urban landscape is remarkably absent until the final scenes. Even then, the cityscape appears more like that of a small town than a major metropolis. In contrast to *Going My Way*, the movie's preoccupations with an earlier historical era and village settings suggest a hesitation to portray religion as a modern urban phenomenon. Indeed, the review in the *Motion Picture Herald*, subtitled "Grassroots and Nostalgia," opined, "Here is a warm, appealing, human drama woven of the stuff that will carry city audiences back to the grass roots of rural America and give solid, small town citizens a nostalgic excursion to a slower paced way of life when the America that lies between the mountains was untroubled by the strains of modern life."[35] Further, *Variety* speculated that the film's treatment of a Protestant clergy "may with proper exploitation attract great numbers of folk who seldom go to picture theaters."[36] *One Foot in Heaven*'s casting of Protestant clergy in a small-town, nostalgic register contrasts markedly with *Going My Way*'s depiction of Catholics in a modern, urban, ethnic setting.

From Hollywood's perspective, therefore, Protestants represented the religion of an older America that was out of step with modern realities. Catholics, by contrast, signified the pluralism and urbanization of the twentieth century. A film of an urban Catholic parish gave moviegoers during the war an attractive story for engaging complex issues about cultural change that Protestant films were not able to provide. But the developments signified by *Going My Way* involved more than religious change; they also involved the character of communal identity and popular culture itself in America during the 1940s. Just as an Americanized priest suggested new ways of being Catholic, the film's modernization of a New York City parish signified alterations in the social meanings of community. By focusing attention on the cool, confident stewardship of Father O'Malley, *Going My Way* redirected communal understandings to new styles of corporate leadership. By normalizing the parish, the movie also displaced Hollywood's urban landscape of cultural modernity and social transformation.

Thus, in the middle of the forties, Bing Crosby and *Going My Way* helped set the stage for a postwar culture in which reform would be incremental and the city would be left behind in favor of the promise of the suburbs. They embodied a Catholic contribution to the formation of the American Century in which the New Deal was consigned to an era the nation was believed to have transcended. In place of social conflict, consensus was imagined. Instead of mutuality and cooperation, community became tailored to security and abundance.

Going My Way would have a remarkable impact in the cultural history of Catholics in subsequent decades, becoming a touchstone for discussions of the representation of priests in American life. Later movies, from Otto Preminger's *The Cardinal* (1963) to John Gregory Dunne's *True Confessions* (1981) to John Patrick Shanley's *Doubt* (2008), all engaged in a significant dialogue with McCarey's movie.[37] Fulton J. Sheen took up Father O'Malley's charge to demonstrate to Americans that Catholic leadership could respond to the challenges of modern life in the 1950s, a subject a later chapter explores.

Perhaps the most significant, though overlooked, sign of *Going My Way*'s importance not only for reshaping the image of Catholics but also for setting a new direction in the relationship between religion and American public culture occurred fifteen years after its release, when another young Catholic leader burst upon the national scene. He too had to overcome doubts about his religious identity. He too encouraged the nation to look to a new generation of leadership. His youthful charisma and confidence spoke deeply to Americans' desires for change and helped usher in the tumultuous decade of the 1960s. But in breaking from the pugnacious public personas of ethnic forebears such as Joe McCarthy and Father Coughlin, this man possessed a calm, self-assured, and pragmatic style more than a little reminiscent of that of the priest at St. Dominic's. Though rarely recognized as such, John F. Kennedy proved to be the Father O'Malley of Irish Catholic politicians for the postwar American consensus.

PRO-*LIFE* CATHOLICS: THE REPRESENTATION OF CATHOLICISM IN *LIFE* MAGAZINE, 1936–1960

Margaret Bourke-White's cover photograph of the Fort Peck Dam in Montana helped introduce *Life* magazine to the American public when the inaugural issue, dated November 23, 1936, hit newsstands. That dramatic image, with its stark modernist rendering of technological achievement, marked the beginning of a new era in American photojournalism. Less well remembered, however, are the six photographs of Catholics also published in that first issue. These included Cardinal George Mundelein of Chicago; Father John O'Hara, president of Notre Dame University; and Cardinal Eugenio Pacelli, Vatican secretary of state and the future Pope Pius XII; in addition, there was a photo-essay by the noted Alfred Eisenstaedt on a school for Chinese immigrant children in San Francisco taught by the Sisters of St. Joseph.[1] Taken together, these photos comprised a remarkable amount of coverage for an individual religious community in the opening issue of American's newest media sensation. But they also manifested a fascination with Roman Catholicism that would inform the magazine over the next three decades. In fact, the newsweekly would repeatedly turn to Catholics at home and overseas as subjects for its visual gaze, testifying to the powerful role Catholicism played in *Life*'s vision of America and the world.

Religion became a staple of America's most influential photojournalist magazine, and Catholicism proved particularly attractive to *Life*.[2] Popes, priests, nuns, and laypeople as well as churches, cathedrals, and monasteries constituted an endless stream of imagery from the magazine's inception in the mid-1930s through the 1950s when *Life* enjoyed its greatest impact in American culture. The deeply material and embodied character of Roman Catholicism intersected with the magazine's efforts to define social life in terms of visual representation to produce numerous photo-essays on Catholics both in the United States and around the globe.

As *Life*'s prospectus asserted, the magazine aimed "to see life; to see the world; to eyewitness great events . . . to see and to take pleasure in seeing; to see and be amazed; to see and be instructed."[3] But as scholars Wendy Kozal, Erika Doss, and other have argued, *Life* did not simply record social experience but also guided its readers to understand that experience in specific ways. Particularly by the early forties, when its founder and editor in chief Henry R. Luce articulated his creed of the American Century, *Life* played an influential role in teaching Americans to imagine the United States as a global power abroad and a materially abundant, harmonious, middle-class society at home. As the success of the magazine indicates, the photographic image proved an especially powerful means to encode an ideological construction of the nation through a representation of seemingly "objective" social reality.

Luce's vision of a new era for the United States represented a very particular understanding of America intended to reestablish capitalist authority in society. In addition to offering a charter for free markets around the world, Luce's vision embodied a powerful rejoinder to progressive beliefs about social organization, economic justice, and the common good that had emerged during the Depression. As an ardent defender of corporate interests, the media mogul fiercely opposed the New Deal state and the insurgent public sphere of the thirties.[4] His belief in the American Century represented a cultural effort to put an end to social reform and encourage a new national order of enlightened capitalist leadership and class consensus.

The numerous photo-essays and images of Catholics in *Life* magazine therefore were more than reflections of the Roman Catholic Church in the twentieth century. They manifested the ideological and cultural value of Catholics in the construction of Luce's larger project of the American Century. Because Catholicism possessed an international character and at the same time was the largest single religious community in the United States, it offered a particularly compelling subject for a magazine that professed to "see the world." Representations of Catholics in the United States allowed *Life* to envision a more encompassing and pluralist religious landscape of the nation than older Protestant understandings had permitted. Americanized images of Catholics therefore contributed to a consensual vision of the nation. Similarly, Catholicism's global nature gave *Life* an opportunity to narrate the Cold War struggle abroad. Popes and the Vatican often served as the magazine's surrogates in the cultural battle with the Soviet Union. In terms of identifying the American mission in the world and envisioning the society worth defending against the communist threat, Catholicism was a powerful, multivalent subject for *Life*'s vision of the United States.

The pages of the magazine provide dramatic evidence that the cultural contest over Americanism in the 1930s and 1940s had a profound influence on the representation of Catholicism in the national imagination. A magazine created and run by Anglo-American Protestants found in Catholics a powerful subject by which to reorient national identity away from the popular social challenges of the Depression era. Turning Catholics into Americans was important not just to Catholics themselves or Hollywood moviemakers but also to cultural interests such as Luce's determination to roll back the reformist allegiances that had emerged in the previous decade. The visually rich, religiously distinctive, international character of Catholicism gave *Life* a useful means to map the world in its own image and encourage its readers to believe they were living in an American Century.

"The American Century" and the Assault on the New Deal

Life magazine began publication in the middle of the Depression. It published its most influential essay, however, in the early forties as World War II raged on the European continent. In the February 17, 1941, issue, Henry Luce issued a clarion call for national revitalization in an essay entitled "The American Century"[5]—a phrase that has become a commonly used term to reference the emergence of American power in the twentieth century.[6] As cultural historian Erika Doss has noted, Luce's essay is "arguably one of the most important declarations of national purpose and identity disseminated in the twentieth century."[7] Although Luce was preoccupied with international events, his statement was far more than a description of the United States in a global age. His essay in fact offered an early articulation of a new cultural formation of capitalist leadership, social harmony, and moral virtue intended to delegitimize the reformist values and ideals of New Deal America. A close look at his essay makes clear that fighting fascism was not Luce's only objective in authoring "The American Century."

The immediate purpose of the essay was to convince Americans in early 1941 that even though the United States was not yet militarily involved in the war in Europe, the nation was already deeply invested in its outcome and consequently should prepare for battle. But Luce's larger objective was cultural, to define the terms of American community and its relationship to the modern world. He insisted that only the United States had the capacity to assume the leadership of democracy in a world where its enemies were determined to destroy it. To claim this responsibility, Luce asserted it was incumbent on the American people to know what they stood for. Toward that end, the editor elaborated his vision of Americanism founded upon freedom, capitalism, and Christianity. He concluded his essay by identifying the four characteristics of the American Century:

> America as the dynamic center of ever-widening spheres of enterprise, America as the training center of the skillful servants of mankind, America as the Good Samaritan, really believing again that it is more blessed to give than to receive, and America as the powerhouse of the ideals of Freedom and Justice—out of these elements surely can be fashioned a vision of the 20th Century to which we can and will devote ourselves in joy and gladness and vigor and enthusiasm.[8]

Free enterprise, the professional and educated skills that generated national productivity, a Christianized charitable commitment to helping the world's poor, and the cultural inheritance of the West constituted Luce's understanding of America and its leadership for modern times. At the center of his expansive vision lay the virtue of freedom. "We have some things in this country," he wrote, "which are infinitely precious and especially American—a love of freedom, a feeling for the equality of opportunity, a tradition of self reliance and independence and also of co-operation." Tellingly, he placed cooperation at the end of his list of uniquely American characteristics as if it were an afterthought and secondary to his larger concerns. He also asserted that the American Century would be one in which "it is for America and America alone to determine whether a system of free economic enterprise—an economic order compatible with freedom and progress—shall or shall not prevail in this century." He thus clearly believed that the purpose of U.S. victory in the war was to secure an economy organized around private leadership and capitalist values.[9]

Luce's American Century marked a dramatic challenge to the reformist Americanism of the 1930s, which emphasized the common good over individual interest, mutuality over self-reliance, and interdependence over independence.[10] His economic vision of enterprise and freedom repudiated public efforts to restrain corporate America. Yet even though Luce's antipathy to the New Deal was evident in his essay, his career as a magazine publisher demonstrated that he understood simple opposition alone would not suffice.

Luce realized that reclaiming the nation for capitalist prerogatives necessitated winning the imagination of the American people. That fight entailed utilizing the mass media, which in the 1930s had become an important cultural vehicle for the new reformist Americanism that sanctioned the New Deal.[11] As a media entrepreneur himself, Luce insightfully understood that popular culture was never simply about entertainment but instead was the symbolic terrain through which politics was waged and social groups won consent for their ideas and values. Although *Time* and *Fortune* were also part of the Luce empire, it was *Life*, as Doss, Kozol, and others have shown, that provided the crucial means for elaborating the American Century to the nation. Particularly in the 1940s and 1950s, *Life* utilized the genre of photojournalism to represent to the American public a compelling, powerful vision of the country and the world profoundly shaped by the values Luce articulated in 1941. The magazine celebrated the success and opportunities of middle-class prosperity founded upon capitalist freedom and organized around a traditional social arrangement of home, family, and religion.[12]

Religion played an enormously important though largely overlooked role in the cultural struggle over Americanism in the middle of the twentieth century. *Life* magazine's treatment of Catholics demonstrated the extent to which the cultural hegemony of the American Century involved the rearticulation of ethnic outsiders into signs of American success. The importance of religion to Luce's vision of America was evident from the references to the Good Samaritan in his essay. In its original formulation of 1941, with its emphasis on the centrality of freedom to national purpose and the American way of life, the American Century suggested a distinctly Protestant character. The son of Presbyterian missionaries who had served in China in the early twentieth century, Luce drew deeply on the tradition of Protestant manifest destiny that had shaped Lyman Beecher and other Protestant nationalists in previous eras.

Yet Luce realized that for traditional social elites to reclaim cultural authority, a simple harkening back to an older Protestant America would not suffice. He understood that if business were to regain legitimacy, it could not propose a return to laissez-faire capitalism and the Victorian culture that sanctioned it.[13] In an age of popular support for social reform and labor, capitalist leaders had to acknowledge that government and unions had some role to play in the economy. Similarly, they needed to embrace rather than deny the pluralism that characterized contemporary American society.

Life's modern attitude toward Catholicism in the forties and fifties consequently reflected a more general intellectual flexibility, for the sake of rehabilitating traditional ideas of national greatness. Luce and his most prominent magazine realized that the high moral purpose they attributed to the United States could not, in a society of religious differences, be borne by Protestants alone but would need to incorporate Catholics as well. It was thus critical to construct a Catholicism appropriate for the American Century, one that would support rather than challenge American mission abroad and capitalist supremacy at home. This effort involved disassociating Catholics from their past identifications with ethnic communities and social reform. Instead, the magazine turned Catholics into symbols of the religious renewal and moral seriousness that characterized the American Century. Indeed, at a time when Protestant-Catholic tensions remained very real, particularly after World War II, *Life* indicated that the American Century mediated those conflicts by Americanizing Catholics into signs of religious variety and moral commitment that paralleled the material abundance and cultural vitality the magazine insisted defined the nation.[14]

To realize the profound impact that Luce's vision of the American Century had upon *Life*'s representations of Catholics, it is helpful first to examine the magazine's early depictions, before his statement of belief of 1941. The cultural semiotics of *Life*'s Catholics of the forties and fifties broke significantly with the magazine's prior treatment, particularly its fascination with Catholic bodies, urban life, and the papacy. Before the American Century made Catholics citizens for a new era, older assumptions about the nation, religion, and public life had to be overcome.

New World Exotics and Old World Figureheads

In *Life*'s initial years in the 1930s, its characterization of Catholics had a diffuse, eclectic character, much like the magazine itself. Yet even in these early years, several preferences emerged. As Terry Smith has argued, *Life*'s photographic stories provided a powerful visual medium through which it delineated normative America.[15] In the thirties, *Life* clearly defined Catholics as the Other to mainstream society. Representations of Catholics not only helped authorize *Life* as the photographic record of the contemporary world for readers but also functioned to mark the boundaries of an older Anglo-Protestant American community.

This characterization of Catholics reflected the sensibilities of *Life*'s editors as well as its middle-class audience in the thirties, for whom the urban, ethnic, working-class culture of American Catholics was a world apart. In the initial years of the magazine, Luce gathered a stable of editors and writers who, like himself, were from Anglo-American backgrounds and often products of the Ivy League. John Shaw Billings, *Life*'s first managing editor, attended Harvard and came from an old South Carolina plantation family. After he had made his fortune as a loyal soldier in Luce's Time-Life empire, Billings bought back the old family plantation and made it his home away from Manhattan. Daniel Longwell, the magazine's original pictures editor, harkened from Omaha, Nebraska, and was educated at Columbia University. Wilson Hicks, who replaced Longwell in the key position of pictures editor, was born in Sedalia, Missouri, and educated at the University of Missouri. So like Luce, *Life*'s editors hailed from places far beyond the major enclaves of Catholic culture in America.[16]

Further, a number of the magazine's prominent photographers were well-traveled professionals with little intimate contact with Catholics. Alfred Eisenstaedt emigrated from Germany after many years of photographing high continental society during the late twenties and early thirties. Wallace Kirkland, the photographer of a major 1937 cover photostory on a Catholic laymen's retreat in Chicago, came from Jamaica and had done a stint in the temple of Anglo-American progressivism, Hull House, in the twenties. Carl Mydans, the photographer for a big story on the Catholic Mass at St. Patrick's Cathedral, had worked for the famed Farm Security Administration as a documentary photographer before joining *Life*.[17] The magazine's early editors and photographers therefore possessed impressive credentials but not much familiarity with the Catholic experience in America. As a result, *Life*'s portrayal of Catholics in the late 1930s had a highly voyeuristic character, as if the journalists were gazing at them with both fascination and disapproval.

One of the most common representations of Catholics in the early years of the magazine portrayed them on their knees, either in prayer or expressing respect to religious authorities. A 1937 story on the American Legion convention in New York City, for instance, included a prominent photograph of Catholic legion women kneeling in pews at Mass, with rosary beads dangling from their hands.[18] Similarly, a story on a popular Chicago novena was topped with a photo of women kneeling before a replica of the Pieta. It concluded with a full-page photograph of a woman on her knees at a side chapel in the Church of Our Lady of Sorrows, where the novena took place, underscoring both the feminine and the supplicant look of Catholic devotionalism.[19]

Poses of reverent and worshipful kneeling also characterized *Life*'s depiction of Catholics around the world. A full-page photo showed the Duke of Norfolk, a Catholic layman, kneeling before Cardinal Hinsley of Westminster, England, with the headline BRITAIN'S NO. 1 CATHOLIC KISSES ITS ONLY CARDINAL'S RING.[20] *Life* rendered Mexican Catholicism as a bizarre spectacle in such stories as "The Catholics of Mexico Crawl to the Shrine of Guadalupe."[21]

But it was not only women and non-American Catholics that *Life* represented kneeling in their religious practice. The first issue of the magazine included a picture of the prominent New Deal urban politician James Farley on bended knee, kissing the ring of Cardinal Pacelli; this was part of a two-page spread entitled "The President's Album," a photo-story on FDR. The caption beneath the photo left no doubt about this kind of gesture and Catholic identity, reading "With great deference, Mr. Roosevelt received Eugenio Cardinal Pacelli, Papal Secretary of State, the man who may be the next Pope. But with even greater deference did good Catholic Postmaster Jim Farley kneel to kiss the Cardinal's ring."[22] Similarly, the magazine's article "Life Goes to a Party" in late June 1938 highlighted the Catholic wedding of a young Polish American couple and included a dramatic full-page shot of the neatly appointed groom alongside his bride kneeling before the priest in front of an elaborate altar.[23]

Through these numerous images of Catholics kneeling, a powerful message was conveyed to *Life*'s readers suggesting that Catholicism was a religion that demanded subordination and deference from its faithful. In a magazine that celebrated youthful vigor, athleticism, and fashionable style, while bulging with ads that reveled in the joys of material abundance, Catholicism appeared out of step with the vibrancy of modern life. Bodies that knelt, genuflected, and bowed not only implied physical subservience but also cultural inferiority and emasculation. The persistence of such images subtly hinted that Catholicism was antithetical to American individuality and independence. The Roman Catholic Church, *Life* seemed to be saying, made bodies do strange things, and those odd-looking bodies helped mark the boundaries of normative America in the pages of the magazine.

In addition to focusing on the Catholic body, *Life* also associated the urban, ethnic character of Catholicism with deviant behaviors—with crime, vice, and corruption. In "Sidewalk Prayers to Governor Save Four out of Six Murderers," a wide-angle photo of women praying outside the Park Avenue apartment of New York's Governor Lehman topped a brief story about calls for clemency for six convicted murderers of a Brooklyn subway collector. A second photo showed the mother of one of the convicted men holding her rosary beads, with her head slumped down on a table, as she listens to the radio for news about her son.[24] Similarly, in a May 1938 "Newspictures of the Week" column, a photo of a priest giving last rites to a stripper dying on a Manhattan street from an attempted suicide linked Catholicism with the seamier side of city life.[25]

A highly critical story on Mayor Frank Hague of Jersey City, New Jersey, with photos by Margaret Bourke-White, described the politician as "a devout Irish Catholic" who ruled "by the old-time boss methods of fear, force and favor." The photo-essay included a picture of Father John P. Sullivan, identified as "Hague's priest"; it showed the cleric with a smug smile on his face beneath a sign reading, "Make Parish Returns Here." The caption of the photo described Sullivan as "spiritual director of the Rosary Confraternity which directs Jersey City's biggest Bingo game." Another photo was of Hague's "$50,000 altar in St. Aedan's Roman Catholic Church," identified as a "personal gift from the Mayor to his parish." In this manner, a story about a notorious political boss turned Catholicism into a sign of a corrupt and morally turgid ethnic, urban world that produced such men.[26]

Not content with equating Catholic politics and urban corruption, *Life* also treated the religious rituals of ethnic Catholics with disdain, as evidenced in the article "'Little Italy' Cloaks Its Healing Saint in Dollars," from September 1937. Describing the street procession of St. Rocco as one of the Italian community's "biggest and most colorful religious festivals," *Life*'s editors transformed the religious devotion into a spectacle of superstition and paganism. Photographs showing dollar bills affixed to the statue of St. Rocco encouraged readers to read the feast as a materialist desecration of religion. Other images of wax legs, heads, and infants, which the devout used as offerings to the saint, suggested a strange world of barbaric rituals.[27] Missing from this photo-essay was any suggestion of the lived religion of ordinary Italian Catholics.[28] Consequently, the magazine's voyeuristic revulsion at the popular saint's feast turned Catholicism into the faith of desperate, uneducated, and gullible Italians.

Even a seemingly innocuous story about nuns and the education of immigrants reduced the complexities of Catholic life to modern exoticism.

The first issue of *Life* contained a brief story, entitled "Chinese School," about young Chinese American children in the "only Catholic parochial school for Chinese children" in San Francisco's Chinatown; the text was illustrated with photographs by Alfred Eisenstaedt, one of *Life*'s most prominent picture-takers. Primarily an exercise in orientalism, the essay made dramatic visual effect of the Catholic nuns of the Order of St. Joseph who taught at St. Mary's school. In one photograph, a young girl stands between two nuns, whose backs are turned to the camera. Eisenstaedt adeptly captures the flowing lines of the drape of the nuns' habits and robes as they lean down to speak with the child, turning the image into an example of modernist formal aesthetics. The placement of nuns on either side of the child helped frame the young girl, making her the focus of the photograph. This visual framing provided by the nuns is underscored by the text, which noted the nuns were teaching the schoolchildren English, thereby functioning as an Americanizing frame for the Chinese pupils.[29]

Focusing on a new generation of Chinese Americans, the story indulged in a double exercise of exhibiting cultural Others while turning Chinese youth and Catholic nuns into exotic, highly gendered specimens of the ethnic ghettos of San Francisco. The feminine character of both the children and the Catholic teachers made the representations of cultural difference appear nonthreatening, thereby diminishing the likelihood that the story about Catholic schools and new immigrants would trouble readers.

Yet the story profoundly distorted the Catholic presence in Chinatown. Although it stressed the role of the nuns in the acculturation of "young Americans" among the Chinese community in San Francisco, the sisters were actually part of a novel parish mission project led by the order of Paulist priests. In addition to the day school in which the nuns taught, the Paulists had established a Chinese-language school run by two Chinese Catholic laymen. The school sought to retain Chinese culture among the children of Chinatown by accepting both Catholic and non-Catholic students, encouraging the use of traditional Chinese musical instruments in playing Chinese music, and publishing a quarterly magazine. St. Mary's Mission Center also had a social services department, which helped provide for the welfare needs of the community. Thus, far from merely serving as an outpost of Americanization in a Chinese ethnic enclave, St. Mary's actively involved the Chinese themselves and their cultural traditions in the religious work. But none of the social complexity of Catholicism in Chinatown was conveyed in *Life*'s story stressing exotic little girls and their maternal Catholic teachers.[30]

The magazine coverage of Catholics in the mid- and late thirties consequently communicated powerful assumptions about ethnicity, religion, and American identity. In much the same way, a cover story from August 1937, "Pious Workers Go on a Retreat," conveyed the class and ideological biases of the magazine as it depoliticized industrial workers by emphasizing their spiritual devotionalism.[31] Photographer Wallace Kirkland captured a group of Chicago industrial workers from Asbestos Workers Union, Local 17, participating in a sixty-hour Catholic retreat outside Chicago. The story recounted how Hugh Mulligan, vice president of the union, got 300 of his fellow union members to engage in the spiritual practice. Yet visually, the focus was on Hugh Patrick Dunn, "Chicago's oldest asbestos worker." In a series of four photos, Dunn was shown entering St. Francis Retreat House and climbing the stairs to his room. Another photo showed Dunn on his knees praying at the third station at the retreat's stations of the cross, described incorrectly by the caption as a "shrine." Interspersed with the images of Dunn were other group photos of the union workers at Mass entering a chapel and kneeling at the thirteenth station of the cross. The story concluded by returning to Dunn on its final page with two more photos of him, one showing him on his knees receiving communion and the last when he was back at work, "covering steam pipes in a Federal housing project at Chicago's Trumball Park."

By highlighting, among all the men on retreat, the elderly Irish Catholic dutifully at prayer, the story reinforced the stereotype of the Irish "Paddy" praying on his beads. But the photo-essay also communicated a subtle political point. Ending a story of Catholic industrial workers on spiritual retreat with a photo of Dunn back at work visually implied that the primary significance of Catholic religion was as spiritual refreshment that provided workers the sustenance needed to be good laborers. Nowhere did the essay suggest either the vibrant industrial labor movement in Chicago or the social reform activism of the Chicago Catholic Church under Cardinal George Mundelein, a friend of Roosevelt's, during the thirties.[32]

Kirkland's own background perhaps contributed to the conventional depiction of Catholic devotion. Born in Jamaica to British parents, the photographer wound up working at the famous Hull House overseeing boys' clubs. He eventually left the settlement house and became a contributing photographer for *Life* during its early years.[33] The condescension toward the Catholic men evident in Kirkland's photographs hints that his notions of religion may have been informed more by the liberal

Protestant social gospel creed of Hull House than by any awareness of Catholic religious life.

In fact, the story and Kirkland's photographs caught only part of the reality of the Catholic workers' retreat. St. Francis Retreat House, which hosted the union men, was actually an estate known as Mayslake Hall that had been sold to the Franciscan order and became an important center in the budding National Catholic Laymen's Retreat Movement during the 1930s. This group was founded in 1926 to cultivate the spiritual life of Catholic laymen. During the 1930s, it held a series of national conventions in an attempt to organize and collaborate on the effort of developing laymen's religious experiences. The Chicago church was a key force of this movement, and within Chicago, Mayslake served as an important site. By 1931, the retreat movement had pursued outreach to industrial workers, particularly in the Chicago area. Hugh Mulligan, whom the story described simply as having led his fellow union men to the retreat house because of a prior positive visit, actually had been president of the St. Francis Laymen's Retreat League of Chicago, one of the local associations of the National Catholic Laymen's Retreat Movement.[34]

The Laymen's Retreat Movement remained rather small within American Catholicism during the 1930s, but it reflected the extensive institution building at a national level in the Catholic subculture of the early and mid-twentieth century. Further, its focus on laymen evidenced an early effort to move Catholic spirituality beyond strictly clerical needs. Equally significant, the Chicago league's attempts to engage union men reflected the intertwining of the labor movement and the Catholic Church during the Depression.

Through such stories as those on the Catholic industrial workers and the San Francisco mission school, therefore, *Life* offered a highly truncated and distorted representation of Catholics in America, draining them of their public and religious legitimacy. Its account of Catholicism abroad in like manner offered a portrait of Old World traditions mired in the past while struggling to cope with a changing world. In the late 1930s, *Life* began a significant investment in covering the papacy. For a magazine devoted to the visual image, Rome proved irresistible. *Life*'s main photo-essay of December 26, 1938, for example, focused on the Vatican, with eleven pages of photo and print offering a glimpse into the center of Roman Catholicism.[35] "From a Roman Hill the Pope Rules His Troubled World," declared the subtitle of the article. On the facing page was a large photo of a somber, sad-eyed Pius XI. Next to the title was a photo of the Swiss Guards of the Vatican in their medieval uniforms. The story described Pius XI as "an old man, sick and sorrowful" who looked out upon a contemporary world "bold with persecution which bears harshly down on daily Catholic life." Fascist aggression in Italy and communist advances in Russia and Mexico had put the church on the defensive. The pope now looked "for aid and comfort" to the "great Protestant democracies," the article asserted, implying a vindication of the Reformation.

Photographs of cardinals' dining rooms and bedrooms as well as the Sistine Chapel took readers inside the seat of Roman papal power. Indeed, images of the vaulted ceilings of the Vatican Library, examples of Renaissance art from papal collections, and the looming dome of St. Peter's all contributed to a portrait of Catholicism as a religion of the past rather than a relevant institution of the present. One photo had Pius XI sitting on the throne of St. Peter's during a canonization ceremony for three saints. The pope seemed all but lost amid the soaring columns and elaborate altar piece of the Basilica, dramatically conveying the spectacle of Catholic power. The caption read, "Surrounded by baroque splendor and breath-taking ceremony the Pope is enthroned at the head of his world."

As the numerous stories and images of Catholics both in the United States and in Europe demonstrated, Roman Catholicism proved a compelling subject through which *Life* asserted its authority to visually render the world to its readers. Unlike Hollywood films of the 1930s, however, it treated Catholics based upon particular assumptions of Catholicism as an Old World religion alien to American culture. Representations of Catholics served to construct a portrait of America by signifying cultural differences of body, urban life, politics, and religion itself that lay outside the imagined community of an Anglo-Protestant nation. In the 1940s, however, as the magazine assumed a sharper editorial vision regarding the United States and its place in the world, *Life* developed a whole new set of meanings for the visual drama that was Roman Catholicism.

The War Makes Good Catholics

During World War II, *Life*'s representations of Catholics broke dramatically from its coverage of the thirties, reflecting the new focus Luce provided the magazine with his vision of the American Century. In this tumultuous period, the magazine increasingly portrayed Catholics as expressing a unified national community. And in the process, *Life* turned Catholics into good citizens by decoupling them from their ethnic and devotional practices and linking them to the symbols of the wartime state.

The magazine's new treatment of Catholics became manifest even before the United States formally entered the war in December 1941. In a photographic story that foreshadowed the association of Catholics with national symbols that became common during the war, *Life* ran a large photo in its August 18, 1941, issue of a Catholic Mass held for American soldiers in Greenland. With American flags prominent in the open-air service, the headline stated, FIRST U.S. TROOPS LAND IN GREENLAND TO PREPARE MAIN ARMY AND AIR BASE. The Catholic chaplain, dressed in military uniform, stood at a pulpit draped with the flag. Tellingly, none of the American soldiers were kneeling.[36]

Similarly, in an essay on the one-year anniversary of Pearl Harbor, *Life* chose to use a full-page photograph of a service at the Catholic St. Cyril and Methodius Church in Bridgeport, Connecticut, to portray a nation at prayer. Titled "U.S. Remembers Pearl Harbor Day with Ships and Prayers," the story used a trio of photos of the launching of three new navy ships to suggest the nation's rebounding from the loss of Pearl Harbor but used only the Catholic service to represent Americans' spiritual mobilization.[37]

By 1943, the wartime Americanization of Catholics was well under way, as demonstrated by a June story, "Life Goes to a Hero's Homecoming," on John Basilone, a young marine who won the Medal of Honor. Basilone gained recognition for his heroic stand against Japanese fighters in the Philippines: the magazine gushed, "Johnny had mowed down 38 Japs singlehanded." The story covered Basilone's return to his hometown, Raritan, New Jersey, where he was greeted by large crowds and a parade. Prominently included in both the photos and the text were references to Basilone's Catholicism. Between photos of the huge gathering and the parade car with the marine waving to well-wishers was an image of Basilone in uniform with his parents and the family's parish priest, Father Russo. The story noted that John had attended St. Bernard's parochial school. Another photo showed the hero at Mass at his boyhood church on the day of his big celebration. Notably, the marine in uniform was standing rather than kneeling during the service. Underscoring the war's reframing of Catholics in America, the caption read, "Johnny requested mass be said at St. Ann's for his buddies at Guadalcanal, not for himself." Unlike so many of *Life*'s Catholics from the 1930s, this Catholic soldier evoked an image of moral strength and national pride. Indeed, this Catholic from an Italian immigrant family was an American hero, a figure *Life* raised up to readers who were eager for signs of American success against their Japanese enemies.[38]

The magazine's coverage of Americans at war transformed the portrayal of Catholic men into soldiers who symbolized national confidence. The war years also saw changes in depictions of Catholic women. No longer emphasizing their alien religious devotions, *Life* incorporated them into the visual landscape of a virtuous domestic front. A story of a Catholic foundling hospital inundated with abandoned children due to the war ended with a compelling shot of a nun cradling a swaddled infant in her arms.[39] A March 1944 story on "The Brides of Christ," about a group of young women entering a Carmelite convent in New York, suggested in exaggerated form the values of female purity and marriage of a traditional gender ideology that reemerged during the war.[40] Using a visual narrative similar to that in the Feast of St. Rocco essay, the article incorporated a series of photographs to show the "picturesque pageant of renunciation" whereby the young women abandoned their secular lives and embraced religious life. This ritual provided dramatic images of rows of women in white kneeling before a priest while he blessed them. Yet the excess of the Italian festival was replaced by the restraint and formality of the ritual of initiation. Wedding veils, nuns' habits, and elongated candles evoked a fusion of female decorum, propriety, and otherworldly spirituality.

Even a story about Catholic women praying for their loved ones fighting in the war abroad linked Catholic devotion to the cause of the war instead of accentuating its ethnic difference from mainstream American worship.[41] Like the images of soldiers' wives, daughters, and girlfriends that populated the pages of *Life* during the war, these Catholic women coded the moral obligations of the conflict in highly gendered terms. The fight against fascism therefore became a struggle to protect a home front where women practiced moral acts of selflessness and religious piety.[42]

Life's voyeuristic treatment of Catholicism in the thirties thus gave way to patriotic and affirmative imagery during the early forties. Visually, this meant the signs of the nation-state increasingly intersected with distinctly Catholic markers, such as Roman collars and elaborate church architecture. This semiotic shift reflected the magazine's effort to promote a unified American people engaged in a virtuous struggle against fascism. Catholics, the magazine suggested, were equally a part of the national endeavor.

Catholicism and the Rise of Cold War Culture

World War II helped Americanize Catholics, just as it did other white ethnic minorities.[43] The pages of *Life* provided ample evidence of this development. Nonetheless, Catholicism remained a troubling and divisive presence in the United States during the 1940s, as revealed by the renewal of Protestant concerns about the Roman Catholic Church.[44] *Life* shared some of these anxieties, as reflected in stories that highlighted Catholic papal spectacle and popular devotionalism.[45] Yet what is more striking, given the photo-journal's cultural roots in Anglo-American Protestantism, was the continuing favorable treatment it accorded Catholicism into the postwar era. *Life* was not the *Nation* magazine, and Henry Luce was not Paul Blanshard.[46] To be sure, the pattern that had emerged in the early forties, in which the magazine created good Americans out of Catholics by detaching them from their ethnic identities, persisted. But issues both global and close to home were also at work in the Luce empire, issues that directed *Life* toward Catholicism.

In 1946, Henry Luce's wife, the glamorous Clare Booth Luce, converted to Catholicism. Her spiritual adviser in the church was none other than Fulton J. Sheen, radio star of the *Catholic Hour* and professor of philosophy at Catholic University of America.[47] The Presbyterian Luce now found that he literally had a partner in Roman Catholicism. Clare served as an important intellectual and political ally for Luce. According to Andrew Heiskell, the publisher of *Life*, Clare's influence on her husband was substantial.[48] Luce therefore may have taken new interest in Catholicism because of Clare. He would even occasionally attend Mass with his wife.[49]

But Clare's was not the only Catholic voice Luce heard. Other Catholics started to invade the Ivy League, Anglo-American citadel of the Luce media empire by the 1940s. These individuals included Roy Alexander, *Time* magazine's managing editor from 1949 to 1960. Alexander was from Omaha and, unlike so many other of Luce's associates, was a product of a Catholic education, a graduate of the Jesuit St. Louis University. In addition, Emmet John Hughes, another Catholic and friend of the Jesuit moral philosopher John Courtney Murray, became a leading writer for Luce by the late 1940s, penning numerous essays for *Life* magazine on European politics. Hughes actually became a Luce confidant during the Eisenhower years, and the two men, along with Murray, sometimes played golf together.[50] Therefore, although *Life* remained an institution informed by Protestant sensibilities, beginning in the mid-forties Henry Luce's world began to include a number of Catholics in prominent positions at home and work.

In addition to personal and professional developments surrounding Luce, larger global and political changes also affected *Life*'s treatment of

Catholics. World War II inevitably brought forth reflections on the spiritual meanings of the American struggle against its enemies. In the early years, *Life*'s commentary conveyed a decidedly Protestant perspective. In late December 1942, for instance, the magazine published John Foster Dulles's "A Righteous Faith," which asserted that the "Protestant Churches of America are awake to the spiritual need that faces our nation. They are determined to do all that lies in their power to assure that out of this war will be born, not just ephemeral passions, but a faith that will endure and that will project us into the world as a great force for righteousness."[51]

But by 1944, *Life*'s editors were already anticipating that America's greatest postwar challenge would be an aggressive Soviet Union. This hardening of attitude toward Russia would have important consequences for the magazine's understanding of Catholicism. The publication of a controversial essay by American diplomat William C. Bullitt, "The World from Rome," for example, demonstrated *Life*'s new respect for Roman Catholicism. Bullitt argued the real threat to the world lay in Soviet domination of Europe, and he portrayed Pius XII as a savvy reader of communist duplicity. From the essay's perspective, the church provided the most important bastion against Soviet incursions in Italy.[52]

In a February 1944 editorial, "The Kremlin and the Vatican," *Life* criticized an attack on the papacy by the official Soviet newspaper, *Izvestia*. It used the Soviet challenge to the pope to reflect upon the virtues of American tolerance, drawing parallels between communist opposition to the Vatican and prejudice against Catholics in America that the editors asserted the United States had largely outgrown. "It is native bigotry and not the Pope, that occasionally makes Catholicism a political question in America. . . . And it is religious tolerance, written into our Constitution, that enables all Catholics to be good Americans and to be as politically free and divided as the non-Catholics are." The editorial concluded by asserting, "An attack on the pope is an unfriendly act not only to Catholics. Because it is intolerant and begets intolerance, it is unfriendly to all freedom–loving Americans."[53] In the eyes of *Life*'s editors, the looming threat posed by Soviet communism to deeply cherished American values displaced older social divisions and encouraged a serious reconsideration of Catholics and American identity.

After the war, *Life* insistently called for waging a new cultural battle against communism. Believing the struggle against the Soviets was fundamentally ideological, it demanded a rededication to American ideals. *Life*'s understanding of this fight, crucial for its treatment of Catholics in ensuing years, gave centrality to religion and spiritual commitment. In a March 1946 editorial, "'Getting Tough' with Russia," the magazine quoted Dulles on the need for a "spiritual drive" in the United Nations that only Americans could supply. Three months later, *Life* published his two-part article on Soviet foreign policy; in it, the magazine's favorite diplomat called for a muscular response to Soviet communism. Dulles sounded the call for spiritual mobilization: "We must show that our free land is not spiritual lowland, easily submerged, but highland, that most of all, provides the spiritual, intellectual and economic conditions which all men want." He also claimed the Soviet challenge necessitated that Americans show their cultural superiority by returning to their religious foundations. "The most significant demonstration that can be made," he asserted, "is at the religious level. The overriding and ever-present reason for giving freedom to the individual is that men are created as children of God in His image."[54] Dulles, like Luce himself, was a dedicated Presbyterian and deeply involved with the Protestant National Council of Churches. Yet by framing the American response to Soviet communism as a spiritual-cultural project that entailed the mobilization of all Americans, *Life*'s postwar ideology provided the opening for moral-cultural rapprochement with Catholicism. Indeed, as its publication of the Bullitt article in 1944 indicated, even before the end of World War II the photo-journal had already turned an approving eye to the Vatican as an ally against communism.

Life's early and intense call for an anticommunist foreign policy as well as a new Catholic presence at Time-Life suggested that the magazine's more favorable treatment of Catholics in the forties was not solely due to wartime exigencies. Hostility toward the Soviet Union in particular sustained *Life*'s willingness to see Catholics as partners in a global struggle against godless tyranny. Cold War quickly supplanted world war for Luce and *Life*, and representations of Catholics reflected this ideological development.

Less than six months after the war ended, the magazine published a celebratory, two-part story on Archbishop Francis Spellman of New York. Spellman himself graced the January 21 cover of *Life* for the first part of the essay, whose subtitle described him as "a great American." The occasion of the article was Spellman's elevation to cardinal by Pius XII, but its purpose was to present the leading American Catholic bishop as an embodiment of the Americanization of Catholicism. Roger Butterfield's account stressed Spellman's international experiences as a young protégé of Pius in Europe battling Italian fascists in the early 1930s and later as a champion of American armed forces during World War II. The admiring essay turned the archbishop of New York into a symbol of a new era of Catholic and American unity, predicated upon a shared moral purpose in the fight against totalitarianism.[55]

The opening photograph depicted Spellman offering Mass at St. Patrick's Cathedral, and other photos conveyed a wholesome Americanism. An image of Spellman's colonial-style boyhood home in Massachusetts looked like something out of an Andy Hardy movie. Another photo of Spellman's parents, listening to the radio in a comfortable parlor, oozed normalcy. A wartime photo of Spellman visiting soldiers on the Italian front showed him in army khakis, no different from the men standing next to him.[56]

The text complemented this visual depiction of Spellman's American identity by describing his "democratic ways" as a parish priest, the "tolerant tone" he gave to "Catholic affairs in the U.S.," and his "broad-minded attitude" in dealing with his fellow Catholics. For all his stature as a representative of the Roman Catholic Church, the essay asserted,

> the Archbishop, too, has never forgotten that he was an American boy who delivered groceries and played shortstop and got his start in the democratic atmosphere of an American small town. . . . Far from feeling that there is any basic conflict between the American form of government and the Church, he has expressed the sincere conviction that they are now united in the same purpose: to bring justice and democracy to all the people of the world. . . . Today, with most of the older Catholic countries ravaged by war, the U.S.—which has always been a great Protestant country—is on the way to becoming the greatest Catholic country as well. American opinion, American influence, American support both spiritual and material, are indispensable to the Church.[57]

If Cardinal Spellman became a favorite of *Life* after World War II, Pope Pius XII provided grist for the magazine's elevation of Catholics into a partner in the Cold War struggle. But Rome proved a more difficult subject, for the papacy did not always play by the rules that *Life* had expected for Roman Catholicism. In such instances, the magazine revealed where the ideology of the American Century continued to struggle with the Catholic Church. At midcentury, Pius XII engaged in a number of dramatic assertions of Catholic power that *Life*'s editors found difficult to swallow. The 1950 Holy Year celebrations in Rome provoked traditional fears about Catholic pomp and spectacle. An article entitled "The Door

A smiling Cardinal Francis Spellman on the cover of a January 1946 issue of Life helped reintroduce Catholic power to readers as a friendly partner to American greatness. (Lisa Larsen/Time & Life Pictures/Getty Images)

"Opens on a Holy Year" had an interesting subtitle—"At 20th Century's Turning Point an Ancient Ritual Calls Believers to Rally and Fortify Catholic Power." The granting of indulgences to pilgrims to Rome as part of the celebration drew suspicion: "Before the year's end up to three million are expected to have fulfilled the prescribed penance and departed— a rich source of income for the tourist trade." Photographs emphasized the Baroque setting of the Vatican and mobs clamoring to see the pope raised high above their heads on his papal chair.[58] A story later that year, "An 11-Year-Old Girl Is Made a Saint," exoticized another aspect of Catholic culture, the cult of saints. Reporting on the canonization of Maria Goretti, a murdered young girl whom the church turned into a modern-day martyr of feminine chastity, *Life* opened its story with a photo of Maria in her coffin with the caption, "Clothed skeleton of the new saint. . . . The head is a likeness in wax." A second photo on the bottom of page offered a wide-angle shot of canonization ceremonies in St. Peter's Square. These two images of Goretti's remains and the Vatican visually framed the story in ways that highlighted Catholic foreignness for readers.[59]

Through such gestures as the Holy Year celebrations and the Goretti canonization as well as the Proclamation of the Dogma of the Assumption, Pius turned the Vatican into a theater of the Cold War in the years from 1945 to 1950. Historians of this pontiff debate whether such actions indicated the centrality of his role for the early Cold War or instead his isolation from real geopolitical developments.[60] Nevertheless, the pope vigorously assumed the media spotlight, and *Life* kept American readers informed of the latest events in Rome.

Despite the appeal to the exotic, however, the magazine was determined to make the pope an international hero in the global struggle against communism. It found the church's opposition to communism too valuable to be distracted by Catholic ritualism. The hardening of lines between East and West in the immediate postwar years served as a crucial context for *Life*'s coverage of the papacy. Paul Hutchinson's lengthy 1946 survey of Western European politics, "Does Europe Face a Holy War?" opened with a photo of a large anticommunist crowd amassed in St. Peter's. Hutchinson, the managing editor of the *Christian Century*, told readers that Western Europe was "fast moving toward a showdown with communism." But the greatest sign of hope lay in the emergence of new Christian Democratic parties that were gaining the allegiance of millions of Europeans who were afraid that communism would destroy their liberties. In Hutchinson's account, Pius XII emerged as "an astute observer of European politics," who was leading the revival of Christian contributions to democracy in Western Europe. Hutchinson recognized that some Protestant readers of Life might consider the incursion of the church into politics as a "shock," but he assuaged their fears by pointing to examples such as the German Democratic Union, which demonstrated "the ability of Catholics and Protestants to cooperate for a common cause." That cause, Hutchinson claimed, was a European future of social justice and freedom from communist control.[61]

Life's supportive coverage of Catholicism as a moral force against communism went into overdrive in 1948 when Italy saw a major political campaign between the Christian Democratic and Communist parties. A story in March during the immediate run-up to the elections focused on Father Riccardo Lombardi; it was titled "A Man of Love Fights Communists in Italy." A small photo above the title showed the animated radio priest positioned before a microphone. Other photos demonstrated the large crowds Lombardi attracted. The story reported that "from Naples to Milan hundreds of thousands of Italians rallied around a small, pale priest who, as a good Christian, proposed to frustrate the Kremlin with love, rather than iron."[62]

After the defeat of the Communists in the elections, an ecstatic Life editorial proclaimed, "Final credit goes to the Pope." It waxed approvingly about the power of the church to get out the vote. What once would have produced only dread now seemed to earn the acclaim of the magazine: "The Pope's legions carried the battle deep into the slums, the farms and the fishing villages." This was all to the good according to Life because the church "reached voters at a level which only the consecrated and hard-working Communists had directly reached before." The editorial also encouraged the pope and his Catholic Action organization of lay political workers to continue their efforts of building a "nonpartisan Christianity." It concluded by asserting, "Let the Pope's legions remain at their posts, fighting for a society in which Communism is no longer a problem, because justice and prosperity are no longer strangers, a society where righteousness and progress are partners again."[63]

Life imagined the pope as a crucial ally in the unfolding of the American Century's battle with Soviet totalitarianism. Even so, the magazine worried that the church's assertiveness might alienate Americans unused to thinking of the papacy as a spiritual comrade in arms. Life therefore drew upon additional resources in its efforts to harness both the pope and the Catholic Church for its Cold War vision of the world.

At the height of Catholic-Protestant tensions of the early 1950s, *Life* published two essays by English Catholic convert and novelist Graham Greene. Greene was fresh from his critical and commercial hit *The Heart of the Matter* as well as his work on Orson Welles's acclaimed movie *The Third Man,* and the magazine provided its readers with his reflections on Pope Pius XII's recently proclaimed Dogma of the Assumption of Mary in late 1950. Few topics were more likely to divide Catholics from Protestants as dogmatic assertions from Roman pontiffs on Mary as the Mother of God. Yet Greene made the new teaching seem like a thoroughly appropriate response to a modern era searching for religious meaning. Pointing to the "general heresy of our time, the unimportance of the individual," his essay concluded that the proclamation amounted to a fulsome resistance to the nuclear age's belief that "the human body is regarded as expendable material, something to be eliminated wholesale by the atom bomb."[64]

Then, a year later, *Life* published another Greene essay on Pius himself. The English novelist portrayed Pius, for all his papal authority, as really just a humble man of God. A full-page photo of the pope born aloft on a chair through St. Peter's, which introduced the essay, conveyed Catholic splendor. But the title of the essay, "The Pope Who Remains a Priest," accompanied by another photo of a solitary Pius clad in simple white robes walking in the Vatican gardens, suggested a more humane dimension to the pontiff. Other photographs depicted the pope years earlier when he was Archbishop Pacelli distributing food to Italian prisoners of war in World War I, as well as a scene of Pius talking to children. Greene's text stressed the man behind the papacy: "Pacelli combines his official work with pastoral work, just as still during his public audience he has been known to go to a corner of the audience hall at a peasant's request and hear his confession." The essay dismissed recent papal condemnations of progressive Catholic theologians as acts "not the immediate work of the Pope but of the civil service" of the Vatican. Greene even asserted that "it is a long time since a Pope has awaked, even in those of other faiths, such a sense of closeness."[65]

The papacy thus provided a central focus for *Life*'s treatment of Catholicism at midcentury. Particularly as East-West divisions settled over Europe and Pius XII used his religious authority to make Rome a prominent site in the cultural battle with totalitarianism, *Life* found in the pope a visually powerful means of concentrating its Cold War understanding for readers. Catholic ritual rested uneasily with *Life*'s more Protestant assumptions about authentic religion. Yet the magazine's ideological vision of an American Century more often than not trumped anticlericalism to harness Catholicism's vivid material culture. The whore of Babylon had been transformed in the pages of *Life* into the Old World's most distinguished religious representative of Cold War Americanism.

Catholics and Consensus

Life's coverage of the papacy after World War II displayed the new cultural semiotics of the Cold War in which the see of Peter assumed a role as America's ally in the moral and spiritual fight against global communism. The magazine's treatment of Catholics in the United States underwent parallel changes. In the late forties and fifties, representations of American Catholics served to celebrate the success and openness of an American way of life characterized by assimilation, prosperity, and religious vitality. Imagery and narratives of consensus turned Catholics into signs of American social and moral achievement. In addition, Catholics functioned to expand the religious landscape of American democracy at a time when the Cold War demanded the spiritual mobilization of the entire nation. In this way, representation of Catholics reflected *Life*'s own vision of America as a harmonious, prosperous, and classless society, capacious enough to include religious outsiders. Catholics therefore helped further the magazine's larger project of celebrating the United States as a free society in contrast to the oppression of Soviet totalitarianism. In the process, the sharp edges of Catholic difference were simultaneously worn down and reworked to elaborate *Life*'s commitment to the American Century.

A lengthy round-table discussion in the July 12, 1948, issue epitomized the magazine's new perspective on American Catholics. The subject for debate was the pursuit of happiness in America, and the discussion included the Jesuit Edmund Walsh of Georgetown University along with such other luminaries as Sidney Hook, Erich Fromm, and Stuart Chase. The story included a photograph of all the participants invited by *Life* to opine on the topic at hand seated around a large table. It provided a none too subtle symbol of the great cultural conversation *Life* believed postwar American democracy represented. The inclusion of Walsh, however, indicated the magazine believed Catholics enjoyed a legitimate place within the national community.[66]

Representations of Catholics in fact helped signify *Life*'s deep investment in a consensus America during the postwar years. Catholics signified the possibilities and freedoms available within existing social arrangements that *Life* worked to sanction. But to turn Catholicism into a marker of the American way of life, its historical associations with social reformism and immigrant culture had to be diminished.

Toward that end, a story from 1953 on Bishop Bernard Sheil of Chicago renarrated the Catholic commitment to economic justice in the 1930s into a celebration of social unity. Sheil founded the influential Catholic Youth Organization in 1931 in response to the devastating consequences of the Depression on Chicago's working-class boys. He also became a strong advocate of labor unions and social justice. Yet the story on his twenty-fifth anniversary suggested those social conflicts were signs of the past and emphasized instead Sheil's popularity across religious and social lines. Admitting the priest had faced hostility from wealthy Catholics and others in earlier times, it also stressed that "leaders of business, labor, government and the church came from all over the U.S. to honor him" and that an "Episcopalian bishop gave the benediction and a rabbi blessed the bishop." Little in the article visually suggested Sheil's involvement in social justice. The large photo of him in bishop's regalia that introduced the story placed him on a street observing a CYO band pass by, reducing the Depression-era organization he founded to a form of entertainment. Another photo showed Sheil and other prelates at a luncheon table with huge American and papal flags behind them. Another image depicted the twenty-five-layer cake in honor of the jubilee celebration.[67]

Similarly, a story on Philip Murray, the head of the Congress of Industrial Organizations (CIO) referenced his Catholicism to suggest his moderate character as a labor leader. A lengthy photo-essay from 1954 on the American Jesuits recognized the role of the clerical order in battling communists who were "infiltrating U.S. labor unions" and encouraging managers and workers to "discuss their mutual problems." A photograph of a Jesuit priest in Philadelphia, gesturing forcefully to a group of dockworkers who were looking up to him attentively, helped convey an impression that labor had left behind its radicalism and become responsible thanks to men such as the Jesuit labor priests.[68]

One of the most telling examples of *Life*'s Americanization of Catholics occurred with a major photographic essay from October 1953, "An Italian Family in America."[69] Focusing on three generations of the La Falce family in Poughkeepsie, New York, the article proclaimed these individuals "stand for something bigger—the whole pattern of trial and triumph followed by all the millions of Europeans, Africans, Asians who have in the last three centuries become Americans." Catholicism served as an important signifier linking ethnics to American community. The opening photograph by Ralph Morse, for instance, depicted a classroom full of kindergarteners at Our Lady of Mount Carmel school looking up to the American flag and pledging allegiance. The second image, a full-page photograph, was a group portrait of the extended La Falce family. All the family members including the children were well dressed in suits and ties or dresses, suggesting middle-class respectability. Right behind the patriarch, Alfonso, and his wife, Rosario, stood their daughter, Sister Mary Rose, in her nun's habit.

A two-page spread within the story under the title "A Church of Their Own" gave particular attention to the Catholic character of this Americanized Italian family. The text and photos emphasized the centrality of the Catholic faith to the La Falces. A large close-up photo captured the "well-worn hands" of the father saying his rosary. Another photo showed the younger La Falce men and their wives singing in the church choir at Mass. But the text also described the family's parish priest, Father Salvatore Cantatore, as "a hustling handsome man who looks something like Spencer Tracy," calling up the image of Tracy's performance as Father Flanagan in *Boys Town* and connecting this family to the mass media that all Americans shared. Other photos surrounding the text extended the connection between Catholicism and modern popular culture. One photo showed the younger La Falce boys playing a game of pool at the "Friday night social of the Catholic Youth Organization." Another depicted teenagers dancing, with a caption that read, "Friday night at the parish hall finds the younger members jumping to music." A phonograph player was visually prominent in the foreground of the image, offering a modern, secular "balance" to the choir singing at Mass shown on the opposite page. In fact, the photograph's gathering of youth, popular music, and the Catholic parish echoed *Going My Way*'s depiction of Father O'Malley's hip embrace of mass culture.

The fusing of Catholic faith and modern America continued in the two following pages with the title "Life, Death and a Sense of Belonging," which presented Catholic religious rituals as part of the fabric of a contemporary, assimilated family. One image showed Father Cantatore baptizing an infant with a respectable-looking godmother holding the child. A candle in the middle of the image gave dignified solemnity to the scene. Father Cantatore was also shown administering extreme unction to a friend of the La Falces at St. Francis Hospital. The oxygen tent enclosing the patient, through which the priest had to reach to bless the man, suggested that modern medical science and Catholic ritual were partners in the care of the physical and spiritual needs of the sick.

The rendering of Catholicism in the life of the La Falce family broke dramatically from prewar images of ethnic Catholic life, such as the 1937 story on the Feast of St. Rocco. There, Catholicism was portrayed as a strange, even grotesque cultism practiced by foreigners in America. Now, almost twenty years later in a story celebrating assimilation, *Life* rendered Catholicism in terms of respectable faith, upward mobility, and popular culture. Narrating the Italian immigrant family as a melting-pot story, the essay visualized Catholics as part of the American dream in which ethnicity was consigned to a fading, older generation and Catholic devotionalism was cleansed of its eccentricities.

The story of the La Falces revealed *Life*'s strategy of making Catholics part of an American consensus through narratives of assimilation and middle-class family life.[70] Another lengthy photo-essay on American Catholicism, "The Biggest U.S. Archdiocese," demonstrated a different approach, which relied upon postwar culture's high regard for corporate America. The story highlighting the size, breadth, and extensive activities of the Archdiocese of Chicago ran the risk of raising anxieties about excessive Catholic power in America.[71] But *Life* sought to diffuse such concerns by rendering the church in Chicago as a well-managed corporate citizen of the city. The photo-essay organized its story around Cardinal Stritch, described as a man with "a rare mixture of tough-minded practicality and unworldly piety." Stressing the numerous jobs and duties the cardinal performed in his role as leader of Catholicism in Chicago, the article portrayed Stritch more like a civic-minded business executive than a prince of the Roman Catholic Church. The corporate image *Life* assigned to the archdiocese extended to Stritch's clerical assistants. Photos of the priests who headed the various agencies of the Chicago church surround a headline that read THE TEAM WHICH AIDS "THE BOSS." Each man looked directly at the camera, like vice presidents of a large corporation. In addition to focusing on the men at the top, the essay also highlighted the archdiocese's ministry to the aged, mentally ill, and hospitalized, further softening the image of Catholicism in Chicago. Emphasizing executive leadership and charitable work, *Life*'s photo-essay Americanized the church by having it echo the postwar corporate social order of the American Century.[72]

Finally, the magazine's most explicit recognition of Catholics as part of a consensus culture occurred in the same issue as the Chicago archdiocese essay. In a lengthy editorial that splashed over two pages with the banner headline THE AMERICAN MORAL CONSENSUS, the magazine's editors claimed the success of American democracy rested upon a shared moral philosophy of limited government. Since that philosophy acknowledged the existence of God, the editorial asserted, the American experiment in self-rule depended on the existence of religious people for its continued success.

Two faces peered from under this editorial's title. One was Supreme Court Justice John Marshall, whom the editorial quoted as asserting that the American Constitution reflected a moral vision imprinted upon mankind by its "Creator." The other face, however, was a Catholic, the late nineteenth-century bishop and first Catholic cardinal in the United States, James Gibbons. The editorial used Gibbons as an example of the long line of Catholic leaders and thinkers who had embraced the American Constitution.

Explicating the genius of the American constitutional arrangement regarding church and state, the editorial also quoted "Father John C. Murray," who described the Constitution's religious provisions as "Articles of Peace." Although most readers would have been unaware of it, Murray at the time was engaged in a revision of Catholic understanding on church and state that would culminate in the major Declaration of Religious Liberty at the Second Vatican Council. *Life*'s editor in chief, Henry Luce, had begun a correspondence and friendship with the Jesuit Murray in the mid-1950s. The very title of the editorial, "The American Moral Consensus," had a decidedly Murray-like quality, since Murray's work attributed just such a moral consensus to the success of the American arrangement in separating church and state. The recognition of Gibbons and Murray in an editorial celebrating limited government and moral agreement offered dramatic evidence that *Life* had found Catholics useful for its rendition of the postwar nation.[73]

The Postwar Catholic Mystique

After World War II, *Life* turned Catholics into symbols of American consensus, encouraging readers to see Catholicism in recognizable and reassuring terms of family, middle-class success, and corporate leadership. Yet not all stories in the magazine stressed the similarity between Catholics and the rest of America. Indeed, a number of essays actually emphasized Catholic difference, particularly those describing the religious orders. But these portraits were still quite different from the condescending stories of the 1930s. Rather than signifying Catholic exoticism as deviancy, the magazine made it appear romantic and compelling. In fact, these representations produced a Catholic mystique that reassured Americans a consensus culture did not have to result in spiritual blandness.

In a November 19, 1947, editorial entitled "The Methodists," the magazine carefully hinted that the mainline American churches might not have all the religious answers. In the accompanying lengthy photo-essay on the Methodists in the United States, *Life* celebrated the "main characteristic of the American Methodist," which, "despite his occasional prejudices, is his friendliness, optimism and practicality." Yet it acknowledged that the "vulnerable point of American Methodism is the vulnerable point of American civilization; its truth is perhaps too closely related to outward signs of health. It sustains men well in fellowship, but is less sustaining to the lonely hero, mystic, martyr or artist."[74] During the postwar years, one place *Life* suggested these alternative spiritual values could be found was Catholicism. Particularly in an American context, the magazine implied, Catholicism's otherworldliness and alternative religious practices functioned as a healthy spiritual complement to mainstream Protestantism's buoyant embrace of social improvement.

Life was not alone in finding new things to like about Catholicism. A wave of high-profile converts—not the least of course being Luce's own wife, Clare Booth Luce, but also Graham Greene and Thomas Merton, among others—gave new élan to Roman Catholicism in the postwar years. The magazine even made use of Merton's best-selling account of how he became a Trappist monk in its own effort to spiritually mobilize the nation for the American Century.

A 1949 editorial entitled "God's Underground" commented on the emergence of a Christian underground in Soviet Russia. This led *Life* to ask, "How goes it with God's underground in the Christian West?" and then deplore the spread of godlessness in Western civilization. Yet the magazine saw new stirrings of a Christian underground even in secular America. As evidence of this new interest in religion, it pointed to the success of Merton's *The Seven Story Mountain,* asserting that "the faith it voices, though it is dogmatically and uncompromisingly Roman Catholic, is also so profoundly Christian that Baptists and Presbyterians can say amen to it." The editorial claimed that it "is hard to see why this quiet, almost devotional book should have aroused so much interest among American readers in this secular age—unless they were somehow predisposed to listen. Perhaps, both within the churches and outside them—who knows?—a deeper commitment to religion is growing."

Life suggested that Merton's account of Catholic monastic discipline and austerity represented a new religious seriousness that might counter the spiritual emptiness of creeping secularism in American life.[75]

A photo-essay, "Trappist Monastery," later that same year extended *Life*'s new interest in Catholic monasticism. As it attended to traditional Catholic practices, it also visually remade them. Clearly attempting to tap into the popularity of Merton's best seller, the story about a new Trappist monastery in Utah turned the monks into robust, dedicated men of spiritual conviction. The essay stressed in text and visual imagery the asceticism and discipline of Catholic monastic life. "Monastery days are spent in meditation and silence," asserted the article. The monks "all have renounced their worldly connections. They gather several times a day in their chapel for mass and prayer and the rest of their time is rigidly scheduled into periods of study, sleep and meals." The essay was accompanied by a dramatic photo of three white-hooded monks, walking in silence down a corridor. Another photo depicted four monks intently studying at their desks in the library. Still another showed the monks in their chapel, with a caption stating, "Day begins at 2 A.M. when monks gather for service in the chapel," underscoring the rigors of monastic life.[76]

The story on Catholic monks suggested different, even conflicting meanings. For some, it might have called to readers' minds older Gothic associations of entrapment and darkness. The story made clear, however, that these men had freely chosen their difficult paths: "Their escape from the outside world is not irrevocable. Even within the monastery walls a young man may decide that the unworldly life is not for him." Further, through visual and textual cues, the essay turned the monks into a compelling image of religious commitment and masculine vigor. Highlighting the Western frontier character of the Trappist venture provided one means of reframing Catholic difference. A photograph on the title page showed the monastery nestled amid the mountains of Utah. In addition, the story described the monks in terms redolent of nineteenth-century pioneers as it recounted how the monastery "was started less than two years ago when 34 Trappist monks journeyed from their Kentucky monastery in a Pullman car, the shades drawn and the porter locked out during their frequent hours of prayer en route."

Equally important, *Life* associated the monks with the recently completed war. It pointed out that "since the last war . . . the Trappists have gained young veterans who turned to them for the peace and quiet they thought they would find at a monastery. There are now 12 veterans of

World War II at the Utah monastery." The caption of the opening photograph pointed viewers to the Quonset style of the new monastery, encouraging further visual linkage between the monks and the military. These Trappists thus were normal, American men—there were certainly no aging clerics telling their beads, no young people held against their will in this Catholic institution.

Through dramatic imagery and words, *Life*'s photo-essay implied that the Trappist monks offered the romantic, intense experience the open frontier and the war once had provided American men. At a time when suburban domesticity and the organization man increasingly defined middle-class America, Catholic monasticism held out an alluring alternative. But the use of familiar national symbols of the Western landscape and the military also sutured the Trappists to a decidedly American context. *Life* turned Catholic difference into a religious mystique that complemented rather than questioned cultural assumptions about the good life in America.

If the Trappists represented for *Life* a new spiritual presence on the American frontier, the Jesuits embodied the romance of religious commitment in the modern world. In 1954, the magazine devoted an extensive essay to the American Jesuits, highlighting their wide-ranging endeavors both in the United States and overseas. Few essays were more celebratory of Catholicism than this piece published during the height of the postwar consensus. Margaret Bourke-White's compelling photographs turned the Counter-Reformation's most famous order of priests into emblems of American religious vigor and adventure.[77]

The first page of the story asserted that the Society of Jesus was "the largest and fastest growing order in the Church and finds its greatest area of growth—in new recruits, new facilities and variety of activities—in the U.S."[78] Above the title of the essay was a small photo of the death mask of Ignatius Loyola, the founder of the order. A large photo on the opposite page contrasts strikingly with the small death mask. Bourke-White captured a young Jesuit seminarian with arms crossed, shoulders squared, staring intensely into the distance through a low-angle shot, accentuating his stature. The full-page photo of this young man dominated the opening two pages of the story, conveying an impression of the Jesuits as youthful, vibrant, and confident. Taken together, these two opening pages visually narrated the article's larger message, for as a reader's eyes moved from the first page to the second, the death mask of Old World Loyola was replaced by a matinee idol–like image of a young America

Jesuit seminarian, implicitly suggesting a robust Catholicism in America displacing an Old World past.

Photos of American Jesuits in subsequent pages demonstrated their involvement with modern society. "Flying Jesuit, Father John Higgins" was shown in the cockpit of a plane at St. Louis University, where he taught aeronautics. "Astronomer, Father Francis J. Heyden of Georgetown" stood next to a large telescope, indicating his area of expertise. Father Daniel Linehan, a seismologist, was captured in layman's khakis leading a line of men up a forest hill doing work for a dam project in Maine. Father Daniel Lord, a writer of songs and stage plays, sat at a piano, surrounded by a group of women, looking like an older Father O'Malley from *Going My Way*.[79] Although the magazine acknowledged the more traditional pursuits of teaching, ministering, and counseling in the religious order, its selection of images wrapped the American Jesuits in contemporary America signified by technology, science, and popular culture.

The story concluded with a full-page photo of a white-robed Jesuit standing in the bow of a sailboat manned by two men, with the sails fully capturing the wind. The dramatic curves of the sails, the taut ropes held by one of the boatmen, and the solitary and erect Jesuit in the front of the skiff offered a powerful image of adventure and romance. A caption identified the priest as a missionary developing cooperatives among fishermen and farmers in British Honduras.

The essay thus ended as it opened, with an intensely romantic image of a youthful American Jesuit, communicating a very different message about priests than traditional notions suggested. These photos complemented the numerous portraits of scientists, educators, and thinkers to portray the American Jesuits as a band of brothers, immersed in the modern world yet committed to higher religious goals. The magazine's representation of the Jesuit priests allowed it to envision America as a society whose religious diversity could generate such complex and fascinating moral commitments as the men who were both scientists and missionaries. The great melting pot of the United States that *Life* so often celebrated, the story implied, need not result in religious impoverishment. Indeed, the Jesuits of this essay echoed to an uncanny degree the vision Henry Luce articulated years before in his famous essay. They were adventurous, worldly, dedicated, sophisticated, scientifically skilled, and morally committed, just as Luce described the United States. In the pages of *Life,* in fact, the Jesuits became the spiritual signs of the American Century both at home and abroad.

Margaret Bourke-White's dramatic image of a Jesuit missionary in the bow of a boat for a big 1953 photo-essay on the Jesuits in America vividly captured Life's *postwar romance with Catholicism (Margaret Bourke-White/Time & Life Pictures/Getty Images)*

Unlike earlier, disparaging images of Catholic difference, photo-essays such as "The American Jesuits" framed Catholics in terms relevant for Americans after World War II.[80] Monks who were veterans seeking transcendent meaning in their lives and Jesuits immersed in scientific progress at home and humanitarian aid in the Third World spoke to deeply felt issues about identity and purpose in an era of middle-class prosperity. But even more, these stories demonstrated that the postwar consensus did not so much erase Catholic particularity as resignify it as an expression of the American Century. Catholic difference in the postwar years became a means of suggesting adventure, youthful vigor, and spiritual renewal. Romanticism replaced alien ethnicity and Old World Catholic power. The combination of familiar American associations and Catholic distinctiveness suggested that religious mystery could exist *within* modern society rather than oppose it. In expressing a new Catholic style appropriate for an age of consensus, the Trappist monks and the Jesuits in *Life*'s pages, with their Catholic mystique, shared a similar project to *Going My Way*'s earlier depiction of the cool, youthful Catholic priest. Both registered a Catholicism that sanctioned rather than challenged the postwar American social order.

Life's treatment of American Catholic clerics contrasted sharply with a major photo-essay, "Priest to the Campesinos," that appeared in 1952 and focused on a Mexican priest, Father Enrique Salazar, who worked among the poor of central Mexico. The difference in the portrayal of Catholic priests in America and Mexico offered stark evidence of how assumptions about American national identity informed representations of Catholicism in America and elsewhere around the world. This story of a lone Mexican priest provided a voyeuristic look into the poverty and destitution south of the border. Although the priest was portrayed sympathetically as attempting to minister to the spiritual and medical needs of the poor he encountered, a tone of hopelessness pervaded this representation of Third World Catholicism. Death, illness, and the isolation of a single priest suggested the enormity of the challenge facing the church in Mexico. A final two-page photograph of the priest heading off into the "hot, steaming rain" on a borrowed mule visually dramatized the bleak state of Mexico and its Catholicism.[81]

If stories about non-American Catholicism such as that highlighted by "Priest to the Campesinos" helped draw distinctions between Catholics in America and those in other places of the world for *Life*'s readers, stories involving American Catholic nuns underscored the highly gendered logic of the magazine's postwar portrayal of Catholics in the United States. Jesuits and monks were often treated in dramatic, romantic fashion as stalwarts of moral seriousness and religious commitment, but American nuns bore the brunt of stereotyping. Their unique outfits were favorite targets of the magazine's treatment. A major photo-essay on Catholic high schools in 1954 opened with a large head-and-shoulder shot of Sister Margaret of Providence. Her homely features encircled by an enormous habit made her appear ridiculous. Other photos in the story that depicted a modern school building and Catholic high schoolers in ordinary teenage apparel only served to heighten the strangeness of Sister Margaret and the other nuns. Similarly, *Life* made the religious women in "Nuns in a Musical Frolic" appear infantile by opening with a large photograph of a chorus of nuns singing and dancing. Even a largely complimentary story on Sister Madeleva, the accomplished leader of St. Mary's College in South Bend, Indiana, utilized the nun's dress to undermine her credibility. A head-and-shoulders shot of the nun in a story entitled "Nun, President and Poet" showed her face enveloped in a huge habit, disproportionately large relative to her head, making the woman look absurd.[82]

Life's representation of Catholics thus was more than a reflection of their movement into the postwar mainstream. Deeply informed by particular ideas about the nation, the world, and gender, the magazine taught its readers to view Catholics through the lens of its own ideological vision, which privileged American exceptionalism and masculine vigor. The popular weekly consequently played a crucial role not only in depicting Catholics for mass audiences but also in shaping how that Catholicism could be viewed and understood. Far from denying the importance of Catholics to America, *Life* actively harnessed Catholic difference to a wider project of postwar national consensus.

Life's approval of Catholicism culminated in the special issue on American Christianity from December 1955. In addition to the editorial proclaiming an American moral consensus that quoted the Jesuit John Courtney Murray and the photo-essay on the Archdiocese of Chicago, there was a story with photographs by the noted Gordon Parks on a Benedictine monastery in Kansas, another complimentary essay on Pius XII by Emmet John Hughes, and even an article by Murray himself on the need for Catholics to move beyond their isolation in American society.[83] Indeed, Catholicism enjoyed so much coverage in the issue that a letter to the editor complained, "When *Life* discusses religion why are the Catholics always given preference over any other church?"[84] Furthermore, as well as being extensive, the portrayal of Catholics in the magazine was deeply respectful. Catholics were no longer subjects against which to construct authentic America; rather, the magazine now construed the nation through its largest religious minority.

By the mid-1950s, therefore, *Life* encouraged its readers to view Catholics in the United States as part of a broader American cultural and moral landscape. To be sure, Catholics often continued to look different, with their Roman collars, habits, and robes and their elaborate church architecture—indeed, their appeal for a magazine predicated on the visual image lay precisely in their rich visual and material culture. Yet *Life* provided numerous ways to interpret this Catholic difference as part of its own vision of the American Century. Highly favorable stories of Pius XII turned him into an ally of the American crusade against Soviet totalitarianism. Essays on American Catholics privileged narratives of social harmony and assimilation into middle-class prosperity. Stories of Catholic religious orders turned older conventions of Gothic darkness on their heads and made Jesuits and monks emblems of religious dedication within the nurturing environment of American freedom.

Anticommunism, consensus, and religious mystique thus provided the basic coordinates in *Life*'s reclamation of Catholics during the postwar years. Such a development within the nation's most influential photojournalism revealed the intensely political character of Catholic representation in the mass media. In Americanizing Catholicism, the magazine harnessed Catholics to its own very particular vision of national greatness and international leadership, intended to erase the popular imaginary of alternative cultural memories and identifications. *Life* had learned to like Catholics and encouraged its readers to do so as well. But what it really wanted was for everyone to love the American Century.

Normal Americans

By the end of the 1950s, *Life*'s treatment of Catholicism had assumed a predictable formula, increasingly making Catholics seem just like other Americans. A lengthy cover story about the Knights of Columbus, for instance, made this Catholic laymen's organization and its elaborate rituals and costumes appear like a college fraternity or one of the many cotillion parties the magazine chronicled throughout the decades. Explicit Catholic imagery actually was minimal in the ten-page story. Men in fancy plumed hats and young women in white robes outnumbered images of the Virgin Mary and the pope. A casual reader may have overlooked the Catholic identity of the Knights by just looking at the photographs.[85]

Even John F. Kennedy's bid for the presidency, which created intense controversy in 1960, generated little anxiety among the editors at *Life*. An essay in 1959 by the Episcopal bishop James Pike raised the traditional fears about Catholic politicians and controversial issues such as birth control and religious freedom. Yet the magazine's editorial "Catholics and U.S. Democracy," in the same issue as Pike's essay, sounded remarkably like it could have been ghostwritten by the Jesuit John Courtney Murray by rooting American Catholics in a distinctly U.S. tradition of "religion freedom in a religious society."[86]

One story from 1959 in particular revealed *Life*'s approach to Catholicism by the late fifties. That photo-essay, "The Altar Boy—Momentary Angel," chronicled the training and preparation of altar boys in a New York parish. Using children as a focus to depict Catholic ritual reflected the magazine's intense emphasis on family in the postwar years. A series of photos by Esther Bubley captured the boys rehearsing their roles, laughing with each other during breaks, dressed in their altar clothes and receiving last-minute instructions before the beginning of Mass. The focus was on the antics of boyhood, and a priest was prominent in only one photo that captured the beginning of the services. Rendering a story on Catholic worship in terms of young boys preparing to become altar servers all but eliminated any hint of Catholic foreignness. The use of children helped to sentimentalize religion and made what might have been seen as a strange ritual of Catholic faith appear identifiable and approachable. A final photo showed one of the new altar boys, after serving at his first Mass, leaping to the arms of his smiling, well-appointed mother. Catholic practice had become enfolded into family bliss.[87] Few stories could more powerfully suggest the domestication of Catholicism into *Life*'s harmonious, middle-class America.

CHAPTER FIVE

PERFORMING CATHOLICISM
IN AN AGE OF CONSENSUS:
FULTON J. SHEEN, TELEVISION,
AND POSTWAR AMERICA

In 1953, during the second season of his popular prime-time television show *Life Is Worth Living*, Fulton J. Sheen, the auxiliary bishop of New York, spoke of the need for all Americans to find new ways to dialogue with one another, in an episode entitled "Liberal or Reactionary?"[1] Reflecting the postwar era's dislike of ideological extremes, Sheen critiqued the sway of both modern liberalism and conservatism in society. He told his viewers that he knew someone who could "restore sanity to the world." In quite suspenseful fashion, he then unfolded the story of this remarkable person. He explained that when this brilliant man was in school, his elders had attempted to dissuade him from his studies by introducing a woman into his room. The virtuous scholar, Sheen recounted, reacted by taking a burning poker and chasing the temptress out, then etching upon the door to his room "a blazing cross." Sheen mimicked this action by tracing a cross in the air for his audience. He then identified this man to whom the modern world should look as none other than the thirteenth-century saint Thomas Aquinas. Sheen walked over to a desk that was a staple of the show's faux study, where the bound works of the medieval Catholic thinker were arranged in numerous high stacks. To underscore the extent of Aquinas's remarkable achievement, Sheen paused and patted each stack of books, which he described as among "the greatest masterpieces of the human mind."

Why would a Catholic bishop clothed in the regalia of the Roman hierarchy appear on prime-time television preaching the virtues of a thirteenth-century theologian? And why would *Life Is Worth Living* turn into one of the biggest television successes of the fifties, running for five seasons on the Dumont and ABC networks from 1952 to 1957? Sheen's show has often been interpreted as a sign of the Americanization of Catholics after World War II. Scholars debate the merits of that achievement, with some emphasizing the Catholic character of his popular success and others highlighting the ironic consequence of Sheen's appeal to mainstream Americans.[2] Yet the coming of age of Catholics in the United States was not the only or even the most prominent dimension of Sheen's television show. Indeed, the cultural significance of *Life Is Worth Living* extended beyond what it revealed about the character of Catholicism in the fifties to illuminate the role of Catholics in the formation of the postwar American consensus.

Sheen's show represented a dramatic break from the reformist, socially conscious Americanism that popular representations of and by Catholics helped imagine during the Depression. The bishop disassociated religious identification from alternative cultural or critical meanings and turned it into a source of collective well-being during the fifties. His presentation of Catholicism encouraged Americans to look to the private realm for identity and happiness, detaching religion from older public commitments. By offering religion as the solution to the problems that plagued Americans—from worries over war to child raising—he preached the social virtues of private life.

Life Is Worth Living therefore did not deny its Catholic character in the promotion of a shared Americanism. Rather, it resignified it, turning the minority faith of Catholicism into a means of making sense of the new social order of the postwar nation. Sheen's translation of Catholicism into an accessible, appealing moral guide intended for all Americans helped smooth over and naturalize what in reality were dramatic changes in national life and identity that reshaped the United States after World War II. Organizing society around anticommunism, consumerism, and the privatization of public life that characterized America in the postwar years demanded an enormous amount of cultural work. Citizens had to be won over to the vision of a harmonious consumer nation rather than passively led to it. As George Lipsitz has shown, early television played a crucial role in this project by drawing upon older cultural identities of ethnic, working-class Americans in order to legitimate the demands of consumer capitalism. Shows such as *The Honeymooners* and *The Goldbergs* taught Americans to embrace private, consumerist identities precisely by first acknowledging the role of ethnic traditions in the lives of their viewers.[3]

Life Is Worth Living represented a very similar project. It was no coincidence that Sheen, like many stars of early television, was already a major figure in popular culture before appearing on TV. He first rose to prominence through his work on the radio show the *Catholic Hour* of the thirties and forties. This was an essential, though often overlooked, dimension of Sheen's significance in America. His work for decades as a promoter of Catholic beliefs and values gave him a cultural authority that *Life Is Worth Living* drew upon in order to harness Catholicism to the ends of the new Cold War Americanism of the fifties.

So turning Aquinas, the symbol of Catholic romance with the medieval past, into prime-time television fodder was not as strange as it may seem. It manifested how the postwar consensus derived its legitimacy by reworking older cultural traditions and memories of ethnic, religious minorities such as Catholics. *Life Is Worth Living* demonstrated that efforts to create a privatized, politically quiescent, consumerist nation were so great that even the country's old Roman nemesis was called upon to offer cultural benediction and spiritual absolution.

From Heartland America to New York Success

Born in El Paso, Texas, in 1895, Sheen grew up in the small cities and rural communities of the Midwest during the early twentieth century.[4] He and his parents, who were children of Irish immigrants, moved to Peoria, Illinois, when he was five. There, Sheen received a Catholic primary and secondary education. He attended St. Viator College in Bourbannais, Illinois, a school run by a teaching order of priests who had fled the French suppression of religious schools in the early twentieth century. After earning a degree, he entered the seminary at St. Paul, Minnesota, in 1917.

Sheen had the misfortune of gaining his clerical training just as the rigorous, antimodernist backlash in Catholic theological circles assumed hurricane force. Pope Pius X had recently reiterated his demand that the philosophy of Aquinas function as the sole model of Catholic intellectual life. In 1917, the year that Sheen entered the seminary, the church's Code of Canon Law had been revised to require that professors of the "sacred sciences" were to "adhere religiously" to "the method, doctrine and the principles of the Angelic Doctor." Consequently, the philosophy and theology of Thomas Aquinas became the reigning standard of Catholic study.[5]

Ordained a priest in 1920, Sheen pursued an advanced degree at the prestigious University of Louvain in Belgium. He published a scholarly work in neo-Thomist philosophy, based on his dissertation, five years later—*God and Intelligence in Modern Philosophy.*[6] In 1925, after Sheen had completed his second dissertation at Louvain, his bishop called him home to Peoria. The following year, he was appointed a chair of apologetics in the School of Sacred Sciences at Catholic University of America.[7] There, he would hold a teaching position for the next three decades. Although life there was perhaps more interesting than in Peoria, a professorship in Washington, D.C., must have seemed like a poor prospect after his years of study in Europe.

The opportunity to appear on the new national radio program the *Catholic Hour,* broadcast from New York City, in 1930 must have been greeted by Sheen as a fortuitous second beginning after his return to the United States. He had already expanded his horizons beyond his teaching responsibilities at CUA by the time he presented his first radio series. In the late 1920s, he delivered the Lenten homilies at the Paulist Church in New York City, which were broadcast on radio. He had also begun traveling around the country giving talks and leading retreats, practices that would consume him throughout his career.[8] Sheen had become ensconced in a privileged position with the world of American Catholics, a far cry from his days busting sod in Illinois. But the opportunity to explain and promote Catholicism through national radio was a major turning point in Sheen's career that would have lasting influence.

The *Catholic Hour* and the Imagined Community of American Catholicism

The *Catholic Hour* itself represented the confluence of a number of cultural and social developments in the late twenties and early thirties. The new medium of radio proved particularly hospitable to religious programming. But the *Catholic Hour,* unlike much religious radio that had a local character, enjoyed the support of the new NBC national radio network, which had itself only been formed a few years earlier. The network offered the Catholic Church its own radio show as part of its project of providing airtime to representatives of the three major religious traditions—Protestantism, Judaism, and Catholicism. The National Council of Catholic Men, an organization under the auspices of the Catholic hierarchy in America, agreed to sponsor a program for the NBC network. The bishops particularly liked the opportunity of having a national forum to explain Catholicism to Americans in light of the pervasive anti-Catholic sentiments that had erupted during the presidential election of 1928.[9]

Sheen was among the first guests on the NBC radio show. He quickly became its most popular speaker, returning yearly for a lengthy series of talks that usually ran from Christmas to Easter Sunday. As early as 1931, a year after Sheen's first appearance on the *Catholic Hour,* he was already being dubbed a celebrity.[10] His early success indicates that he realized the power of the emerging mass media to shape popular discourse in America.

Beyond providing a vehicle for Sheen's own fame, his participation on the *Catholic Hour* represented an important project of cultural formation, crafting an imagined community of American Catholicism in the thirties and forties out of religious devotionalism and moral theology.[11] Radio gave a range of cultural actors means of reaching mass audiences in the thirties. Entertainers, musicians, politicians, and above all advertisers could speak beyond local communities to a whole nation wired together through the electronic airwaves. The new medium helped foster in very immediate ways a sense of collective American identity as listeners tuned in to the same programs at the same time each week. But as Michele Hilmes and others have shown, it also allowed competing understandings of what that shared national belonging meant. Fundamentalist Protestant ministers and Popular Front writers as well as commercial sponsors all sought to use radio to broadcast their different visions of American society.[12]

Sheen proved highly effective in adapting the medium to the needs of a changing Catholic population in the United States. As Robert Orsi has argued, the postimmigrant generation of Catholics between the wars faced new challenges as they sought a cultural identity beyond the older ethnic enclaves of their parents.[13] Devotion to new saints such as St. Jude aided in this process. But Sheen's rise to popularity on the *Catholic Hour* indicates the new medium of radio also helped Catholics imagine themselves as part of a transethnic Catholic community in America.

Sheen's contribution to this cultural formation was based in the antimodern Catholic romance he dramatized of spiritual rejuvenation and moral adventure. Through florid and evocative language, his talks encouraged his audiences to understand themselves as a people of redemptive suffering, cultural humility, and sacred desires. Early in one radio series, Sheen said, "In religious matters the modern world believes in indifference. Very simply this means it has no great loves and no great hates; no cause worth living for and no causes worth dying for."[14] On another occasion, he observed, drawing upon the Catholic love of the medieval, "This world of ours is full of half-completed Gothic Cathedrals, of half-finished lives and half-crucified souls."[15]

Sheen placed the blame for this spiritual declension on the pernicious modern philosophies of empiricism, Freud, and Marx.[16] He told his audiences that a "bad psychology told man he had no soul, then no mind and finally no consciousness but that he was only a complex machine made up of actions and reactions . . . he became only an atom dissolved in the mass of a two-dimensional universe of space and time."[17] Similarly, he said that communism, "the last of the enemies," offered an equally important symbol of modernity's dangers. It was, Sheen described, the "late season fruit of the tree of spiritual bankruptcy."[18]

Against the failed project of modernity, Sheen repeatedly turned to traditional Catholic symbols and practices, including the cross and Calvary, the Eucharist, the Virgin Mary, and the Sacred Heart of Jesus, to imagine an alternative national community. In 1936, Sheen had introduced his seven-week discussion of Christ's last words on the cross with a dramatic invitation to his audience: "Picture then the High Priest Christ leaving the sacristy of heaven for the altar of Calvary. He has already put on the vestment of our human nature, the maniple of our suffering, the sole of priesthood and the chasuble of the Cross . . . Christ is going to His altar. We shall assist at His First Mass."[19] In his 1941–1942 radio talks entitled "Peace," he repeatedly requested that his Catholic listeners devote one hour each day to the adoration of the Eucharist. He asked his audience members to make this devotion their spiritual contribution to the tough fight the nation faced overseas.[20] By tailoring his radio addresses to the tangible symbols and practices of Catholic life, Sheen connected his radio discussions to the lived religion of his Catholic listeners.

Scholars of radio have noted how the medium functioned to confuse boundaries between public and private, and Sheen's *Catholic Hour* broadcasts clearly evidenced this essential characteristic of radio.[21] They gathered together devotionalism and social understanding, personal spirituality and political ideology. Sheen linked individual Catholic radio listeners into a national Catholic community, forging their inner lives of faith into an alternative spiritual resource to modernity's secularism. His deeply antimodern narrative gave cultural shape to the emotionally elusive yet powerful nature of Catholic devotionalism for a generation of individuals searching to make sense of their dual identities as Catholics and Americans.

Sheen's radio shows, therefore, proved to be far more than pious entertainment that filled the airwaves at midcentury. They translated familiar Catholic practices and images into a new discursive space of spiritual and cultural rejuvenation. By means of the new medium of radio, Sheen infused national significance into traditional Catholic devotions and beliefs, repeatedly reminding his listeners they possessed the resources of both personal and social transformation for a modern America that was descending into moral chaos. The cross became a repudiation of shallow individualism in favor of self-abnegation, humility, and spiritual abandonment. The Sacred Heart of Jesus signified the great sacrificial love his listeners could embrace as they struggled through a materialistic world hostile to compassion, mercy, and charity. The Virgin Mary embodied the selfless sanctity of motherhood and family besieged by modern culture's absorption with sexual freedom.

It is telling that the title of Sheen's first radio series in 1930, which initially earned him national popularity, was *The Divine Romance,* for he equated Catholicism with high ideals, great heroic quests, and invisible but very real spiritual powers. This was a world where grand emotional hopes and longings were recognized as signs of sacred presence. Speaking of the human heart, Sheen wrote, "Something God-like is mirrored there—for whatever is best in the treasured lives of heroic men and the serene unwritten lives of innocent women . . . is but the dim reflection, the far-off echo, the faint shadow of that which in God is perfect."[22] Week after week, year after year, Sheen's radio lectures identified Catholicism with the adventure, romance, and mystery that modernity had drained from the world.

The cross and Calvary proved particularly resonant symbols that Sheen used to trace his alternative spiritual landscape. They embodied the drama of faith with its difficult commitments, personal demands, and acceptance of struggle. "Take the danger and doubt away from life and where would be the heroism and faith? Let there be no sorrow by night, no malady by day, and where would be kindness and sacrifice?" Sheen told his audience, "A world without contingency could have no hero or no saint."[23] Along the same lines, during his 1936 series he bluntly stated:

> We have been sent into this world for only one purpose, namely, to assist at the Holy Sacrifice of the Mass. We are to take our stand at the foot of the Cross, and like those who stood under it the first day we are asked to declare our loyalties. . . . There must be harvest in our hands after the springtime of the earthly pilgrimage. That is why Calvary is erected in the midst of us, and we are on its sacred hill. We were not made to be mere on-lookers . . . but rather to be participants in the great Drama of Redemption.[24]

By privileging Christ on the cross, Sheen's radio discourse oriented his listeners to suffering and self-abnegation as redemptive spiritual values in a world deformed by materialism. Christ, he told his audiences, manifested how divinity existed "in simplicity, in the unexpected, in defeat and in frailty."[25] Indeed, Sheen spoke of the "joy of defeat" and the "hymn of the conquered" to describe Christ's actions on Calvary that all Christians were commanded to follow.[26] The cross was not just a religious symbol but also a pattern upon which he asked his listeners to model their lives, an alternative form into which they were to pour themselves against the distorted formulas of psychoanalysis and Marxism.

Sheen encouraged his audiences to imagine their lives as expressions of contemporary saintly holiness, now lived out in their own kitchens, homes, families, and everyday experiences. "We can all become saints to a certain degree," he told his listeners, and his talks encouraged them to commit themselves to making that a reality in their own lives.[27] By focusing on the redemptive suffering of the cross, Sheen counseled his listeners to realize that their devotions, their prayers and offerings, their sacrifices and self-denials were part of a glorious spiritual adventure that the modern world was incapable of providing. He turned the inner lives of his listeners into emotional spaces of quiet triumph over modernity's shallow illusions.

Sheen's broadcasts also offered an ideal of humility through which to view and judge the modern world. God could be found in the things and people modernity overlooked or dismissed. Commenting on Christ's option while on earth for the people on the margins, he told his audience, "Had you and I walked down the street with Him, we would have noticed that it was principally only what our modern sociologists call the dependents, the defectives, and the delinquents that interested Him."[28] Sheen taught his audiences how to embrace their sufferings and see them as signs of grace. He encouraged a rejection of worldly success as dangerous to the religious and moral life of his listeners. His list of heroes shared a marginal social status. They became spiritually glamorous in his eyes precisely because their lives of sacrifice and selflessness were so ordinary and mundane.

Sheen linked the emotionally rich and complex world of his Catholic listeners' devotional lives to a narrative of cultural critique and revitalization, in the process forging a distinctly Catholic public sphere through radio that transcended local and ethnic attachments. Yet to enter into the spiritual landscape Sheen offered was to become immersed in an emotionally charged, volatile world, one characterized by deep and often confusing feelings. The cross symbolized the path to spiritual happiness but also an intense infatuation with self-erasure. Sheen spoke of "the violence of our Blessed Lord," and also "the pure Mother Immaculate, the starry treachery of whose eyes 'tempt us back to Paradise.'"[29]

Sheen's rendering of Calvary and Christ's suffering often, in fact, assumed a voluptuous, almost erotic quality. His talks dwelled upon excessive and even lurid descriptions of bodily pain and anguish. Yet such imagery was crucial to Sheen's theology of the cross, whereby redemptive suffering assumed spiritual and cultural primacy. He would speak of Christ's despair at Gethsemane that resulted in "crimsoning olive roots with drops of blood, each like a bead forming the great Rosary of Redemption."[30] Likewise, he noted that "the blood drops that fell from the Cross on Good Friday in that Mass of Christ, did not touch the spirits of the fallen angels."[31]

Sheen's dramatic constructions of Christ's passion created an emotional space in which his audiences were to vividly imagine his anguish and, beyond that, to identify themselves as the true agents of that pain. This moral complicity in the suffering of the truly innocent God was painted in rich, evocative language. Sheen asked his listeners to consider "if we did know that every sin of pride wove a crown of thorns for the Head of Christ . . . if we knew that every grasping avaricious act nailed His hands, every journey into the byways of sin dug His feet."[32]

Sheen's infatuation with suffering was intended to spiritually connect his audiences' own struggles with the anguish of Christ on the cross. "There is nothing more tragic in all the world than wasted pain," he commented. Consequently, he asked his listeners to consecrate their sufferings to God, and using vivid Eucharistic language, he told them to say, "Transmute the poor bread of my life into Thy Divine Life, thrill the wine of my wasted life into Thy Divine Spirit; unite my broken heart with Thy Heart."[33]

Yet his mysticism of suffering encouraged a disturbing acquiescence to actual human pain. His talks were replete with advice to embrace one's struggles as part of a virtuous life, as if suffering represented the price of God's love. He counseled his audience to recognize that the moral life entailed realizing that in "the short time of our bodily life every tree may be a cross, every bush a crown of thorns, and every friend may be a Judas."[34] Similarly, he encouraged Catholics to see their sufferings as essential to their spiritual life: "If our heart beat in unison with His then it too shall show the riven side which the wicked lance of jealous earth had pierced. Blessed indeed are they who carry in their Cross-marked hands the bread and wine of consecrated lives signed with the sign and sealed with the seal of Redemptive Love. But woe unto them who come from Calvary with hands unscarred and white."[35]

The tense, emotionally ambiguous constructions of Sheen's religious devotionalism extended to his description of the Virgin Mary's body. It was both sexualized and brutalized. Indeed, as Robert Orsi has argued, the devotionalism of Catholic clerical leaders expressed a subconscious anger against the female body precisely because they eroticized it.[36] For instance, Sheen spoke of Mary's body as "a Paradise so beautiful and sublime that the Heavenly Father would not have to blush in sending His Son into it" and as a "flesh-girt Paradise in which there was to be celebrated the nuptials, not of man and woman but of humanity and divinity." Yet he also proclaimed that "the womb of the Blessed Mother was the anvil of flesh upon which the Divine and human nature of Christ were united."[37]

Sheen's *Catholic Hour* talks therefore deployed Catholic devotionalism and moral teaching to unite Catholics into a new discursive community in the 1930s and 1940s. The spiritual narrative he elaborated sought to discipline his audiences against the temptations of modern culture. It valorized a war against the self in opposition to modern people's supposed selfishness. Love became spiritualized to distinguish it from modernity's identification with sex. A "thrill of monotony" was encouraged because progressive thinking, in Sheen's formulation, sought only the new and novel.[38] By asking his audience to deny themselves and accept monotony in their lives, however, he betrayed a deep resentment toward his listeners, as if routine and sacrifice were all they deserved in this world. His talks often suggested a sustained effort to deny, denigrate, or even punish his audiences' interests in the contemporary world. Within Sheen's vision, the cross of Christ functioned not only as a sign of sacred contradiction but also as a boundary marker etched in antimodern suspicion and distrust.

Popular Success

By the 1940s, Sheen had become a major Catholic figure in the religious landscape of the United States. The secular press, especially Henry Luce's *Time* magazine, had already taken to following his exploits, particularly his success at winning converts to Catholicism and the popular following he gathered through the *Catholic Hour* broadcasts. *Time* described him in 1940 as "one of the most brilliant U.S. pulpit and radio orators, and one of the most astute Catholic minds."[39] That same year in another article devoted to Sheen, the magazine called him "a persuasive, lucid speaker, with a well-cultivated voice, who can make religion sensible and attractive to great masses of people." It also favorably contrasted Sheen to Father Charles Coughlin, the infamous radio priest and anti-Semite from the thirties. Unlike the parochial Coughlin, Sheen was "one of the Church's ablest converters."[40] Five years later, *Time* described him as "probably America's best-known priest with an audience of millions for his Sunday preaching on NBC's Catholic Hour and a fan mail of 3,000 to 6,000 letters a Sunday."[41] Likewise, *Newsweek* noted that Sheen's "eloquence, wit, and persistence have made him an ace interceder for the Catholic faith."[42] That description referred to Sheen's success in winning a number of notable converts to the church, including the liberal newspaperman Heywood Broun, Henry Ford II, and Louis Budenz, editor of the communist *Daily Worker*. Perhaps the most prominent convert proved to be the bad girl of Manhattan social life in the thirties and the wife of media magnate Henry Luce, Clare Booth Luce, with whom Sheen enjoyed a lasting friendship.[43]

As the accounts in the secular press indicated, Sheen's radio broadcasts helped win him national attention. Yet his work extended beyond radio to include numerous lectures and personal appearances. His sermons at St. Patrick's and talks to various groups brought him widespread recognition. He was a frequent speaker at Catholic associations and conventions.[44] Indeed, by 1940, *Time* reported, Sheen had 150 speaking dates a year.[45] Many of these appearances served to organize Catholics for public action and protest. In the late thirties, he became active in the Catholic opposition to the Loyalist cause in the Spanish civil war. In 1938, he spoke before a rally at New York's Carnegie Hall on the dangers of socialist violence. In January 1939, Sheen addressed a large gathering in Washington's Constitution Hall to encourage the maintenance of the arms embargo on Spain.[46] As his involvement in the Catholic effort to oppose the Spanish republic indicates, Sheen's public addresses sought to mobilize Catholics in the United States into a forceful, united bloc against modern progressives and liberals.

One of his most significant public addresses occurred in 1935 at the Eucharistic Congress in Cleveland, Ohio. There, before a crowd of over 40,000 packed into Municipal Stadium, Sheen rallied his listeners to the Mystical Body of Christ embodied by the Roman Catholic Church in confronting the threat of communism. Exemplifying the Catholic front, Sheen's speech offered a rebuttal to the newly formed Popular Front emerging in Europe and the United States. Like many Americans in the thirties, Sheen believed that the present order of rugged individualism was passing away and that a new social order premised on a communal understanding of humanity would emerge. But he directed the search for social alternatives toward the church. He claimed the reigning secular solution of the day, communism, denied the dignity of the person. Only the church as the Mystical Body of Christ expressed a truly social conception of human existence predicated on the recognition of God and the value of every human being. Sheen asserted, "If you want to be a real Communist then be a Communicant, and bring your hearts to the anvil of Divine Life." In a similar vein, he told the audience gathered in Cleveland to celebrate the Eucharist, that this central sacrament of the church, "age-long symbol of the common mean," embodied the "basis of the brotherhood of man." Sheen concluded his address by predicting that in the future, there would be "only two great capitals in the world, Moscow and Rome." By offering a vision of the competing "tabernacles, the Red Square and the Eucharist," he encouraged Catholics to imagine their own American society as the arena for a wider struggle between the two transnational forces of communism and the church.[47]

Over the course of the thirties and forties, therefore, thanks to the *Catholic Hour* and his numerous books and public speaking engagements, Sheen became a major celebrity in the Catholic world. After World War II, he enjoyed both fame and notoriety for his staunch advocacy of traditional religion against psychology. He rode the wave of interest in therapy with his best-selling *Peace of Soul,* which offered a Catholic counter to Rabbi Joshua Leibman's *Peace of Mind.* He also became embroiled in a very public squabble with psychiatrists over the merits of psychoanalysis.[48]

In 1950, Sheen became national director of the Society for the Propagation of the Faith, which served Catholic missions around the world. He left Washington, D.C., and Catholic University and made his permanent home in New York City, where he had been making his living for decades as a religious celebrity. Then, a year later, Sheen was named auxiliary bishop of New York, serving the powerful Cardinal Spellman.[49] Now centered in the media capital of the world, with an elite ecclesiastical title, Sheen projected an image of Catholic success both within and outside the church. His own personal fortunes, however, once again became entwined with the changing character of the mass media as television took hold of the popular imagination in the 1950s. His star would only rise higher, suggesting a new era of acceptance for Catholics in the United States. But the very sign of this accomplishment spoke as deeply about the transformation of cultural difference under conditions of Cold War nationalism as it did about Catholic achievement.

Life Is Worth Living and Why Americans Needed to Know It during the Fifties

Billing itself as a "program devoted to the everyday problems of all of us," *Life Is Worth Living* initially appeared on the Dumont network beginning in 1952 and switched to ABC in 1955, where it would run until 1957. For five seasons, Sheen presented himself to national audiences for a half hour each week, discoursing on topics ranging from juvenile delinquency to the atomic bomb. The success of the show quickly earned him a cover story in *Time* magazine in 1952.[50] That same year, he won an Emmy as the most outstanding personality. Between 1953 and 1958, Sheen consistently made the top-ten lists of the most admired men in America according to the Gallup Poll. In 1956, in fact, he ranked third, standing above both Pope Pius XII and Billy Graham and behind only President Dwight Eisenhower and Winston Churchill.[51] At the height of its popularity, *Life Is Worth Living* reached up to 30 million viewers.[52]

Sheen's show appeared at a particularly propitious time for the television industry. By the early fifties, a number of Americans viewed television with rising moral concern. Unlike movies, television programming entered directly into living rooms and therefore threatened the intimate spaces of the home. The new medium generated widespread anxiety about its effects on family life. Some feared television would disrupt family unity as members fought over what to watch. Even more important, critics complained, the available programming jeopardized the moral health of young children who were transfixed by their TV sets.[53]

Many Catholics voiced concern about the influence of television in the home. The Catholic call for a reform of television programming was evident in the hearings on radio and television programs held by the Subcommittee on Interstate and Foreign Commerce of the House of Representatives in 1952. Among the invited speakers at the hearing was Winifred D. Smart, representing the National Council of Catholic Women.[54] Smart testified on two extensive surveys conducted in 1952 by the local chapter of the NCCW at her Catholic parish, St. James, in Falls Church, Virginia. She and a group of her fellow parishioners had surveyed the viewing habits of children who attended St. James's parish school and collected parent responses to their children's television programs. She told the subcommittee, "The results of these surveys are greatly disturbing to us" as they demonstrated parents' belief that television represented a real danger to children. The new medium, she claimed, "has, on occasion, overstepped the bounds of normal morality and decency. Most important of all, at least to parents, television has woefully neglected its responsibility to children."

The rise of television after the war therefore inspired moral anxiety on the part of some Americans. That Congress called hearings to consider the new medium testifies to the social concerns it engendered. In an effort to protect itself from further criticism and in hopes of forestalling government regulation, the television industry had established a voluntary code of censorship in early 1952. Yet television remained a subject of investigation and moral concern well into the decade. Estes Kefauver's Senate subcommittee hearings on juvenile delinquency, for example, included in its investigations an examination of television's impact on youth crime.[55]

Changes in the scope and reach of television in the early fifties also shaped the context for Sheen's show. In 1952, the Federal Communications Commission (FCC) rescinded its freeze on granting television station licenses. This move led to the growth of stations throughout the nation, extending TV beyond its largely northeastern regional base and transforming it into a truly national medium of communication.[56]

Finally, Sheen's appearance on television coincided with the tail end of a flare-up in Protestant-Catholic tensions during the early postwar period. As Robert S. Ellwood had described the era, "Interreligious relations in the United States were at a low ebb" in the early 1950s.[57] Protestants worried anew about the Catholic Church as a political power, as evidenced by the formation of Protestants and Other Americans United for the Separation of Church and State in 1947. Senator Joe McCarthy and the large amount of support he received from Catholics seemed indicative of the antidemocratic tendencies of American Catholics in the eyes of some. Paul Blanshard had just published his second volume of hyperbolic criticism of Catholicism, *Communism, Democracy and Catholic Power*, which poured further fuel on an already combustible religious climate.[58]

Consequently, when *Life Is Worth Living* hit the television screens on February 12, 1952, many social factors encouraged its commercial success. The industry could not have hoped for a better response to criticism that television lacked moral and educational programming than Sheen's weekly religious counsel. The show particularly appeased Catholics who worried that television posed a threat to morality. Representative of much Catholic response, the *Catholic World* declared that *Life Is Worth Living* was "probably the most amazing program on TV."[59] And though Sheen— the Catholic agent provocateur for some Protestants—may not have diminished tensions with Protestant and other Americans, his upbeat, affirmative presence on television helped counter some of the most egregious ethnocultural animosities that trailed in the wake of the ascendant Catholic population in America during the early fifties.

But the show's success did not lie solely in offering a positive image of Catholics at a time of residual religious tensions. Indeed, an attractive, nonthreatening representation of Catholicism was, by the 1950s, really nothing new. Bing Crosby and Pat O'Brien had already seen to that.

Unlike the portraits of Catholics these stars offered, Sheen's Americanized Catholicism was expressed in a medium central to the reorganization of social life in the late 1940s and 1950s. Recognizing the role of early television in postwar culture, in fact, is central for explaining the larger significance of Sheen's show, for television was a powerful new vehicle for advancing the interests of corporate capitalism after World War II by linking advertisers with consumers in the privacy of their own homes.

Television embodied the triumph of a consumerist understanding of American democracy over more public and producer orientations. As Alan Brinkley has argued, the politics of consumption that emerged during the forties marked the end of New Deal social reform in American life. Lizabeth Cohen similarly has shown that a "consumers' republic" defined American society after World War II. Indeed, throughout American culture in the forties and fifties, citizens were encouraged to look to a materially abundant, robust private sphere as their primary source of social identity.[60]

This postwar equation of mass consumption with American democracy demanded that individuals abandon their earlier identifications with the public realm and social reform as evidenced in the labor movement and the New Deal. It also entailed a dramatic break from older cultural habits (including class, ethnic, and religious traditions) that viewed consumerism with suspicion. Early television helped lead Americans into this new postwar social order, as George Lipsitz has argued, by reimagining those alternative cultural memories as justification for a privatized, consensual America. The hopes and desires of the past, the new medium insisted, could be realized more effectively by abandoning public commitments and identifying with a prosperous, melting-pot nation.[61]

Sheen's television show therefore must be seen as directly embedded in these cultural, social, and political developments. Tailoring Catholicism to a rhetoric of national unity and religious virtue, *Life Is Worth Living* instructed viewers in how to find meaning within the constricted social landscape of Cold War America. Sheen translated his Catholic difference into friendly counsel that encouraged his audience to identify the collapse of progressive social change as opportunity for moral renewal and spiritual enrichment.

More than simply offering "stability in the midst of change," as Christopher Owen Lynch has argued, *Life Is Worth Living* epitomized the particular cultural formation of Cold War consensus.[62] In the context of the fierce debates over national definition that characterized popular culture at midcentury, the moral clarity of the show's Catholic ethos represented a cultural project to protect the new postwar social order against political challenge and reform. Sheen's Americanized Catholicism was therefore equally a rendering of the nation itself, one determined to discredit the alternative Americanism that had emerged out of the struggles of the 1930s. At the heart of this project lay Sheen's replacement of the virtues of public life with the private allegiances of faith, home, and family as the foundation for collective American identity. *Life Is Worth Living*'s ability to turn Catholicism into a sanction of the Cold War consensus rested upon its blending of distinctly Catholic referents and shared American sentiments. This effort began with the look of the set on his show and of Sheen himself. Each episode opened with a shot of a book cover with the title of the show displayed in prominent letters. After a voice-over introduction, the television camera cut to a shot of the studio set, complete with desk, armchair, bookcases, fireplace, and a statue of the Madonna and Child. Noticeably absent were windows in the study as well as any reference to the urban landscape of ethnic Catholicism that had been so central to earlier depictions of Catholics in the Hollywood movies of the 1930s. Indeed, *Life Is Worth Living* completed *Going My Way*'s visual efforts to remove Catholicism from the gritty, contentious associations of the city streets through its particular construction of a genteel study as Sheen's stage.

After a pan shot that allowed viewers to take in the nicely appointed set, Sheen would enter stage right in his cape, robe, zucchetto, and pectoral cross. The juxtaposition of the normalcy of the study with the Roman ecclesiastical garb offered a striking contrast. The familiarity constructed by the set highlighted the alien appearance of Sheen. That of course was the point of the show's effort to win the viewers' interest in Catholic difference, which Sheen maximized. He played up his uniqueness, with his dark eyes, lilting speech, and dramatic voice all intended to leave a lasting impression on his audience.

Sheen began his talks with jokes, often at his own expense, sometimes making reference to letters that he had received or people he had encountered who commented on his show. These prefatory remarks helped make the bishop, who of course represented the Roman church, appear warm and personable.[63] After such openings, Sheen would commence his exploration of the particular topic that was the focus of the episode.

Because the program never ventured beyond the study, Sheen was limited in terms of what he could actually do in each episode. Yet within such constraints, he found clever ways of putting on a show. A favorite running joke referenced his "angel," the unseen stage assistant who cleaned his chalkboard whenever Sheen stepped away from it. The bishop was also quite adept at using the space of the study. Within each episode, he frequently moved about the set—sometimes standing at the chalkboard, sometimes beside the desk, at other times in the middle of the study— in order to add dynamism to his presentations. Almost always, Sheen concluded the episode by offering some final remarks of a general religious nature, delivered in dramatic fashion. And he usually did this while standing beside a statue of the Virgin Mary and Christ child. The statue in the background of the set functioned as a visual and spatial prop that helped orient both Sheen and the viewer. By standing next to it, he left viewers with a final sign linking his moral discourse with Roman Catholicism. This gesture exemplified the entire series, calling forth an inclusive Americanism with specifically Catholic accents to demonstrate consensus as both recognizable and compelling.

One central means by which Sheen eased Americans into the new postwar social order was by identifying the spiritual stakes in the nation's fight against communism. He offered a Cold War discourse saturated in moral assumptions about personal responsibility and ethical practice. In an episode entitled "Why Some Become Communists," he asserted that "communists seek to destroy morality and in so doing prepare the way for persecution and hate and apparent love of social justice while the individual himself is given over to moral abandonment."[64] He also described communist sympathizers as elite, affluent individuals who supported Marxist revolution in order to ease their guilty consciences for the "wealth that was not acquired except by avarice."[65] In another episode, "Man, Captain of His Own Destiny," he reiterated this belief that fellow traveling was an exercise in personal irresponsibility by claiming that its politics represented a projection of feelings of moral guilt upon others in society.[66]

In much the same way, Sheen portrayed the Soviet Union itself as a

Bishop Fulton J. Sheen doing what he did best: holding an audience for Life Is Worth Living *in the midfifties. Courtesy of Photofest.*

perversion of moral conscience. In the "Russian Lullaby of Co-existence," he highlighted the Soviets' duplicity in geopolitical relations. The Soviets, he said, pursued coexistence to lull the West into complacency so they could continue "nibbling, nibbling away at Korea, China, Vietnam."[67] All the while, Sheen insisted, the Soviets broke international treaties, which he recounted by offering a long list of agreements violated by the communists. In "Communism and Russia," he depicted the Soviet Union as a despotic Marxist tyranny that held the Russian people captive and manipulated their deepest moral impulses. The Russians themselves, he told his audiences, possessed a deep sense of universal brotherhood as well as souls sensitive to guilt and the need for confession. Yet the Soviets corrupted these two admirable qualities, turning identification with the "oneness of the world" into imperialism and the longing to confess sins into the practice of torture "in which the soul itself was spoiled." Sheen's identification of the suffering Russian people with a desire for confession lent a clearly Catholic element to his drama of Soviet persecution.[68]

In contrast to the communist perversion of morality in the Soviet Union, Sheen described the United States as an instrument of virtue in the world. Reflecting on why ordinary Americans might want to pursue coexistence with the Soviets, he said, "We want harmony, we want peace, simply because we are human beings. We are not imperialists."[69] The American flag, Sheen insisted in the episode "Teenagers," represented important spiritual realities, namely, "the traditions and institutions for which it stands."[70] But as he did with the Soviets, he also utilized Catholic referents to describe the moral character of the United States. He concluded "War As a Judgment of God" by reminding his audience to "love America because I believe America is destined to be a secondary cause under Providence for preserving all the liberties of the world."[71] That use of the phrase *secondary cause* echoed traditional Catholic terminology derived from neo-Thomist philosophy. Similarly, he drew upon his use of Crucifixion imagery from the *Catholic Hour* when he claimed that Christ's saving of the thief crucified alongside him on the hill at Calvary embodied the "foundation of democracy, the worth of a single soul."[72]

Life Is Worth Living therefore preached a familiar Cold War division of the world. But by drawing upon Catholic categories and beliefs, he dramatized the struggle against the Soviet Union as a great moral and spiritual project that demanded constant commitment. Sheen's discourse was not about containment or realism. Instead, he encouraged his viewers to see the fight against godless communists as part of their own moral obligation as both religious believers and citizens. Opposing communism was about much more than balancing global interests, Sheen told his audience; it was a profound cultural contest that demanded their spiritual identification. Insisting that the soul of humanity was at stake, his show served as a catechism in the ethics of anticommunism, and his constant attention to Marxist corruption called viewers to engage in their own examination of the national conscience.

Life Is Worth Living extended beyond communism to address other prominent issues of postwar America, including the turn toward middle-class domesticity and the ethos of psychology. But as with the question of communism, Sheen converted these subjects into an arena for a great moral and spiritual adventure that rested in the hands of his viewers. The burden of the nation's social well-being, *Life Is Worth Living* told viewers, depended upon their commitment to family, their spiritual devotion, and their personal character.

Sheen portrayed family life as a crucial institution in which the moral stakes for America were enormous. In episodes such as "Teenagers" and "A Cure for Selfishness," he addressed the prevalent issue of juvenile delinquency and adolescent youth. Parents, Sheen insisted, possessed a profound responsibility in cultivating the God-given ends toward which their children were created. He encouraged his viewers to have sympathy for their teenage children's transitions to adulthood. Sheen acknowledged young people's urge to develop their own friendships and social circles, separate from their parents, insisting that it was "good and right. God put it there and it is not to be crushed." But he also insisted that teenagers needed firm guidance and direction if they were to develop properly. He told parents of their moral obligation to discipline their adolescents in order that they might realize their true end in life, namely, "love of God, love of country and love of neighbor."[73]

Sheen's discussion of marriage also framed that institution as a great drama of heroic sacrifice and spiritual idealism. In "For Better or Worse," for instance, he addressed the difficulties of married life. He encouraged viewers to see the normal tensions that afflict a marriage as natural expressions of deeper longings for unity, love, and fulfillment that would only be truly satisfied in the next life with God.[74] The everyday, ordinary struggles of couples, he suggested, were actually indications of the human desire for the transcendent. Although Sheen recognized that some problems in marriage (such as alcoholism or money troubles) were more challenging than others, he urged married couples in his audience to "stick it out." Tellingly, he turned to the ongoing war in Korea for an analogy of the virtues of sacrifice in marriage. "Our grand army does not desert soldiers wounded on the battlefield," he asserted. "So too it behooves us that there be other heroes than on the battlefield alone, namely heroes in the home." He ended with reference to the "tradition of the sea" in which a captain goes down with the ship, and he pleaded with his viewers that "we have that kind of tradition in the home where the husband or wife . . .

will go down with the ship, for the sake of the honor, for the sake of God, for the sake of America." Equating the difficulties of marriage with the struggles of war, Sheen fused the private and public, directing his audience to see their roles as husbands and wives in the context of the larger moral good of society.

Life Is Worth Living reserved some of its most excessive rhetoric for the virtues of motherhood. Reproducing common sentiments of the fifties, Sheen described mothers as moral educators in the home and as more sensitive to virtue than men because of their ability to create life. But he also imparted to mothers a spiritual vocation that drew on traditional Catholic beliefs. In "The Training of Children," he described a mother as a "flesh and blood ciborium," referring to the chalice that in Catholic worship holds the Eucharist.[75] In "How Mothers Are Made," Sheen celebrated the virtues of motherhood by assuming the persona of a pregnant woman who says to "the young within, 'Take and eat. This is my body. This is my blood,'" echoing the very words of Jesus recited in the Catholic liturgy of the Eucharist. At the end of the episode, when Sheen turned to a reflection on Mary as the true model for all mothers, he recited a deeply sentimental poem by Mary Dixon Thayer, which he had used in his radio broadcasts. In the poem, a person asks Mary to teach him how to pray. As Sheen recited the entire poem, slowly and with effect, the music of "Ave Maria" played in the background.[76]

Life Is Worth Living therefore assigned enormous moral and religious significance to the turn in the 1950s to the private realm of motherhood, marriage, and family life. Some experts legitimated the depoliticization of postwar America by identifying the home as an arena for personal expression, and Sheen contributed to this project by teaching television audiences to embrace the home as a site for spiritual dedication and personal heroism.[77] The everyday realm of spouses, children, and parenting offered more than freedom from the expectations of work: it offered the context for the pilgrimage of the soul.

Another area in which Life Is Worth Living gave spiritual significance to the privatist turn in postwar America involved its attention to psychology and to matters of the self. Episodes such as "Fears and Anxieties," "Is Self-Expression Always Right?" and "The Psychological Effects of the Hydrogen Bomb" manifested the show's preoccupation with personal psychology. Frequently, Sheen made reference to Sigmund Freud, Carl Jung, and other major thinkers in his television talks. Indeed, he proved quite adept at riding the interest in existential philosophy in an era in which Paul Tillich and Søren Kierkegaard assumed new stature as prominent philosophers.[78] He genuinely appreciated the search for meaning that characterized twentieth-century modernity. He spoke of the need for people to develop a "philosophy of being" rather than a "philosophy of habit," in order to address the difficulties in their lives.[79] At times, he could sound like a habitué of the Left Bank of Paris, noting that "modern man does not know where he is going. He is always in danger of being thrown back into the nothingness from which he came, and so he lies in a terrible sense of dread."[80]

But Sheen made use of modern thinking on the self to draw a distinction between contemporary philosophers of despair and traditional religion, which he told his viewers offered authentic hope. He repeatedly asserted that even though psychiatry and psychoanalysis might be helpful for "abnormal people," his talks were directed at normal people, such as his viewers at home. Likewise, he told them the dread of modern life derived ultimately from the individual's abandonment of orthodox Christianity.

In Sheen's hands, religion offered psychological aid for ordinary people as they dealt with everyday problems. It gave people moral purpose and direction, which countered the despair and confusion of modern life. Similarly, Sheen presented religion as offering high ideals and demanding challenges that could provide meaning and stability to people confused by a culture that valued freedom and tolerance. Thus, he could tell his viewers in one episode that "we are going to try to put man together"—no small goal for a commercial television show. To accomplish this, he encouraged his viewers to realize, as the title of that episode asserted, that "man, [is] captain of his destiny." "What is primary," he asserted, "is what happens to a man's thoughts, his choices, his decisions, his resolutions and his character; man is what he makes himself."[81]

The popular turn to psychology in the postwar era therefore afforded Sheen an opportunity to imbue the search for authentic life with religious meaning. Psychological attention to people's personal struggles, he insisted, did not have to lead to modern isolation and individualism. Indeed, he taught that the contemporary focus on the self provided a new context to pursue a grand adventure in which even the largest issues of the day lay within the responsibility of each person. Only if the conflicts within were addressed, Sheen liked to comment, would the larger social tensions and wars in the world be truly overcome. In "War As a Judgment of God," he concluded by proposing that the roots of war lay within modern man's disregard for the transcendent. "Maybe the fault is inside ourselves," he told his viewers, "and maybe it's because we have forgotten God." Addressing the possibility of nuclear war and the effects of deploying a hydrogen bomb, he asserted, "No crisis ever creates character. It merely reveals character." And character could only be realized by following the precepts of sacrifice, responsibility, and duty of religious morality.[82]

Sheen's insistence that traditional religion offered the solution to the problems of the self—whether cast as existential doubt, emotional unease, or psychological difficulty—channeled Catholicism into the postwar project of detaching citizens from public life and social struggle. Sheen's neo-Thomist moral philosophy offered a metaphysics of the psyche that may have contested Freud but that also granted theological sanction to the depoliticization of national life in the fifties. *Life Is Worth Living* thus demonstrated the deployment of alternative cultural traditions in directing Americans to identify their needs and hopes with a refurbished private realm. Utilizing Catholicism to depict this sphere as a site for moral idealism and spiritual achievement, Sheen encouraged television viewers to imagine new possibilities within the postwar social order rather than search outside it.

For all its efforts to harness Catholicism to a Cold War American way of life, however, *Life Is Worth Living* could not always contain the alternative cultural values that Sheen brought to television. In fact, the more distinctive elements of his Catholicism, such as the belief in redemptive suffering and a theology of the cross, impinged at times upon the affirmative vision of America that the show promoted. The tensions between the two worldviews became manifest in moments of rupture and instability that disturbed *Life Is Worth Living*'s smooth surface of consensus.

Indicative of how Sheen's Catholic sensibility troubled the dominant narrative of postwar America, his call for spiritual dedication sometimes collided with the reigning ethos of popular consumerism. In certain episodes, Sheen challenged the middle-class ideology that happiness could be found through consumption. In "Fears and Anxieties," for example, he warned his viewers that modern people sought to suppress the existential dread informing their lives through recourse to "sleeping tablets, opiates, constant love of past time and pleasures." In the American culture of the fifties, in which an expanded leisure sphere was equated with the good life, Sheen's condemnation of the pursuit of private consumption might easily have struck a discordant note with some viewers.[83]

Even more dramatically, in "Communism and Russia," Sheen turned a conventional Cold War narrative of competing American and Soviet worlds into a critique of consumer abundance. Imagining what ordinary Russians might say to the U.S. government–funded Voice of America if they could freely speak their minds, Sheen assumed the role of the collective Russian people: "Please America do not talk to us about economics . . . whenever your Voice of America talks of dropping Sears-Roebuck's catalogues on us, [or] whenever you talk about the superiority of your television sets." In this case, Sheen's moral vision slipped into an implicit challenge not only to consumerism but also to the very medium intended to link consumers to the new world of products advertised before their own eyes.[84]

But it was in another episode devoted to Cold War concerns, "The Russian Lullaby of Co-existence," that Sheen's skepticism toward middle-class consumerism appeared to practically spin out of control before his viewers' eyes. In a lengthy and bizarre interlude to a program devoted to the duplicities of Soviet calls for peace, Sheen reflected on the impulse that drove many Americans to embrace coexistence with the communists. He began by observing, "We are living in psychological fear. Sometimes the ways the newscasts are is to heighten our fear." He also pointed to ads on television and radio that contributed to this collective sense of fear as well. Sheen then dramatically began to act out a series of advertising pitches, moving in an agitated manner around the entire television set. At one point, to stress his mockery of a particular ad, he walked close to the camera and leered into its lens. A moment later, he mimicked ads intended to scare women about their "dishpan hands" and young husbands who were "fearful of your jobs, fearful of your security, fearful of what your boss will say to you looking at your shirt and that tattletale gray." Sheen's humorous performance elicited laughter and applause. Yet so dramatic was his acting and so energetic and unpredictable were his movements about the small set that he appeared on the verge of losing control. His usually careful placement of his body unwound as he assumed in exaggerated form the persona of various product pitchmen. While making comedy out of advertising, Sheen's role-playing also inadvertently highlighted the artificial character of the show itself.[85]

Performance actually functioned as a crucial means by which Sheen's traditional Catholic devotionalism, with its stress on the Crucifixion of Christ and the virtue of suffering, returned within a show offering an affirmative discourse of moral uplift. Although the theology of the cross that informed his radio broadcasts of the thirties and forties was largely elided for his television shows, Sheen did make use of the cross on several occasions. For instance, in "Pain and Suffering," he performed the conversation between Christ and the two thieves crucified alongside him on Calvary from the Gospel of Luke. He assumed the voice of all three characters as he elaborated the scene of the Crucifixion. He gave particular dramatic intonation to Christ's plea for mercy to God, slowly drawing out each word for effect, "Father, forgive them, they know not what they do." Similarly, he underscored the importance of the good thief on a cross by assuming his persona of sorrowful repentance and dramatically recited his prayer to Christ while assuming the pose of a man nailed to a cross. He then reverted to the role of narrator, and in language reminiscent of his radio talks, he painted a rich, Baroque image of Christ's suffering: "The thief looked at the crown of thorns and saw a royal diadem, the nails were a scepter between power and authority, his crucifix was his installation, his blouse was royal purple and he asked only to be remembered." He finished the performance by reciting in dramatic fashion Christ's words to the good thief: "This day, thou shall be with me in paradise."[86]

Sheen's point in performing the story of the good thief was to encourage viewers to find religious meaning in their own ordinary struggles. Yet without actually asserting that, as sinners, people were called to place themselves at the foot of the cross in penitence and sorrow, Sheen articulated a traditional Catholic understanding of the Crucifixion. Acting out the scene on Calvary gave him the opportunity to express in drama and imagery elements of his popular Catholic theology of the cross, which privileged embodied suffering and redemptive self-abnegation.

Episodes such as "Pain and Suffering" actually demonstrated that *Life Is Worth Living*'s efforts to balance Catholicism with a generalized piety occasionally faltered. In drawing upon Catholic difference to cement allegiance to the private realm, the show ran the risk of opening audiences to dramatically different values and beliefs. When Sheen told his viewers that personal difficulties could be understood in spiritual rather than psychological terms, he introduced them to distinctly Catholic ideas. He taught them two ways of using pain, first through "expiation," the offering up of one's sufferings for atonement for "one's failings and sins," and second through reparation, offering one's sufferings "for others and not just ourselves." These terms of *expiation* and *reparation,* as well as the notion of offering up one's sufferings for personal and collective sin, were staples of Catholic religious practice at midcentury. Later in the episode, Sheen asked his viewers to "think of all the sick in hospitals . . . who might sanctify their pain by correlating it to a crown of thorns. . . . All the wounded hands that might sacramentalize that agony by correlating it in some way with the hands riven by steel." Such language shifted Sheen's discourse from generic moral counsel to a specifically Catholic register that emphasized redemptive suffering. Though such moments were ideologically contained within the episode by more general elements of humor, jokes, and conventional moral platitudes about worshipping God, they nonetheless marked the presence of an alternative moral and spiritual sensibility that hovered just beneath *Life Is Worth Living*'s project of incorporating Catholicism into the common faith of fifties America.[87]

Another America

One of early television's most significant attractions was its promise to bring the wider world into people's homes.[88] *Life Is Worth Living* clearly embodied this impulse. Sheen's dress, the props including the statue of the Virgin Mary, the dramatic performances that conveyed Sheen's Catholic ethos, and the language of sacrament and Catholic ritual all functioned to create a distinctive world on television that allowed viewers a peek into Catholic difference. Every week, the show gave television audiences the opportunity to tune in to Catholic perspectives on the contemporary world. Sheen allowed Americans a means to encounter some of the religious sensibilities of their Catholic neighbors within the comfort of their own homes. As much as it worked to present him as a moral counselor to all Americans, *Life Is Worth Living* also contributed to the "range of difference" that television scholar Horace Newcomb argues characterized early television.[89]

Fulton Sheen actually embodied a version of the Catholic mystique that characterized American popular culture in the 1940s and 1950s. Like Bing Crosby's hip priest in *Going My Way* and the romantic Jesuits of *Life* magazine, *Life Is Worth Living* indicated the resignification of Catholic difference by a culture of consensus. Straddling the line between Catholic outsider and American insider, Sheen encouraged Americans to see themselves as part of a great spiritual, moral project played out within the intimacies of their own lives. His presence on countless household television screens communicated his most crucial message—the private realm had become the real stage of the national imagination.

Sheen therefore placed a heavy burden on Americans in the 1950s. *Life Is Worth Living* encouraged them not to look to the public realm or politics or new institutions or the state for help in navigating the complexities of the postwar era. Instead, Sheen taught them that the responsibility for creating a good society rested in their own hands. His show was a weekly exercise in learning how to live within the social constraints of consensus. He counseled viewers in vigilance against communism at home and abroad. He instructed them in their moral duties to raise children, to be good mothers and committed spouses, and to care for their own souls. Their fate, Sheen proclaimed to his audience, was in their own control. But unlike those who promoted traditional notions of individual self-improvement, Sheen told viewers that their own moral destinies were intimately linked to an iridescent sacred order that structured human existence, the world, and even the cosmos. Consequently, he proposed a transcendent vision to Americans and offered himself as guide to help them see the religious drama of their own everyday experiences.

Yet *Life Is Worth Living* paradoxically subverted its own consensus commitments, for by insisting that Americans were responsible for their society, Sheen also granted them enormous agency.[90] In the context of the fifties, this meant redoubling their efforts to forge good homes, attend church, and work on their own character. But implicitly, Sheen's counsel suggested that individuals had the power to change their world if it failed to meet the high standards they were taught to apply to their own lives. In the following decade, many Americans did just that. Thus, from the grainy black-and-white image of a Catholic bishop on television emerged intimations of other social possibilities.

CHAPTER SIX

FROM PUBLIC DILEMMAS TO PRIVATE VIRTUE: LEO MCCAREY, HOLLYWOOD COMEDY, AND THE HOUSEHOLD OF AMERICANIZATION

In 1946, *Saturday Evening Post* gave celebrity treatment to film director Leo McCarey in a lengthy article entitled "Going His Way," by Pete Martin. The popular magazine portrayed the director at the top of his game after having just made *The Bells of St. Mary's* (1946), the successful sequel to *Going My Way*. It pointed out, however, that McCarey was "paying last year's biggest income tax" on the profit from these two films and therefore was unable to fully enjoy the material rewards of his achievement. Martin also explained that McCarey initially had trouble getting his original Father O'Malley movie off the ground, since "for some reason, a belief existed in movie circles that a religious picture wouldn't even return production costs." The article informed readers that despite his difficulties, the director remained a genial, upbeat man, noting, "Bitterness is no part of his stock in trade." Martin, in fact, quoted McCarey indicating he had no interest in using movies to address social problems: "'Let other people take care of sordidness and ugliness . . . I string along with Disney. I think the biggest message of all is Who's Afraid of the Big Bad Wolf. The way I look at it, it's larceny to remind people how lousy things are and call it entertainment.'"[1]

McCarey's insistence on always looking on the bright side expressed a sentiment very much in tune with the emerging conservative reaction in Hollywood. His refusal to make movies that addressed "sordidness and ugliness" echoed the position taken by Eric Johnston, the head of the Motion Picture Producers' Association who, also in 1946, asserted, "We'll have no more *Grapes of Wrath*, we'll have no more *Tobacco Roads*, we'll have no more films that deal with the seamy side of American life." McCarey's identification with Walt Disney also indicated his growing conservatism, for Disney had moved dramatically to the right after cartoonists at his studio went on strike. Both McCarey and Disney belonged to the reactionary Motion Picture Alliance for the Preservation of American Ideals (MPA), an organization within the film industry determined to counter liberal sentiments in movies.[2]

The image of Leo McCarey, the movie spinner of American happiness and affirmation, thus hides a more complex story of one of Hollywood's most important filmmakers between the 1930s and 1950s, one that connects Catholicism and ethnicity to a cultural politics of the American Century. *Going My Way* and *The Bells of St. Mary's* were but the most visible expressions within McCarey's film corpus, the tip of a much wider investment in elaborating popular Americanism through ethnic and religious representation. The attention to pluralism placed his work at the center of Hollywood cinema's revision of national identity. But as McCarey's comments in the *Saturday Evening Post* article intimated, during the 1940s and 1950s the director subordinated his sensitivity to ethnicity and religion to affirmations of traditional American society. Far from merely offering sentimental pieties or comforting hilarity, McCarey and his comic movies revealed that laughter expressed the most serious of cultural concerns in the struggle to represent the nation.

Of all the major filmmakers of Hollywood's classical period, McCarey remains one of the least studied.[3] A director of some of the most noteworthy films of the 1930s, including the screwball comedy *The Awful Truth* (1937), for which he won his first Academy Award for best director, McCarey found that his career had all but collapsed by the 1950s. In the postwar era, his output slowed considerably, and the few films he did make—such as *Good Sam* (1948) and the Cold War melodrama *My Son John* (1952)—never enjoyed the same commercial or critical success of his earlier movies.

Scholars are at a loss to explain his shift from sophisticated comedies to reactionary anticommunism. Some minimize his later conservative politics as uncharacteristic in a career marked by warm, humane humor. Others construe his interest in religion starting with *Going My Way* as a fatal artistic decline that accelerated in the postwar period. Yet such assessments tend to isolate McCarey's work from the broader context of popular cinema itself.[4]

To understand the dramatic changes in McCarey's corpus, it is useful to situate them in what Lary May has identified as the public sphere of Hollywood cinema between the Depression and the Cold War.[5] McCarey's movies of the thirties exemplified the new pluralist Americanism of popular film, which imagined ethnic minorities and cultural outsiders as central to a reformist national community. As an Irish American Catholic, McCarey understood the inadequacies of Anglo-Saxon Protestant conceptions of the nation. Unlike other ethnic Catholic filmmakers, such as Frank Capra or John Ford, however, he eschewed overt political symbols or grand collective myths in favor of smaller, more personal themes. The intimate spaces of the couple, the home, and marriage instead served as the primary imaginative terrain upon which his films examined the relationship between ethnic difference and American society. The romantic couples and comic households that populate McCarey's movies, in fact, exemplified an ethnic discourse in American culture in which national belonging was rendered through romance.[6]

Initially, McCarey's treatment of the household produced a comic vision of society characterized by fluidity, adaptability, and mobility. Films such as *Ruggles of Red Gap* and *The Awful Truth* stressed the unstable character of modern life, resonating with an ethnic awareness of displacement and struggle. In their comic intimations of breakdown and transformation, they also conveyed a Depression-era openness to exploring new arrangements in social life.

But beginning in the late thirties and forties, McCarey's movies turned quite conservative, exemplifying the cultural shift toward consensus that characterized the nation during World War II and the Cold War. In the process, they dramatically revised their renderings of ethnicity and American allegiance. They utilized the romantic couple to portray social identities of the past as dangerous and to encourage traditional values of domesticity and patriotism. They proposed marriage, home, and religion as safe refuge in a dangerous public world. Commitment and responsibility replaced the social inversions and antic energy of the Depression. Affirming rather than questioning the existing American order became the central preoccupation of McCarey's movies by the late thirties, breaking from an earlier, more capacious vision of society.

Through their renderings of romantic and household relations, therefore, McCarey's films participated in the cultural conversion from social experimentation to national retrenchment that May has shown characterized much of Hollywood cinema from the New Deal to the Cold War eras.[7] These films were particularly significant for their ethnic Catholic mediation of this larger cultural transformation in midcentury America. In the comic world where McCarey's movies unfolded, a privatized, domesticated nation arose out of the dilemmas of ethnic assimilation.

Irish American Catholic, Southern Californian Roots

A brief biography of McCarey reveals a life shaped by ethnic, religious difference and mainstream aspirations. Born in 1898, the son of an Irish American father and French immigrant mother from the Pyrenees, McCarey grew up in Los Angeles. His father, Thomas Jefferson McCarey, owned a renowned West Coast boxing arena in the city and enjoyed a reputation as a leading sports promoter. One of the most famous fights he arranged involved the first African American boxing champion, Jack Johnson, in a contest against Jack Jeffries. He eventually sold the boxing business but continued in his role as an urban entrepreneur by running a liquor store. The family was thus part of an ethnic middle class whose success rested upon catering to the new urban, popular culture organized around commerce, sports, and entertainment.[8]

A product of both Catholic and secular schooling, Leo McCarey attended St. Joseph's Catholic grammar school, Los Angeles High School, and the University of Southern California. His father's sister, whom Leo claimed had a great influence on him, was a nun at the Immaculate Heart Convent in Hollywood, suggesting the wider McCarey family's immersion in a Catholic world. His two siblings both attended Catholic colleges in Los Angeles, further evidence of the Catholic milieu in which the director was raised. McCarey continued the practice of providing Catholic education for his only daughter, Mary Virginia. On a trip to Europe in 1939, after his successful *The Awful Truth,* McCarey and his wife had an audience with the pope in Rome, testifying to his ongoing ties to the church.[9]

Given his middle-class background and his education in public schools, McCarey reflected a Catholicism that was more fluid and permeable than that of others in his era who were raised in the deeply bounded cultural enclaves of the Northeast. He was more Southern Californian than New Yorker, and his religious identity trafficked between Catholic difference and mainstream participation. That hybrid experience would leave its imprint on a number of his films beyond the famous *Going My Way,* to include *Love Affair* (1939) and *My Son John* (1952), and it helps account for the persistent concern with Old World/New World tropes and assimilationist stories that informed his movies.

A failed attempt at a career as a lawyer after graduating from USC resulted in his employment in the film industry, working for Tod Browning at Universal. Hired by Hal Roach in 1922 to join his studio, known for its comedy shorts, McCarey worked with Charles Chase, an Irish American vaudevillian from Baltimore, Maryland. Chase's own earlier career in movies entailed a stint at Keystone Studios, founded by Mack Sennett, an Irish Canadian who migrated to the United States and eventually landed in Los Angeles. McCarey directed Chase in a series of successful slapstick comedies at the Roach studio, including *His Wooden Wedding* (1925), which allowed him to develop his talents as a comic filmmaker. In 1926, he became vice president of the Roach operation, overseeing all film production. In this position, McCarey proved instrumental in developing the team of Laurel and Hardy. In 1929, he left the Roach studio and signed a contract with Paramount. So by the time McCarey became a director of feature-length films in the 1930s, he already had years of experience honing his comic skills in a film milieu shaped by ethnics and immigrants.[10]

That experience served him well in the following decade as he directed several important comedies, including the Marx Brothers' movie *Duck Soup* (1933) and *Ruggles of Red Gap* (1935). McCarey proved a particularly adept creator of one of the key genres of the Depression era, the screwball comedy, with such movies as *The Awful Truth* (for which he won the Academy Award for best director in 1937) and *My Favorite Wife* (1940). Late in the decade, he turned his hand to romantic comedy with *Love Affair* (1939). Then, in the 1940s, he enjoyed even greater success with his two movies about Catholics, *Going My Way* and *The Bells of St. Mary's*. At the same time, he joined the conservative Motion Picture Alliance for the Preservation of American Ideals, indicating his opposition to leftist politics in Hollywood. After the war, he served as a friendly witness in the House Un-American Activities Committee's investigation of communism in the film industry. In 1949, he made a short film entitled *You Can Change the World,* highlighting the work of Father James Keller and his popular organization, the Christophers, a group intended to promote Christian values in everyday life. The film featured Bing Crosby, Bob Hope, Irene Dunne, Loretta Young, and others discussing the merits of Keller's project.[11] In 1950, McCarey participated in a deeply contested ideological drive led by Cecil B. DeMille to enact loyalty oaths in the Screen Directors Guild.[12] Two years later, he made a virulently anticommunist film, *My Son John,* which failed at the box office. Although he enjoyed renewed success with *An Affair to Remember,* a 1957 remake of his 1939 romantic melodrama *Love Affair,* his last film, *Satan Never Sleeps,* about Catholic missionaries facing the communist takeover in China, met a hostile reception.

The film scholar Robin Wood has suggested that McCarey's films "raise the question, 'What does it mean to be an American?' in all its complexity and all its impossible contradictions."[13] Wood correctly identifies the central problematic of McCarey's work over three decades. Yet he misses a key source for these films' exploration of American identity, namely, their ethnic mediation of national belonging. He asserts that McCarey believed himself to be a "staunch and committed Yankee Roman Catholic" without noting his Irish American heritage, thereby reproducing the very assimilationist project that McCarey's films simultaneously achieved and interrogated.[14] Further, the subject of commitment that Wood ascribes to McCarey's self-presentation as a Catholic is actually the historically central dilemma of "hyphenated Americans" around which his movies continually revolved.

The paradoxical character of McCarey's films, in which anarchy and conformity are coupled, therefore rests upon a textually embedded impulse that repeatedly rehearses the question of ethnic allegiance to the nation during an extended period when the bonds of patriotic affection were profoundly reformulated, first by the Depression and later by the Cold War. The importance of McCarey's movies in this cultural project of national redefinition will become evident through examining a series of films, beginning with two comedies of the 1930s that staged the desires and anxieties of Americanization in often disguised and indirect ways that Mark Winokur has argued informed other screwball comedies of the decade.[15] This will be followed by a consideration of *Love Affair* and *Once upon a Honeymoon,* two films in which romantic conversion stood in for and exemplified cultural conversion to traditional Americanism. Finally, I will offer an analysis of two postwar movies, *Good Sam* and *My Son John,* in which the retreat to the private sphere folded back upon itself to produce claustrophobic accounts of American virtue. By the time of this last film, at the height of the Cold War, the American Century had exacted its price on McCarey's ethnic Catholic imagination. He had learned to serve the nation dutifully, only to find his own place within it gutted of all the screwball, subversive glee he had demonstrated when questioning its adequacy in the years prior to World War II.

Immigrant Travelers, Ethnic Journeys: *Ruggles of Red Gap* and *The Awful Truth*

Long before *Going My Way,* McCarey had become deeply preoccupied with issues of ethnic cultural difference and American identity. Yet unlike his work from the 1940s, his films of the Depression utilized ethnicity to question traditional conceptions of national belonging. These earlier movies demonstrate that ethnic sensibilities in Hollywood film did not always promote consensus understandings of the nation. In fact, a close look at two of his films from that era, *Ruggles of Red Gap* (1935) and *The Awful Truth* (1937), makes clear McCarey's participation in what Lary May has identified as the new civic arena of thirties cinema that encouraged an alternative, inclusive Americanism.[16]

A story about an English manservant, Ruggles, who finds himself thrown into Red Gap, a frontier town of the American Northwest, *Ruggles of Red Gap* enjoyed excellent reviews and became one of the most successful movies of 1935. The film gained particular attention for its lengthy, dramatic scene of Ruggles reciting Lincoln's Gettysburg Address to a barroom audience. *Variety* called that scene "so dangerous and audacious that it almost startles" and described it as "the high spot of the picture." The *Hollywood Reporter* called the scene "unquestionably the picture's most memorable highlight." The *Daily Variety* reviewer claimed that "the sequences brought sustained applause from the audience" at the showing he attended. And the *Chicago Tribune* titled its review, "One of the Best Films Ever Produced."[17]

The popular and critical response indicated that the film's story of the immigrant as American hero struck a chord with Depression-era audiences. Like other movies during this period that May has shown challenged Anglo-American definition of American community, *Ruggles* promoted a vision of the nation that included outsiders and "foreigners." By privileging a character originally identified with European hierarchy and Old World tradition as the voice of Lincoln's democratic sentiments, the film gave an ethnic Catholic accent to Hollywood's new Americanism.

The film constructed its ethnic rendering of American community through a familiar division of Old World/New World identities. Ruggles is an English lord's manservant who embodies one set of cultural habits derived from traditional European society. Through the course of the film, he learns another set of cultural codes rooted in American democracy whose key text is Lincoln's Gettysburg Address and whose models are Egbert Floud, a folksy citizen of Red Gap, and his mother-in-law, Ma Pettingill, a self-made businesswoman. Interfering with this cultural shift are the American imitators of Old World aristocracy who want to reproduce class hierarchy and cultural exclusion, embodied by Floud's wife and Ma's daughter, Effie, who has taken charge of Ruggles as her new house servant.

Though the English Ruggles may seem as close to the dominant Anglo-American norm as possible, the valet actually functions as a safe form of alterity by which to encode deeper concerns of cultural otherness. Ruggles's identity as manservant to an English lord equates Old World Europe with undemocratic practices of hierarchy and servitude, an association that decades of anti-Catholicism both reflected and helped foster in the American imagination. Charles Laughton's adept performance of the English servant attuned to deference and authority might have been influenced by his own upbringing by a Catholic mother and his schooling by the Jesuits at Stoneybrook, England.[18] On another historical plane, Ruggles's fate as an immigrant who is employed within a Victorian, middle-class household echoes the experience of Irish Americans (particularly women) as domestic servants in the homes of Anglo-Americans throughout the nineteenth and twentieth centuries. Therefore, though superficially Ruggles is an Englishman, the servant also suggests a "disguised ethnicity" referencing wider cultural and class differences, including those of Irish American Catholics.[19]

The film emphasizes and derives much of its comedy from the clash of cultures when Ruggles attempts to transfer his Old World practices as servant to his New World employer. Indeed, for the lengthy early scenes set in Europe, the humor highlights Ruggles's difference from his new employer, Floud, the folksy egalitarian from America's northwestern frontier. Yet Floud refuses to allow Ruggles to continue his patterns of deference and subservience and tries to teach him how to act like an American. This confuses Ruggles, who has been so habituated into a different cultural way of life that he has trouble letting go of his Old World behavior.

Once the Flouds, with Ruggles in tow, return to America, the cultural differences are heightened. This retention of the Old World in the New is visibly conveyed through Ruggles's traditional servant attire, complete with morning coat, high collar, and bowler hat, which marks him off from the western frontier cowboys once the film moves to the Floud's residence in Red Gap, Washington. When Floud takes Ruggles to Nell's, a popular bordello in town, he gives Ruggles the cane and gloves that Effie insisted her husband carry. Floud explains to the Englishman that if his buddies saw him with such European accoutrements, they would run him out of town. But they would not give it another thought if they saw them on Ruggles.

If Ruggles at first appears as an alien in the egalitarian New World, Floud is not without his own difficulties. For all his populist sentiments, he finds himself subordinated to his wife's demands for middle-class respectability. He may be a "natural" democrat at heart, but he is continually frustrated by his wife's cultural pretensions, extending even to Effie's insistence that she dress him properly. Though he treats Ruggles with equality when the two associate alone, in the presence of his wife he succumbs to her more powerful elitist expectations. Floud therefore is the expression of a frustrated American democratic ethos incapable of realizing its egalitarian aspirations on its own.

As Ruggles settles into his life in Red Gap, the frontier landscape works its magic, and he soon finds himself chafing at his restraints as Effie's servant. His announcement to Floud and Ma Pettingill at the local bar that he has decided to "stand on my own two feet" marks a turning point in the film. Floud applauds this change by telling him he sounds like Lincoln at Gettysburg. But his inability to remember what Lincoln actually said introduces the scene, noted by critics, in which Ruggles the European outsider recites the entire Gettysburg Address. Shots of the men in the bar, standing two and three deep, listening in awe to Ruggles's performance evoke the social realist photography of the 1930s. Indeed, the scene gathers together the iconic figure of Lincoln, frontier Americana, working-class laborers, and ethnic outsiders to construct a Depression-era image of popular democracy.

As a demonstration of his newfound independence, Ruggles commits to opening a restaurant with the help of his lady friend, Prunella, as well as Floud and Ma Pettingill. Yet when Lord Burnstead arrives in Red Gap to take Ruggles back to England, the former servant confronts a difficult decision. As he tells Prunella, service to the former employer is more than simply labor; it is intimately tied to family honor, for the men of the Ruggles family have been servants to the Burnstead lords for generations. "I'd be the first member of my family ever to let his family down," he tells Prunella. "It isn't just keeping a man buttoned up but about heredity and loyalty and I guess you could call it habit if you wanted to." Ruggles thus voices the central conflict confronting immigrants and ethnics in America—the competing claims of family, descent, and heritage versus freedom and individualism.[20]

Yet Ruggles's choice is really no choice at all, as demanded by American culture. We know what the only available option is for him: the price of Americanization is the severing of family heritage. Prunella's questioning of Ruggles's manhood (already complicated by Charles Laughton's fey performance) if he returns to Burnstead's service only underscores the overdetermined nature of his choice. Ruggles does of course stand up to his former employer, and not surprisingly, he manages to enjoy a smashing success with the opening of his new restaurant, which concludes the film.

If there really is no choice for Ruggles, what then is the meaning of democracy suggested by the movie? Is the ethnic who vocalizes democratic sentiments merely the ventriloquist of nationalist ideology? Indeed, the film's most famous scene entails a recitation by Ruggles of famous words written by someone else. However, if leaving behind the Old World and its traditions is the cost of assimilation, the film also suggests a revisionist Americanism akin to the "composite personalities and interdependent publics" May identifies in many films of the 1930s.[21] A mutual correction is enunciated by the movie's ethnicized American hero, for Ruggles recites the Gettysburg Address only because all the native citizens have forgotten it. The memory of democracy is in this way located in the immigrant. That combination produces a recognition of cultural outsiders as part of the community, as suggested by the film's final scenes when the townspeople turn out to celebrate Ruggle's new venture. In addition, Ruggles's performance of Lincoln's famous speech inspires Floud to challenge the class pretensions of his wife. Confronting Effie, he too refers to the Gettysburg Address. Floud, the epitome of American folk populism, quotes Ruggles, the immigrant worker quoting Lincoln, the icon of democracy. Furthermore, the figure of the immigrant serves to elaborate the movie's understanding of a cooperative, communitarian public sphere. Ruggles's success depends upon the material aid of Ma Pettingill and Floud as well as the assistance of Prunella. Within the ideological world of this film, individual freedom is tempered by democratic mutuality. Ruggles's moment of Americanization—his recitation of the Gettysburg Address—notably takes place in a public space (the town bar), as does the fruit of his labor, the restaurant he opens as a sign of his independence. Similarly, Nell's bordello is envisioned as a kind of public arena where Egbert can escape the pretensions of Effie's faux-aristocratic household. In fact, it is at the bordello that Lord Burnstead falls in love with Nell, thereby performing another of the film's inversions of social class and hierarchy.

And so, the movie turns Ruggles into an emblem of American freedom. But Lincoln's values of "government by the people," which Ruggles recites, give democratic content to that freedom. Enunciated by an ethnic laborer, those cultural ideals are materialized in the struggle of an immigrant negotiating the strange landscape of American society. In the middle of the 1930s, when the nation's focus had turned to the "people," against economic elites, *Ruggles of Red Gap* imagined an America grounded in the aspirations of its ethnic outsiders.

Cultural difference and assimilation also deeply informed McCarey's successful 1937 movie, *The Awful Truth*. Film scholars consider this film one of the defining examples of screwball comedy of the 1930s.[22] With the movie's wealthy, young characters and New York high-society settings, the last subject it would seem to be about is ethnicity. But the intensity of its identification with these markers of American success suggests a more complex story just below its smooth and attractive surface. The movie actually epitomizes Mark Winokur's insight that 1930s film comedy was a genre deeply shaped by the structuring absence of ethnicity. Banished from explicit content, ethnic concerns return as the cultural repressed through the film's preoccupations with public failure within "proper" society.[23]

Americanization therefore is figured in *The Awful Truth* as a comedy of humiliation and displacement.[24] Here, the comedy of ethnic unease assumes so-called screwball form in a story of a posh couple, Jerry and Lucy Warriner, who decide to end their marriage only to discover in the process of divorcing that they actually love each other. The comic premise of the Warriners' inability to decide, until the very end, how they are to relate to one another points to a complicated and uncertain consciousness redolent of ethnic and hyphenated American identity. As Lucy observes to Jerry in the movie's final scene, "You're all confused, aren't you?" Audiences know, of course, that Jerry and Lucy love each other and will ultimately reunite, but the humor of the film is generated through watching *them* stumble, awkwardly and embarrassingly, toward this end.

The film's opening shot of the New York skyline and the Brooklyn Bridge indicates the modern, cosmopolitan landscape that both confronts and is constructed by ethnic peoples. This image dissolves to a close-up of a giant wall clock, its ticking noticeable on the sound track. The first two shots of the film firmly locate its story within the place and time of industrial, mechanized society. The movie then cuts to a men's club, where Jerry (Cary Grant) is getting a treatment under sunlamps. We quickly learn that he is in quite a bind, one that entails his own complicity. Jerry has lied to his wife, Lucy (Irene Dunne), saying that he had been on a trip to Florida when he really had been pursuing his own pleasures about town. He hopes that a quick treatment under the sunlamps at his club will provide him with a tan that can disguise his deceit. Time is of the essence, however, because his wife is expecting him to arrive from

Florida later that day. Though ostensibly a member of New York's bright set, Jerry is introduced to us as an urban figure trapped by the strictures of modern, mechanical time, hiding his true identity under a pose—Jerry Warriner, twentieth-century ethnic American.

Indeed, Jerry is a man who does not quite fit into the world around him. The scene in the Warriners' swank residence, following Jerry's desperate efforts to cover his trail, highlights his predicament. When he arrives home with some friends he has invited for brunch, Jerry finds Lucy is absent. This causes him some embarrassment in front of his companions. One of his friends observes that letters on the desk addressed to Lucy remain unopened, indicating a lengthy absence from home. When Jerry tries to dismiss the insinuation of infidelity, another friend needles him even more. Jerry attempts to save face by insisting that Lucy is probably at her aunt's cabin, only to have the aunt enter the room behind him, inquiring where Lucy is. When Lucy does show up, she has a male friend in tow, her music teacher, Armand Duvalle (Alexander D'Arcy). This only worsens appearances for Jerry in front of his friends, making him look like a cuckold. The impression of Lucy's deceit toward Jerry also inverts his own effort to pass himself off as the wily husband who can confidently mask his own indiscretions, conveyed in the previous scene at the men's club.

But what makes this scene particularly noteworthy is the public character of Jerry and Lucy's marital difficulties. In its comic rendering of Jerry's discomfort in front of his friends, the scene suggests an ethnic anxiety about hidden truths of identity becoming sources of public shame. Not only does Jerry seek to hide his own past, he needs to cover for his wife's as well. But the guests take delight in watching the spectacle of Jerry's failing efforts to maintain a pose of respectability. Jerry is left to squirm in front of them, his best laid plans to keep up his public face, with which the film opened, left in tatters.

Jerry signifies the ethnic dilemma that assimilation does not necessarily entail acculturation. The latter involves its own conflicted and difficult work. Jerry is the "disguised ethnic," whose plight involves the continuous struggle to reassert his legitimacy among the people around him.[25] Even amid the splendor of the material comfort and privilege of the Warriner apartment, complete with an African American servant and Greek columns, Jerry is an outsider in his own home, with the wider world able to peer in and chuckle.

The entire movie is a sustained chronicling of Jerry's public embarrassments. After he and Lucy trade accusations, they agree to divorce. While they await the finalization of the divorce proceedings, their paths repeatedly cross, leading to several humiliating encounters for Jerry. When he and a date run into Lucy and her new boyfriend, Daniel Leeson (Ralph Bellamy), a wealthy oilman from Oklahoma, at a nightclub, Jerry chides her for her taste in picking a country bumpkin. But when Jerry's date turns out to be the club's singer, Dixie Lee, who does a bawdy routine, he finds the table turned on him. Jerry's pretense of sophistication is subverted by his own poor judgment in choosing women.

Perhaps the most intense example of this comic expression of ethnic anxiety occurs at a turning point in the film when Jerry learns that Lucy is to meet Armand, the music teacher. He is convinced that Lucy is actually pursuing an assignation with Armand. He goes to the hotel room where the two are meeting and barrels in, only to find that Lucy is giving a public recital with Armand playing the piano. Jerry is brought up short and takes a chair in the rear of the room. As Jerry leans back in his chair, it slips from under him, leading to a loud crash. The concertgoers who fill the room turn to look at him as he sits splayed on the floor, the object of their ire. The public embarrassment of Jerry that began in the early scene in the apartment with his friends is amplified into a much larger, blue-blooded disdain for the man, who is rendered comically as the barbarian crashing the gates of high-brow culture.

But it is at this point that Lucy realizes that she actually loves Jerry. At the very moment when he reaches a nadir in humiliating himself and has demonstrated his inability to fit comfortably into the high-society world around him, his wife wants him back. Lucy's attraction for Jerry may be grounded in her awareness of their similarity. For Lucy, too, has trouble keeping up appearances and finds herself continually reacting to forces beyond her control. The early scene in the Warriner apartment when she arrives with Armand casts public doubt on her own virtue. Her fiancé's middle-American ways and his close attachment to his mother, whom he has brought with him to New York, cause Lucy intense discomfort, which Jerry takes pleasure in exacerbating. The mother in fact suspects Lucy is a scheming gold digger. Furthermore, Lucy's effort to balance Jerry, Leeson, and Armand and their differing claims on her results in the ground constantly shifting beneath her feet. Scenes of different men entering her apartment, confronting each other as well as her, comically highlight Lucy's unsteady grip on the world around her.

Thus, when Lucy decides to win Jerry back from Barbara Vance, a young wealthy socialite of the polo and horse-racing set, she uses the one

The man who does not quite fit within respectable society: Jerry Warriner (Cary Grant) finds himself in an embarrassing moment under public scrutiny in Leo McCarey's The Awful Truth *(1937). Courtesy of Photofest.*

strategy she and Jerry know only too well—public embarrassment. On the night their divorce is to be final, Lucy shows up at the Vance mansion, where Jerry and Barbara are having dinner with Barbara's parents. She pretends to be Jerry's sister. She makes Jerry intensely uncomfortable by asking for a drink in the teetotaling household, putting on a record, and performing the same dance routine that Jerry's nightclub date had done earlier in the film. Realizing that Lucy is shredding the Vances' impression of him, Jerry quickly whisks her away. On the drive back to city, their car runs out of gas, and they are forced to spend the night at Lucy's family cabin, far from the Vances, Dan Leeson, and Manhattan's high-society crowd. There, they decide to stick together.

In a film that encodes an ethnic perspective on Americanization, explicit incorporation of ethnicity is largely relegated to brief appearances of the Warriners' African American maid and Armand's Japanese manservant. The movie thus reproduces the traditional Hollywood and American racial hierarchy whereby blacks and Asians are reduced to the role of domestic laborers. The most explicit elaboration of white ethnicity is Armand, the French music teacher with whom Jerry believes Lucy is having an affair. Though a secondary character, Armand proves significant for the film's implicit preoccupations with assimilation.

Armand is Jerry's ethnic double, the man he fears has Lucy's true affections but who is also clearly culturally different. In the early scene at the Warriner home that introduces Armand, the Frenchman is initially impressed with Jerry for not being jealous. He tells Lucy, "Your husband is not like the average American man. . . . He is free of all mean suspicion. Yes, he has more the Continental mind." Jerry *is* in fact jealous, but Armand equates him with a non-American difference that implicitly structures his character and governs *The Awful Truth*.

The similarity between Armand and Jerry extends to their shared appearance and dress. This is particularly evident when the two are contrasted with Leeson, the good old boy from Oklahoma. Both Jerry and Armand are slim and dark-haired, and both are impeccably dressed in elegant dark suits, in comparison with Leeson's larger build and dull clothing. The film thereby more than hints at the correspondence between the American Jerry and the ethnic Armand.

Jerry has to beat the ethnic, signified by Armand, out of his marriage to Lucy if he is to regain his place within the well-bred world he and Lucy inhabit. In one scene, Lucy is meeting with Armand in her apartment. When Jerry shows up, Lucy quickly sends Armand into her bedroom to hide before her husband enters. But when Leeson arrives thereafter, Jerry volunteers to hide so as not to cause Lucy embarrassment. He sneaks away to Lucy's bedroom, where Armand waits. As Lucy is distractedly trying to get the oafish Leeson to leave, we hear Jerry and Armand engage in violent fisticuffs. Soon, Armand makes a mad dash out of the room and the apartment, with Jerry in quick pursuit.

The movie therefore allows Jerry an assertiveness and strength he otherwise lacks when he is determined to defeat Armand from winning Lucy, as if the issue of the wife masks deeper, unspoken fears on Jerry's part about his own ethnic identity that his other, Armand, signifies. But if Jerry is most forceful in his dealings with his ethnic double, he proves inept at being the cultured New York sophisticate. As the film comically demonstrates, he has a difficult time making himself into a proper member of high society. Repeatedly, his efforts at presenting a dignified and reputable face to the world fail miserably. Jerry's efforts to separate from unspoken ethnic entanglements is not accompanied by a comparable achievement of mainstream respectability. The comic depiction of Jerry Warriner derives from his plight as a man caught between a suspect past and a social norm he cannot quite achieve.

Further, Jerry compensates for Lucy's perceived betrayal by pursuing the wealthy young socialite Barbara Vance. Ostensibly, Jerry's involvement with the polo crowd makes sense given the wealthy circles in which the film locates him. But the film's montage of Jerry and Barbara's courtship so soon after his beating of Armand in Lucy's apartment suggests the extremities of the cultural poles Jerry is implicitly ricocheting between—ethnic fears and Anglophilic desires.

Indeed, the cultural associations of the individuals that Jerry and Lucy both ultimately reject in order to reunite are telling. Lucy turns down the representative of heartland America, whereas Jerry leaves Barbara Vance, the ultrawealthy East Coast heiress. These refusals on their part help distance Jerry and Lucy from class hierarchy even while the film encourages viewers to feel comfortable with their wealth. But their dual rejections also signal the spectrum of Anglo-America against which *The Awful Truth* defines Jerry and Lucy. Ultimately, the couple turn out to be urban people struggling to maintain their hold not only upon one another but also upon their place in society, a society that seems all too willing to cast a suspicious gaze upon them. Romantic reunion thus encodes ethnic Americanization.

The film culminates in a scene of wondrous verbal playfulness that on the surface provides a resolution to Jerry and Lucy's marital problems. Stanley Cavell has argued this concluding scene provides a sophisticated philosophical meditation on marriage and reconciliation.[26] However, the dialogue also suggests an astute reflection on the complex character of ethnicity and American identity. At Aunt Patsy's country cabin, Jerry and Lucy have retired to separate rooms for the evening, minutes before their divorce is finalized. A door whose lock does not work properly is all that physically separates them. Repeated attempts to fix the problem allow Jerry and Lucy to indirectly convey their true feelings for each other. It is here, as Jerry enters Lucy's room, that she tells him that he is "all confused." Jerry agrees but also asks for another chance: "Things are different except in a different way. . . . So long as I'm different don't you think, well, things could be the same again but only a little different?" Jerry is telling Lucy that he promises to be different by changing his philandering and suspicious ways so that the two of them can again be the husband

and wife they were before, except that he will not be a cheating husband in the future.

Yet considered as the words of a disguised ethnic American, Jerry's promise resonates with the dilemmas of assimilation. They aptly describe the demands and realities of Americanization. Ethnics are offered the dream of American identity so long as they promise to change and be different from who they are so that the same Americanism that national ideology promotes as timeless can be replicated. Yet in fact—and as the ethnic subconscious of this film insists—ethnic Americanization is a repetition of that ideology with a difference grounded in the struggle and conflicts experienced by cultural outsiders. If the movie is read as an allegory of ethnicity, the title of the film assumes additional significance. *The Awful Truth* refers as much to the painful and contradictory experience of Americanization as it does to marriage.

Leo McCarey's screwball hit from 1937 therefore offers a comedy of displacement that stems from an ethnic awareness of the difficulties of assimilation when one remains haunted by cultural difference. Largely erased from the story of an American couple, ethnicity returns in a comic mode. Cary Grant's famous double takes and slapstick humor manifest physically the anxieties that Americanization generates from those the nation embraces in truncated form. The wages of acculturation are thus borne upon the body itself. The jokes deflect the pain; the laughter is the anguish.

A Conversion to Remember: *Love Affair* and *Once upon a Honeymoon*

Two years after *The Awful Truth*, McCarey directed the romantic comedy *Love Affair* (1939) about an American woman, Terry McKay (Irene Dunne), and a French bon vivant, Michel Marnet (Charles Boyer), who meet by accident aboard a transatlantic ocean liner and fall in love. It was McCarey's first effort to align ethnicity and religion with a privatized vision of modern life, for Catholicism grants spiritual and moral value to traditional social roles as an alternative to the confusions of the contemporary world. *Love Affair* anticipated the conversion pattern that Lary May has identified in forties Hollywood cinema, in which the progressive identifications of the thirties were repudiated in favor of cultural traditionalism.[27]

The film emerged in a period of increasingly restricted social options both abroad and at home. As Elizabeth Kendall notes, historical events "hovering on the edges of the story, [are] the source of the potent aura of melancholy that permeates the movie."[28] McCarey directed the film after a lengthy trip to Europe, where he had an audience with Pope Pius XI as well as an opportunity to witness the growing power of fascism sweeping the Continent. Production occurred during the fall and winter of 1938, a time marked by the Munich Agreement and Kristallnacht overseas and a resurgent political conservatism at home. The film was released in March 1939, the same month that the Germans abrogated their agreement, made only months before, with England and France and took over the rest of Czechoslovakia.

The story of *Love Affair*'s Old World/New World couple suggests that the dangers threatening the Atlantic world could be met by a rededication to traditional values and moral commitment. The movie introduces its narrative of cultural conversion by portraying Terry and Michel as denizens of a shallow, directionless, modern culture signified by sexual promiscuity. Terry is a "kept woman," whose benefactor has sent her off to Europe on an extended shopping trip. Michel is a French playboy, enjoying a romantic dalliance on Lake Como with a woman who is not his fiancée.

The film therefore implies that the contemporary world on both sides of the Atlantic suffers from moral declension. Only Michel's grandmother's home on the island of Madeira (complete with not one but two Catholic chapels) provides, as Terry observes on her visit, "another world." And it is here, within space explicitly marked as Catholic, that Terry and Michel's relationship begins to change from playful flirtation to true love.

In a key scene, *Love Affair* draws upon the spiritual and sacred associations of Catholicism to signal Terry and Michel's transformation. While their ship has a short stop at the island of Madeira, Michel runs into Terry on his way to visit his grandmother. He invites her to join him, and they arrive at the older woman's house only to find that she is praying in one of the family chapels. While they wait for her to finish, Terry looks around and is powerfully moved by the place. A medium-distance shot of her, with her back to the camera, facing the entrance of the chapel locates her as well as Michel in clearly Catholic space. Above the chapel's entrance door is a mural of the Madonna and Christ child. The chapel wall is also sketched with a figure of a saint holding a cross. After the grandmother leaves the chapel and greets Michel and Terry, she encourages them both to make their own visit to the sanctuary.

The film cuts to the interior of the chapel, introducing a scene that constructs Terry and Michel's relationship in spiritual terms. An establishing shot depicts Terry standing partially in shadows on the right side of the frame, facing an altar and looking up at a statue of the Virgin Mary. Michel enters from the left, and the film cuts to a low-angle shot of the statue. In front of the Virgin Mary, a crucifix is prominently displayed. A cut back to a medium-distance shot depicts Terry on one of the kneelers in front of the altar. Michel follows her lead and lowers himself onto the other kneeler. Through a series of shots of Terry in prayer, with both the Virgin and Michel observing her, the sequence renders Terry as religiously sincere and Michel as transformed by recognizing her true worth. The transatlantic couple tossed together by fate is brought into union through the mediation of the Virgin. They leave the chapel together, transformed by their newfound appreciation of each other. Tea with the Catholic grandmother afterward only draws the couple closer.

In light of their new relationship, Terry and Michel each agree to alter their lives. Terry leaves her sugar daddy and becomes a singer. Michel, who had confided to Terry that he had never worked a day in his life, buckles down and gets a job as a painter. The modern sophisticates therefore renounce their former, shallow lives for traditional morality and conventional social roles.

But the couple pays for their past transgressions when Terry, on her way to meet Michel at the Empire State Building after several months of separation, is brutally injured in a traffic accident that leaves her paralyzed. As she tells the priest at her bedside, "While I was on my way to being a good girl, I got hit. . . . It wasn't anybody's fault but my own." Close-up shots of Terry as she conveys her self-punishing regret heighten the purgative role of her suffering. Actually, her punishment was demanded by Joe Breen, head of the Production Code Administration, who insisted that Terry's past indiscretions as a kept woman be thoroughly condemned.[29] But her anguish also fits with the film's larger effort to dramatize the value of private commitments against public distractions.

Because he is not told of Terry's accident, Michel concludes she has stood him up at the Empire State Building. While Terry remains paralyzed, she takes a job teaching music to orphans. Scenes of her with the children deepen the reconstruction of Terry as a woman of traditional values and family that had begun with the chapel conversion. Michel meanwhile has become a successful painter, indicative of his own path to respectable living. In fact, the larger love affair this film encourages is toward traditional social roles of gender, work, and family. The couple's reunion at the end announces the completion of their conversion to established cultural norms.

*Conversion through Catholicism: the transatlantic cosmopolitan couple, Terry and Michel
(Irene Dunne and Charles Boyer), at prayer in a Catholic chapel in* Love Affair *(1939).
Courtesy of Photofest.*

The film's break from the screwball anarchy of McCarey's *The Awful
Truth* suggests a new seriousness that matched the growing anxieties of
the late thirties. Whereas the earlier film accepted the precariousness of
marriage in a modern age and assumed a playful attitude toward gender relations, *Love Affair* seems to have a much sterner attitude toward
modern sexual relations. Jerry and Lucy Warriner did not have to pay for
their moral failings by renouncing their way of life. But the American
Terry and the European Michel, seared by suffering and misfortune, are
united through their commitment to giving up their old, frivolous lives
and dedicating themselves to traditional values of hard work, productivity,
religion, and domesticity.

Love Affair therefore captured an emergent mood of cultural retrenchment that would only grow in subsequent years, and it helped elaborate a
conservative reaction to the social experiments that had characterized the
1930s.[30] The recurring image of Terry and Michel standing alone at the

ocean liner's railing amid the fog in the middle of the Atlantic epitomized the somber, disquieted emotional tone of the film. Unmoored in a modern world, they sought refuge from history by hoping to turn the Empire State Building into their own private chapel.

Cultural conversion was even more apparent in McCarey's *Once upon a Honeymoon,* made in 1942. By then, the United States had entered World War II, and the movie invested ethnic identity with new significance as an expression of American unity.

The film stars Ginger Rogers as a working-class, Irish American stripper named Katie O'Hara who passes as a refined, elegant woman, Catherine Butt-Smith, living in Europe; she is engaged to the Austrian Baron Von Luber (Walter Slezak). Cary Grant plays a radio reporter named Pat O'Toole. He is chasing down a big story about Hitler's right-hand man, who turns out to be O'Hara's fiancé. The comic premise of *Once upon a Honeymoon*—that upward mobility might inadvertently entail marrying a Nazi—therefore rests upon a profoundly ethnic anxiety, namely, that assimilation might be a treacherous endeavor. Yet the intense wartime patriotism of the film resolves these doubts by casting love of country as a return to one's true roots.

Katie, as her efforts to present herself as a refined woman indicate, is a fraud, and she learns to exchange her fake persona not with her original, working-class ethnic identity but with a new one that pays fealty to the nation-state. After escaping the baron, she learns to embrace the fight against fascism, as signaled by her eschewing her false name for her real Irish American name of O'Hara. Eventually, she even becomes a spy, working for the American government. By taking up the cause of the nation, the working-class Irish American Katie O'Hara embodies the new meaning of ethnicity within wartime Americanism. Ethnic outsiders now represent the pluralist basis of national unity promoted by the film.[31] To achieve that role, however, the film asserts that ethnics have to undergo a cultural transformation and cleanse themselves of compromised pasts and material desires of worldly success. Katie's heroic Americanism rests upon her rejection of prior attachments and aspirations, signified by both her working-class background and her earlier social climbing.

Within this new Americanism, identity likewise must become clear and unambiguous. Like *Ruggles of Red Gap* and, implicitly, *The Awful Truth,* *Once upon a Honeymoon* is preoccupied with the fluidity and changeability of identity. Katie O'Hara's unsuccessful attempt to remake herself as a refined, upper-crust lady is but the most extended example of this theme. However, unlike McCarey's earlier films, which participated in Hollywood's wider reconstruction of personal identity as part of an energetic, expansive social arena, this film offers an overdetermined nationalism to secure identity.[32] "You love your country, don't you?" the head of the American spy ring asks Katie, who responds affirmatively. Then, as if the film fears such assurances may not be enough, the agent has Katie recite the Pledge of Allegiance.

At the end of the movie, Katie and O'Toole are onboard an ocean liner taking them back to the United States. Secretly, the baron is also on the ship, hoping to plot a Nazi invasion of America. When Katie comes upon him on deck, he attempts to throw her overboard. But it is actually she who tosses him into the ocean. She runs to O'Toole, and together they inform the captain, who turns the ship around. In the final scene, O'Toole notes that the Germans would never turn around an ocean liner to save an American lost at sea. Katie's response—"Maybe that's what makes us different from them"—serves as the coda for the entire film, not only reminding viewers of the common identity all Americans supposedly shared but also indicating that the war itself rested upon fixing sharp cultural distinctions.

Private Virtues, Public Enemies: *Good Sam* and *My Son John*

After the successes of *Going My Way* and *The Bells of St. Mary's*, McCarey's career veered dramatically rightward. At the peak of his commercial success and popular recognition, he became a significant player in the culture war against progressives and liberals in Hollywood. Already a member of the Motion Picture Alliance, he associated with archconservatives who warned of a left-wing threat to the nation from movies that criticized the American way of life. Then, in the immediate postwar years, he helped legitimate the political crusade against the film industry by cooperating with the House Un-American Activities Committee in 1947. In May, as committee leaders gathered information for their investigation in Los Angeles, McCarey met with Congressmen J. Parnell Thomas and John McDowell. He told the *New York Times*, "I only came down because I was glad of an opportunity to cooperate with the committee." Then, in October of the same year, he testified, along with Gary Cooper, as a friendly witness to the HUAC hearing in Washington, D.C.[33]

When McCarey and Cooper cooperated with HUAC, they were in the middle of making the film *Good Sam*, a story of a middle-class department store manager who tries to translate the Good Samaritan ethos into his daily life. Released in 1948, that movie participated in Hollywood's turn to addressing postwar readjustment, exemplified by such films as *The Best Years of Our Lives* and *Mr. Blandings Builds His Dream House*. *Good Sam*'s treatment of this subject offered a deeply conservative Americanism that pushed back against reformist and liberal demands for resuming the New Deal at war's end.[34] Although it would be a mistake to read the film as a direct reflection of McCarey's appearance before HUAC, the movie's cultural politics is nonetheless evident in its privileging of private solutions to pressing social problems of postwar America. In fact, *Good Sam* represents a continuation of the cultural conversion to traditional values evidenced in McCarey's earlier films, *Love Affair* and *Once upon a Honeymoon*. Now, however, the renewal of traditional values takes place on the nation's emergent suburban frontier.

The film's defense of American traditionalism is organized around a reworked figure of displacement that informs much of McCarey's work. But here, cultural difference is rendered through Sam Clayton (Gary Cooper), a middle-class department store manager and family man determined to practice the Good Samaritan's alternative value of selfless giving. Like Jerry Warriner in *The Awful Truth*, Sam is a man who does not quite fit into his surroundings. His wife, Lou (Ann Sheridan), continually reminds him that he is too good for this world. Her words are confirmed through a series of incidents in which Sam's charity is repeatedly abused and taken for granted. Through the character of Clayton, *Good Sam* remakes the cultural outsider in America as the mainstream, middle-class individual who embraces traditional notions of generosity and goodwill to all. The odd man out now is the guy who tries to live charitably in a grasping, self-centered world. Unlike Jerry, however, Sam Clayton is rock-solid. Gary Cooper's performance only underscores the impassive, unchanging strength of character Sam possesses. The world around him may be chaotic and uncertain, but Clayton does not manifest any of its "screwiness," as the hero of *The Awful Truth* did. Instead, he is the constant center of goodness in a society that takes advantage of his charity.

But more is at stake in this film than simply a comedy about a man misunderstood and exploited. In its portrayal of Sam's generosity to people in need, *Good Sam* references very real social challenges facing postwar Americans. Sam's brother-in-law, Claude, is an injured war veteran suffering psychological difficulties whom Sam invites to live at the Clayton home for six months. Though presumably disabled, Claude is a handsome young man who acts perfectly normal and sleeps late into the morning before going down to the government office to pick up his relief check. Similarly, an ungrateful neighbor who crashes the car Sam lent him has lost his job, has difficulties paying bills, and shirks his responsibility for the accident. Through such unsympathetic depictions of veterans and the unemployed as freeloaders, the film implies that collective problems such as veteran disability and joblessness are, at root, matters of individual bad character.

The unworthiness of the people Sam helps makes his own generosity all the more virtuous. But more important, Sam's acts of goodness also represents very private solutions to complex social problems. The film's opening scene is set in a church, with Sam and his family listening to the minister reflect on the challenges of the "difficult world we live in" and making a call for more charity. But the rest of the film takes place beyond the church, offering a portrait of how that moral and religious charge can be implemented in everyday life through the daily trials and tribulations of Sam Clayton. The Good Samaritan story offers pretext, both narratively in the film and more broadly speaking culturally, to reconfigure the responsibilities and obligations of citizenship and the common weal in a period of postwar economic and social transition.

The movie's privileging of private virtue as solution to social problems is particularly evident in the enormous attention it pays to the struggles and desires for good housing in the immediate postwar years. Addressing a very real dilemma facing millions of Americans after World War II, the world depicted in *Good Sam* revolves around homes, homeowners, renters, and the homeless. Claude, the brother-in-law, lacks his own place to live. A young woman at Sam's department story is abandoned by her boyfriend and is evicted from her apartment. In addition, a young expectant couple whom Sam befriends try to establish a home of their own.

The Clayton residence itself is depicted as tight and cramped. The space of the house is small, characters appear physically close to each other, even at the dining table and in the living room, suggesting that Sam and his family experience both a physical and a psychological squeezing in their domestic quarters. Though it initially seems that the family owns the home, we learn that they are only renters hoping to move up. In fact, Lou keeps reminding Sam about her desires to finally get a home of their own. When a real estate agent takes them to a well-appointed ranch with a large yard and a master bedroom with its own bath, Lou exclaims, "This is paradise."

Yet the film insists that such collective problems as decent housing can be handled through the goodwill and charity of individual citizens. Sam opens his residence to his homeless brother-in-law. Likewise, he allows the abandoned young woman working at the department store to stay at his house. The young couple Sam has befriended is only able to get started on a life of their own thanks to his charity. Even the Claytons' own housing problems are rectified in the end by the town banker making an exception for Sam and extending him a loan after he had been robbed of the down payment on Lou's suburban dream house.

Good Sam exemplifies the dramatic turn toward the private realm that characterized American culture in the postwar years in general. McCarey's movies had moved in this direction even before the war. But *Good Sam* demonstrates that as the nation confronted housing shortages, unemployment, and returning veterans, McCarey believed it was time to put away public solutions and reaffirm traditional values. As the minister tells his congregation in the opening scene of the film, the world does not need any more "plans"—an implicit critique of New Deal social reform—but rather needs "better people." The movie makes clear that McCarey's testimony before HUAC did not emerge in a vacuum but stemmed from the director's deeper commitments to rolling back progressive politics in society and in culture as well.

In its sustained portrait of self-absorbed people benefiting from Sam's charity, *Good Sam* in reality offers a barely concealed rage against liberal assumptions about the possibilities of collective action. Far from suggesting a capacious, expansive view of human relations, the film turns the Good Samaritan ethos into a covert club with which to beat a selfish world and justify private responses to the difficult problems of postwar America. In the process, it renders religious values in intensely individualistic terms, curtailing any possibility of a socially or politically oriented faith. As the minister sympathetically sides with Lou when she confides her frustration at her husband's generosity to strangers, "No question, but the happiness of the home comes first."

Like *Going My Way, Good Sam* privileges religion as an alternative rather than a complement to social reform. But Father O'Malley's confident, tolerant, open-ended approach to the world has, by 1948, been replaced by a smug, self-righteous, individualistic moralism. The problem facing America, the film implies, is not ethnic prejudice or social inequality but the existence of a society of slackers. *Good Sam* displaces older, Depression-era renderings of society as a conflict between elites and the people by imagining an America divided by morally committed individuals besieged by the irresponsibility and self-interest of their fellow citizens.

The only hope for the world, the movie suggests, lies in the continued goodwill of souls such as Sam Clayton who persevere with their individual acts of charity and thoughtfulness even amid all the human selfishness. The movie concludes with the family ensconced in Lou's suburban dream house, awaiting Sam's arrival for dinner. But Sam, having been rejected for a bank loan, goes on a despondent tear at the local bar. Stumbling out of the tavern, he encounters members of the Salvation Army, one more sign of privatized charity the movie privileges, who march him safely home. Reunited with wife and family in their new suburban ranch, Sam returns back to where he began. The American dream, the film reassures viewers, is not jeopardized by Sam's radical notion of a truly selfless life. Indeed, the two fuse together in McCarey's postwar vision, to keep the public realm out of the picture.

By 1952, McCarey's vision became even more constricted, as evidenced by his fevered, anticommunist screed *My Son John*. Although *The Bells of St. Mary's* (1946) offered a sequel to *Going My Way* by having Bing Crosby's priest tussle with an attractive, headstrong nun (Ingrid Bergman), the real companion to the original Father O'Malley film was this movie from the height of the Cold War. That the movie's creators clearly had *Going My Way* on their minds was manifest through the presence of the actor Frank McHugh, who played O'Malley's clerical friend, Father Timmy O'Dowd; McHugh again played a priest named Father O'Dowd in this film, too. Indeed, *My Son John* read as a photographic negative to *Going My Way*. Both films were deeply invested in the logic of assimilation, both organized those concerns through the tensions between generations—*Going My Way* in terms of the gentle jostling between the elderly and young clerics, *My Son John* as a fierce struggle between parents and rebellious son—and both focused their ideological commitments on the privatization of American society. But whereas *Going My Way* conveyed an upbeat confidence in the ability of the private sphere to satisfy public needs, *My Son John* anxiously insisted such identifications could only be sustained through social practices of self-policing and surveillance.

As in most of McCarey's movies, *My Son John* focused ethnic preoccupations with assimilation upon the family household—in this case, a highly Americanized Catholic middle-class family, the Jeffersons, whose very name signifies the intensity of the film's compulsions toward consensus. Within this home, the mother, Lucille (Helen Hayes), attempts to sustain a degree of normalcy. Two of her sons have enlisted in the army, but a third, John (Robert Walker), has a mysterious preoccupation that keeps him from visiting his parents. John's difference—signified through his dark hair and suits, his slightly effete mannerisms, and his college education in contrast to his brothers, who have lighter hair and all-American looks and wear military uniforms—causes anguish for his parents, particularly his father, Dan (Dean Jagger), who suspects he is a communist.

As it turns out, the ultrapatriotic, American Legion–attending father is correct. John is a part of a spy ring within the U.S. government in Washington, D.C. Lucille suspects that her son's difference might indicate nefarious proclivities, but she attempts to convince herself that her husband is wrong. However, the arrival of an FBI agent, Stedman (Van Heflin), leads her into a process of careful monitoring of her own son to uncover the truth about John before the FBI can catch him. When she learns that he is indeed guilty of what Stedman claims and Dan insinuates, she attempts to convince her favorite son to "get in the game" and abandon his treason. In the confrontation scene with John, Lucille opens her clenched fist to reveal rosary beads. Thrusting them before her son's face, with the crucifix dangling from the beads, the mother marshals her Catholic faith to convince John of the depths of his crimes and persuade him to repent. When he refuses, she abandons him, concluding, "Take him away. You need to be punished John." John is eventually killed by mysterious assailants, but not before he records a confession of his treasonous ways that is played at the graduation ceremony of his alma mater. Lucille and Dan are in attendance, and the film's final scene depicts the parents walking toward the school chapel to pray for their son John.

My Son John elaborates the dark implications of *Going My Way*'s consensus dreams through its reworking of the earlier film's own assimilation narrative. But in this movie, the traditional logic of assimilation of New World sons rejecting Old World fathers is turned upon its head. The young Catholic son of New World America, Father O'Malley, kept venturing forth from St. Dominic's to gather a wider America around private identifications. He crossed the parish boundary in order to combine Catholicism with leisure activities, entertainment, and traditional high culture. But John Jefferson is the inverse of O'Malley—the young communist son who has rejected the church and embraced a public realm of political commitment portrayed as deceitful and unpatriotic.

The communist John is the cultural Other to the American father. The son signifies the dangerous limit of assimilation—the realm of radical politics beyond which all Americanization must not gravitate. As in McCarey's other films since the forties, the public realm is emptied of all

My Son John *(1952), the real sequel to* Going My Way: *The Catholic Lucille and Dan Jefferson with their communist spy son John (Helen Hayes, Robert Walker, and Dean Jagger) chat with their parish priest after Mass. The priest, Father O'Dowd, has the same name as Father O'Malley's clerical friend in* Going My Way *and is played by the same actor, Frank McHugh. Courtesy of Photofest.*

attraction. But in *My Son John,* it is also imagined as a site of danger and the source of secretive allegiances. In such a world, the heavy hand of the state, symbolized by the FBI agent, becomes necessary to safeguard a virtuous private realm. But ultimately, the film suggests through Lucille's willingness to turn in her own son that private institutions themselves, such as the family, must assume the role of active monitors.

My Son John locates Americanism where consensus understandings typically encouraged citizens to look—the realm of family, religion, and the private sphere. But it identifies a belief in the nation with parents rather than rebellious sons. In so doing, however, the film reflects the profound rearrangement that Cold War imperatives demanded in the terms of American identity. Dissent and consent, similarity and difference, public and private assume new meanings that reveal the tortured logic of postwar culture. Assimilation of outsiders such as the Catholic Jeffersons no longer entails the rejection of the Old World father but instead requires parents' betrayals of sons to compensate for the sons' own betrayals of an American national ideology that demanded immigrants betray their pasts. Yet the intensity of McCarey's insistence that individuals attach themselves to privatized conceptions of the nation even if it results in a culture of surveillance and self-policing ironically produces a movie that displays, for all to see, the enormous costs that Americanism has come to demand from its citizens in the 1950s. Against its own zealous patriotic impulses, *My Son John* turns Americanization into film noir.

The End of the Affair

McCarey would continue to make films after *My Son John*, including *An Affair to Remember* (1957), a hit remake of his own *Love Story*. Yet his anticommunist diatribe marked a particularly significant culmination of McCarey's explorations of American life. Before his career lost its way in the 1950s, Leo McCarey proved one of the most successful and highly regarded directors in Hollywood. But his success was not due simply to his skill as a filmmaker; it also was the result of a wider cultural transformation in popular values. As an Irish American Catholic director, he helped articulate a pluralist revision of national community during the Depression. His films resonated with audiences because they communicated in a comic mode the social hopes and experiences of a nation being remade by ethnic and religious minorities. Their embrace of cultural flux, change, and combination reflected the wider reality of an Anglo-Saxon America dissolving before the new claims for participation by cultural outsiders. Aware of the power of ethnic and religious identities in American culture, however, McCarey harnessed pluralism to national resolve beginning in the late thirties. Ethnicity and religion became aligned to belief in a unified, harmonious country. In the process, they lost their protean powers to signal cultural change and social transformation.

Leo McCarey's films and career therefore exemplified the "politics of the American way" that Lary May has argued characterized American film between the 1930s and 1950s.[35] Long before Will Herberg wrote of a triple melting pot of Protestant, Catholic, and Jew, McCarey's movies imagined a nation predicated upon its ethnic and religious minorities.[36] But his films also demonstrated that American unity involved the erasure of alternative, more capacious conceptions of society that cultural outsiders helped signify during the Depression.

The consequences proved enormous. Public life diminished in the shadow of an expansive private sphere. Ethnic and religious identities fell subject to the nation's primacy and lost their critical voices. As a result, the energetic, comic spirit of thirties America faded. In its place emerged the uncertain laughter of a nation wondering if the comforts of cultural agreement could compensate for the thrill of screwball experimentation.

JOHN FORD'S IRISH AMERICAN CENTURY: ETHNICITY, CATHOLICISM, AND THE BORDERLANDS OF NATIONAL IDENTITY

Religion is an unbroken thread running through the films of John Ford, providing his movies with some of their most compelling moments. From the Yankee churchgoing of *Doctor Bull* (1933) to the devotions of industrial miners of *How Green Was My Valley* (1941) to the frontier worship of *My Darling Clementine* (1946), religious imagery deeply informs Ford's representation of human behavior and social community. His movies are also notable for the diverse assortment of religious faiths and traditions that appear in his depiction of the people of America, including Italian Catholics in New England, Mexican Catholics in the Southwest, Indians on the frontier, Mormons in the West, and Protestants in small towns. Taken together, these religious rituals, institutions, and identities indicate Ford's role within popular culture as a major observer of American religion.

That preoccupation was no accident but stemmed from Ford's own background as an ethnic Catholic. As the son of Irish immigrants growing up in Yankee Portland, Maine, he understood the complexities and tensions of religion in American life. He realized the power of religious values and beliefs both to organize and divide society. The representation of religion in his films therefore signified more than simply local detail in the larger canvas he painted of American life; rather, it was a crucial means through which Ford imagined national community and belonging.

Yet the religious significance of Ford's films remains a largely unexplored subject. Treatment of religion by film scholars pales in comparison to explorations of myth, ideology, and history.[1] Even recent cultural studies on Ford that address the construction of gender, race, and ethnicity pay scant attention to religion. This is particularly unfortunate because religious differences confirm Charles Ramirez Berg's insight that for all their problematic treatment of race, Ford's films provide a "richly textured multicultural vision."[2] The few works that acknowledge a Catholic dimension to his movies are exceptions, but they tend to focus on theological themes such as "sacramental imagination."[3] Understanding the centrality of Catholicism in Ford's films is about more than merely giving religion its due in the work of an important filmmaker, for Ford's significance in Hollywood's construction of popular American identity derives from, rather than diminishes, his sensitivity to ethnic and religious difference.

Recognizing the importance of religion in Ford's engagement with national myths and symbols also challenges notions that the Americanization of religious minorities entailed assimilation into an American way of life marked by individualism, freedom, and material success. Ford originally became a major filmmaker during the 1930s precisely by directing movies that questioned the legitimacy of Anglo-American, middle-class culture. His sensitivity to ethnic and religious difference actually placed him at the center of what Lary May has identified as the "recreation of America" by Hollywood cinema during the Depression.[4] From the early thirties to the eve of World War II, Ford directed films that leveled trenchant critiques against competitive individualism and class privilege, among them *Judge Priest, Stagecoach,* and *How Green Was My Valley.* In the place of traditional conceptions of American community rooted in Anglo-Puritan assumptions, he drew upon memories of ethnic Catholicism in the United States to imagine a cooperative, interdependent community that voiced the reformist aspirations materialized in the New Deal. Ford's movies therefore helped link religious identity to a politics of progressive change.

Only beginning in the forties did his films suggest a common faith that all citizens, including ethnic and religious minorities, shared. Ford's Irish Catholic sensibility proved particularly adept at turning cultural outsiders into signs of national strength in such films as *Fort Apache* and *Wagon Master.* In the process, however, pluralism was drained of its political challenge, reflecting a wider pattern in movies as May has shown.[5] Religion simultaneously lost its association with alternative social values and became an emblem of American virtue.

These postwar Ford movies manifested the enormous pressures toward cultural conformity demanded by America's emergence as a global superpower in the forties and fifties. Yet even during the height of Cold

War unity, these movies could strike a discordant note. Alongside their embrace of American community lurked continuing unease and skepticism. Some of his films questioned facile celebrations of national goodness and echoed his critique of social injustice from the 1930s. Films overlooked at the time, such as *The Sun Shines Bright* (1953) and *The Man Who Shot Liberty Valence* (1962), indicate that memories of religious difference and alienation could not be completely subsumed within consensus Americanism.

Ford's films thus exemplify the intense struggle over national definition that May argues characterized Hollywood cinema in the mid-twentieth century. They reveal that the postwar assimilation of religious minorities into the nation's mainstream represented a dramatic transformation of the relationship between ethnic, religious outsiders and American culture. The melting-pot ideal of the fifties rested upon a significant denial of the reformist, cooperative visions of American society that had emerged during the Depression, which ethnic artists such as Ford helped imagine. Recognizing the Catholic difference at the center of Ford's films illuminates the complexities of popular Americanization between the 1930s and 1950s, when the nation's pluralism represented the possibility of political and social change before succumbing to a Cold War consensus.[6]

Religion therefore proved central to Ford's search for a home in America as an ethnic outsider. It provided an essential vantage point from which he gave witness to the American experiment. On the surface, his films appeared to provide cinematic poems to the United States and its people. But ultimately, these movies revealed a troubled and contentious Catholic journey into the American Century.

Early Years

Born John Feeney in 1894 in Cape Elizabeth, Maine, just outside Portland, Ford grew up in a deeply Irish Catholic environment. When he was four, his family moved to Portland, where he would live until he left for Hollywood in 1914. His parents were both Irish immigrants who met in Portland, married, and raised six children to adulthood. His father, John Feeney, born in Spiddal, a small village outside Galway, in 1854, emigrated to the United States in 1872. Ford's mother, Barbara Curran, also born in Spiddal but in 1856, arrived in Portland in 1872 as well. Though John and Barbara were both born after the worst of the famine in their homeland, they surely were shaped by its profound consequences. They each brought memories and stories of an Ireland devastated by hunger and death. Displacement, exile, and the search for home—characteristic themes in the Irish imagination—would be central preoccupations in Ford's own renderings of the American experience as well.[7]

By the time of Ford's parents' arrival, Portland had become a prominent port city on the eastern seaboard of the United States. Ships from Europe as well as other American cities docked in the local harbor. Maine was actually the largest supplier of fish in the nation. In addition, rail lines connected Portland to the entire northeastern United States and beyond. The city consequently participated in a wider Atlantic economy that included New York, Boston, Canada, and England, trading in foodstuffs, timber, granite, and immigrants.[8]

Because of its far-reaching economic networks, Portland possessed a polyglot population. In addition to the Irish, who often worked the docks, the residents of Portland included Italians, French Canadians, Jews, and African Americans. Yet these immigrants and minorities remained outside the established social and political order dominated by Anglo-Protestants. Testimony to the cultural power of older Anglo elites in both the city and the state was the Prohibition law enacted in 1851. Indeed, ethnocultural tensions informed relations between the Protestant middle class and the newcomers. Ford's niece recalled that the Irish Catholics in Cape Elizabeth confronted the sting of bigotry, noting that "kids would run up and see if we had horns." Ford himself once claimed that he left Portland because of the difficulties Irish Americans faced. In the 1920s, the city enjoyed the dubious honor of being the headquarters of the Ku Klux Klan in Maine.[9]

Ford's youth reflected the social realities that were shaping Portland. His father, originally a farmer who took numerous jobs to support his growing family, eventually ran a series of saloons in the city. The saloons would be affected by the temperance politics in the city, occasionally being raided by the police due to the power of the dry forces in Portland. Not surprisingly, Ford's father became involved in city politics, with his saloons serving, in good Irish fashion, as a base for the local Democratic Party. And one of Ford's favorite relatives, Joseph Connolly, was a lawyer who, with the support of the Democratic Party, served as a judge on the municipal court and eventually was appointed by the governor of Maine to the Cumberland County Superior Court. Between his father's saloon-based ward politics and his uncle's ascent in the legal world, Ford imbibed a thoroughly Irish American political education, one that mingled localism, advocacy for social outsiders, and the tenets of the Democratic Party.[10]

In addition to politics, Catholicism provided the foundation of Ford's Irish Americanism. The Feeneys were practicing Catholics and belonged to St. Dominic's, a church built to serve the burgeoning Irish population in the city. According to one of Ford's most thorough biographers, his father hoped John would become a priest. Ford did, in fact, serve as an altar boy for morning Mass at St. Dominic's while a youngster, and that experience brought him particularly close to the ritual character of Catholicism.[11] The formative influence of this religious practice on his imagination was suggested in a letter he wrote to his wife, Mary, years later, where he described a Mass he attended aboard a ship to Ireland: "Just as the priest lifted the host, the clouds and fog lifted and three miles away we could see the shores of our beloved fatherland, 'The Emerald Isle,' as green and fresh as dew on the down. Even the priest stopped . . . [and] gazed."[12] Ford's dramatic description hinted at a liturgical basis for the sensitivity to the mise-en-scène and visual composition that informed much of his filmmaking.

His Catholic upbringing had a lasting impact on his personal life as well. Once in Hollywood, Ford joined the Knights of Columbus. He became a parishioner of the Church of the Blessed Sacrament in Hollywood and, later in life, St. Martin of Tours in Brentwood (also the parish of Frank Capra). As he increasingly struggled with alcoholism, Ford more than once signed oaths of abstinence that he had witnessed by priests. Further, according to one of his wife Mary's friends, the Ford house "was full of priests." Mary Ford, born a Presbyterian, would eventually convert to Catholicism. Because she had been divorced when she married Ford, the two were not married in the Catholic Church, but after the death of her first husband, she and Ford retook their marriage vows, administered by a priest. Finally, in one of the most direct intersections of Catholic practice and filmmaking in his career, Ford had priests say Mass on the set while filming *The Iron Horse* (1924) and *My Darling Clementine* (1946).[13]

The Irish family and Catholicism were formative elements in Ford's life, but unlike many other Catholics of the early twentieth century, he was not bound by a parochial setting. Evidence of the wider world that informed his life included the public school education he obtained in Portland. There, he encountered an awareness of his difference from his Anglo-American schoolmates. But he also experienced sympathetic teachers who encouraged his interest in American history, including the role of ethnic groups in the development of the nation.[14]

The legacies of Irish immigration, ethnic politics, Catholicism, and public schooling all intermingled in Ford's youth. He was a second-generation Irish American Catholic in a city defined by New England Anglo-Protestants. Raised in both a distinctly Catholic milieu and a multiethnic environment, Ford took with him to Hollywood the experiences and perspectives of a religious outsider straddling the complex fault lines of twentieth-century urban America.

Getting Started with the West

After graduating from high school in 1914, Ford set out for Los Angeles, seeking a job with his brother Francis, who had become a successful director of serials at Universal Studio. Under Frank, Ford was introduced to Hollywood, working in a series of acting, stunt, and assistant directorial jobs. By 1917, he had become a director in his own right at the studio. Particularly significant for Ford was his collaboration with the cowboy star Harry Carey Sr. Over the next four years, Ford worked intensely with Carey on a series of films, many of them westerns. The two men, along with Carey's new wife, Olive Golden, set up camp in the Newhall, outside Los Angeles, filming on location and returning only periodically to the greatly expanded studio that Universal chief Carl Laemmle had created to showcase his movie enterprise. In what must have seemed to the two of them in later years as a prelapsarian moment in Hollywood cinema, they filmed their movies in the open air and thrashed out ideas and stories at night under the stars while Olive kept a makeshift home for the film production crew. As Joseph McBride has noted, this period proved enormously fruitful for Ford and Carey. They collaborated on twenty-four films between 1917 and 1921, including five feature-length movies in 1917, seven in 1918, and seven more in 1919.[15]

The older Carey had a profound influence on the young Ford. Carey's low-key, homespun interpretation of the western hero—a contrast to the highly stylized, moralistic figure presented by William S. Hart—appealed to Ford's sense of Irish realism. McBride also suggests the Carey characters in these early Ford films embodied a kind of noble outlaw, a hero outside a corrupt society who "confronted class prejudices and enabled society to behave in a more humane manner"—a figure with whom the Irish American Catholic outsider Ford could easily identify.[16]

Given the centrality of westerns in this early collaboration with Carey, it is not surprising they assumed a significant role in Ford's later career. The western functioned as a touchstone by which Ford would constantly take measure of his deeply ambivalent attitudes toward success, home, and society. As the son of immigrants seeking to make his own way in the world, Ford assumed a workmanlike attitude toward the business of moviemaking, turning out popular serials and longer films in quick succession. But in addition to providing the immediate opportunity to develop his craft, Hollywood also functioned as the arena in which he began to negotiate his relationship to his ethnic past and his American identity. Within the emerging film studio system, the western was the primary form through which Ford pursued his own ambitions. Thus, beyond its national and ideological importance, the western genre possessed deep personal significance for Ford. Every later western that he made was a return not only to his early years as a filmmaker but also to the complex emotional and cultural landscape of his second-generation Irish Americanism.[17] As he left home in Portland, breaking from the ethnic Catholic environment of his youth, moviemaking and in particular the western genre provided a psychic context to negotiate cultural identity. On the West Coast, the more established Harry Carey offered the young, uncertain Ford a surrogate father, standing in for the real, immigrant one he had left behind in Portland as he pursued his own migration to the new world of Hollywood. And just as Ford left his Irish father to support himself, he also left Carey in order to prove his worth in the wider film industry. Westerns therefore carried a particularly complex emotional and cultural resonance for Ford, etched in ethnic memory, ambition, pain, and ambivalence.

Many commentators have noted the psychologically nuanced and rich character studies of Ford's westerns, yet far less recognized are the cultural origins of his achievements in this genre. But in observing that "the frontier in Ford's cinema is not only a geographical place but a psychological state of mind" born from Ford's ethnic outsider status, Paul Giles insightfully recognizes the cultural basis for this achievement. Ford's westerns emerged out of an encounter between his identity as a second-generation Irish American and the emerging Hollywood film system in which familiar idioms of American mythology became the imaginative terrain on which to negotiate ethnic, religious, and generational tensions.[18]

The end of the close, familial relationship between Ford and Carey in the open spaces outside Los Angeles also marked Ford's ascent into mainstream success.[19] In 1921, Ford left Universal and signed a contract at Fox, seeking to move beyond making westerns. His marriage to Mary McBryde Smith, a Presbyterian woman from an old southern family, also represented a preference for domestic stability over the loose, independent ways he had enjoyed with the Careys. As much as Ford liked to pose as a rebel, his marriage and new movie contract indicated a desire for respectability and security. For the rest of the decade, Ford served as a proficient, commercially reliable director at Fox. His most important film, *The Iron Horse* (1924), another western, celebrated Anglo-American progress, which, as Lee Lourdeaux has noted, was appropriate for the reigning conservative cultural ethos of the era.[20]

Spiritual and Political

Ford was a successful and dependable director in the twenties, but the early 1930s entailed a dramatic change of fortune. Both Ford and Hollywood experienced profound crisis in the initial years of the Depression. Ticket sales plummeted, and studios scrambled to survive as Americans cut back on movie attendance. The film industry quickly realized that the formulas that had brought box office success in the twenties failed to sustain moviegoers' interests when national prosperity gave way to social collapse. Consequently, producers were forced to find new stories and stars to win back their audiences. Filmmakers discovered that Americans were eager for movies that voiced the discontent many felt about their society. Gangster movies, anarchic comedies, and "fallen" women's stories all enjoyed enormous success. Their hard-edged realism and skepticism toward middle-class respectability captured the mood of a nation hungry for alternatives to conventional portraits about American progress and prosperity.[21]

However, at a time when Edward G. Robinson and James Cagney catapulted to fame by giving a new, urban ethnic look to modern America cinema with films such as *Little Caesar* and *The Public Enemy*, the Irish American Ford experienced deep personal and creative malaise. As a sign of this emotional confusion, in early 1931 Ford took his friend and actor George O'Brien on an extended trip to the Far East, providing the director with an excuse to engage in a punishing, self-destructive drinking binge.[22] Back home from his Far East trip, Ford's problems only deepened. Fox loaned him to Samuel Goldwyn to direct *Arrowsmith*. However, this time, in a very uncharacteristic move, Ford began drinking while the film was in production. Alarmed at this change in the director, Goldwyn had him removed from the movie. Ford's home studio, Fox, was forced to pay back to Goldwyn the fees it had earned for loaning Ford out. In turn, Fox terminated Ford's contract in late 1931. As Joseph McBride has noted, "Ford's career had hit its lowest ebb."[23] The director responded to this humiliation by embarking on another long voyage, going to Hawaii and the Philippines with Mary from late 1931 to early 1932. Yet on this trip, his self-destructive tendencies again emerged. Ford's drinking become so dangerous that his wife had him hospitalized to recover.[24]

His determination to escape, evidenced in the long journeys to the Pacific, his extensive and dangerous drinking binges, and the loss of his studio contract, suggests that Ford suffered a profound spiritual crisis in the early thirties. As Tag Gallagher has noted, Ford's "personal depression was not financial but moral."[25] His achievements of the previous decade—his development as a filmmaker, his commercial successes and critical acclaim, his ability (unlike his brother Frank) to navigate the Hollywood studio system—all had unraveled. Indeed, Ford's behavior indicated a deep ambivalence to the achievements he had won. After more than a decade of proving himself in Hollywood, the Irish Catholic filmmaker was uncertain as to the meaning of his ambitions, just as the nation as a whole confronted the collapse of the New Era illusions of the twenties.

Ford's spiritual breakdown at the beginning of the decade suggested the director initially responded to the changes in Hollywood and America with confusion. Mainstream success in the previous decade had not prepared him to take advantage of shifts in the popular tastes of a nation in crisis. But in 1933 and continuing through the Depression era, he struck back with a vengeance with a series of films, beginning with *Pilgrimage* (1933) and continuing through to *How Green Was My Valley* (1941). Ford would move forward by going backward, drawing upon alternative ethnic and religious memories to construct new portraits of American community grounded in social justice and the perspective of religious outsiders.

In doing so, Ford participated in the broader transformation of popular Americanism in the 1930s. As Lary May has shown, Hollywood became a major public sphere where a "new multicultural republic," characterized by ethnic pluralism and social reform, moved to the center of popular representation. Filmmakers such as William Dieterle, William Wyler, Mervyn LeRoy, and Frank Capra, who came from European Jewish and Italian Catholic backgrounds, moved to the forefront of Hollywood by creating movies that privileged urban, ethnic, and class experiences of modern life. Collectively, they and many others turned movies into a forum where aspirations for a more equitable and just America assumed popular expression.[26] Ford's own renewal as a filmmaker, therefore, coincided with and exemplified the new ethnic remaking of modern American imagination in the thirties.

Catholic Margins, Puritan Centers

Ford's participation in the new critical Americanism of Hollywood in the 1930s rested heavily upon an Irish Catholic awareness of religious and cultural difference in national life. Rarely employing them as the primary focus of any one film, Ford nonetheless repeatedly turned to religious institutions and practices in his movies to elaborate their social vision. Indeed, his films articulated their critique of middle-class culture and suggested more inclusive alternatives *through* religious imagery and characters, turning his movies into sustained Depression-era reflections on the intersection of religion and society in America. Religion, in fact, provided a crucial means by which Ford's films mapped social identity, staged cultural contests, and expressed moral and spiritual meanings.

A central feature of Ford's use of religion was its delineation of social hierarchy and cultural tension. Mainstream, middle-class society in many of his films was marked as Protestant, particularly Puritan. Joseph McBride's observation that "Ford's portraits of Protestant reformers and Boston Yankees are caustic in the extreme" is particularly applicable to his films of the Depression era, when Ford was especially attuned to class politics.[27] The respectable social center of the Fordian world was often associated with churchgoing, scripture quoting, and personal piety. Yet this dominant culture was also depicted as exclusionary, static, and emotionally dead. In contrast, the social margins were marked through Catholic signs in such films as *Doctor Bull* and *Stagecoach*. These sites, in turn, were associated with alternative values of mutuality, renewal, and festivity.

Ford's films made great use of the emotional and symbolic power of religious space to dramatize these social differences. The mise-en-scène of these films was notable for the inclusion of religious signs to elaborate character and stage conflict. Churches functioned as significant public arenas, where community members gathered together or laid bare underlying social tensions, as in *How Green Was My Valley*. Other spaces, including homes and alternative venues such as inns, also assumed religious, particularly Catholic, significance through the use of Catholic iconography and material culture. Such Catholic spaces were associated with life-affirming activities, for example, childbirth and collective celebration. Place therefore was laden with religious association in Ford's movies and was a central means by which they represented America as a religiously diverse and conflicted society.

Ford's films of the thirties thus rendered society as a struggle between

Puritan centers and implicitly ethnic Catholic margins. Their explorations of social conflict pitting elites against "the people" consequently resonated with additional cultural references to the country's contentious religious history. Because public religion was usually signified in Anglo-Puritan terms in Ford's movies, the true moral leader of society was often a "secular" figure, such as a lawyer or doctor, who represented a more authentic generosity of spirit and concern for the dispossessed than religiously identified characters. This shift in moral focus from representatives of mainstream religion to civic figures reflected the ethnic skepticism toward Anglo-Puritan virtue that ran throughout Ford's movies. At times, Ford's heroes were even located within a recognizably Catholic devotional world of crucifixes and religious art, as in *Doctor Bull* and *Stagecoach,* exemplifying what May has identified as characters of "interpenetrating opposites" who combined progressive American ideals and cooperative values of cultural minorities.[28] In the case of Ford's films, this cultural exchange produced a public-minded citizen accented by a Catholic ethos of corporate mercy and spiritual vulnerability.

Ford's heroic American figures of the thirties actually echoed a traditional Catholic priority of communal good over individual achievement through their willingness to serve the needs of others. Characters such as Abe Lincoln, Judge Billy Priest, and Dr. Bull were members of mainstream society who were alienated from their own class and who identified with the lowly and forgotten. They were frequently haunted by personal loss, which translated into an acceptance of weakness in others, finding in the outcasts of society a mirror of their own emotional displacement. Their acquaintance with suffering also gave them a more inclusive understanding of community than that felt by respectable members of society who espoused progress, achievement, and success.

Ford's attention to the plight of social outcasts—a major preoccupation of his Depression-era films—therefore suggested as much an ethnic Catholic moral economy as it did a thirties consciousness. His films are populated with characters such as Dallas in *Stagecoach* and the Joads in *The Grapes of Wrath* who were social sinners in the eyes of an older, middle-class Protestant moral order that valued sobriety, restraint, and individual effort. Outlaws, prostitutes, failed doctors, poor farmers—frequent figures in Ford's movies—all shared an exclusion from proper, respectable society. Yet their social marginalization led them into collaborative alliances with others that indicated a need for communal cooperation over private individualism.

Through the rendering of social hierarchy, depictions of mise-en-scène, and dramatization of character, Ford's films of the thirties materialized a hybrid Catholic sensibility. They placed the nation under ethnic Catholic judgment and found it wanting. Fusing a Catholic ethos of redemptive suffering with a wider Depression-era concern for the people, they produced an Americanism organized around social justice and the incorporation of cultural outsiders. By creating films steeped in the dominant myths of the nation (such as the western frontier and small-town Americana) but imbued with ethnic Catholic memory, Ford embodied a key agent of twentieth-century American culture—the Irish Catholic outsider as insider. During the thirties, that shifting alignment between ethnic religious minority and mainstream America entailed the articulation of cultural critique and social reform through representations of religious difference.

The Ethnic Deal and the Thirties Imaginary

Indicative of the spiritual preoccupations that informed his conversion to a politically engaged artist, in 1933 Ford made *Pilgrimage,* his first significant film of the decade. The story of a strong-willed mother, Hannah Jessup, who cannot let go of her adult son, Jim, the film offers a powerful tale of destructive family relationships, transformation, and redemption. Consumed by her own love for Jim, Hannah cannot acknowledge the legitimacy of his desire to marry a woman from a nearby farm. Instead, she secretly enlists Jim in the army. He is sent overseas during World War I and is killed. Hannah's own selfish love results in the devastating loss of the one person she wanted for herself. Her despair is only deepened when she participates in a Gold Star Mothers' pilgrimage to France to attend a memorial for fallen American soldiers. Trapped within her own spiritual torment and guilt, Hannah is able to find redemption when, one lonely night, she prevents another young man from committing suicide. She assists him in returning to his girlfriend and prevents his mother from ruining the man's plans for marriage. Hannah returns to her hometown, where she reunites with her son's lover and the young woman's son, who turns out to be Jim's own boy and therefore Hannah's grandson.

A tale of parents and children that explores ethnic preoccupations of intergenerational conflict, *Pilgrimage* also portrays the destructive impulses of selfish individual desires upon home and community. Hannah is one of Ford's most complex characters, embodying powerful familial emotions that turn back upon themselves with devastating results. The home—a perennial value in the Fordian world—becomes a claustrophobic force of emotional violence. Hannah has to confront the limitations of her own certainties and realize the value of self-transformation and adaptation to a changing world, symbolized by her adult son's desire for another woman. In its grappling with the contradictions of family and home, the film also suggests Ford's own search for new alternatives in a morally confusing and unstable society.

Pilgrimage marked the beginning of a new period in which Ford responded to the social crises around him. After this movie, he began a fruitful collaboration with Will Rogers that resulted in three important films, *Doctor Bull* (1933), *Judge Priest* (1934), and *Steamboat 'Round the Bend* (1935). Rogers's laconic, down-to-earth style that voiced the hopes and concerns of ordinary folk influenced many of Ford's later films, including *Stagecoach* and *Wagon Master*.[29] His tragic death in an airplane crash in 1935 dealt a devastating loss to a remarkable artistic friendship. As evidence of the esteem Ford possessed for Rogers, the Catholic director had a memorial Mass said for the actor when he learned of his death.[30]

Working with Rogers, who laced homespun humor with liberal politics, allowed Ford to combine his own outsider sensibility with the common–man ethos of traditional populism. The three films they made together represented Ford's examination of small-town America from an ethnic Catholic perspective. Their depiction of American communities riven by religious hypocrisy and zealotry, cultural prejudice, and class injustice offered a sustained critique of the cult of traditional Americana that had characterized the nativist assault on immigrants, ethnics, Catholics, and Jews in the 1920s.[31] In contrast to the pious, righteous characters that dominated conservative evocations of small-town life, these films suggested a new kind of hero, a mainstream figure, alienated from his own middle-class environment, who identified with the cultural margins and social outcasts. Not surprisingly, both Rogers and Ford enthusiastically embraced Franklin Delano Roosevelt, who was often accused by his enemies of being a "traitor" to his class in the early 1930s.[32]

Central to these films' portrait of Americana are religious imagery and characters. Indeed, *Doctor Bull*, *Judge Priest*, and *Steamboat 'Round the Bend* all make important use of religion to critique social injustice and imagine new forms of social connection. The very title of *Judge Priest*, for instance, associates the compassionate and heroic judge, played by Rogers, who defends the town's social outcasts, with religious connotations. As it happens, the judge does play a priestly role as a celibate man who mediates the conflicts in the town, leading the community to real-ize its potential for decency and inclusion. In contrast, the town's elites are identified with the local church, keeping up their moral respectability, all the while protecting their community from contamination by social outcasts.

Steamboat 'Round the Bend includes a character known as the New Mo-ses (Berton Churchill, who in the 1930s often played unlikable characters in Ford films), an evangelical preacher. Rogers captains a steamboat on the Mississippi in the late nineteenth century, which functions as an al-ternative community to the intolerant, bigoted social order that exists in the regions the steamboat traverses. As Martin Rubin has noted, the so-cial order on the banks of the Mississippi that Rogers and his steamboat travel "is represented almost exclusively by Puritan images," including the New Moses and the morals committee of angry men who board the steamboat with guns in an attempt to shut down a popular entertainment show.[33]

But it is the first film in the Ford-Rogers trilogy, *Doctor Bull,* that most clearly reflects Ford's ethnic Catholic rendering of small-town America. Unlike the other two Rogers films, the setting of *Doctor Bull* is New Eng-land, the region of the country most familiar to Ford. Indeed, the imagi-nary town in which the film takes place, New Winton, dominated by Anglo-American elites with social margins signified in Catholic terms, echoes the Portland, Maine, of Ford's youth. And as was characteris-tic of the director's most prominent explorations of community, *Doctor Bull* utilizes the representation of religion to elaborate a critical vision of America.

The film offers the story of a doctor (Will Rogers) who is more con-cerned with helping the destitute and broken than winning the approval of the town's stifling respectable class. The movie's early sequence, set in the town's mainline church and adjoining graveyard, not only communi-cates the icy relationship between the doctor and New Winton's "best peo-ple" but also identifies the Anglo-Protestant character of the town's social elites. Alienated from his own genteel New England middle-class society, Bull actually feels more comfortable with the people he doctors, including the poor and the workers as well the town's young college students, all of whom live far beyond New Winton's proper society.

One sequence in particular vividly captures the film's use of religious difference to imagine Bull's connections with the town's cultural margins. As the doctor travels to a night call, he is pulled over by men in front of a house where a woman is about to give birth. Bull enters the home and finds it crowded with people and alive with noise. In the foreground is a table around which sit numerous men with bottles of wine and glasses. Unable to speak English, the Italian inhabitants of the house are nonetheless able to communicate their need. The room is replete with Catholic imagery. On one wall is a painting of Christ on the cross, on another there is a crucifix and a holy water container.

This space therefore is noticeably ethnic and Catholic. Drawing upon the convention of Italians as emotional people, the setting is nevertheless also dramatically different in tone and meaning than the earlier Anglo-Protestant imagery. Here, after Bull has successfully delivered a baby boy, one of the men offers him a glass of wine, which he gladly takes. He tells the Italian men that he likes delivering Italian babies because he is always offered something more than coffee. Unlike in the earlier scene with New Winton's respectable churchgoers, Bull is welcomed by the working-class Italian Catholics with enthusiasm. He is invited to share in the joy of the family. This scene, surrounded with traditional Catholic imagery, is a space of new life, festivity, wine, and connection, an explicit contrast with the emotional and moral frigidity Bull faced at the cemetery of the mainline Protestant church earlier in the movie. Locating the doctor in the ethnic space of Italian immigrants, the film utilized Catholicism to represent values of reciprocity and generosity as alternatives to the privileged self-sufficiency of New Winton's elites.

In addition to his role as a doctor, however, Bull is also the town's health inspector. He finds himself under attack from New Winton's most successful businessman, Herbert Banning (Berton Churchill), who rails against Bull for standing in the way of his plan for a major commercial development in town. The doctor is skeptical of Banning's twenties-style business boosterism, since Bull has cared for one of the man's employees who had been worked to exhaustion. Yet Banning mobilizes public opinion against Bull and calls for a vote to relieve him of his duties as health inspector. Bull is forced to step down, signaling a triumph of the elites in town. In the end, however, the doctor is vindicated when his efforts to help an injured worker, Joe, prove successful, and the town's paper celebrates him as a hero.

In its evocation of a New England town, *Doctor Bull* critiqued that most sacrosanct symbol within the collective American imagination—the small-town community—to intimate alternative social possibilities. At a time when the Depression had caused many Americans to question basic assumptions about their nation, Ford contributed his own rethinking of Americanism. In his assessment, the traditional guardians of national community—the descendants of Puritan Christianity, businesspeople, the respectable middle class—were deeply flawed. Bull's enemies—cultural elites, the religiously pious, and promoters of private business—embodied an older Anglo-American world that had lost its authority. In their place, the film offered Doctor Bull and his expanded sense of community, which included ethnic Catholics, workers, and the poor.

Tellingly, at the end of the movie when Bull boards a train out of New Winton, a small group of friends including the working-class couple he had aided sees him off. Though Joe has regained his ability to walk, a cut from Bull to the station platform shows the young man walking with a cane. That image of vulnerability both echoes Bull's own life of struggle with the town's sanctimonious elites and signified the "small" people on the margins with whom the alienated doctor found support and encouragement. At the depths of the Depression, the film turned weakness into strength in order to broaden the boundaries of American identity.

The social critique of *Doctor Bull* reflected a broader turn to the left on Ford's part during the 1930s. Throughout the decade, Ford worked with a number of other prominent liberals and progressives in Hollywood besides Rogers. These individuals included the screenwriter Philip Dunne; Liam Flaherty, the Irish novelist and author of *The Informer*; screenwriter Dudley Nichols; and Walter Wanger, a maverick film producer who worked with Ford on *Stagecoach*.[34]

Off screen, Ford also became politically active in a number of liberal causes. In 1933, he helped form the Screen Directors Guild, a union to protect directors against the studios. At the time, Ford gave a fiery speech calling for solidarity of the directors with other workers in the film industry, condemning the banks for engaging in a "sitdown strike" to provoke a "financial crisis" so that "wages and wage earners [could be pushed back to] 1910."[35]

Ford's participation in the labor struggles in Hollywood led to involvement in additional liberal efforts throughout the decade. He helped found the Motion Picture Artists Committee to Aid Republican Spain. His support for the Loyalists was particularly striking given how most Catholics of the era opposed the republican government in Spain. Writing to his nephew, Bob, a member of the International Brigade in Spain in 1937, Ford asserted, "*Politically*, I am a definite socialist democrat—*always* left."[36]

The late thirties saw Ford deepen his support for progressive politics.

In 1938, he served as vice president, along with Philip Dunne, of the Motion Picture Democratic Committee. He became active in the Hollywood Anti-Nazi League, an organization of liberals opposed to fascism and supportive of the Spanish Loyalists. In January 1938, Ford spoke against Nazis to crowds at the Shrine Auditorium in Los Angeles. He also joined the picket line in support of the Newspaper Guild workers striking against the *Hollywood Citizen-News*. These activities indicated that the social justice Americanism of Ford's films emerged from a wider concern for reform during the Depression years.[37]

Liberal politics gave Ford a means by which to direct his own sense of cultural alienation as a religious outsider into a broader critique of social inequality. They also proved quite beneficial to his career. Collaborations with progressives helped sharpen his own social understanding and resulted in several well-received and commercially successful films in the midthirties, such as *Judge Priest* and *Steamboat 'Round the Bend*. Particularly significant, Ford won the Academy Award for best director for his version of the Irish Marxist Liam Flaherty's novel *The Informer* in 1935, thereby establishing his reputation as a serious artist in the eyes of both critics and the movie studios.

In the late thirties, Ford's artistic skill and political beliefs converged in a series of influential films, beginning with *Stagecoach* in 1939 and culminating with *How Green Was My Valley* in 1941. The western, Abe Lincoln, the colonial settlement of the American frontier, and the plight of Dust Bowl victims and industrial workers all dominated Ford's imagination during a short but intensely creative span of three years. Not surprisingly, these films, which also included *Young Mr. Lincoln* (1939) and *The Grapes of Wrath* (1940), have been dubbed Ford's Popular Front period. But if his work with Dudley Nichols and Philip Dunne led him into an alliance with the Popular Front, these left-wing films possessed decidedly ethnic Catholic accents.[38]

In fact, the confident liberalism of the late thirties provided a second important context in which Ford could elaborate his ethnic Catholic Americanism. Just as Rogers's heartland populism earlier in the decade allowed Ford to explore small-town Americana through the lens of a religious minority, the Popular Front's cultural ambitions gave Ford an opportunity to blend an ethnic outsider sensibility with modern progressivism. Two films in particular, *Stagecoach* and *How Green Was My Valley*, demonstrated the role of Catholicism in Ford's revision of the national imaginary in the era of reform.

Stagecoach is considered one of Ford's most important achievements, but the role of religion in the film has been widely overlooked. Joseph McBride's insight about the movie's "metaphorical reflection of the American immigrant experience" needs to be extended to recognize the film's awareness of religion within that history.[39] The movie's story of a group of people thrown together on a stagecoach, traveling from Tonto to Lordsburg, Arizona, across hostile Indian territory, relies heavily upon religious associations and signs. *Stagecoach* offers a cultural journey from an Anglo-Puritan society of intolerance and individualism to a New Deal community of mutual assistance. Through the genre formula of the western, Ford proposes an ethnic and religious mediation of progressive impulses reshaping American identity during the Depression. If *Doctor Bull* critiqued small-town America from the perspective of ethnic, religious outsiders, Ford's late-thirties western shows what an alternative social community could look like. The cultural margins are allied with a new collective realm, and beyond that, they actually infuse and transform it with their cooperative values.

Stagecoach signals its revisionist interpretation of American religion and culture through its early sequence set in Tonto, the starting place of the trip across the frontier. An initial pan shot of the town's main street includes a church prominently positioned in the background. That image helps visually describe the town in religious terms. But the introduction of two main characters, Dallas (Claire Trevor), a prostitute, and Doc Boone (Thomas Mitchell), the irascible, boozy town doctor, suggests the particular character of religion that prevails in Tonto.

Dallas is marched out of Tonto by the town's guardians of traditional morality, the Ladies of the Law and Order League. Recognizing Doc Boone, who has also suffered the moral opprobrium of the Victorian women for his drinking, Dallas pleads for his assistance. Taking her by the arm, Doc tells her they are the "victims of a foul disease of social prejudice." As they are being run out of town, a jaunty rendering of the traditional religious hymn "Gather at the River" on the sound track musically subverts the moral piety of the women and associates their treatment of Dallas and Doc with religious discord.

The opening scenes of *Stagecoach*, therefore, establish its narrative tension between elites and "common folk" by drawing heavily upon cultural memories of religious conflict in American life. With their intolerance of Doc's drinking, their self-righteous treatment of Dallas, and their pious demeanor, the Ladies of the Law and Order League suggest the Anglo-Puritan efforts to impose moral order on the country that during the 1920s culminated in Prohibition and immigration restrictions. The expulsion of Doc and Dallas mark these two characters as religious and social Others to this traditional Americanism. Originating in Tonto, a cauldron of moral intolerance and prejudice, the journey begins as an escape from religious and cultural oppression.

Once the stagecoach sets out for Lordsburg, it becomes a vehicle for competing social relations and values. The real conflict of the film is not between the travelers and hostile Indians, looming on the horizon, but among the members of the coach itself. The banker Gatewood (Berton Churchill), who has stolen money from his own bank, as well as two other characters, Mrs. Mallory (Louise Platt), the wife of a cavalry officer traveling alone, and Hatfield (John Carradine), a shady southern gambler, epitomize an older, corrupt, and intolerant middle-class culture of individual effort, competition, and propriety. The outcasts Doc, Dallas, and Ringo (John Wayne), the escaped convict tracking down the killers of his family, express what Robert S. McElvaine has described as a moral economy of cooperation and mutuality.[40]

Stagecoach utilizes ethnic and religious references to dramatize this social struggle over democratic community. Gatewood the banker spouts off about the importance of business for America, echoing traditional conservative apologetics for the marketplace, all the while clutching a briefcase that holds the money he has stolen from his own bank. In his arrogant treatment of others, he embodies business-class smugness and hypocrisy. Mrs. Mallory, who barely speaks throughout the movie, symbolizes the cultural condescension of genteel silence toward disreputable people such as Dallas. Hatfield plays the role of the chivalrous southern man who protects Mallory from contamination by the social underclass. Gatewood, Mallory, and Hatfield thus extend the social elitism of Tonto's Anglo-Puritanism into the stagecoach itself.

Conversely, Doc's implicitly Irish character becomes more apparent as the film progresses through his extensive drinking, his loquaciousness, his subversive humor, and a jaded facade that hides a deep and compassionate sentimentality. "I'm not only a philosopher but a fatalist," he announces during the luncheon rest stop when the travelers debate whether to continue their journey to Lordsburg, while also telling Dallas he is the last person worthy of judging her own desires for happiness. Dallas and Ringo are more conventional western types, but their own marginalization complements Doc's failed efforts at respectability.

The ethnic allusions in *Stagecoach* are accompanied by sacramental and religious references that impart a moral character to the alliance of outcasts suffering the contempt of the coach's genteel travelers. The meal scene at the rest stop, for instance, uses Ringo's serving of food to Dallas to suggest a communion of the lowly. Similarly, the passing of the flask of water between the outlaw and the prostitute back in the coach connotes a biblical symbol of moral generosity the two share, in contrast to the selfishness of the respectable Mrs. Mallory and Hatfield.

Stagecoach's investment in ethnicity and religion is particularly demonstrated in the representation of the distinctly Catholic space of the second rest stop, Apache Wells. The use of Catholic detail in this segment of the movie is especially notable because the sequence represents a key moment of conversion for many of the travelers. The segment begins with a camera shot of the opened gate of the rest stop as the coach approaches. Spanish voices, belonging to the men in charge of the gate, are heard on the sound track, marking this as a space of ethnic difference in contrast to the Anglo-Puritanism of Tonto. The Mexican Catholic character of this part of the film is riddled with contradictions. On the one hand, the scene trades upon stereotypes of Mexicans as untrustworthy. On the other, one of the Mexicans is a friend of Ringo's, deepening the film's alliance of outsiders to include explicitly ethnic characters. Even more, this Mexican space is the site of new life and rebirth.

As she disembarks from the coach, the proper Mrs. Mallory collapses on the ground. The men quickly arrange for her to be taken to a bedroom at the inn. To the surprise of everyone else, she is actually pregnant and has started her labor. Doc Boone (improbably) sobers up enough to deliver her baby. Dallas assists and tends to the mother after the birth. A shot of Boone and Dallas in the room where Mallory lies prominently displays a crucifix and kneeler in the background.[41] In this room marked as Catholic space, the two social outcasts care for the genteel woman who has demonstrated her contempt for both of them throughout the journey. A later shot reinforces the Catholic practice of mercy by arranging Dallas in the foreground combing Mallory's hair while above her shoulder is the crucifix in the background. Visually, Dallas appears to be at the foot of the cross, selflessly ministering to the bodily needs of the woman who rebuffed her earlier offers of help.

Similar to *Doctor Bull*'s linkage of the town doctor and the poor Italian family, this scene in *Stagecoach* articulates new life, ethnic Catholicism, and compassionate personalism. The Apache Wells segment functions as

Stagecoach (1939): Dallas (Claire Trevor) at the foot of the cross, assisting Mrs. Mallory (Louise Platt), who has just given birth. Courtesy of Photofest.

a crucial moment in the film where the outcasts assume leadership and display alternative values that sustain human connection and community, in opposition to the prejudice and individualism of the middle-class travelers. Even Hatfield, who had aligned himself with Gatewood and Mrs. Mallory at the luncheon, recognizes Doc Boone's work in delivering the baby, indicating a changed attitude toward the people he once dismissed.

The transformation that occurs among the travelers in the Mexican Catholic rest stop is extended in the following scenes when the coach must quickly leave to escape the approaching Indians. To make a swift escape, cooperation is necessary. Hatfield realizes that he must assist the very individuals he earlier thought worthless. The characteristics of mutuality and selflessness that Doc, Dallas, and Ringo have demonstrated throughout the film become the means by which the coach survives. Working as a team, the travelers are able to ford a river and keep ahead of the pursuing Indians. Interdependence defeats the elitism with which the journey began.

Once the merits of a cooperative ethos, in stark contrast to a bankrupt individualism, have been demonstrated in the Mexican Catholic Apache Wells and the river-crossing scenes, generic conventions of the western quickly move to the forefront. Thus, the cavalry bursts upon the scene to rescue the coach from attacking Indians and provide melodramatic excitement. But the arrival of the coach in Lordsburg provides a final accounting of the characters. Gatewood is arrested for his crime; Mrs. Mallory lies prostrate on a stretcher, passive and ashamed before Dallas as she is taken off the coach. Hatfield has been killed by an Indian arrow in the earlier attack on the coach. All the characters who had represented the established, traditional Anglo-Puritan Americanism have been brought low by the time the coach arrives at its destination.

In good western fashion, Ringo wins his shoot-out with the Plummer boys, the men responsible for killing his family. But if the Lordsburg sequence entails a certain kind of rough justice for the villains, the final scenes of *Stagecoach* also suggest the town is a place of charity as well. Ringo keeps his promise to Dallas to return for her, even after having walked her back to her bordello in the red-light district of town. Then, at the conclusion of the film, Curly, the sheriff, and Doc Boone, in another sign of collaboration, arrange a horse and wagon for Dallas and Ringo to escape Lordsburg and cross the border to Ringo's ranch in Catholic Mexico. As they ride off, Doc quips that the couple is "saved from the blessings of civilization." With this concluding scene, *Stagecoach* tempers the American frontier justice of Lordsburg with the unseen promise of Mexico and gratuitous acts of mercy.

Some critics have found Ringo and Dallas's escape to be evidence of the film's inability to imagine a viable, alternative social order to the advancing, individualistic American society.[42] Yet the film's investment in ethnic Catholicism suggests that Doc Boone's quip about being saved from the blessings of civilization is actually a cultural critique of Anglo-Puritan America. The line reflects and sums up the film's entire ethnic outsider sensibility. The flight into Catholic Mexico is less a failure of social imagination than an expression of a transnational ethnic religious perspective that situates American identity in a broader cultural landscape.[43] *Stagecoach* critiques national purity in favor of an Americanized hybridity in which the values of the margins, signified in ethnic Catholic terms, suggest the resources necessary to sustain humane community. Just as the Mexican Apache Wells exists inside Arizona, Ringo's ranch operates on the other side of the national boundary. The film's social vision is far from absent. Rather, it is expressed in the border-crossing sensibilities in which ethnicity, the alternative moral ethos of Catholicism, and liberal social justice continually traffic through and within each other.

Stagecoach demonstrates that Ford's renewed interest in the national mythology of the western harnessed ethnic and religious memories to imagine a more inclusive Americanism. *How Green Was My Valley,* made two years later, in 1941, manifests the ethnic religious mediation of Ford's critical portrait of industrial capitalism. In fact, the film, about a devout, working-class family in a mining community, represented the culmination of Ford's work as a public theologian of Hollywood's New Deal America.

The ethnic character of Richard Llewellyn's novel, set in Wales, about a family of coal miners clearly spoke to Ford's own sensibilities. As he told Philip Dunne, the screenwriter, "The Welsh are just another lot of micks and biddies, only Protestant."[44] Ford surely sensed a family resemblance between the Welsh Protestant Morgans and the Irish Catholics. Though set overseas, *How Green Was My Valley* resonates with ethnic and working-class struggles in thirties America. The film portrays industrial capitalism, cultural intolerance, and religious rigidity as the primary threats to life-affirming traditions of family and communal life. Thus, although the locale is Old World, the movie represents a transference to a foreign setting of very American concerns about economic justice, workers, and ethnic communities of the Depression era. Indicative of the film's intention to speak directly to class and ethnic concerns in America is the fact that its producers, Twentieth Century–Fox, held special prerelease showings of the movie in the mining cities of Scranton and Wilkes-Barre, Pennsylvania, in late 1941.[45] That the film became a commercial and critical success further indicates the American appeal of a movie about Welsh miners.

The film depicts the human consequences of economic exploitation through the story of the religiously devout, working-class Morgan family—the patriarch, Gwilym (Donald Crisp); his strong-willed wife, Beth (Sara Allgood); their adult sons, who follow in their father's footsteps into the mines; a daughter, Angharad (Maureen O'Hara); and their youngest son, Huw (Roddy McDowall). Easily mistaken for nostalgia for a simpler era, *How Green Was My Valley* actually suggests the complex interrelationships between ethnic, class, and religious identities in modern industrial society.[46] Its extensive use of religious ritual, for instance, conveys the deeply communal bonds of ethnic, working people. But the conflict between a harsh, unforgiving church deacon (Arthur Shields) and the Morgan sons, who seek to organize a labor union among the miners, also dramatizes the political dimensions of religious faith. The deacon's condemnations of their efforts and his belief that the liberal town minister (Walter Pidgeon) has no role in the labor dispute show the use of religion as a weapon of class domination. Conversely, a Morgan son's references to scripture justifying the rights of workers communicates a socially conscious and politically engaged form of Christianity.[47] Even the death of Gwilym when a mine collapses is rendered in religious terms, imbuing his loss with spiritual and moral meaning. Shots of Huw clasping his father's dead body in his arms in the mine elevator as they ascend the pit are intercut with images of the women of the family wearing shawls around their heads and looking off camera, suggesting the pious depictions of the Crucifixion at Calvary. Religious imagery and references therefore are central to *How Green Was My Valley*'s portrayal of working-class community and its destruction by industrialization. The extensive role and representation of religion in the film renders the brutalities of rapacious capitalism as religious tragedy and turns religious identity into a site of political struggle.

The Crucible of War

The completion of *How Green Was My Valley* marked another important turning point in Ford's career. When filming ended, Ford put commercial moviemaking aside and entered actively military service in the navy. Between 1941 and 1945, he directed his skills as a filmmaker toward the fight against the nation's enemies. As head of a film and photographic unit in the Office of Strategic Services (OSS), he documented combat operations for the military and made numerous educational and propaganda films for the war effort. He would win two Academy Awards for directing two documentaries, *The Battle of Midway* (1942) and *December 7th* (1943), about the attack on Pearl Harbor. Ford also covered some of the most important theaters of war, including North Africa, Normandy, and Southeast Asia.[48]

However, the move from Hollywood director to navy officer also entailed a significant reorientation in Ford's focus—from making movies that critically examined religion, class, and ethnicity in American life to directing films that mobilized the nation for war. These years had a profound impact on Ford that would have lasting consequences for how he understood America. His service in the navy and the OSS brought him success and recognition without the taint of Hollywood commercialism. For an Irish American Catholic taught the sins of individual ambition and pride, the military offered redemption through sacrifice and discipline.

Active service also produced a shift in Ford's personal affiliations, from Hollywood progressives to military commanders and officers, as the director spent the early forties far from California recording the Allied campaigns against Germany and Japan. Ford's best work had always been the product of partnerships and collaborations. Will Rogers, Dudley Nichols, and Philip Dunne in the thirties and early forties drew out the radical dimensions on Ford's Irish American rebellious impulses. Now, however, as head of a military film unit, he joined forces with men who were leading the nation's war, including the Irish Catholic, Wall Street lawyer turned spy William Donovan, head of the OSS, and the deeply anticommunist general Albert C. Wedemeyer, the chief of staff for Chiang Kai-shek and commander of American forces in China.[49] This militarization of Ford and his filmmaking had a decisive influence on how he would view the world and the films he made after the war.

The war thus drew Ford away from liberal progressivism and led him toward the political right. This shift extended beyond his military affiliations to include his ties back in Hollywood. In 1944, Ford signaled his growing conservatism by agreeing to be a founding member of the arch-right-wing Hollywood group known as the Motion Picture Alliance for the Preservation of American Ideals, dedicated to protecting "the American way of life" against "Communists, radicals and crackpots." This organization also included the director Leo McCarey and James Kevin McGuinness, both of whom would later serve as friendly witnesses during the House Un-American Activities Committee's witch hunts against leftists in Hollywood. McGuinness worked closely with Ford on *They Were Expendable* (1945), and they became close friends.[50]

Unlike other members of the MPA, Ford did not actively take up the anticommunist crusade in Hollywood after the war. In fact, his stance against Cecil B. DeMille's efforts to demand loyalty oaths in the Screen Directors Guild in 1950 has been seen as a courageous fight against the Red Scare. But Ford's position in this conflict was actually more ambivalent than is sometimes suggested. DeMille sought a recall of Joseph Mankiewicz, president of the guild, for his opposition to DeMille's demands that all guild members take an anticommunist loyalty oath. Mankiewicz sensed that such an oath would consign directors who did not take it to a blacklist maintained by industry producers. On the evening of October

22, 1950, during an intensely contentious general membership meeting held to vote on whether to recall Mankiewicz, Ford made a dramatic (and subsequently famous) speech to denounce blacklists and support Mankiewicz against DeMille. This speech played a key role in shifting opinion against DeMille. Mankiewicz survived the recall effort, and Ford's proposal that the entire board of directors of the guild step down and a new slate be elected carried the day.

But as Joseph McBride has pointed out, Ford hedged his opposition to DeMille by privately contacting the director almost immediately afterward and congratulating him on his performance at the meeting amid hostile attacks from opponents. So although Ford played a pivotal role against the anticommunist hysteria within his own directors' guild, he seemed eager to disassociate himself from the more liberal elements in the cultural battles afflicting Hollywood. Indeed, in 1949, he had become a member of the executive committee of the Motion Picture Alliance at a time when the MPA pursued an aggressive campaign against liberal sentiment in the motion picture industry.[51]

Ford's own role in the anticommunist battles, therefore, was ambiguous. He opposed blacklists and the most egregious forms of red-baiting, including that of Senator Joe McCarthy. Yet his political commitments and friendships also clearly indicate that in the years after World War II, he abandoned his strong liberal sympathies from the thirties. Even more significant, his movies helped reimagine the stories and symbols of the nation for an age of Cold War consensus. As in earlier Ford films, religion played a central role in this postwar Americanism.

Reimagining Religious Difference in Cold War America

The years between 1946 and 1950 produced some of the most self-consciously religious films in Ford's career. *The Fugitive* (based on Graham Greene's novel about a priest in Mexico, *The Power and the Glory*) and *Three Godfathers* (a western allegory of the Gospel account of the Three Wise Men) demonstrate Ford's interests in explicitly religious subject matter, which has led a number of scholars to concentrate their consideration of religion in Ford's films on these movies. Particularly in regard to *The Fugitive,* many critics acknowledge his Catholicism as an influence. Scott Eyman writes, for example, "The problem with the picture . . . was only amplified by Ford's protective attitude toward the Church—an attitude far removed from Graham Greene's more singular brand of Catholicism." Indeed, most commentary equates the religiosity of these postwar movies with bad filmmaking. Joseph McBride goes so far as to assert, "If not the worst film of Ford's career, *The Fugitive* is a leading candidate for that distinction." Similarly, *Three Godfathers* has received harsh criticism. Tag Gallagher dismisses it as a "minor movie." And McBride, while admiring its stunning color cinematography, describes the movie briefly as "unabashedly sentimental."[52]

The fact that none of these films has held up very well in the eyes of critics has discouraged a more comprehensive examination of religion in Ford's postwar works. But rather than demonstrate the limits of his cinematic engagement with religion, these movies actually indicate that in the immediate postwar era, religion intensified as a central concern for Ford. As with many other Americans in the postwar era, religion provided him a means of understanding a world shaken by war and fears of totalitarianism. Religion continued to inform many of Ford's films from this period, and as with his prewar movies, it was inextricably bound to questions of American national definition. Less explicitly religious films, such as *My Darling Clementine* and *Fort Apache,* reveal the deep role that Ford's ethnic Catholicism played in his exploration of American identity after World War II. Precisely because religion functioned in oblique, indirect ways in these films, they testify to the subtle influence of ethnic Catholicism in organizing Ford's vision of America.

In the immediate postwar years, Ford's treatment of religion and ethnicity underwent a marked transformation. Because these subjects helped constitute his understanding of America, changes in their representation pointed to important shifts in the director's Americanism. Ethnic and religious outsiders no longer signified alternatives to a bankrupt middle-class society. Instead, they now served as defenders of a virtuous American civilization. Cultural difference was highlighted only to be resolved into united fronts against external enemies. Religion functioned as a sign of the promise of the nation that ethnics defended against attack. The reworking of ethnicity and religion in fact provided a crucial means through which Ford's films of the forties, like much of Hollywood cinema, moved from Depression-era concerns with cultural critique and social justice to Cold War consensus.[53]

My Darling Clementine is a revealing example of this postwar change. A retelling of the story of legendary western hero Wyatt Earp and the famous shoot-out at the O.K. Corral, it marks the beginning of Cold War Americanism in the director's work. Early in the film, the renegade Doc Holliday (Victor Mature) confronts Wyatt Earp (Henry Fonda) in his saloon in Tombstone. Sizing up the new marshal, Holliday challenges the lawman, "You haven't taken it into your head to deliver us from all evil?" Earp replies, "I haven't thought of it quite like that but it ain't a bad idea." This contest of wills between confident moralism and profane skepticism highlights the film's subtle use of religious difference to frame the relationship between Earp and Holliday. The film's logic of consensus, in fact, unfolds through the complex interaction between the two men.

Earp and Holliday symbolize two different cultural types in Ford's world—the respectable Anglo-American figure of mainstream society and the ethnic outsider. Earp embodies American law and order, seeking justice in Tombstone for the murder of his brother. Morally upright, controlled, and clean-cut, *My Darling Clementine*'s Earp is, in many regards, the successor to the Anglo-Puritan characters that Ford's 1930s films critiqued. Doc, by contrast, suggests ethnic associations. Mature's swarthy looks contrast strikingly with Fonda's Anglo features. Doc is a failed, drunken doctor, a reject from proper Boston society—echoing *Stagecoach*'s Irish-inflected Doc Boone—who robs banks and enjoys a reputation as a dangerous gunman. If Earp signifies American justice, law, and success, Doc suggests the ethnic margins, criminality, and failure.

Yet the film stages the cultural differences implied by these two characters in order to reconcile them into a shared project of defeating larger threats to the community. As rendered by *My Darling Clementine*, the tension between Earp's Anglo-American rectitude and Holliday's ethnic Catholic moral ambiguity pale in comparison to the malevolence of the Clanton gang members who hover outside Tombstone. Ultimately, Wyatt Earp and Doc Holliday achieve an uneasy partnership to vanquish the town's enemies and pave the way for civilization on the frontier.

Doc's death in the gunfight at the O.K. Corral suggests the film's uncertainty about where ethnic outsiders fit in the emerging civilized society that Holliday and Wyatt Earp have saved from outside threat. Yet Holliday's conversion from outlaw to partner with the forces of law also transforms ethnic difference into a support for established social institutions. Indeed, the inclusion of Doc's ethnically affiliated character in Wyatt Earp's crusade against the Clantons expands the terms of law and order in a dangerous world. Protecting traditional community is no longer identified solely as the project of traditional Anglo-American elites. Ethnics and outsiders, once considered beyond the boundaries of respectability, now play an important role in defending society and securing its future.

The film's most visually striking scene demonstrates the moral and social stakes of consensus in the fight with the evil Clanton gang. A lengthy segment in the middle of the movie depicts the people of Tombstone gathering for Sunday worship at the town church. The skeletal frame of the church steeple rises prominently on the landscape. The partially constructed church building dramatizes the incomplete character of civilization on the frontier, helping to justify the importance of ethnic outsiders such as Doc in subduing threats to social order. The film accentuates the central role of religious worship in communal life through long, slowly paced shots of frontier folk gathering at the church. The graceful, elegant sequence of Earp escorting Clementine to the service underscores the social importance of religious institutions in the film's conception of American civilization and visibly articulates masculine law, female gentility, and religious authority as a cluster of essential cultural values.

The lay preacher's words that conclude the service indicate a revision of Ford's depiction of mainstream religion. In prewar films such as *Doctor Bull* and *How Green Was My Valley*, Ford depicted the religion of respectable classes as intolerant and cold. But just as Earp's Puritanism is humanized in order to suggest a moral legitimacy of law and order, the deacon embodies an attractive form of Protestant religious practice. He tells the congregants, "I've read the good book from cover to cover and back again and I've nary found one word against dancing." *My Darling Clementine* thus shifts the cultural associations of the Bible from the Victorian moral hypocrisy of New Winton, Connecticut, depicted in *Doctor Bull*, to a religious sanction for communal festivity and popular celebration.

The religious service at the center of the town functions as a crucial sign of the civilization unfolding on the American frontier. Its ritual character communicates the film's assumption that religion is a corporate, communal activity and not simply an individualistic pursuit. The church scene is complemented by a second ritual—the shoot-out at the O.K. Corral at the end of the film. The two are intimately bound to one another narratively. The former legitimates the latter, even as secular violence ensures the continuation of the sacred. Further, the two rituals dramatize Doc's transformation from social outlaw to agent of justice. While Earp dances with Clementine at the church celebration after Sunday services, Doc is conspicuously absent. Instead, he is enjoying the morning in bed with Chihuahua (Linda Darnell), the local barmaid. However, Holliday's participation in the shoot-out reunites him with Earp and by extension incorporates him into a project of civil defense against the illegitimate aggression represented by the Clantons.

Joseph McDonald's noirish cinematography gave *My Darling Clementine* a brooding, ambiguous character echoing the wider unsettled mood of a United States still absorbing the enormity of World War II. But the darkness may also have stemmed from Ford's own sense, if only subconscious, that the war had defeated not just the nation's foreign enemies but also the social justice aspirations that had dominated the preceding decade. The death of the ethnic-inflected Doc Holliday may therefore have signified both the demise of a legendary outlaw and Ford's own farewell to his earlier hopes for a reformist Americanism as well.

My Darling Clementine utilized ethnic memory through complex, indirect signs to revitalize an American western mythology of righteous lawmen and frontier civilization. Two years later, Ford made ethnic difference explicit in *Fort Apache* (1948). In the first of what became known as his Cavalry trilogy, Ford depicted ethnic outsiders as the true guardians of the nation's safety in an era of dangerous external threats. But even though ethnicity occupied a privileged role in this western, its centrality also demonstrated the contradictions of cultural difference in an age of national consensus.

Fort Apache was, in fact, an Irish American Catholic romance of the Cold War. Ethnic consciousness and militarism weighed heavily upon the film's rendering of the American frontier. It reconciled ethnic outsiders to America through valorizing a martial ethos of duty, sacrifice, and defense. Simultaneously, it articulated a postwar understanding of American community as military power *through* ethnic difference. It extended *My Darling Clementine*'s reworking of ethnicity into support for traditional American civilization by turning ethnic outsiders into defenders of the nation-state.

The film's critique of bigotry and its privileging of Irishness as a central component of American identity was ultimately a double-edged achievement, however. On the one hand, the film suggested that the inclusion of ethnic outsiders was the condition for the advance of American society. Yet on the other, the agency of ethnics that the film valorized rested on a prior founding assumption of the rightfulness of national power. The representation of Irish Americans, standing for all ethnic outsiders, therefore gave new legitimacy to expansionist understandings of American identity in a historical moment when national purpose was directed toward a global conflict with the Soviet Union.

The film opens with shots of a stagecoach speeding across the western landscape. It appears that *Fort Apache* picks right up where Ford's prewar

The town of Tombstone in John Ford's My Darling Clementine *(1946), where the dreams of social transformation go to die. Note the partially constructed church. Courtesy of Photofest.*

Stagecoach left off. Indeed, by invoking moviegoers' memories of that film, the opening scene encourages a continuation with the past. Yet *Fort Apache* is engaged in a very different Americanism than Ford's Depression-era films, and the impression of continuity helps ease the profound transformation of cultural meaning it enacts. This early postwar film offers a vision of ethnic difference folded into a project of national security rather than the social justice concerns of the thirties.

A fictionalized rendering of Custer's last stand, with the fort's commanding officer, Colonel Owen Thursday (Henry Fonda), standing in for Custer, *Fort Apache* utilizes Irish American ethnicity to figure a new American consensus. Thursday has been sent, with his adult daughter Philadelphia (Shirley Temple) in tow, to Fort Apache, an assignment he feels is beneath his stature and dignity. There, he finds a military post populated by Irish American soldiers, including the young lieutenant Michael O'Rourke (John Agar), and for the well-bred Thursday, that only deepens his disgust at his plight. A chance to return the Native American chief Cochise and his tribe to their reservation allows Thursday to dream of glory and believe he has found his ticket out of Fort Apache. He leads his men in a suicide charge against the Indians over the protests of the wiser Captain Kirby York (John Wayne). Few soldiers survive, and York is left to assume the leadership of Fort Apache. Yet the foolish and vain-glorious Thursday is transformed in death by journalists visiting the fort into a national hero. York's words to the press, however, prevail, redirecting attention away from Thursday to the dog soldiers, whose "faces may change" but who are the real American heroes advancing the cause of the nation.

Thursday functions as an emblem of an older exclusionary American community against which the movie offers an alternative Americanism predicated on the successful reconciliation of Anglo-Americans and Irish outsiders. In fact, he is really the only figure at the fort who is uncomfortable with the Irish. York, one of the officers at the outpost, has no difficulty respecting the Irish who serve at Fort Apache and practically functions as an honorary Irishman himself. His acceptance of the Irish is matched by his nuanced dealings with the Indians, recognizing that their reasons for leaving the reservations have some justification. Just as Thursday suggests a correspondence between ethnic intolerance and incompetent leadership, York brings together a respect for cultural differences and smart military command.

The film's use of ethnicity to represent a new national collectivity organized around the military is evident as well in its depiction of life at the fort. Fort Apache is practically an Irish enclave on the American frontier. Besides young O'Rourke, there is his father, Michael Shannon O'Rourke (Ward Bond), and his mother (Irene Rich), as well as Sergeant Mulcahy (Victor McLaglen), and Sergeant Quincannon (Dick Foran). All these Irish are tied to the rituals of military life and symbols of the nation. The film imagines a world where ethnicity and national allegiance easily intermingle. In reality, the fort is a place where Irish boys can become American men, as Michael O'Rourke's transformation from fresh-faced son to experienced military officer and married man demonstrates. Fort Apache is also where U.S. soldiers can indulge in Celtic play as the army grunts engage in traditional antics of Irish masculinity—fistfighting, drinking, singing, and horse riding.

Finally, O'Rourke's courtship of and marriage to Philadelphia offers an image of social harmony that contrasts with the ethnic divisions represented by Thursday. From the opening minutes of the film, when the genteel Philadelphia furtively looks through her mirror at O'Rourke, *Fort Apache* hints at a desire for American and Irish combination. By the end of the film, the two have not only married but have produced a child, striking a hopeful note that the union of historically opposed cultural groups will generate a promising American future. Indeed, Thursday's death, which the film shows to be actually ignoble, suggests the defeat of his exclusionary patriotism, whereas O'Rourke and Philadelphia's fecundity implies a new Americanism founded upon the reconciliation of former antagonists.

Many commentators analyzing *Fort Apache* stress that the movie's complex ending is a sign of Ford's critique of the military. Yet concentrating both on how the film records the myth of national military glory and the lies upon which it is founded obfuscates Ford's larger ethnic preoccupations. Despite all the flaws in Thursday that are condemned, the movie insists that the military is a viable form of American community for traditional outsiders. Most interpretations miss how the famous ending reflects a very ethnic Catholic rendering of institutional authority.[54] Kirby York's complicity in the reporters' mistaken belief that Thursday was a military hero is actually his nuanced response as the new leader of the fort. As much as York knew Thursday was a poor commander, he presents the dead officer in the larger context of the good of the soldiers he leads. He does not challenge the newspapermen's fantasy of Thursday as a heroic leader because he knows that would undermine the work of the military on the frontier. The sins of one individual are absolved by the merits of the larger community. But Ford allows us to witness York's disgust at Thursday's action, evidenced by the flat monotone of his voice and the controlled expression on his face as he tells the reporters they are "correct in every detail" regarding their description of a painting back in Washington, D.C., celebrating Thursday's charge.

This response is itself revealing. York's comments focus on the specifics of the heroic accounts of Thursday, which in a sense are accurate because Thursday rode off to his death imagining himself as just the kind of leader that the reporters' gushing accounts convey. What York does not agree with is the belief that these renderings actually capture the larger truth about the regiment. For that, York steers the discussion away from Thursday toward the "regular" army men whom the reporters have overlooked. For this more important reality, he offers a memorial for the dead, correcting the reporters who believe the grunts have been forgotten: "They aren't forgotten because they haven't died. They're living right out there [gesturing beyond the window]. . . . And they'll keep on living as long as the regiment lives." York's final words to the journalists suggest a cavalry version of the communion of saints, transposed to soldiers whose lives do not really end but continue in the memory of the faithful. Far

From Irish boys to American men by way of the U.S. Cavalry: the O'Rourkes (Irene Rich and Ward Bond) welcome home their officer son, Michael Shannon O'Rourke (John Agar), on the frontier in Fort Apache *(1948). Note the religious statue on the wall behind Michael's left shoulder. Courtesy of Photofest.*

from encouraging a prophetic denunciation of American state power, *Fort Apache*'s ending actually harnesses ethnic Catholic moral understanding to a militarized vision of the nation.

A third film from the postwar period, *Wagon Master* (1950), reveals the depths of Ford's own conversion to a new consensual Americanism at the beginnings of the Cold War era. But as with most of his work, the representation of that shared, virtuous America rests upon the articulation of religious and cultural difference. As in so many of his films, ethnic Catholicism lurks just below the surface here, shaping and organizing the movie's depiction of American community. The story of a group of Mormon outsiders who journey across the rugged landscape to establish a new home for themselves on the American continent, the film offered one of Ford's most loving, poetic evocations of the western. *Wagon Master* transposes Ford's Catholic identity to persecuted Mormons in a celebration of America as a promised land of religious liberty and virtuous pioneers. If *Fort Apache* articulates an American community in terms of ethnic union and militarism, *Wagon Master* makes analogous use of religious minorities to render national myths of the frontier spirit and providential mission appear inclusive and pluralist. Indeed, as with the other postwar films *My Darling Clementine* and *Fort Apache*, *Wagon Master* draws upon memories of cultural difference and struggle in order to sanction a new American unity. The result is a film that turns religious minorities into emblems of godly national triumph.

Wagon Master represents the apotheosis of Ford's postwar embrace of American goodness. It demonstrates the pressures for national affirmation that Cold War ideology placed upon even a skeptical outsider such as Ford. It also suggests the complex role that religious difference played in organizing American unity. *Wagon Master* recognizes the challenges that religious minorities confront even as it blunts their critical implications. By addressing religious difference, the film embodies the delicate and unstable work of consensus that rests upon memories of cultural exclusion only to contain their disruptive associations.

Postwar Doubts about the American Century

In the immediate postwar years, therefore, Ford's films broke from his earlier reformist Americanism to envision a Cold War nation. Ethnicity and religion remained crucial elements in his movies. However, he reworked these perennial concerns in light of new preoccupations with social reconciliation and collective unity. Major threats and conflict became projected outside American communities to lawless gangs or Native Americans who loomed just over the horizon. Ethnic outsiders assumed new roles as defenders of communities threatened by such malevolent forces. Representations of religion symbolized the virtuous society that ethnics were called upon to protect.

Yet Ford's identification with consensus Americanism proved deeply ambivalent. Even during the era when he seemed most supportive of Cold War nationalism, his films evidenced a complex perspective on America, as *Fort Apache* testified. Then, in the 1950s and early 1960s, a number of Ford's movies manifested a renewed critical awareness. Many scholars point to Ford's influential *The Searchers* (1956) as an effort to address racism.[55] Even *The Quiet Man* (1952) struck a discordant note by having its hero leave America and settle in Ireland to find a true home. To the proud, aspiring Irish American soldiers of the cavalry westerns, such a move would have been considered unpatriotic. Two films in particular from Ford's postwar period, *The Sun Shines Bright* (1953) and *The Man Who Shot Liberty Valence* (1962), are noteworthy for their dissent from the complacencies of consensus America.

Nothing more clearly demonstrated the lasting impact of the 1930s on Ford than his remake of his own *Judge Priest* during the height of the American Century, in *The Sun Shines Bright*. A film that gained little attention when it was released and that is largely overlooked in Ford filmography, the movie nevertheless allowed the director to critique the inequalities and prejudices that his identification with a Cold War consensus had initially repressed.[56] Though ostensibly its main character served as judge in a small river town of Fairfield, Kentucky, Billy Priest acted more like a denizen of the urban, ethnic Catholic world of Ford's boyhood home, Portland, Maine. Priest headed a political machine composed of a motley group of townsmen including the Jewish department store owner and a compassionate doctor, both of whom were looked down upon by the genteel citizens of Fairfield. His reelection campaign pitted the tolerant judge against an opponent determined to take back the town for the respectable class. As with Ford's prewar films, the movie identified social privilege with Puritan religion and the cultural margins with a religion of mercy and generosity. Ford's reclaiming of Priest and the memories of social justice and public life from the thirties that he signified was more than nostalgia. It indicated the director's dissatisfaction with the spirit of national complacency that had triumphed by the 1950s. Retelling the story of Billy Priest and his compassionate, inclusive vision of the law signaled Ford's continuing investment in Depression-era values for assessing the character of postwar society.

A very late film in Ford's career, *The Man Who Shot Liberty Valence* further demonstrated his deepening disenchantment with America. In fact, the whole film conveyed a profound sense of loss and regret over the failed promise of American democracy that Ford's work had helped imagine since the thirties. The aged countenances of the main characters—the lawyer and politician Ransom Stoddard (James Stewart), the gunman Tom Doniphon (John Wayne), Stoddard's wife, Hallie (Vera Miles), and the town marshal Link Appleyard (Andy Devine)—the staginess of film studio sets, and the unadorned mise-en-scène all communicated a world drained of life and vitality.[57] One of Ford's last returns to the western genre proved to be one of his bleakest as well.

The film begins amid the settled, civilized town of Shinbone with U.S. Senator Ransom Stoddard and his wife returning home to bury the forgotten Doniphon. Then a flashback to the wild early frontier days is introduced via Stoddard's account to newspaper reporters of his first arrival in town. We learn that as a young idealistic lawyer, Stoddard took Horace Greeley's famous adage to go west and headed out to the frontier. There, he is viciously beaten by the brutal Liberty Valence and his outlaw gang. Befriended by Doniphon in Shinbone, Stoddard is determined to bring Valence to justice under the law. Doniphon counsels the young attorney that the law is held in little esteem in the frontier territory and that the gun is a more effective form of protection. Stoddard's and Doniphon's opposing views provide the central conflict around which the film's exploration of the character of justice revolves.

As many critics have noted, the film offers a rich, intensely complex exploration of the classic theme of civilization and wilderness, law and violence in American culture.[58] But this meditation on American identity, as is typical of Ford's films, is rendered in terms of ethnic and implicitly religious difference. The law book–toting, teetotaling Stoddard suggests an Anglo-Puritan understanding of America predicated upon idealistic principles of justice and moral right. The film's rendering of Stoddard in ethnic-religious terms is explicitly evoked by Doniphon's repeated identification of the lawyer as "pilgrim." Conversely, Doniphon's skepticism about Stoddard's legal abstractions and the particular religious nickname he assigns the lawyer suggest an ethnic sensibility, suspicious of radical transformations of local community.

Doniphon's differences with Stoddard, however, do not translate into opposition to statehood for the frontier territory. At the town meeting to debate the issue, Doniphon is as enthusiastic as Stoddard. He does not, therefore, represent a violent, frontier justice in contrast to Stoddard's civilized commitments. Rather, Doniphon suggests an ethnic understanding of society that is founded upon an appreciation of local custom and practical wisdom, in contrast to Stoddard's abstract and formal approach to law.

Stoddard's confrontation with Liberty Valence culminates, against the lawyer's own best efforts, in a shoot-out, with the outlaw killed, seemingly, by the easterner's gun. The death of Valence turns Stoddard into a hero, leads Hallie to shift her affections from Doniphon to him, and launches him into a successful political career that years later culminates in a U.S. Senate seat. However, Stoddard's growing reputation among the people of Shinbone is unwarranted, although even the lawyer does not recognize this until his friend Doniphon tells him that it was he, hiding in the shadows the night of the shoot-out, who shot Valence, knowing that Stoddard was no match for the criminal. But Stoddard is unable to correct the public's mistaken impression that he was the man who shot Liberty Valence. His subsequent achievements are therefore predicated on a lie. Doniphon, having lost Hallie, fades away from Shinbone to die a forgotten man.

Stoddard's entire account to newspaper reporters who want to know why the senator has returned to Shinbone is, in reality, his confession of complicity in the illusion of his heroism. Near the end of the film, as it cuts from the flashback to the present, a three-quarters shot of Stoddard sitting in a chair dramatically isolates the lawyer, underscoring the fact that what viewers have just witnessed is an admission of guilt. Yet the newspaper editor refuses to publish Stoddard's confession, ripping up the notes from the interview and telling him, "This is the West, sir. When the legend becomes fact, print the legend."

Perhaps the most famous lines of dialogue in any Ford film, this pronouncement encapsulates the director's ability to self-consciously reflect on the myth-making power of the western and of movies themselves. But as a response to Stoddard's effort to confess his sins and move toward reconciliation with this past, the line is especially powerful.[59] The editor refuses to acknowledge Stoddard's attempt to publicly admit responsibility and atone for his moral transgressions. Without the possibility of confession and penance, Stoddard is left in his own personal hell.

The Man Who Shot Liberty Valence offers a wintry assessment of American democracy, told through the prism of an Irish Catholic conscience familiar with guilt and regret. Made in the final years of Ford's career, it suggests the director's growing alienation from the nation whose stories and history he had chronicled for over four decades. But just as in earlier periods when ethnic and religious difference mediated Ford's belief in the hope in America, cultural diversity frames his later disenchantment.

The film remains attached to ethnic and cultural pluralism even if it seems that pluralism has become overwhelmed by spectacle and illusion in American public life. One character, Duncan Peabody (Edmond O'Brien), especially concentrates the implicit ethnic religious character of Ford's vision of American community. Peabody is the town's loquacious, boozy newspaper editor, dubious of Stoddard's high-minded confidence in the law but also a fierce proponent of the cause of statehood and democracy. At Shinbone's town meeting when he is nominated as the town's second representative to the territorial convention, he protests vociferously, claiming the primacy of his role as newspaperman, which he likens to being the town's "father confessor." As he pleads with his fellow citizens to reconsider his nomination, he stumbles about for another descriptor fitting his role in the community, to which Doniphon replies, "Town drunk."

One sequence involving Peabody in particular dramatizes the film's reliance on ethnic religious memory to mitigate its despair over the fate of democracy in America. After he and Stoddard have been elected to attend the convention, Peabody is alone in his office, copyediting the next day's newspaper edition. With the editor drunk, stumbling about and talking to himself, much of the scene relies on broad humor. But a more somber note is struck when Peabody admits his fears stemming from Liberty Valence's presence in town and acknowledges that alcohol gives him courage. The drunken editor, confessing his fears even while pursuing his public duty to the community by preparing his newspaper, suggests an image of democracy predicated not upon illusions of strength, mastery, and individual will but upon the realities of human weakness and vulnerability.

Realizing his jug of booze is empty, he walks across the street to the Mexican cantina in search of a refill, where he is warmly greeted. When he returns to his office, he finds Valence and his men waiting in the dark. The outlaw beats Peabody to a bloody pulp, leaving him for dead while his men trash the newspaper office, demonstrating their contempt for the institutions of civic life. Stoddard subsequently enters the office to find Peabody on the ground. Valence's attack on the editor jolts Stoddard into taking up the gunman's challenge for a duel later that night.

In a final shot of the sequence, remarkable for its formal and cultural power, the bloodied newspaperman lies on a cot in his office. Compositionally, a diagonal line within the frame connects the injured man, through ruined newspapers on the ground, out the door of the office to townspeople across the street in the background giving witness to Valence's destruction. But as they return to their own business, Mexican women rush in to minister to the broken body of the "father-confessor" and "town drunk" champion of democracy in Shinbone.

Lyman Beecher's Worst Nightmare

Unlike the triumphalism of Catholic leaders such as Fulton Sheen who insisted that America needed the certainties of the church, Ford's films expressed a Catholicism voiced in a "minor" key. Rarely the explicit subject, Catholicism lurked beneath and within familiar stories of western frontiers and small-town communities, covertly untying the bounds that sutured Anglo-American Protestantism to American identity. His films translated ethnic Catholic cultural memories of exclusion and marginalization into new understandings of national community. Quietly and far less ostentatiously than many other Irish Americans toiling in twentieth-century popular culture, Ford through his movies enacted his own Catholic acculturation to America. These films revealed that the historical transformation from religious outsiders to mainstream insiders was neither straightforward nor simple. Instead, they implied the cultural process entailed ambivalence, indirection, and displacement.

Ford's films thus provided the symbolic coordinates for a nation transformed by ethnic, religious Americanization. They imagined the United States as a society of differences, characterized less by cultural purity and orthodox boundaries than by hybridity, exchange, and border crossings.[60] By continually rendering religion in America from the perspective of an ethnic Catholic outsider, his films produced a new national subject of religious and ethnic pluralism.

Ford's sensitivity to the cultural complexity of America gave his films particular resonance in the struggles over national definition in the twentieth century. Ethnicity and religious difference served as the grounds on which his movies addressed the realities of the Depression, world war, and the Cold War between the 1930s and 1960s. The significance of Ford's Catholic-inflected movies lay precisely in their use of religion and ethnicity to represent American community in a period of fierce cultural contest over national purpose. American pluralism was at the very center of Ford's films. But their meanings changed over time as aspirations for social reform gave way to the demands of Cold War unity. Like many of the most important chroniclers of the nation, Ford understood the deeply religious character of the United States. But as his movies made clear, his own plea for the West counseled Americans to embrace rather than escape the challenges of their own impure cultural diversity.

CATHOLICS AND THE AMERICAN COMMUNITY AT THE TURN OF A NEW CENTURY

The role of Catholics in popular culture's creation of twentieth-century America is a subject that has slipped through the cracks in the study of both Catholics and American culture. Historical considerations of Catholics and public life often remain focused on intellectuals, leaving aside the popular engagement with the nation. Yet studies of Catholicism in popular culture tend to consider its significance for Catholics rather than broader social and political implications. Cultural studies, in turn, often resist taking religion seriously as a subject for investigation.[1]

This book has brought religion, popular culture, and politics together to argue that popular representations of and by Catholics provided an important cultural arena for expressing competing understandings of Americanism between the New Deal and Cold War eras. Depictions of Catholics as participants in an American national consensus at midcentury marked a dramatic rejection of socially conscious, reformist conceptions of the nation that Catholic representations had helped forge during the Depression.

I argue, therefore, that popular visual narratives of and by Catholics communicated not only religious signs but also social meanings about the definition and character of national community. Indeed, movies, photographs, and television articulated ideas about the character and priorities of American society through images of Catholic leaders, space, and institutions. Simultaneously, Catholic filmmakers made movies about America informed by memories of ethnic, religious difference and cultural struggle. Both popular depictions of Catholicism and Catholic portraits of America placed Catholics at the very center of the contest over Americanism between the 1930s and 1950s.

The extensive role of Catholics in the construction of popular American identity demonstrated that the ideological justification of the modern nation could no longer be sufficiently articulated by Protestants alone. When the Depression precipitated a crisis in traditional conceptions of the United States as a land of rugged individuals and free markets, reformist efforts to create a more equitable and just society drew upon the Catholic presence in America. And as reformist desires suffered defeat, Catholics proved equally important in the elaboration of postwar conceptions of democracy predicated upon mass consumption and consensus.

Popular culture thus proved an enormously productive space for Catholic outsiders to help shape the imagined community of twentieth-century America.[2] In the end, popular culture itself became their home. The ties between Catholics and the mass media were, in fact, so tight that it is easy to overlook their significance for both Catholicism and American culture. Indeed, what once surprised and delighted now seems contrived. Bing Crosby's priest has long since left the parish. He now serves as a useful foil against which contemporary artists such as John Patrick Shanley have pursued their own relationships with America.

The decline of Father O'Malley's stature, however, involved more than simply restlessness with Hollywood conventions. The key moment for this cultural shift occurred in the 1970s when the social conditions and ideological imperatives that made old St. Dominic's parish a model for American consensus collapsed under their own contradictions. As testimony to the significance of Catholicism in the construction of postwar American identity, when the American Century could no longer be sustained, Catholics assumed a relevancy in the popular imagination they had not enjoyed since the 1940s. Popular and influential movies such as *The Godfather* films and *The Exorcist* conveyed a longing for the cultural clarity of the old ethnic Catholic world that the postwar era had replaced with suburban, middle-class dreams.[3] To many people, it seemed that the star on which Father O'Malley encouraged his followers to swing had imploded amid racial strife, economic dislocation, and the erosion of American power in Vietnam.

The recourse to older depictions of Catholics in the seventies showed that Father O'Malley and the popular Catholicism of the forties were always about more than simply Catholicism. Mass-mediated Catholics of this earlier era provided influential signs of a very particular version of the American nation and its values of consensus, social order, and moral goodness. When that postwar vision of the nation lost its cultural authority, popular culture targeted Bing Crosby's affirmative portrait of Catholics to register discontent with the American Century and suggest alternative values.

But the revisionist understandings of both nation and church succumbed to reaction by the late twentieth century. In its wake, the popular representation of Catholics once again underwent transformation. But some of these new expressions had remarkable parallels with the earlier, postwar era. The papacy of John Paul II in particular marked a dramatic rejection of the experimental, modernist look of the Catholic Church that had emerged with the reforms of the Second Vatican Council of the early 1960s.

The late twentieth century did not witness any popular, influential movies about Catholics comparable to *The Godfather* or *Going My Way* of earlier eras. Perhaps a reason for this absence was that the biggest, most important Catholic performance of the era never hit the screens but instead was signified by the church's most charismatic leader of the modern age, John Paul II. Nobody performed Catholicism like the Polish pope. An actor turned priest, John Paul II astutely understood the importance of culture and symbol in the creation of social identity. The pontiff functioned as an enormous representational black hole, drawing to himself all the powerful semiotic energies inherent in Roman Catholicism, including his very body. The history of his papacy could, in fact, be told through the compelling visual images of his numerous, far-flung journeys around the world—to the United States, Poland, a Roman synagogue, Cuba, Israel.

John Paul's performance of Catholicism was, it turned out, Fulton J. Sheen writ large on a global stage. And like Sheen, John Paul was an ardent anticommunist, staring down Stalinists of his own country of Poland, thereby repeating Sheen's protests on *Life Is Worth Living* about the communist mistreatment of Eastern European Catholics.

But it was not only Sheen's dramatic religious anticommunism that John Paul's Catholicism echoed. His papacy encouraged a Catholic mystique akin to *Life*'s romantic portrait of American Jesuits. His call for a heroic, committed faith prepared to sacrifice all for the sake of the transcendent turned Catholic identity into an adventure, religion into alternative culture, and piety into edgy, risky commitment.

John Paul's particular construction of Roman Catholicism, however, came at a high price. As E. J. Dionne has argued, the pope actually offered highly critical assessments of capitalism and championed the rights of the poor, immigrants, and the dispossessed around the world.[4] Yet his adept use of cultural representation to cultivate an image of the church focused upon papal leadership all too often overshadowed his social teaching of economic justice and the common good in the popular imagination.

The American Century's construction of Catholicism in the 1940s and 1950s therefore found unexpected new life in the popular papacy of John Paul II. But with the declining health of the pope in the early years of the twenty-first century, not only did the Catholic Church lose its vigorous leader but the mass media lacked good Catholic material. Into this cultural void, a Catholic filmmaker once again stepped to capture the popular attention. Unlike the films of John Ford and Leo McCarey, a movie by Mel Gibson unleashed a religious fury that deeply divided the nation. *The Passion of the Christ* (2004) about the final hours of the life of Jesus on his way to crucifixion, treated moviegoers to an unrelenting stream of torture, bloodshed, and bruised human flesh. A cinematic version of the traditional Catholic Lenten devotion of the stations of the cross, *The Passion* generated intense controversy for its excessive violence and anti-Semitic imagery.[5]

No one could have anticipated that a movie with dialogue in the ancient languages of Aramaic and Latin would become a huge box office hit. Gibson's film proved that the visual culture of Catholicism still had power to entice popular tastes. But it also signaled something new, for the film's commercial success rested heavily upon the support of evangelical Christians. This cultural alliance between Catholics and evangelicals provided an important basis for the political victory of the conservative George W. Bush as the new century began, once again demonstrating the deep bonds between religion, popular culture, and politics in modern America. But Gibson's movie about a bloody Jesus encouraged a very different America than that envisioned by John Ford's Popular Front Catholicism of *Stagecoach* and *How Green Was My Valley*. Indeed, *The Passion of the Christ* suggested that the cultural fortunes of Catholics in early twenty-first-century America had come to rest more upon the evangelical nation than on solidarity with the forgotten man.

NOTES

INTRODUCTION. PRIESTS, GANGSTERS, AND COWBOYS

1. Mrs. James Dant to Eric Johnston, 23 August 1946, MPAA Breen Office Files, Box 2, Folder: Religion, Margaret Herrick Library, Academy of Motion Picture Arts and Sciences, Beverly Hills, Calif. (hereafter cited as AMPAS) (emphasis in the original).

2. Charles R. Morris discusses the popularity of these Catholic films in his *American Catholic: The Saints and Sinners Who Built America's Most Powerful Church* (New York: Vintage Books, 1997), 196–200.

3. On Ford and Capra as Catholic filmmakers, see Lee Lourdeaux, *Italian and Irish Filmmakers in America: Ford, Capra, Coppola and Scorsese* (Philadelphia: Temple University Press, 1990), and Richard A. Blake, *AfterImage: The Indelible Catholic Imagination of Six American Filmmakers* (Chicago: Loyola University Press, 2000). On Ford, see also Paul Giles, *American Catholic Arts and Fiction: Culture, Ideology, Aesthetics* (New York: Cambridge University Press, 1992), 296–308. McCarey has received far less study than Ford or Capra, but see Wes D. Gehring, *Leo McCarey: From Marx to McCarthy* (Lanham, Md.: Scarecrow Press, 2005), and Jerome M. McKeever, "The McCarey Touch: The Life and Films of Leo McCarey," Ph.D. diss., Case Western Reserve (Ann Arbor, Mich.: UMI, 2000).

4. On the cultural significance of *Life* magazine, see Erika Doss, ed., *Looking at "Life" Magazine* (Washington, D.C.: Smithsonian Institution Press, 2001); Wendy Kozol, *"Life's" America: Family and Nation in Postwar Photojournalism* (Philadelphia: Temple University Press, 1994).

5. On Sheen, see Christopher Owen Lynch, *Selling Catholicism: Bishop Sheen and the Power of Television* (Lexington: University Press of Kentucky, 1998); Mark Massa, *Catholics and American Culture: Fulton Sheen, Dorothy Day and the Notre Dame Football Team* (New York: Crossroad Publishing, 1999); Thomas C. Reeves, *America's Bishop: The Life and Times of Fulton J. Sheen* (San Francisco: Encounter Books, 2001).

6. The concept of the nation as an "imagined community" derives from Benedict R. Anderson, *Imagined Community: Reflections on the Origin and Spread of Nationalism* (London: Verso, 1983). The term *visual terrain* is from Shawn Michelle Smith, "Photographing the 'American Negro': Nation, Race, and Photography at the Paris Exposition of 1900," in *Looking for America: The Visual Production of Nation and People*, ed. Ardis Cameron (Malden, Mass.: Blackwell Publishing, 2005), 62. On the role of visual images in the construction of American identity more generally, see also the other essays and introduction in *Looking for America*.

7. Lary May, *The Big Tomorrow: Hollywood and the Politics of the American Way* (Chicago: University of Chicago Press, 2000); Michael Denning, *The Cultural Front: The Laboring of American Culture in the Twentieth Century* (New York: Verso, 1996); Wendy L. Wall, *Inventing the "American Way": The Politics of Consensus from the New Deal to the Civil Rights Movement* (New York: Oxford University Press, 2008); Lizabeth Cohen, *Making a New Deal: Industrial Workers in Chicago, 1919–1939* (New York: Cambridge University Press, 1990).

8. See May, *Big Tomorrow*, 55–99.

9. Ibid., 139–174.

10. Ibid., 175–213. See also Kozol, *"Life's" America*, and Elaine Tyler May, *Homeward Bound: American Families in the Cold War Era* (New York: Basic Books, 1988).

11. On nineteenth- and early twentieth-century American nationalism as an imagined community of middle-class, Anglo-American, Protestant men, see David W. Noble, *The Death of a Nation: American Culture and the End of Exceptionalism* (Minneapolis: University of Minnesota Press, 2002).

12. On Beecher and the Charlestown riots, see Morris, *American Catholic*, 56.

13. Lyman Beecher, "A Plea for the West," in *God's New Israel: Religious Interpretations of American Destiny*, revised and updated edition, ed. Conrad Cherry (Chapel Hill: University of North Carolina Press, 1998), 123–124.

14. On the metaphor of two worlds in the writing of American history by Anglo-American intellectuals, see David W. Noble, *The End of American History: Democracy, Capitalism and the Metaphor of Two Worlds in Anglo-American Historical Writing, 1880–1980* (Minneapolis: University of Minnesota Press, 1985).

15. On anti-Catholicism and antebellum American culture, see Jenny Franchot, *Roads to Rome: The Antebellum Protestant Encounter with Catholicism* (Berkeley: University of California Press, 1994).

16. John Higham, *Strangers in the Land: Patterns of American Nativism, 1860–1925*, 2nd ed. (New Brunswick, N.J.: Rutgers University Press, 1988), 264–330.

17. In addition to the works by May and Cohen, see Robert S. McElvaine's discussions of the transformation of values in Depression-era America in his *The Great Depression: America, 1929–1941* (New York: Times Books, 1993), 196–223.

18. On the history of Catholic social reform thought in the thirties, see David J. O'Brien, *American Catholics and Social Reform: The New Deal Years* (New York: Oxford University Press, 1968). On Coughlin, see Alan Brinkley, *Voices of Protest: Huey Long, Father Coughlin and the Great Depression* (New York: Vintage, 1983); on Ryan, see Francis L. Broderick, *Right Reverend New Dealer, John A. Ryan* (New York: Macmillan, 1963); on Rice, see Kenneth J. Heineman, *A Catholic New Deal: Religion and Reform in Depression Pittsburgh* (University Park: Pennsylvania State University Press, 1999).

19. See Robert Anthony Orsi, *The Madonna of 115th Street: Faith and Community in Italian Harlem, 1880–1950* (New Haven, Conn.: Yale University Press, 1985); John McGreevy, *Parish Boundaries: The Catholic Encounter with Race in the Twentieth-Century Urban North* (Chicago: University of Chicago Press, 1996).

20. See James Terence Fisher, *The Catholic Counterculture in America, 1933–1962* (Chapel Hill: University of North Carolina Press, 1989).

21. May, *Big Tomorrow*, 11–135.

22. On the eclipse of social reform in the 1940s, see Alan Brinkley, *The End of Reform: New Deal Liberalism in Recession and War* (New York: Vintage Books, 1995); Wall, *Inventing the "American Way"*; May, *Big Tomorrow*, 139–213. On the immediate postwar era and the conservative challenge to reform, see Jonathan Bell, *The Liberal State on Trial: The Cold War and American Politics in the Truman Years* (New York: Columbia University Press, 2004); Robert Griffith, "Forging America's Postwar Order: Domestic Politics and Political Economy in the Age of Truman," in *The Truman Presidency*, ed. Michael J. Lacey (New York: Cambridge University Press, 1989), 57–88; Elizabeth Fones-Woolf, *Selling Free Enterprise: The Business Assault on Labor and Liberalism, 1945–1960* (Urbana: University of Illinois Press, 1994). On the 1950s consensus, see Godfrey Hodgson, *America in Our Time: From World War II to Nixon* (Garden City, N.Y.: Doubleday, 1976), 67–98; and Wall, *Inventing the "American Way."*

23. On *Life* magazine, see Doss, *Looking at "Life" Magazine*; Kozol, *"Life's" America*.

24. See May, *Big Tomorrow*, 139–174.

25. Will Herberg, *Protestant-Catholic-Jew: An Essay in American Religious Sociology*, rev. ed. (Garden City, N.Y.: Anchor Books, 1960). See also Jay Dolan, *The American Catholic Experience: A History from Colonial Times to the Present* (Garden City, N.Y.: Doubleday, 1985). For a reassessment of the Catholic movement into the center of American life, see Massa, *Catholics and American Culture*.

26. In addition to May, *Big Tomorrow*, see Noble, *End of American History*, and Lary May, ed., *Recasting America: Culture and Politics in the Age of Cold War* (Chicago: University of Chicago Press, 1989).

27. James T. Fisher's work is exceptional in its sensitivity to the complexities of popular culture and its recognition of Catholics as important actors in the creation of postwar America. See his *Dr. America: The Lives of Thomas A. Dooley, 1937–1961* (Amherst: University of Massachusetts Press, 1997).

28. On the Legion of Decency, see Gregory D. Black, *Hollywood Censored: Morality Codes, Catholics and the Movies* (New York: Cambridge University Press, 1994); Frank Walsh, *Sin and Censorship: The Catholic Church and the Motion Picture Industry* (New Haven, Conn.: Yale University Press, 1996); Leonard J. Leff and Jerold L. Simmons, *The Dame in the Kimono: Hollywood Censorship and the Production Code*, 2nd ed. (Lexington: University of Kentucky Press, 2001); Francis G. Couvares,

"Hollywood, Main Street, and the Church: Trying to Censor the Movies before the Production Code," in *Movie Censorship and American Culture*, ed. Francis G. Couvares (Washington, D.C.: Smithsonian Institution Press, 1996), 129–158; Morris, *American Catholic*, 200–209.

29. Couvares, "Hollywood, Main Street, and the Church," 129–158.

30. On the central role of ethnicity in American literature, see Werner Sollors, *Beyond Ethnicity: Consent and Descent in American Literature* (New York: Oxford University Press, 1986). On the importance of ethnicity for American film, see Mark Winokur, *American Laughter: Immigrants, Ethnicity and 1930s Hollywood Film Comedy* (New York: St. Martin's Press, 1996), and Lester D. Friedman, ed., *Unspeakable Images: Ethnicity and the American Cinema* (Urbana: University of Illinois Press, 1991).

31. See Lourdeaux, *Italian and Irish Filmmakers*, 88–124; Blake, *AfterImage*, 129–176.

32. Colleen McDannell, ed., *Catholics in the Movies* (New York: Oxford University Press, 2008).

33. Lynch, *Selling Catholicism*; Massa, *Catholics and American Culture*, 82–101.

34. On visual images as "narratives of national belonging," see Smith, "Photographing the 'American Negro.'" 62.

35. See Ella Shohat's important essay in which she argues that "ethnicity is culturally ubiquitous and textually submerged" in American film, "Ethnicities-in-Relation: Toward a Multicultural Reading of American Cinema," in Friedman, *Unspeakable Images*, 215–250.

36. For an important account of ethnic memory in cultural expression more generally, see Michael M. J. Fischer, "Ethnicity and the Post-modern Arts of Memory," in *Writing Culture: The Poetics and Politics of Ethnography*, ed. James Clifford and George E. Marcus (Berkeley: University of California Press, 1986), 194–233. Mark Winokur's insightful *American Laughter* is particularly significant for recognizing the complexities of ethnicity within 1930s comedies.

37. On Irish American Catholics more generally as brokers between insider and outsider groups in America, see Timothy J. Meagher, "The Fireman on the Stairs: Communal Loyalties in the Making of Irish America," in *Making the Irish American: History and Heritage in the United States*, ed. J. J. Lee and Marion R. Casey (New York: New York University Press, 2006), 609–648.

CHAPTER ONE. THE CATHOLIC FRONT

1. Agnes K. Maxwell, "Advertising Catholic Principles," *Commonweal*, 8 January 1935, 431.

2. Alfred W. Hommel, "The Catholic Press," *Commonweal*, 21 December 1932, 217; Henry B. Sullivan, "The Catholic Press," *Commonweal*, 22 February 1933, 468.

3. See William M. Halsey, *The Survival of American Innocence: Catholicism in an Era of Disillusionment, 1920–1940* (Notre Dame, Ind.: University of Notre Dame Press, 1980); Philip Gleason, *Contending with Modernity: Catholic Higher Education in the Twentieth Century* (New York: Oxford University Press, 1995); Paula Kane, *Separatism and Subculture: Boston Catholicism, 1900–1920* (Chapel Hill: University of North Carolina Press, 1994); Robert Orsi, *The Madonna of 115th Street: Faith and Community in Italian Harlem, 1880–1950* (New Haven, Conn.: Yale University Press, 1985); John T. McGreevy, *Parish Boundaries: The Catholic Encounter with Race in the Twentieth-Century Urban North* (Chicago: University of Chicago Press, 1996).

4. Michael Denning, *The Cultural Front: The Laboring of American Culture in the Twentieth Century* (New York: Verso, 1996). My argument that Catholicism itself became a cultural front draws upon Denning's revisionist work on the Popular Front of the 1930s.

5. McGreevy, *Parish Boundaries*.

6. On Ryan, see Francis L. Broderick, *Right Reverend New Dealer, John A. Ryan* (New York: Macmillan, 1963); on the Bishops' Program of Social Reconstruction, see Joseph M. McShane, *Sufficiently Radical: Catholicism, Progressivism and the Bishops' Program of 1919* (Washington, D.C.: Catholic University of America Press, 1986).

7. On Catholic intellectual and cultural opposition to modern thought and culture, see Halsey, *Survival of American Innocence*. For another perspective on Catholic intellectual life and its institutional history within higher education, see Gleason, *Contending with Modernity*.

8. John Higham, *Strangers in the Land: Patterns of Nativism, 1860–1925*, 2nd ed. (New Brunswick, N.J.: Rutgers University Press, 1988), 264–330.

9. John T. McNicholas, "Justice and the Present Crisis," *Catholic Mind*, 22 October 1931, 476.

10. "The New Deal," *America*, 24 June 1933, 266.

11. "The Gains of Labor," *America*, 2 September 1933, 506.

12. George Stuart Brady, "NRA's Moral Code," *Sign*, December 1934, 273.

13. David O'Brien, *American Catholics and Social Reform* (New York: Oxford University Press, 1968), 3–28.

14. McNicholas, "Justice and the Present Crisis," 480.

15. "Governor Roosevelt's Sermon," *America*, 15 October 1932, 31; "Religion in Politics," *Commonweal*, 12 October 1932, 545–546.

16. "The President," *Commonweal*, 15 March 1933, 533–535.

17. "Recovery and Reformation," *Commonweal*, 17 November 1933, 58.

18. "Over the Top," *America*, 16 September 1933, 553.

19. "The New Deal," *America*, 24 June 1933, 266.

20. John A. Ryan, "Are We on the Right Road?" *Commonweal*, 12 October 1934, 549.

21. Wilfrid Parsons, "The Roosevelt Revolution," *America*, 6 January 1934, 323. For additional examples of Catholic support for the New Deal in its early years, see O'Brien, *American Catholics and Social Reform*, 47–69.

22. On Coughlin, see Alan Brinkley, *Voices of Protest: Huey Long, Father Coughlin and the Great Depression* (New York: Vintage Books, 1983).

23. "What Will Happen Next?" *America*, 19 March 1938, 564–565; "Fireside Chat in Reverse," *Catholic World*, December 1938, 260–261.

24. On Day and the Catholic Worker movement in the 1930s, as well as Furfey and Michel, see O'Brien, *American Catholics and Social Reform*, 182–211.

25. George Mundelein, "Catholic Action for Social Justice," *Catholic Mind*, 8 February 1938, 48.

26. Edward Mooney, "The American Tradition," *Catholic Mind*, 8 June 1938, 219–220.

27. Raymond A. McGowan, "Government and Social Justice," *Catholic Mind*, 8 June 1938, 222–226.

28. John A. Ryan, "Economics and Ethics," *Commonweal*, 6 October 1933, 521.

29. Francis X. Connolly, "Thunder on the Left," *America*, 2 June 1934, 184–186.

30. William J. O'Neil, "A Planned Theater," *Commonweal*, 18 May 1934, 61–62.

31. Mary Fabyan Windeatt, "The Catholic Play—Where Is It?" *Commonweal*, 12 March 1937, 557–558.

32. M. Helfen, "The Catholic Dramatic Movement," *Commonweal*, 25 February 1938, 497, and "Professional Catholic Theater," *America*, 5 February 1938, 426.

33. Emmet Lavery, "Theatre Dividends," *Commonweal*, 22 October 1937, 591–593.

34. Emmet Lavery, "The Catholic Theater: New Thought on Old Dream," *America*, 5 December 1936, 197–199.

35. Emmet Lavery, "The Curtain Goes Up on the Catholic Theater," *America*, 6 March 1937, 506–507. See also *America*, 19 June 1937, 243, and 26 June 1937, 267.

36. Emmet Lavery "The Baby Walks!" *America*, 25 September 1937, 593; *America*, 26 June 1937, 267.

37. See, for instance, Joseph F. Healey, "The Catholic Daily," *Commonweal*, 1 February 1933, 371–372; Catholicus, letter to editor, *Commonweal*, 27 July 1934, 330; T. O'Donnell, letter to editor, *Commonweal*, 27 July 1934, 330.

38. "Let Catholics Take Warning!" *Commonweal*, 5 April 1933, 617–619.

39. Stuart D. Goulding, "Indictment," *Commonweal*, 1 September 1933, 422–424.

40. Healey, "The Catholic Daily," *Commonweal*, 372.

41. Murray Powers, "Catholic Publicity," *Commonweal*, 14 September 1934, 462.

42. Ibid.

43. Clem Lane, "How to Handle Catholic News," *Commonweal*, 3 November 1933, 12–14.

44. Edward J. Heffron, "Ten Years of the Catholic Hour," *Ecclesiastical Review* 102 (March 1940): 243.

45. Ibid., 238–239.

46. Ibid., 240.

47. Ibid., 245.

48. John A. Ryan, *The Catholic Teaching on Our Industrial System* (Washington, D.C.: National Council of Catholic Men, 1934); "Rev. Daniel A. Lord to Succeed Dr. Sheen on Catholic Hour Broadcast," *Catholic Action*, April 1934, 18.

49. Joseph C. Walen, "A Ball, A Bat—and God," *Catholic Digest*, March 1937, 77.

50. See ibid., 72–77; Edward Doherty, "The Bishop and the Wolves," *Catholic Digest*, May 1938, 1–6; on CYO art exhibits, see "The Church," *Commonweal*, 2 April 1937, 635.

51. On the Catholic crowds in Los Angeles, see Augustine C. Murray, "Fiesta in Los Angeles," *Commonweal*, 3 October 1931, 612–613. My account of the Holy Name parade in Cincinnati is indebted to Roger Fortin, *Faith and Action: A History of the Catholic Archdiocese of Cincinnati, 1821–1996* (Columbus: Ohio State University Press, 2002), 267. On the Assumption Day devotion, see Leslie Woodcock Tentler, *Seasons of Grace: A History of the Archdiocese of Detroit* (Detroit, Mich.: Wayne State University Press, 1990), 410.

52. On the Marian devotions in Chicago and Detroit, see Tentler, *Seasons of Grace*, 409.

53. On the cessation of mayoral race politics in honor of the Eucharist Congress, see "Peace of God in Cleveland," *America*, 5 October 1935, 604.

54. Frank S. Adams, "100,000 in Cleveland Hail Hayes As the Pope's Eucharistic Legate," *New York Times*, 24 September 1935, 1, 18.

55. Ibid., 18.

56. Ibid. On the size of Cleveland's Public Hall, see Frank S. Adams, "43,000 Hear Smith Assail Communism As Foe of Church," *New York Times*, 25 September 1935, 1.

57. Frank S. Adams, "Pope Makes Plea for World Peace," *New York Times*, 27 September 1935, 1, 16.

58. On the Legion of Decency, see Gregory D. Black, *Hollywood Censored: Morality Codes, Catholics and the Movies* (New York: Cambridge University Press, 1994); Frank Walsh, *Sin and Censorship: The Catholic Church and the Motion Picture Industry* (New Haven, Conn.: Yale University Press, 1996); Leonard J. Leff and Jerold L. Simmons, *The Dame in the Kimono: Hollywood Censorship and the Production Code*, 2nd ed. (Lexington: University of Kentucky Press, 2001); Francis G. Couvares, "Hollywood, Main Street, and the Church: Trying to Censor the Movies before the Production Code," in *Movie Censorship and American Culture*, ed. Francis G. Couvares (Washington, D.C.: Smithsonian Institution Press, 1996), 129–158; Mark A. Viera, *Sin in Soft Focus: Pre-code Hollywood* (New York: Harry N. Abrams, 1999).

59. P. J. C., "What the Public Wants," *Ave Maria,* 7 April 1934, 437.

60. My discussion of the origins of the Legion and the Production Code draws heavily upon Walsh, *Sin and Censorship,* and Couvares, "Hollywood, Main Street, and the Church."

61. A copy of the "Working Draft of the Lord-Quigley Code Proposal" is included in Black's *Hollywood Censored,* 302–308.

62. "Code's Birthday" *America,* 8 April 1933, 5.

63. "Clean Up the Movies!" *America,* 24 June 1933, 265–266.

64. "The New Deal," *America,* 24 June 1933, 266.

65. John T. McNicholas, "The Episcopal Committee and the Problem of Evil Motion Pictures," *Ecclesiastical Review* 91 (August 1934): 113.

66. My account of the details of the studio agreement is derived from Walsh, *Sin and Censorship,* 104.

67. Jonathan Munby, *Public Enemies, Public Heroes: Screening the Gangster from Little Caesar to Touch of Evil* (Chicago: University of Chicago Press, 1999), 97.

68. Owen A. McGrath, "Catholic Action's Big Opportunity," *Ecclesiastical Review* 91 (September 1934): 284.

69. John McGreevy, *Catholicism and American Freedom: A History* (New York: W. W. Norton, 2003), esp. 163–188. Reference to the *New Republic*'s editorial "Is There a Catholic Problem?" can be found on 165.

70. My description of a "Catholic tendency" in American culture is indebted to the title of Robert B. Ray's *A Certain Tendency of the Hollywood Cinema, 1930–1980* (Princeton, N.J.: Princeton University Press, 1985).

CHAPTER TWO. A NEW DEAL IN MOVIE RELIGION

1. Spyros P. Skouras, "Religion and the Movies," *Christian Herald,* June 1952, 71.

2. "The Picture of the Year: 'David and Bathsheba,'" *Christian Herald,* March 1952, 101; "Picture of the Year: 'Quo Vadis,'" *Christian Herald,* March 1953, 97.

3. Skouras, "Religion and the Movies," 71.

4. Ibid.

5. On biblical epics and the construction of Cold War American identity during the 1950s, see Melanie McAlister, *Epic Encounters: Culture, Media and US Interests in the Middle East, 1945–2000* (Berkeley: University of California Press, 2001); Alan Nadel, *Containment Culture: American Narrative, Postmodernism and the Atomic Age* (Durham, N.C.: Duke University Press, 1995).

6. Lary May, *The Big Tomorrow: Hollywood and the Politics of the American Way* (Chicago: University of Chicago Press, 2000).

7. Robert S. McElvaine, *The Great Depression: America, 1929–1941* (New York: Times Books, 1993), 196–223.

8. See, for instance, Gregory D. Black, *Hollywood Censored: Morality Codes, Catholics and the Movies* (New York: Cambridge University Press, 1994); Thomas Doherty, *Pre-Code Hollywood: Sex, Immorality and Insurrection in American Cinema, 1930–1934* (New York: Columbia University Press, 1999); Mark A. Vieira, *Sin in Soft Focus: Pre-Code Hollywood* (New York: Harry N. Abrams, 1999); Frank Walsh, *Sin and Censorship: The Catholic Church and the Motion Picture Industry* (New Haven, Conn.: Yale University Press, 1996).

9. May, *Big Tomorrow*; see also Jonathan Munby, *Public Enemies, Public Heroes: Screening the Gangster from "Little Caesar" to "Touch of Evil"* (Chicago: University of Chicago Press, 1999).

10. On gangsters, see Munby, *Public Enemies, Public Heroes*; David E. Ruth, *Inventing the Public Enemy: The Gangster in American Culture, 1918–1934* (Chicago: University of Chicago Press, 1996). On romantic comedy of the thirties, see Elizabeth Kendall, *The Runaway Bride: Hollywood Romantic Comedy of the 1930s* (New York: Cooper Square Press, 2002); Mark Winokur, *American Laughter: Immigrants, Ethnicity, and 1930s Hollywood Film Comedy* (New York: St. Martin's Press, 1996); James Harvey, *Romantic Comedy in Hollywood from Lubitsch to Sturges* (New York: Knopf, 1987); Stanley Cavell, *Pursuits of Happiness: The Hollywood Comedy of Remarriage* (Cambridge, Mass.: Harvard University Press, 1981).

11. Les Keyser and Barbara Keyser, *Hollywood and the Catholic Church: The Image of Roman Catholicism in American Movies* (Chicago: Loyola University Press, 1984).

12. Charles Morris, *American Catholic: The Saints and Sinners Who Built America's Most Powerful Church* (New York: Vintage Books, 1997), 196–209.

13. Colleen McDannell, ed., *Catholics in the Movies* (New York: Oxford University Press, 2008); Judith Weisenfeld, *Hollywood Be Thy Name: African American Religion in American Film, 1929–1949* (Berkeley: University of California Press, 2007).

14. Lary May, *Screening Out the Past: The Birth of Mass Culture and the Motion Picture Industry* (Chicago: University of Chicago Press, 1980).

15. May, *Big Tomorrow*, 17; Doherty, *Pre-Code Hollywood*, 31.

16. Doherty, *Pre-Code Hollywood*; May, *Big Tomorrow*, 55–85; Kendall, *Runaway Bride*.

17. Doherty, *Pre-Code Hollywood*. On the new depiction of women in early 1930s films, see also May, *Big Tomorrow*, 70–72.

18. May, *Big Tomorrow*, 68–69; Munby, *Public Enemies, Public Heroes*, 39–65.

19. May, *Big Tomorrow*, 65.

20. See, for instance, Doherty, *Pre-Code Hollywood*; Vieira, *Sin in Soft Focus*.

21. Quoted in Doherty, *Pre-Code Hollywood*, 106.

22. Walsh, *Sin and Censorship*, 79.

23. Charles Morris highlights these films as evidence of the growing Catholic presence in American culture in his *American Catholic*, 197–209.

24. Doherty, *Pre-Code Hollywood,* 318.

25. On Sheil, see Roger L. Treat, *Bishop Sheil and the CYO* (New York: Messner, 1951); on Rice, see Kenneth J. Heineman, *A Catholic New Deal: Religion and Reform in Depression Pittsburgh* (University Park: Pennsylvania State University Press, 1999); Les and Barbara Keyser also note the wider Catholic social reformism in their discussion of the film; see Keyser and Keyser, *Hollywood and the Catholic Church,* 63, 68.

26. See Thomas J. Ferraro's insightful "Boys to Men: 'Angels with Dirty Faces' (1938)," in *Catholics in the Movies,* ed. Colleen McDannell (New York: Oxford University Press, 2008), 59–82. Ferraro stresses this representing of the priest's own Christian beliefs through and upon the body of Rocky itself. He argues that there is a sophisticated theological significance to the movie, whereas I am particularly interested in the public and social reformist doubling that the ending also enacts.

27. "Boys Town," *Film Daily,* 6 September 1938, 11.

28. "Boys Town," *Motion Picture Herald* (hereafter cited as *MPH*), 10 September 1938, 55.

29. "'Boys Town'—One Man's Work," *Newsweek,* 19 September 1938, 23; "Boys Town," *Time,* 12 September 1938, 45–46.

30. McElvaine, *Great Depression,* 196–223.

31. This account of the premiere is drawn from newspaper clippings in *Boys Town* Premier, 1938, Clippings File of *Omaha World-Herald,* Historical Society of Douglas County, Omaha, Nebraska.

32. "'Boys Town' Gains Civic Approval," *MPH,* 12 November 1938, 68.

33. Ibid.

34. Ibid., 64.

35. "'Boys Town' Prize to Cashier; Brown Promotes Election," *MPH,* 3 December 1938, 51.

36. "Honor Pupils Selected on 'Boys Town' Tie-In," *MPH,* 24 December 1938, 57.

37. E. J. Flanagan, "The Story behind 'Boys Town,'" *Photoplay,* November 1938, 22–23, 85.

38. Edward J. Flanagan, "I Meet Spencer Tracy," *Catholic Digest,* November 1938, 39.

39. Philip T. Hartung, "Answer to 'Dead End,'" *Commonweal,* 23 September 1938, 561.

40. Leonard A. McMahon, "This Business of the Movies," *Sign,* January 1939, 331.

41. On the ethnic character of the social worlds in gangster films of the 1930s in contrast to the corporate milieu of postwar crime films, see Munby, *Public Enemies, Public Heroes.*

42. "New Twists Save Hackneyed Story," *Hollywood Reporter,* 2 December 1940, in *San Francisco Docks* File, PCA Collection, Special Collections, Academy of Motion Picture Arts and Sciences, Beverly Hills, Calif. (hereafter cited as AMPAS).

43. Historians debate the extent to which social reform informed American political culture in the 1940s. But many agree that the war shifted the political landscape for reform. See, for example, Jonathan Bell, *The Liberal State on Trial: The Cold War and American Politics in the Truman Years* (New York: Columbia University Press, 2004); Alan Brinkley, *The End of Reform: New Deal Liberalism in Recession and War* (New York: Vintage Book, 1995).

44. This phrase is the title of Michael Sherry's book, *In the Shadow of War: The United States since the 1930s* (New Haven, Conn.: Yale University Press, 1995).

45. See Brinkley, *The End of Reform*; Wendy L. Wall, *Inventing the "American Way": The Politics of Consensus from the New Deal to the Civil Rights Movement* (New York: Oxford University Press, 2008), 104–131; Lewis A. Erenberg and Susan E. Hirsch, eds., *The War in American Culture: Society and Consciousness in World War II* (Chicago: University of Chicago Press, 1996); May, *Big Tomorrow*.

46. "'Fighting 69th' of the Screen Arrives in Town," *New York Times*, 23 January 1940, 16; "Veterans of 69th Recall War Days," *New York Times*, 25 January 1940, 23.

47. "Veterans Associations Tied to '69th' Dates," *MPH*, 24 February 1940, 56.

48. Ibid.

49. "Msgr. Sheen Scores Youth Congress," *New York Times*, 4 March 1940, 5.

50. Doherty, *Pre-Code Hollywood*, 85, 129–130.

51. Thomas Doherty, *Projections of War: Hollywood, American Culture and World War II* (New York: Columbia University Press, 1993).

52. On predicating public obligations on private interests during World War II, see Robert B. Westbrook, "Fighting for the American Family," in *The Power of Culture: Critical Essays in American History*, ed. Richard Wightman Fox and T. J. Jackson Lears (Chicago: University of Chicago Press, 1993), 195–221.

53. For my account on the story of Bernadette and Lourdes, I draw heavily on Ruth Harris, *Lourdes: Body and Spirit in the Secular Age* (New York: Viking, 1999).

54. See Colleen McDannell, *Material Christianity: Religion and Popular Culture in America* (New Haven, Conn.: Yale University Press, 1995), 132–162.

55. John T. McGreevy, "Bronx Miracle," *American Quarterly* 52 (September 2000): 415–418.

56. See "Modern Miracle," *Time*, 8 June 1942, 90; Franz Werfel, "Writing 'Bernadette,'" *Commonweal*, 29 May 1942, 125–126. On the religiously plural character of the movie, particularly in regard to its production, see Paula M. Kane, "Jews and Catholics Converge: 'The Song of Bernadette' (1943)," in *Catholics in the Movies*, ed. Colleen McDannell (New York: Oxford University Press, 2008), 83–105.

57. On Lourdes and pilgrimage, see Dorothy N. Dixon, "At Lourdes," *Commonweal*, 18 August 1933, 389; Rose Marie, "Lourdes in Springtime," *Commonweal*, 39 March 1934, 600–601; Leo R. Ward, "Things of Earth at Lourdes," *Ave Maria*, 13

February 1937, 201–203; A. Bruens, "A Side Trip to Lourdes," *Ave Maria*, 13 February 1943, 199–202. On Lourdes and illness, see Joseph B. McAllister, "A Haven of the Afflicted," *Ave Maria*, 9 November 1935, 592–596. On the miraculous at Lourdes, see Grace L. May, "Finding Faith at Lourdes," *Ave Maria*, 6 June 1931, 705–709, and 13 June 1931, 745–750; Carla Zawisch, "The Crowds at Lourdes," *Catholic Digest*, January 1944, 45–48. On Lourdes and war and peace, see Eugene P. Murphy, "The Great Tridium," *America*, 20 April 1935, 33–34. On the privileging of redemptive suffering within Catholic devotional culture, see Robert Orsi, "'Mildred, is it fun to be a cripple?': The Culture of Suffering in Mid-Twentieth-Century American Catholicism," *South Atlantic Quarterly: Catholic Lives/Contemporary America* 93 (Summer 1994): 547–590.

58. "Get 'Bernadette' Portraits," *MPH*, 8 April 1944, 42; "Big Ad Campaign for 'Bernadette' in Toledo," *MPH*, 24 June 1944, 96.

59. "'Bernadette' Opens in New York," *MPH*, 29 January 1944, 37; "Eye-Intriguing Displays," *MPH*, 22 April 1944, 46; "Some Sure-Fire Promotions," *MPH*, 20 May 1944, 64; "Showmen Promotions," *MPH*, 1 April 1944, 52.

60. *Christian Herald*, January 1944, 3.

61. William Weaver, "Song of Bernadette," *Motion Picture Daily*, 22 December 1943, in Song of Bernadette File, Production Code Administration, Special Collections, Margaret Herrick Library, AMPAS.

62. Promotion literature in Song of Bernadette File, Henry King Collection, Special Collections, Margaret Herrick Library, AMPAS.

63. *Variety*, 22 December 1943, in Song of Bernadette File, Production Code Administration, Special Collections, Margaret Herrick Library, AMPAS.

64. Terry Ramsaye, "Bernadette," *MPH*, 29 January 1949, 7.

65. Philip T. Hartung, "The Song," *Commonweal*, 11 February 1944, 421.

66. Jerry Cotter, "Stage and Screen," *Sign*, February 1944, 416.

67. "What the Picture Did for Me," *MPH*, 22 July 1944, 38.

68. *MPH*, 19 August 1944, 52.

69. *MPH*, 17 June 1944, 70.

70. "'Bernadette' to Continue at Advanced Admissions," *MPH*, 22 April 1944, 30.

71. Kane notes this point as well in her "Jews and Catholics Converge," 101–102.

72. May, *Big Tomorrow*, 139–174.

73. On the role of movies in developing a new Americanism, see May, *Big Tomorrow*.

74. Catherine Brown, Toledo, Ohio, to Eric Johnston, 25 January 1947; Virginia Griffin, Cedartown, Ga., to Johnston, 27 May 1946; Lucy Ann Morgan, no address, to Johnston, 19 May (no year) (emphasis in original). All letters are in Religion File, MPAA Breen Office Files, Special Collections, Margaret Herrick Library, AMPAS.

1. On Wilder, film noir, and the origins of the postwar counterculture, see Lary May, *The Big Tomorrow: Hollywood and the Politics of the American Way* (Chicago: University of Chicago Press, 2000), 230–256.

2. See, for instance, Eric Michael Mazur, "Going My Way? Crosby and Catholicism on the Road to America," in *Going My Way: Bing Crosby and American Culture,* ed. Ruth Prigozy and Walter Raubicheck (Rochester, N.Y.: University of Rochester Press, 2007), 17–33; Lawrence J. McCaffrey, " 'Going My Way' and Irish-American Catholicism: Myth and Reality," *New Hibernia Review* 4 (Autumn 2000): 119–217; Mary Gordon, "Father Chuck: A Reading of 'Going My Way' and 'The Bells of St. Mary's', or Why Priests Made Us Crazy," in "Catholic Lives/Contemporary America," special issue, *South Atlantic Quarterly* 93 (Summer 1994): 591–601. For a useful discussion of Jewish assimilation in *The Jazz Singer,* see Michael Rogin, *Blackface, White Noise: Jewish Immigrants in the Hollywood Melting Pot* (Berkeley: University of California Press, 1998), 73–120.

3. May, *Big Tomorrow*, 139–174. For May's own discussion of *Going My Way*, see 157–158, which has influenced my analysis of the film.

4. "'Going My Way' Heads for New Paramount Record," *Motion Picture Herald* (hereafter cited as *MPH*), 8 July 1944, 39.

5. According to *MPH, Going My Way* was the box office champion for the months of June, July, and August; see *MPH*, 16 September 1944, 46.

6. *MPH*, 21 October 1944, 39.

7. *MPH*, 11 November 1944, 58.

8. *MPH*, 18 November 1944, 44.

9. "Young Father Crosby," *Newsweek*, 15 May 1944, 78.

10. "Movie of the Week: 'Going My Way,'" *Life*, 1 May 1944, 69.

11. *Christian Herald*, August 1944, 47.

12. Manny Farber, "Fathers and Song," *New Republic*, 8 May 1944, 629.

13. "New Picture," *Time*, 1 May 1944, 90.

14. Philip T. Hartung, "Your Way Is My Way," *Commonweal*, 28 April 1944, 41.

15. "Comics in Cassocks!!" *Extension*, August 1944, 10 (italics in original).

16. Ibid.

17. John Clarence Petrie, "Is Catholicism 'Going My Way'?" *Christian Century*, 4 October 1944, 1132–1134.

18. Francis Alstock to Russell Pierce, 9 October 1944, Motion Picture Society for the Americas Liaison Project File, Box 952, Office of Inter-American Affairs Archives, National Archives, Washington, D.C.

19. *Going My Way* Press Book, 10, 14–15, Special Collections, Margaret Herrick Library, Academy of Motion Pictures Arts and Sciences, Beverly Hills, Calif. (hereafter cited as AMPAS).

20. See Armstrong's introductory essay and chapters by contributors in Elizabeth Armstrong, ed., *Birth of the Cool: California Art, Design, and Culture at Midcentury,* Orange County Museum of Art (New York: Prestel Publishing, 2007). Benjamin Schwarz's review of the Armstrong volume influenced my thinking on this point. See Benjamin Schwarz, "California Cool," *Atlantic Monthly,* March 2008, 87–89. On West Coast jazz, see Ted Gioia, *West Coast Jazz: Modern Jazz in California, 1945– 1960* (Berkeley: University of California Press, 1998).

21. On Crosby's background and early life, see Gary Giddins, *Bing Crosby: A Pocketful of Dreams—The Early Years, 1903–1940* (Boston: Little, Brown, 2001), 27–28, 53–75.

22. Kevin Starr, *The Dream Endures: California Enters the 1940s* (New York: Oxford University Press, 1997), 174.

23. See Leo McCarey, "Comedy and a Touch of Cuckoo," *Extension,* November 1944, 5, 34. On McCarey, see also William H. Mooring, "What McCarey Forgot to Tell," *Extension,* 1944, 5; Jerry Cotter, "Hollywood's Other Leo," *Sign,* December 1944, 236–237; Jerome M. McKeever, "The McCarey Touch: The Life and Films of Leo McCarey," Ph.D. diss., Case Western Reserve, 2000 (Ann Arbor, Mich.: UMI, 1999), 8–14.

24. On Burke, see Giddins, *Bing Crosby,* 422, 581.

25. Patrick Duffy to Leo McCarey, 26 September 1944, Correspondence to and from Leo McCarey, 1956 Folder, Gen. Box 5, Leo McCarey Collection, American Film Institute, Los Angeles (emphasis in original).

26. See May, *Big Tomorrow,* 55–99, and Robert S. McElvaine, *The Great Depression: America, 1929–1941* (New York: Times Books, 1993), 196–223.

27. May is particularly interested in reading *Going My Way*'s redirection of popular culture as a sanction for private consumerism; see May, *Big Tomorrow,* 157–158. But equally important is how the film harnesses popular culture to a project of traditional cultural enrichment and moral improvement through its association with religion and high culture.

28. This analysis of the familiar, nonthreatening character of Catholic space depicted in *Going My Way* is from my essay "America's Favorite Priest: 'Going My Way' (1944)," in *Catholics in the Movies,* ed. Colleen McDannell (New York: Oxford University Press, 2008), 111–116.

29. See Lary May's discussion of Hollywood movies of the thirties, *Big Tomorrow,* 55–99. On the "alternative spirituality" of *Angels with Dirty Faces* in particular, see Thomas J. Ferraro, "Boys to Men: *Angels with Dirty Faces* (1938)," in McDannell, *Catholics in the Movies,* 59–82.

30. Ibid., 157–158. Although May identifies *Going My Way* as an example of the cultural conversion pattern of forties movies, his analysis is quite brief and does not attend to the many dimensions of the film's revision of culture.

31. On the containment of popular culture in Hollywood films more generally, see May, *Big Tomorrow*, 139–174.

32. See May, *Big Tomorrow*, 55–99; see also Elizabeth Kendall, *The Runaway Bride: Hollywood Romantic Comedy of the 1930s* (New York: Cooper Square Press, 1990).

33. May, *Big Tomorrow*, 11–53, 89.

34. This analysis of *One Foot in Heaven* is from my "America's Favorite Priest," 122–123.

35. "One Foot in Heaven" *Motion Picture Herald*, 4 October 1941, in *One Foot in Heaven* File, Production Code Files, Margaret Herrick Library, AMPAS.

36. "One Foot in Heaven," *Variety*, 30 September 1941, in *One Foot in Heaven* File, Production Code Files, Margaret Herrick Library, AMPAS.

37. On *Going My Way*'s influence in the subsequent history of American popular culture, see my "America's Favorite Priest," 107–109, 124–125. On *True Confessions* as a dialogue with *Going My Way*, see Timothy J. Meagher, "Cops, Priests and the Decline of Irish America, *True Confessions* (1981)," in McDannell, *Catholics in the Movies*, 227–249.

CHAPTER FOUR. PRO-*LIFE* CATHOLICS

1. *Life*, 23 November 1936, 20, 24–25, 27, 34.

2. On religion, including Catholicism, in *Life*, see David Morgan, "The Image of Religion in American 'Life,'" in *Looking at "Life" Magazine*, ed. Erika Doss (Washington, D.C.: Smithsonian Institution Press, 2001), 139–157.

3. Quotation is in Doss, *Looking at "Life" Magazine*, 2. On *Life* magazine, see Wendy Kozol, Life's *America: Family and Nation in Postwar Photojournalism* (Philadelphia: Temple University Press, 1994); and the essays in Doss, *Looking at Life Magazine*.

4. On Luce, see Robert Edwin Herzstein, *Henry R. Luce: A Political Portrait of the Man Who Created the American Century* (New York: Charles Scribner's Sons, 1994); W. A. Swanberg, *Luce and His Empire* (New York: Scribner, 1972).

5. Henry R. Luce, "The American Century," *Life*, 17 February 1941, 61–65.

6. See, for instance, Martin Marty, *Modern American Religion*, vol. 3, *Under God, Indivisible, 1941–1960* (Chicago: University of Chicago Press, 1996).

7. Erika Doss, "Introduction," in Doss, *Looking at "Life" Magazine*, 11.

8. Luce, "American Century," 65.

9. Ibid.

10. See, for instance, Robert McElvaine, *The Great Depression, America, 1929–1941* (New York: Times Books, 1993), 196–223. Similarly, Lizabeth Cohen argues that industrial workers in Chicago pursued a "moral capitalism" in the efforts to form the CIO

and in their support for the New Deal; see her *Making a New Deal: Industrial Workers in Chicago, 1919–1939* (New York: Cambridge University Press, 1991), esp. 251–289.

11. In addition to McElvaine, *Great Depression*, 196–223, see Lary May, *The Big Tomorrow: Hollywood and the Politics of the American Way* (Chicago: University of Chicago Press, 2000), 11–135.

12. In addition to the essays in the Doss volume, *Looking at "Life" Magazine,* see Wendy Kozol, *"Life's" America: Family and Nation in Postwar Photojournalism* (Philadelphia: Temple University Press, 1994).

13. On Luce's efforts to encourage business leaders to rethink their Victorian assumptions about themselves and the relationship between business enterprise and the rest of society, see Michael Augspurger, *An Economy of Abundant Beauty: "Fortune" Magazine and Depression America* (Ithaca, N.Y.: Cornell University Press, 2004).

14. On Protestant-Catholic tensions in the postwar era, see Marty, *Modern American Religion*, vol. 3; and John McGreevy, *Catholicism and American Freedom: A History* (New York: W. W. Norton, 2003), 166–188.

15. Terry Smith, "Life-Style Modernity: Making Modern America," in Doss, *Looking at "Life" Magazine,* 30.

16. On Longwell, see "Daniel Longwell, A Founder of 'Life,'" *New York Times,* 22 November 1968, 47; on Billings, see "John S. Billings of 'Life' Is Dead; First Managing Editor Was 77," *New York Times,* 27 August 1975, 42; on Hicks, see "Wilson Hicks, a Former Editor of *Life* Magazine, Dies at 73," *New York Times,* 7 July 1970, 39.

17. "Solemn High Mass Is Celebrated in St. Patrick's Cathedral," *Life,* 21 March 1938, 32–36.

18. "The American Legion Takes New York City," *Life,* 4 October 1937, 28.

19. "Chicago's Perpetual Novena Is Now the Biggest U.S. Religious Service," *Life,* 7 March 1938, 54–55.

20. "Britain's No. 1 Catholic Kisses Its Only Cardinal's Ring," *Life,* 31 January 1938, 52.

21. "The Catholics of Mexico Crawl to the Shrine of Guadalupe," *Life,* 10 January, 1938, 48. See also "Mexico: Can a Socialist at Home Be a Good Neighbor Abroad?" *Life,* 11 April 1938, 53. A story on Ireland also included the image of the kneeling Catholic; see "Ireland: A New Flag Brings Hope to an Old and Pious Land," *Life,* 24 July 1939, 59.

22. "The President's Album," *Life,* 23 November 1936, 27.

23. "'Life' Goes to a Party," *Life,* 21 June 1937, 88–90; see also "Pious Workers Go on a Retreat," *Life,* 2 August 1937, 70–74.

24. "Sidewalk Prayers to Governor Save Four out of Six Murderers," *Life,* 18 January 1937, 18.

25. "Newspictures of the Week," *Life,* 2 May 1938, 17.

26. "City's Mayor Hague: Last of the Bosses, Not First of the Dictators," *Life,* 7 February 1938, 44–51.

27. "'Little Italy' Cloaks Its Healing Saint in Dollars," *Life*, 6 September 1937, 71–72.

28. On Italian Catholic popular devotion, see Robert Orsi, *The Madonna of 115th Street: Faith and Community in Italian Harlem, 1880–1950* (New Haven, Conn.: Yale University Press, 1985).

29. "Chinese School," *Life*, 23 November 1936, 24.

30. On St. Mary's Chinese Mission, see Jeffrey M. Burns, Ellen Skerrett, and Joseph M. White, eds., *Keeping Faith: European and Asian Catholic Immigrants* (Maryknoll, N.Y.: Orbis Books, 2000), 230, 234–239; William A. Lynahan, "A Home Foreign Mission," *Extension* (October 1936): 18, 36–38.

31. "Pious Workers Go on a Retreat," *Life*, 2 August 1937, 70–74.

32. On the labor movement in Chicago, see Cohen, *Making a New Deal*.

33. On Kirkland, see Mary Ann Johnson, ed., *The Many Faces of Hull-House: The Photographs of Wallace Kirkland* (Urbana: University of Illinois Press, 1989), 1–7.

34. On the National Laymen's Retreat Movement, see *Proceedings of the Sixth National Conference: Laymen's Retreat Movement in the United States of America* (Chicago: n.d.). On Mulligan, see *Proceedings*, 140. On outreach to Chicago workers, see William I. Lonergan, "A Catholic Laymen's Conference," *America*, 31 January 1931, 403.

35. "The Vatican," *Life*, 26 December 1938, 36–47.

36. "First U.S. Troops Land in Greenland to Prepare Main Army and Air Base," *Life*, 18 August 1941, 26.

37. "U.S. Remembers Pearl Harbor Day with Ships and Prayers," *Life*, 21 December 1942, 34–35.

38. "Life Goes to a Hero's Homecoming," *Life*, 11 October 1943, 126–129.

39. "Foundlings," *Life*, 21 February 1944, 115.

40. "The Brides of Christ," *Life*, 6 March 1944, 77–79.

41. "The Women Say Their Wartime Prayers," *Life*, 13 September 1943, 69–91.

42. On the gendered encoding of *Life*'s depiction of the obligations of war, see Kozol, *'Life's' America*, 56–69.

43. See, for instance, Philip Gleason, *Speaking of Diversity: Language and Ethnicity in Twentieth-Century America* (Baltimore, Md.: Johns Hopkins University Press, 1992), 153–187; Gary Gerstle, "The Working Class Goes to War," in *The War in American Culture: Society and Consciousness during World War II*, ed. Lewis A. Erenberg and Susan E. Hirsch (Chicago: University of Chicago Press), 105–127.

44. For instance, Harold E. Fey wrote a series of eight articles under the title "Can Catholicism Win America?" in the *Christian Century* from 29 November 1944 to 17 January 1945. The editors of the *Christian Century* also expressed anxiety about Catholic separatism in "Pluralism—National Menace," *Christian Century*, 13 June 1951, 701–703. On tensions surrounding Catholicism during the 1940s, see also John McGreevy, *Catholicism and American Freedom: A History* (New York: W. W. Norton, 2003), 166–168.

45. "An 11-Year-Old-Girl Is Made a Saint," *Life*, 17 July 1950, 107–113.

46. Paul Blanshard wrote two books highly critical of the Catholic Church, *American Freedom and Catholic Power* (Boston: Beacon Press, 1949), and *Communism, Democracy, and Catholic Power* (Boston: Beacon Press, 1951). The former initially was published as a series of articles in the *Nation* magazine in 1948. See Blanshard, *American Freedom and Catholic Power*, 7.

47. Thomas C. Reeves, *America's Bishop: The Life and Times of Fulton J. Sheen* (San Francisco: Encounter Books, 2001), 176–178.

48. Jessica Holland, interview with Andrew Heiskell, Columbia University Libraries Oral History Research Office: Notable New Yorkers, 1987, available at http://www.columbia.edu/cu/lweb/digital/collections/nny/heiskella/transcripts/heiskella_1_17_802.html, accessed 13 December 2006.

49. Swanberg, *Luce and His Empire*, 238; John K. Jessup, ed., *The Ideas of Henry Luce* (New York: Atheneum, 1969), 30.

50. See Swanberg, *Luce and His Empire*, 149–150 for more on Alexander, and 327, 333–334, 360, and 402 for more on Hughes.

51. John Foster Dulles, "A Righteous Faith," *Life*, 28 December 1942, 49. See also the editorial "Christmas," *Life*, 27 December 1943, 28.

52. William C. Bullitt, "The World from Rome, " *Life*, 4 September 1944, 94–109. On the controversy surrounding the essay, see Swanberg, *Luce and His Empire*, 218–219.

53. "The Kremlin and the Vatican," *Life*, 14 February 1944, 32.

54. "'Getting Tough' with Russia," *Life*, 18 March 1946, 36; John Foster Dulles, "Soviet Foreign Policy," *Life*, 3 June 1946, 112–122, and "Soviet Foreign Policy, Part II," *Life*, 10 June 1946, 119–130, Dulles quote is on 122.

55. Roger Butterfield, "Cardinal-Designate Spellman, Part I," *Life*, 21 January 1946, 100–112, and "Cardinal-Designate Spellman, Part II," *Life*, 28 January 1946, 87–98.

56. Butterfield, "Cardinal-Designate Spellman, Part I," 102, 106.

57. Butterfield, "Cardinal-Designate Spellman, Part II," 88, 92, 98.

58. "The Door Opens on a Holy Year," *Life*, 9 January 1950, 26–29.

59. "11-Year-Old-Girl Is Made a Saint."

60. See, for instance, two essays in *Religion and the Cold War*, ed. Dianne Kirby (New York: Palgrave Macmillan, 2003): Frank J. Coppa, "Pope Pius XII and the Cold War: The Post-war Confrontation between Catholicism and Communism," 50–66, and Peter C. Kent, "The Lonely Cold War of Pope Pius XII," 67–76.

61. Paul Hutchinson, "Does Europe Face Holy War?" *Life*, 23 September 1946, 61–68.

62. "A Man of Love Fights Communists in Italy," *Life*, 22 March 1948, 37.

63. "Italy's Victory," *Life*, 3 May 1948, 36.

64. Graham Greene, "The Assumption of Mary," *Life*, 30 October 1950, 50–58.

On Greene's transatlantic success in these years, see Norman Sherry, *The Life of Graham Greene*, vol. 2, *1939–1955* (New York: Viking 1994), 301.

65. Graham Greene, "The Pope Who Remains a Priest," *Life*, 24 September 1951, 146–162. On Protestant-Catholic tensions in the late forties and early fifties, see Robert S. Ellwood, *The Fifties Spiritual Marketplace: American Religion in a Decade of Conflict* (New Brunswick, N.J.: Rutgers University Press, 1997), 51–60.

66. Russell W. Davenport, "A 'Life' Round Table on the Pursuit of Happiness," *Life*, 12 July 1948, 96.

67. "'People's Bishop' Has a Silver Jubilee," *Life*, 18 May 1953, 63–66. On Sheil, see Roger L. Treat, *Bishop Sheil and the CYO* (New York: Messner, 1951).

68. John Chamberlain, "Philip Murray," *Life*, 11 February 1946, 80; "The Jesuits in America," *Life*, 11 October 1954, 142–143.

69. "An Italian Family in America," *Life*, 5 October 1953, 135–151.

70. On the centrality of the middle-class family to *Life*'s vision of America, see Kozol, *"Life's" America*.

71. See, for instance, Blanshard, *American Freedom and Catholic Power*.

72. "The Biggest U.S. Archdiocese," *Life*, 26 December 1955, 62–69.

73. "The American Moral Consensus," *Life*, 26 December 1955, 56–57. Murray's own ideas on consensus and American public philosophy were published as *We Hold These Truths: Catholic Reflections on the American Proposition* (Kansas City, Mo.: Sheed & Ward, 1988).

74. "The Methodists," *Life*, 10 November 1947, 33.

75. "God's Underground," *Life*, 18 April 1949, 34.

76. "Trappist Monastery," *Life*, 23 May 1949, 84–89.

77. "The Jesuits in America," *Life*, 11 October 1954, 134–148.

78. Ibid., 134.

79. Ibid., 138–141.

80. Another example of *Life*'s highly favorable treatment of Catholic religious orders is its photo-essay of a Benedictine abbey, with photographs by Gordon Parks, "A Cloistered Life of Devotion," *Life*, 26 December 1955, 119–123.

81. "Priest to the Campesinos," *Life*, 14 July 1952, 97–103.

82. "Parochial High School," *Life*, 18 January 1954, 63–70; "Nuns in a Musical Frolic," *Life*, 6 August 1956, 115–116, "Nun, President and Poet," *Life*, 10 June 1957, 1, 29–132.

83. "A Cloistered Life of Devotion," 119–123; Emmet John Hughes, "The 'Strange, Mute Magic' of Pius XII: The Impact of a Shy, Scholarly Pope," *Life*, 26 December 1955, 158–160; John Courtney Murray, "Special Catholic Challenges," *Life*, 26 December 1955, 144–146.

84. Letter to editor, *Life*, 16 January 1956, 8.

85. "Knights of Columbus in 75th Year," *Life,* 27 May 1957, 54–67.

86. James A. Pike, "Should a Catholic Be President?" *Life,* 21 December 1959, 78–85; "Catholics and U.S. Democracy," *Life,* 21 December 1959, 30.

87. "The Altar Boy—Momentary Angel," *Life,* 23 March 1959, 103–106.

CHAPTER FIVE. PERFORMING CATHOLICISM IN AN AGE OF CONSENSUS

1. "Liberal or Reactionary?" *Life Is Worth Living,* videocassette, Sheen Productions, Rochester, N.Y. Each season of Sheen's series was published by McGraw-Hill as a separate volume also entitled *Life Is Worth Living,* with the exception of the third season, which was entitled *Thinking Life Through.* However, my analysis of the television show is based primarily upon video- and audiocassette copies from Sheen Productions and from the Fulton J. Sheen Archives, St. Bernard's Seminary, Rochester, N.Y.; I have used the written texts to supplement my study.

2. Will Herberg noted Sheen's popularity as a sign of Catholicism having become one of the great religions of America's triple melting pot; see Herberg, *Protestant-Catholic-Jew,* rev. ed. (Garden City, N.Y.: Anchor Books, 1960), 161. See also Christopher Owen Lynch, *Selling Catholicism: Bishop Sheen and the Power of Television* (Lexington: University Press of Kentucky, 1998); Mark S. Massa, *Catholics and American Culture: Fulton Sheen, Dorothy Day and the Notre Dame Football Team* (New York: Crossroad Books, 1999), 82–101. Sheen often appears in histories of American religion of the 1950s as symbolic of the culture religion of the era; see, for instance, James Hudnut-Beumler, *Looking for God in the Suburbs: The Religion of the American Dream and Its Critics, 1945–1965* (New Brunswick, N.J.: Rutgers University Press, 1994), 62–63.

3. George Lipsitz, "The Meaning of Memory: Family, Class and Ethnicity in Early Network Television," in Lipsitz, *Time Passages: Collective Memory and American Popular Culture* (Minneapolis: University of Minnesota Press, 1990), 39–75.

4. This account of Sheen's life draws heavily upon Thomas C. Reeves, *America's Bishop: The Life and Times of Fulton J. Sheen* (San Francisco: Encounter Books, 2001), and Sheen's memoir, *Treasure in Clay: The Autobiography of Fulton J. Sheen* (Garden City, N.Y.: Doubleday, 1980).

5. Quoted passages are from Philip Gleason, *Contending with Modernity: Catholic Higher Education in the Twentieth Century* (New York: Oxford University Press, 1995), 113. On the neo-Thomist character of seminary life while Sheen was at St. Paul, see also Reeves, *America's Bishop,* 32–33.

6. Reeves, *America's Bishop,* 37–38, 50, 53, 59.

7. Ibid., 59.

8. On Sheen's restlessness at CUA and the beginnings of his wider public work, see Reeves, *America's Bishop,* 62–65. On Sheen's early radio broadcasts, see Sheen, *Treasure in Clay,* 63–64.

9. Edward J. Heffron, "Ten Years of the Catholic Hour," *Ecclesiastical Review* 102 (March 1940): 238–249.

10. Margaret Mary Gannon, "Dr. Fulton Sheen, Philosopher and Catholic-Hour Celebrity," *Queen's Work* 23 (April 1931): 1. I am grateful to Matt Minix for bringing this source to my attention.

11. The concept of "imagined community" derives from Benedict Anderson's work on the cultural dimensions of nationalism; see his *Imagined Communities: Reflections on the Origin and Spread of Nationalism* (London: Verso, 1983). Michelle Hilmes has used this concept in her important work on the cultural history of radio in America. Consequently, I am drawing on Hilmes in arguing that the *Catholic Hour* constructed an imagined community of American Catholicism in the 1930s and 1940s. See Hilmes, *Radio Voices: American Broadcasting, 1922–1952* (Minneapolis: University of Minnesota Press, 1997), esp. xiii–33.

12. See essays in Michele Hilmes and Jason Loviglio, eds., *Radio Reader: Essays in the Cultural History of Radio* (New York: Routledge, 2002).

13. On this postimmigrant generation of American Catholics between the wars, see Robert Orsi, *Thank You St. Jude: Women's Devotions of the Patron Saint of Hopeless Causes* (New Haven, Conn.: Yale University Press, 1996), 30–31.

14. Fulton J. Sheen, *Hymn of the Conquered* (Washington, D.C.: National Council of Catholic Men, 1933), 26. Sheen's yearly radio broadcasts were published in written form by the National Council of Catholic Men. My analysis of his talks is based on these texts. For an excellent study of the romantic impulse in American Catholicism, see James Terence Fisher, *The Catholic Counterculture in America, 1933–1962* (Chapel Hill: University of North Carolina Press, 1989).

15. Fulton J. Sheen, *The Prodigal World* (Washington, D.C.: National Council of Catholic Men, n.d.), 116.

16. Sheen's critique of modern intellectual life reflected a wider Catholic hostility to modern thought; see William M. Halsey, *The Survival of American Innocence: Catholicism in the Era of Disillusionment, 1920–1940* (Notre Dame, Ind.: University of Notre Dame Press, 1980).

17. Sheen, *Prodigal World*, 34.

18. Ibid., 24.

19. Ibid., 75–77.

20. Fulton J. Sheen, *Peace* (Washington, D.C: National Council of Catholic Men, n.d.), 11, 47–48, 95.

21. See Hilmes and Loviglio, *Radio Reader*.

22. Fulton J. Sheen, *The Divine Romance* (New York: D. Appleton-Century, 1940), 16.

23. Sheen, *Hymn*, 22–23.

24. Sheen, *Prodigal World*, 120.

25. Sheen, *Hymn*, 9.

26. *The Hymn of the Conquered* was the title of Sheen's 1933 radio series. The final talk of that series was entitled "The Joy of Defeat." See Sheen, *Hymn*, 107–115.

27. Fulton J. Sheen, *Manifestations of Christ* (Washington, D.C.: National Council of Catholic Men, 1932), 47.

28. Sheen, *Prodigal World*, 133.

29. Sheen, *Hymn*, 26, 49.

30. Sheen, *Peace*, 23.

31. Sheen, *Prodigal World*, 78.

32. Ibid., 78–79.

33. Ibid., 103.

34. Sheen, *Hymn*, 25.

35. Sheen, *Prodigal World*, 121.

36. Orsi, *Thank You, St. Jude*, 73–83.

37. Sheen, *Manifestations of Christ*, 9; Sheen, *Hymn*, 53.

38. Sheen, *Manifestation of Christ*, 14–21.

39. "Biography by Sheen," *Time*, 1 January 1940, 33.

40. "Monsignor's Tenth," *Time*, 11 March 1940, 60–61.

41. "Reconversion," *Time*, 22 October 1945, 60.

42. "Worker's Loss," *Newsweek*, 22 October 1945, 100.

43. See Reeves, *America's Bishop*, 110–111, 135, 170–172, 175–178.

44. Sheen appears to have been one of the hardest-working men in American Catholicism during the 1930s, given how often his name appeared in notices and articles in Catholic magazines. For instance, Sheen's address to the National Conference of Laymen's Retreat Movement was mentioned in William I. Lonergan, "The Key to National Reform," *America*, 19 January 1935, 354. His talk at the Jesuit magazine *America*'s twenty-fifth anniversary celebration was noted in "Thanks for Everything," *America*, 21 April 1934, 28. Sheen conducted a retreat for the unemployed, promoted by Dorothy Day's Catholic Worker movement in the winter of 1937. See "Toasts within the Month," *Sign*, March 1937, 453.

45. "Monsignor's Tenth," 61.

46. On the Carnegie Hall and Washington rallies, see Reeves, *America's Bishop*, 105.

47. On the National Eucharistic Congress in Cleveland, see Frank S. Adams, "43,000 Hear Smith Assail Communism as Foe of Church," *New York Times*, 25 September 1935, 1. Sheen's address was published in two parts as "The Mystical Body" in *Commonweal* 1 November 1935, 7–9, and 8 November 1935, 36–39.

48. On *Peace of Soul*, see Robert S. Ellwood, *The Fifties Spiritual Marketplace: American Religion in a Decade of Conflict* (New Brunswick, N.J.: Rutgers University Press, 1997), 12–13. The debate between Sheen and psychiatrists, including some

Catholic doctors who deeply resented his condemnation of their field, raged in the pages of the *New York Times* in 1947. See, for instance, "Sheen Denounces Psychoanalysis," *New York Times,* 10 March 1947, 18; "Msgr. Sheen's Attack Hit by Psychiatrists," *New York Times,* 2 July 1947, 17; "Dr. Brill Replies to Msgr. Sheen," *New York Times,* 6 July 1947, 42; "Psychiatrist Quits in Catholic Clash," *New York Times,* 20 July 20 1947, 5; "Msgr. Sheen Lays Error to Press," *New York Times,* 21 July 1947, 8; "Sheen Criticized by Psychoanalyst," *New York Times,* 22 July 1947, 16.

49. Reeves, *America's Bishop,* 211–212, 218.

50. "Microphone Missionary," *Time,* 14 April 1952, 72–79.

51. George H. Gallup, *The Gallup Poll: Public Opinion, 1935–1971,* vol. 2, *1949–1958* (New York: Random House, 1972), 1113, 1296, 1387, 1462, 1536; on the 1956 ranking, see 1462.

52. Kathleen Riley Fields, "Bishop Fulton J. Sheen: An American Catholic Response to the Twentieth Century," Ph.D. diss., University of Notre Dame (Ann Arbor, Mich.: UMI, 1988), 355.

53. Lynn Spigel, *Make Way for TV: Television and the Family Ideal in Postwar America* (Chicago: University of Chicago Press, 1992), 50–72.

54. See ibid., 148–150, and House Interstate and Foreign Commerce Committee, *Hearing before a Subcommittee of the Committee on Interstate and Foreign Commerce: Investigation on Radio and Television Programs,* H.Res. 278, 82nd Cong., 2nd sess., 25 September 1952, 323–357.

55. Spigel, *Make Way for TV,* 54–55.

56. Ibid., 32.

57. Robert S. Ellwood, *The Fifties Spiritual Marketplace: American Religion in a Decade of Conflict* (New Brunswick, N.J.: Rutgers University Press, 1997), 54.

58. See John McGreevy, *Catholics and American Freedom: A History* (New York: W. W. Norton, 2003), 166–188.

59. Robert Kass, "Film and Television," *Catholic World,* May 1952, 146. See also Larry Newman, "Bishop Sheen and the TV Camera," *Catholic Digest,* May 1952, 115–117; "Editorial in Pictures and in Print," *Sign,* May 1952, 5.

60. Alan Brinkley, *The End of Reform: New Deal Liberalism in Recession and War* (New York: Vintage Books, 1995); Lizabeth Cohen, *A Consumers' Republic: The Politics of Mass Consumption in Postwar America* (New York: Vintage Books, 2004); Lary May, *The Big Tomorrow: Hollywood and the Politics of the American Way* (Chicago: University of Chicago Press, 2000); Elaine Tyler May, *Homeward Bound: American Families in the Cold War Era* (New York: Basic Books, 1988); Robert Westbrook, "Fighting for the American Family: Private Interests and Political Obligation in World War II," in *The Power of Culture: Critical Essays in American History,* ed. Richard Wightman Fox and T. J. Jackson Lears (Chicago: University of Chicago Press, 1993), 194–221.

61. Lipsitz, "The Meaning of Memory."

62. See Lynch, *Selling Catholicism*. One of Lynch's chapters is entitled "Quest for Stability in the Midst of Change." His study is a rhetorical analysis of *Life Is Worth Living*, astutely showing how Sheen offered his viewers a Catholic romance and adventure rooted in Sheen's attraction to the Middle Ages. Lynch is, however, more interested in arguing that Sheen provided Americans a rhetoric of clear moral boundaries and certainties rather than in connecting Sheen's romantic Catholic medievalism to the particular ideological project of postwar consensus culture that actively opposed the social values and democratic politics of the 1930s and 1940s. My understanding of the postwar consensus draws upon May, *Big Tomorrow*. Nor does Lynch see *Life Is Worth Living* as part of a wider pattern of early television that recuperated older, alternative ethnic traditions in order to legitimate the new privatized social order of the postwar period. On this interpretation of television, see Lipsitz, "The Meaning of Memory," which has influenced my analysis of Sheen's show.

63. Lynch notes this as well. See Lynch, *Selling Catholicism*, 130.

64. "Why Some Become Communists," *Life Is Worth Living*, videocassette, Sheen Productions, Rochester, N.Y.

65. Ibid.

66. "Man, Captain of His Own Destiny," *Life Is Worth Living*, videocassette, Sheen Productions, Rochester, N.Y.

67. "The Russian Lullaby of Co-existence," *Life Is Worth Living*, videocassette, Sheen Productions, Rochester, N.Y.

68. "Communism and Russia," *Life Is Worth Living*, audiocassette, Sheen Productions, Rochester, N.Y.

69. Ibid.

70. "Teenagers," *Life Is Worth Living*, audiocassette, Sheen Productions, Rochester, N.Y.

71. "War As a Judgment of God," *Life Is Worth Living*, videocassette, Sheen Productions, Rochester, N.Y.

72. "Pain and Suffering," *Life Is Worth Living*, videocassette, Fulton J. Sheen Archives, St. Bernard's Seminary, Rochester, N.Y.

73. "Teenagers."

74. "For Better or Worse," *Life Is Worth Living*, videocassette, Sheen Productions, Rochester, N.Y.

75. "The Training of Children," *Life Is Worth Living*, videocassette, Sheen Productions, Rochester, N.Y.

76. "How Mothers Are Made," *Life Is Worth Living*, audiocassette, Sheen Productions, Rochester, N.Y.

77. See May, *Homeward Bound*.

78. On Sheen as an existentialist, see James T. Fisher, "American Religion since 1945," in *A Companion to Post-1945 America,* ed. Jean-Christophe Agnew and Roy Rosenzweig (New York: Blackwell, 2002), 46.

79. "Pain and Suffering."

80. "Fears and Anxieties," *Life Is Worth Living,* audiocassette, Sheen Productions, Rochester, N.Y.

81. "Man, Captain of His Destiny."

82. "War As a Judgment of God."

83. "Fears and Anxieties."

84. "Communism and Russia."

85. "Russian Lullaby of Co-existence."

86. "Pain and Suffering."

87. Ibid.

88. See Spigel, *Make Way for TV.*

89. Horace Newcomb, "Meaningful Difference in 1950s Television," in *The Other Fifties: Interrogating Midcentury American Icons,* ed. Joel Foreman (Urbana: University of Illinois Press, 1997), 113.

90. In this regard, Sheen's television show resembled the contradictions within the domestic ideology of containment that Elaine Tyler May has argued characterized 1950s American culture. See May, *Homeward Bound.*

CHAPTER SIX. FROM PUBLIC DILEMMAS TO PRIVATE VIRTUE

1. Pete Martin, "Going His Way," *Saturday Evening Post,* 30 November 1946, 12–13, 64–66, 68–70.

2. Johnston quoted in Lary May, *The Big Tomorrow: Hollywood and the Politics of the American Way* (Chicago: University of Chicago Press, 2000), 177. On Disney, see 207–208. On the Motion Picture Alliance for the Preservation of American Ideals and McCarey's participation, see Larry Ceplair and Steven Englund, *The Inquisition in Hollywood: Politics in the Film Community, 1930–1960* (Berkeley: University of California Press, 1983), 209–215, 258–259.

3. Full biographies of McCarey are rare. One recent work is Wes D. Gehring, *Leo McCarey: From Marx to McCarthy* (Lanham, Md.: Scarecrow Press, 2005). For another overview of McCarey, his life, and films, see Jerome M. McKeever, "The McCarey Touch: The Life and Films of Leo McCarey," Ph.D. diss., Case Western Reserve University, 2000 (Ann Arbor, Mich.: UMI, 1999). Additional, shorter studies of McCarey include Margaret Smith, "Laughter, Redemption, Subversion in Eight Films by Leo McCarey," *CineAction* (Summer–Fall 1990): 84–90; Robin Wood, "From 'Ruggles' to 'Rally'; or America, America! The Strange Career of Leo McCarey," *Film International* 5 (May 2007): 30–34.

4. See Gehring, *Leo McCarey*; Charles Silver, "Leo McCarey: From Marx to Mc-Carthy," *Film Comment* 9 (September–October 1973): 8–11.

5. May, *Big Tomorrow*.

6. Werner Sollors, *Beyond Ethnicity: Consent and Descent in American Culture* (New York: Oxford University Press, 1986).

7. May, *Big Tomorrow*.

8. On McCarey's biography in general and his father particularly, see Gehring, *Leo McCarey*, 1–18. See also McKeever, "McCarey Touch," 8–14.

9. On McCarey's Catholic upbringing and schooling, see Leo McCarey, "Comedy and a Touch of Cukoo," *Extension*, November 1944, 34; McKeever, "McCarey Touch," 11–12; Gehring, *Leo McCarey*, 9. On McCarey's audience with the pope, see Sidney Carroll, "Everything Happens to McCarey," *Esquire*, May 1943, 142.

10. On McCarey's early career, see McKeever, "McCarey Touch," 18–25; Gehring, *Leo McCarey*, 19–68.

11. Gehring, *Leo McCarey*, 208–209.

12. On McCarey testifying to HUAC and participation in the drive for loyalty oaths in the Screen Directors Guild, see McKeever, "McCarey Touch," 77–82, 88–93.

13. Wood, "From 'Ruggles' to 'Rally'," 27, 30.

14. Ibid.

15. Mark Winokur, *American Laughter: Immigrants, Ethnicity, and 1930s Hollywood Film Comedy* (New York: St. Martin's Press, 1996).

16. May, *Big Tomorrow*, esp. 55–99.

17. Reviews of *Ruggles of Red Gap* in *Variety*, 13 March 1935; *Hollywood Reporter*, 2 February 1935; *Daily Variety*, 2 February 1935, in *Ruggles of Red Gap* Clippings File, Core Collection, Margaret Herrick Library, Academy of Motion Picture Arts and Sciences, Beverly Hills, Calif. (hereafter cited as AMPAS). The *Chicago Tribune* review is cited in Gehring, *Leo McCarey*, 120–121, where other laudatory reviews are also referenced. *Ruggles*'s commercial success is indicated by its inclusion in "Box Office Champions for First Six Months of 1935," *Motion Picture Herald*, 10 August 1935, 32–33.

18. Charles Higham, *Charles Laughton: An Intimate Biography* (Garden City, N.J.: Doubleday, 1976), 4–5.

19. On disguised ethnicity in American film, see Winokur, *American Laughter*, esp. 179–234.

20. See Sollors, *Beyond Ethnicity*.

21. May, *Big Tomorrow*, 85–99.

22. Stanley Cavell, *The Pursuit of Happiness: The Hollywood Comedy of Remarriage* (Cambridge, Mass.: Harvard University Press, 1981), 231–263; Elizabeth Kendall, *The Runaway Bride: Hollywood Romantic Comedy of the 1930s* (New York: Cooper Square Press, 2002), 182–209.

23. See Winokur, *American Laughter*.

24. McKeever argues that McCarey "developed slapstick into a comedy of embarrassment" early in his career, and he identifies *The Awful Truth* as an example of this comedy of embarrassment during the thirties. However, he does not develop the possibility, as Mark Winokur does in *American Laughter*, that such comedy may have signified a larger cultural expression on the part of ethnic filmmakers who translated their unease as hyphenated Americans into comic portraits of American society. See McKeever, "McCarey Touch," 2, 104, 232–235. My analysis therefore draws upon Winokur's analysis of thirties comedy, which does not address McCarey, and McKeever's insight into McCarey as a director of comic embarrassment to offer a cultural interpretation of *The Awful Truth*.

25. Winokur offers an insightful reading of William Powell as a disguised ethnic in *The Thin Man* screwball comedies of the thirties, which has influenced my interpretation of Grant's character in *The Awful Truth*. See Winokur, *American Laughter*, 181–195.

26. Cavell, *Pursuit of Happiness*, 253–263.

27. See May, *Big Tomorrow*, particularly his analysis of the World War II conversion narrative in Hollywood film on 139–174.

28. Kendall also reads the growing threat of war of the late thirties as a source for the film's treatment of traditional marriage. However, she is more concerned with questions of gender than of ethnicity or religion in her account in *Runaway Bride*, 210–228. Quoted passage is on 223.

29. The PCA's anxieties about the kept woman theme and demands that the script be changed so that the characters' immorality would be punished are evident from memos from Joe Breen to J. R. McDonough, RKO studio executive; see *Love Story*, Production Code Administration Files, Special Collections, AMPAS.

30. May, *Big Tomorrow*, 139–174.

31. On the "Americans All" ideology that shaped the discourse of American identity during the war, see Philip Gleason, "Americans All," in his *Speaking of Diversity: Language and Ethnicity in Twentieth-Century America* (Baltimore, Md.: Johns Hopkins University Press, 1992), 153–187. See also Richard W. Steele, "The War on Intolerance: The Reformulation of American Nationalism, 1939–1941," *Journal of American Ethnic History* 9 (Fall 1989): 9–35.

32. May, *Big Tomorrow*, 55–99.

33. McKeever, "McCarey Touch," 77–81, 88–93; Ceplair and Englund, *Inquisition in Hollywood*, 258–259.

34. For an account of the growing opposition to the resumption of New Deal social initiatives in the postwar period, see Jonathan Bell, *The Liberal State on Trial: The Cold War and American Politics in the Truman Years* (New York: Columbia University

Press, 2004); Elizabeth Fones-Wolf, *Selling Free Enterprise: The Business Assault on Labor and Liberalism, 1945–1960* (Urbana: University of Illinois Press, 1994).

35. See his *Big Tomorrow.*

36. Will Herberg, *Protestant-Catholic-Jew* (Garden City, N.Y.: Anchor Books, 1960).

CHAPTER SEVEN. JOHN FORD'S IRISH AMERICAN CENTURY

1. On the nation as an imagined community, see Benedict Anderson, *Imagined Communities: Reflections on the Origins and Spread of Nationalism* (London: Verso, 1983). Lindsay Anderson, *About John Ford . . .* (London: Plexus, 1999); Tag Gallagher, *John Ford: The Man and His Films* (Berkeley: University of California Press, 1986); Peter Stowell, *John Ford* (Boston: Twayne Publishers, 1986); Scott Eyman, *Print the Legend: The Life and Times of John Ford* (New York: Simon and Schuster, 1999); Joseph McBride, *Searching for John Ford: A Life* (New York: St. Martin's Press, 2001).

2. See, for instance, Gaylyn Studlar, "Sacred Duties, Poetic Passions: John Ford and the Issue of Femininity in the Western," in *John Ford Made Westerns: Filming the Legend in the Sound Era,* ed. Gaylyn Studlar and Matthew Bernstein (Bloomington: Indiana University Press, 2001), 44–74; Charles Ramirez Berg, "The Margin As Center: The Multicultural Dynamics of John Ford's Westerns," in Studlar and Bernstein, *John Ford Made Westerns,* 75–101; quoted passage is on 75.

3. Lee Lourdeaux, *Italian and Irish Filmmakers in America: Ford, Capra, Coppola, and Scorsese* (Philadelphia: Temple University Press, 1990), 88–124; Paul Giles, *American Catholic Arts and Fiction: Culture, Ideology and Aesthetics* (Cambridge: Cambridge University Press, 1992), 1–31, 296–308; Richard Blake, *AfterImage: The Indelible Catholic Imagination of Six American Filmmakers* (Chicago: Loyola University Press, 2000).

4. Lary May, *The Big Tomorrow: Hollywood and the Politics of the American Way* (Chicago: University of Chicago Press, 2000). The quote is from the title of chapter 2, 55.

5. Ibid., 139–213.

6. On the dramatic changes in popular Americanism within Hollywood cinema between the 1930s and 1950s, see May's *Big Tomorrow*

7. Background details on Ford's birth and his parents are based upon McBride, *Searching for John Ford,* 20–24. On the memory of the famine on postfamine generations, see J. J. Lee, "Introduction: Interpreting Irish America," in *Making the Irish American: History and Heritage of the Irish in the United States,* ed. J. J. Lee and Marion R. T. Casey (New York: New York University Press, 2006), 17–20.

8. Ibid., 33, and Eyman, *Print the Legend,* 31.

9. For Ford's niece's comments and Ford's claim, see McBride, *Searching for John Ford,* 41, 61. On the Ku Klux Klan in Portland, see Joel W. Eastman, "From Declining Seaport to Liberty City: Portland during Depression and War," in *Creating Portland:*

History and Place in Northern New England, ed. Joseph A. Conforti (Durham: University of New Hampshire Press, 2005), 275.

10. McBride, *Searching for John Ford,* 33–36.

11. Ibid., 58, 67.

12. Quoted in Eyman, *Print the Legend,* 69–70.

13. On Ford joining the Knights of Columbus, see ibid., 54. On Ford's attendance at the Church of the Blessed Sacrament and St. Martin of Tours, see ibid., 300; the quote about the house full of priests is on 105. On Ford's pledges of abstinence before a priest, see ibid., 153. On his abstinence pledges, also see McBride, *Searching for John Ford,* 134, 201; in the same book, see 126 regarding Ford's wife's conversion to Catholicism and 347 regarding the Fords's marriage in the Catholic Church. On having priests say Mass on the sets of his films, see Eyman, *Print the Legend,* 313; Dan Ford, *Pappy: The Life of John Ford* (New York: DaCapo Press, 1998), 31; Gallagher, *John Ford,* 381.

14. McBride, *Searching for John Ford,* 64.

15. My account of Ford and his brother Frank and particularly Ford's relationship with Carey draws heavily upon ibid., 77–83, 98–100, 106–109.

16. Ibid., 103–104.

17. McBride notes Ford's grandson Dan's belief that Hollywood success created an "identity crisis" for Ford as he left his ethnic past in favor of American acceptance. See McBride, *Searching for John Ford,* 120.

18. Giles, *American Catholic Arts and Fiction,* 304–306. Giles's book is also a valuable study of Catholic artistic encounters with dominant American myths more generally.

19. On the reasons for the Ford-Carey breakup, see McBride, *Searching for John Ford,* 117, 127–129.

20. On Ford's marriage to Smith, see ibid., 122–129, and Eyman, *Print the Legend,* 67–69. On Ford's move to Fox, see Eyman, *Print the Legend,* 72–73. On *The Iron Horse,* see Lourdeaux, *Italian and Irish Filmmakers in America,* 96–98.

21. May, *Big Tomorrow,* 55–77.

22. McBride, *Searching for John Ford,* 182–184.

23. On Ford and the *Arrowsmith* production, see ibid., 186–188.

24. Ibid., 188–189.

25. Gallagher, *John Ford,* 74. McBride quotes Gallagher on this as well, in his *Searching for John Ford,* 181.

26. May, *Big Tomorrow,* 55–99.

27. McBride, *Searching for John Ford,* 54.

28. May, *Big Tomorrow,* 77–99.

29. On Rogers as a new kind of popular figure and not simply a backward-looking traditionalist, see ibid., 11–53, from which my account of Rogers heavily draws.

30. McBride, *Searching for John Ford*, 213.

31. See John Higham, *Strangers in the New Land: Patterns of American Nativism, 1860–1925*, 2nd ed. (New Brunswick, N.J.: Rutgers University Press, 1988), 264–299.

32. See May's reading of Rogers's films more generally in *Big Tomorrow*, 11–53.

33. Martin Rubin, "Mr. Ford and Mr. Rogers: The Will Rogers Trilogy," *Film Comment* 10 (January–February 1974): 57. See also May, *Big Tomorrow*, 41–43.

34. On Dunne, see Philip Dunne, *Take Two: A Life in Movies and Politics* (New York: Limelight Editions, 1992); on Nichols, see Charles J. Maland, "'Powered by a Ford?': Dudley Nichols, Authorship and Cultural Ethos in Stagecoach," in *John Ford's 'Stagecoach,'* ed. Barry Keith Grant (New York: Cambridge University Press, 2003), 48–81; on Wanger, see Matthew Bernstein, *Walter Wanger: Hollywood Independent* (Minneapolis: University of Minnesota Press, 1994), 129–150.

35. Ford's speech quoted in McBride, *Searching for John Ford*, 194–195.

36. Ibid., 271 (italics in the original).

37. Ibid., 271–273.

38. On the characterization of this period as part of Ford's Popular Front period, see McBride, *Searching for John Ford*, 309.

39. Ibid., 287.

40. Robert S. McElvaine, *The Great Depression, America, 1929–1941* (New York: Times Books, 1993), 219.

41. Lee Lourdeaux also notes this in his analysis of *Stagecoach*. However, he describes the use of religious symbols as "at best secretive and at worst clumsy." I would argue instead that this is indicative of how Ford incorporated signs of religious differences to elaborate the cultural worlds of his characters and films. See Lourdeaux, *Italian and Irish Filmmakers*, 120.

42. See, for instance, Gaylyn Studlar, "'Be a Proud, Glorified Dreg': Class, Gender and Frontier Democracy in 'Stagecoach,'" in *John Ford's "Stagecoach,"* ed. Barry Keith Grant (New York: Cambridge University Press, 2003), 132–157.

43. On Catholic universalism and national particularity, see Giles, *American Catholic Arts and Fiction*, 505–531.

44. Quoted in McBride, *Searching for John Ford*, 330.

45. "'Valley' Opens; Plans Set for Other New Films," *Motion Picture Herald*, 6 December 1941, 51.

46. Sara Kozloff, quoting Tag Gallagher and J. A. Place, also challenges overly simple interpretations and notes the "nuanced" treatment of the church offered by the film in her "1941: Movies on the Edge of War," in *American Cinema of the 1940s*, ed. Wheeler Winston Dixon (New Brunswick, N.J.: Rutgers University Press, 2006), 69–72.

47. Robert S. McElvaine interprets *How Green Was My Valley* as an example of what he calls the "moral economics," of thirties American culture and notes the role of religion in the film, in his *The Great Depression: America, 1929–1941* (New York: Times Books, 1994), 219–220.

48. On Ford's wartime service, see McBride, *Searching for John Ford*, 335–415.

49. On Donovan's and Wedemeyer's influence on Ford, see ibid., 336–341, 387–388.

50. On Ford and the MPA, see ibid., 371–373, 473.

51. Ibid., 472, 479–484.

52. Eyman, *Print the Legend*, 325–326; McBride, *Searching for John Ford*, 427, 441; Gallagher, *John Ford*, 261.

53. On the broader conservative Americanism in Hollywood movies in the 1940s and 1950s, see May, *Big Tomorrow*, 139–214.

54. See, for instance, Douglas Pye, "Genre and History: 'Fort Apache' and 'The Man Who Shot Liberty Valence,'" in *The Book of Westerns*, ed. Ian Cameron and Douglas Pye (New York: Continuum, 1996), 117–119; Gallagher, *John Ford*, 246–254.

55. See, for instance, Gallagher, *John Ford*, 324–338.

56. McBride, *Searching for John Ford*, 526.

57. See ibid., 623–626.

58. See, for instance, Gallagher, *John Ford*, 392; Cheyney Ryan, "Print the Legend: Violence and Recognition in *The Man Who Shot Liberty Valence*," in *Legal Reelism: Movies as Legal Texts*, ed. John Denvir (Urbana: University of Illinois Press, 1996), 23–43.

59. McBride also notes the Catholic confessional quality to Stoddard's action; see McBride, *Searching for John Ford*, 624.

60. Charles Ramirez Berg is also sensitive to this dimension of Ford's films; see Berg, "The Margin as Center," 75–101.

EPILOGUE. CATHOLICS AND THE AMERICAN COMMUNITY
AT THE TURN OF A NEW CENTURY

1. On Catholics and public life, see John McGreevy, *Catholicism and American Freedom: A History* (New York: W. W. Norton, 2003); David J. O'Brien, *Public Catholicism* (New York: Macmillan, 1989); Philip Gleason, "Pluralism, Democracy, and Catholicism: Religious Tensions," in Gleason, *Speaking of Diversity: Language and Ethnicity in Twentieth-Century America* (Baltimore, Md.: Johns Hopkins Press, 1992), 207–228. On Catholics and popular culture, see Mark S. Massa, *Catholics and American Culture: Fulton Sheen, Dorothy Day, and the Notre Dame Football Team* (New York: Crossroad Publishing, 1999); Richard Blake, *AfterImage: The Indelible Catholic Imagination of Six American Filmmakers* (Chicago: Loyola Press, 2000). The lack of attention to religion in cultural studies led the *American Quarterly*, journal of the American

Studies Association, to devote an entire issue to the question. See "Religion and Politics in the Contemporary United States," special issue, *American Quarterly* 59 (September 2007). There are exceptions to these tendencies, which have influenced my own study; see particularly James T. Fisher, *Dr. America: The Lives of Thomas A. Dooley, 1927–961* (Amherst: University of Massachusetts Press, 1997); Colleen McDannell, ed., *Catholics in the Movies* (New York: Oxford University Press, 2008).

2. Benedict Anderson, *Imagined Communities: Reflections on the Origin and Spread of Nationalism* (London: Verso Books, 1983).

3. Several essays in McDannell, *Catholics in the Movies,* address these seventies films: Carlo Rotella, "Praying for Stones Like This: The 'Godfather' Trilogy (1972, 1974, 1990)," 177–196; Colleen McDannell, "Catholic Horror: 'The Exorcist' (1973)," 197–225; Timothy J. Meagher, "Cops, Priests and the Decline of Irish America ('True Confessions,' 1981)," 227–249.

4. E. J. Dionne Jr., *Souled Out: Reclaiming Faith and Politics after the Religious Right* (Princeton, N.J.: Princeton University Press, 2008), 126–139.

5. See S. Brent Plate, ed., *Re-viewing the Passion: Mel Gibson's Film and Its Critics* (New York: Palgrave Macmillan, 2004); Kathleen E. Corley and Robert L. Webb, eds., *Jesus and Mel Gibson's "The Passion of the Christ": The Film, the Gospels and the Claims of History* (New York: Continuum, 2004).

BIBLIOGRAPHY

"The Altar Boy—Momentary Angel." *Life*, 23 March 1959, 103–106.

"The American Legion Takes New York City." *Life*, 4 October 1937, 23–28.

"The American Moral Consensus." *Life*, 26 December, 56–57.

American Quarterly, special issue, "Religion and Politics in the Contemporary United States," 59 (September 2007).

Anderson, Benedict R. *Imagined Communities: Reflections on the Origin and Spread of Nationalism*. London: Verso, 1983.

Anderson, Lindsay. *About John Ford . . .* London: Plexus, 1999.

Armstrong, Elizabeth, ed. *Birth of the Cool: California Art, Design, and Culture at Midcentury*. Orange County Museum of Art. New York: Prestel Publishing, 2007.

Augspurger, Michael. *An Economy of Abundant Beauty: "Fortune" Magazine and Depression America*. Ithaca, N.Y.: Cornell University Press, 2004.

Beecher, Lyman "A Plea for the West." In *God's New Israel: Religious Interpretations of American Destiny*, rev. and updated ed., edited by Conrad Cherry, 122–130. Chapel Hill: University of North Carolina Press, 1998.

Bell, Jonathan. *The Liberal State on Trial: The Cold War and American Politics in the Truman Years*. New York: Columbia University Press, 2004.

Berg, Charles Ramirez. "The Margin as Center: The Multicultural Dynamics of John Ford's Westerns." In *John Ford Made Westerns: Filming the Legend in the Sound Era*, edited by Gaylyn Studlar and Matthew Bernstein, 75–101. Bloomington: Indiana University Press, 2001.

"'Bernadette' to Continue at Advanced Admissions." *Motion Picture Herald*, 22 April 1944, 30.

"'Bernadette' Opens in New York." *Motion Picture Herald*, 29 January 1944, 37.

Bernstein, Matthew. *Walter Wanger: Hollywood Independent*. Minneapolis: University of Minnesota Press, 1994.

"Big Ad Campaign for 'Bernadette' in Toledo." *Motion Picture Herald*, 24 June 1944, 96.

"The Biggest U.S. Archdiocese." *Life*, 26 December 1955, 62–69.

"Biography by Sheen." *Time*, 1 January 1940, 33.

Black, Gregory D. *Hollywood Censored: Morality Codes, Catholics and the Movies*. New York: Cambridge University Press, 1994.

Blake, Richard A. *AfterImage: The Indelible Catholic Imagination of Six American Filmmakers*. Chicago: Loyola University Press, 2000.

Blanshard, Paul. *American Freedom and Catholic Power*. Boston: Beacon Press, 1949.

"Boys Town." *Film Daily*, 6 September 1938, 11.

"Boys Town." *Motion Picture Herald*, 10 September 1938, 55.

"Boys Town—One Man's Work." *Newsweek*, 19 September 1938, 23.

"Boys Town." *Time*, 12 September 1938, 45–46.

"'Boys Town' Gains Civic Approval." *Motion Picture Herald*, 12 November 1938, 68.

Brady, George Stuart. "NRA's Moral Code." *Sign*, December 1934, 273–275.

"The Brides of Christ." *Life*, 6 March 1944, 77–79.

Brinkley, Alan. *Voices of Protest: Huey Long, Father Coughlin and the Great Depression*. New York: Vintage Books, 1983.

———. *The End of Reform: New Deal Liberalism in Recession and War*. New York: Vintage Books, 1995.

"Britain's No. 1 Catholic Kisses Its Only Cardinal's Ring." *Life*, 31 January 1938, 52.

Broderick, Francis L. *Right Reverend New Dealer, John A. Ryan*. New York: Macmillan, 1963.

Bruens, A. "A Side Trip to Lourdes." *Ave Maria*, 13 February 1943, 199–202.

Bullitt, William C. "The World from Rome." *Life*, 4 September 1944, 94–109.

Burns, Jeffrey M., Ellen Skerrett, and Joseph M. White, eds. *Keeping Faith: European and Asian Catholic Immigrants*. Maryknoll, N.Y.: Orbis Books, 2000.

Butterfield, Roger. "Cardinal-Designate Spellman, Part I." *Life*, 21 January 1946, 100–112.

———. "Cardinal-Designate Spellman, Part II." *Life*, 28 January 1946, 87–98.

Cameron, Ardis, ed. *Looking for America: The Visual Production of Nation and People*. Malden, Mass.: Blackwell Publishing, 2005.

Carroll, Sidney. "Everything Happens to McCarey." *Esquire*, May 1943, 57, 140–142.

"Catholics and U.S. Democracy." *Life*, 21 December 1959, 30.

"The Catholics of Mexico Crawl to the Shrine of Guadalupe." *Life*, 10 January, 1938, 48–49.

Catholicus. Letter to editor. *Commonweal.*, 27 July 1934, 330.

Cavell, Stanley. *Pursuits of Happiness: The Hollywood Comedy of Remarriage*. Cambridge, Mass.: Harvard University Press, 1981.

Ceplair, Larry, and Steven Englund. *The Inquisition in Hollywood: Politics in the Film Community, 1930–1960*. Berkeley: University of California Press, 1983.

Chamberlain, John. "Philip Murray." *Life*, 11 February 1946, 78–90.

"Chicago's Perpetual Novena Is Now the Biggest U.S. Religious Service." *Life*, 7 March 1938, 54–55.

"Chinese School." *Life*, 23 November 1936, 24–25.

Christian Herald, August 1944, 47.

"Christmas." *Life*, 27 December 1943, 28.

"The Church." *Commonweal*, 2 April 1937, 635.

"City's Mayor Hague: Last of the Bosses, Not First of the Dictators." *Life*, 7 Feruary 1938, 44–51.

"Clean Up the Movies!" *America*, 24 June 1933, 265–266.

"A Cloistered Life of Devotion." *Life*, 26 December 1955, 119–123.

"Code's Birthday." *America*, 8 April 1933, 5.

Cohen, Lizabeth. *Making a New Deal: Industrial Workers in Chicago, 1919–1939*. New York: Cambridge University Press, 1990.

———. *A Consumers' Republic: The Politics of Mass Consumption in Postwar America.* New York: Vintage Books, 2004.

"Comics in Cassocks!!" *Extension*, August 1944, 10.

Connolly, Francis X. "Thunder on the Left." *America*, 2 June 1934, 184–186.

Coppa, Frank J. "Pope Pius XII and the Cold War: The Post-war Confrontation between Catholicism and Communism." In *Religion and the Cold War*, edited by Dianne Kirby, 50–66. New York: Palgrave Macmillan, 2003.

Corley, Kathleen E., and Robert L. Webb, eds. *Jesus and Mel Gibson's "The Passion of the Christ": The Film, the Gospels and the Claims of History*. New York: Continuum, 2004.

Cotter, Jerry. "Stage and Screen." *Sign*, February 1944, 416.

———. "Hollywood's Other Leo." *Sign*, December 1944, 236–237.

Couvares, Francis G. "Hollywood, Main Street, and the Church: Trying to Censor the Movies before the Production Code." In *Movie Censorship and American Culture*, edited by Francis G. Couvares, 129–158. Washington, D.C.: Smithsonian Institution Press, 1996.

Dant, Mrs. James, to Eric Johnston, 23 August 1946. MPAA, Breen Office Files, Box 2, Folder: Religion, Margaret Herrick Library, Academy of Motion Picture Arts and Sciences, Beverly Hills, Calif.

Davenport, Russell W. "A 'Life' Round Table on the Pursuit of Happiness." *Life*, 12 July 1948, 94–113.

Denning, Michael. *The Cultural Front: The Laboring of American Culture in the Twentieth Century*. New York: Verso, 1996.

Dionne Jr., E. J. *Souled Out: Reclaiming Faith and Politics after the Religious Right*. Princeton, N.J.: Princeton University Press, 2008.

Dixon, Dorothy N. "At Lourdes." *Commonweal*, 18 August 1933, 389.

Dixon, Wheeler Winton, ed. *American Cinema of the 1940s*. New Brunswick, N.J.: Rutgers University Press, 2006.

Doherty, Edward. "The Bishop and the Wolves." *Catholic Digest*, May 1938, 1–6.

Doherty, Thomas. *Projections of War: Hollywood, American Culture and World War II.* New York: Columbia University Press, 1993.

———. *Pre-Code Hollywood: Sex, Immorality and Insurrection in American Cinema, 1930–1934.* New York: Columbia University Press, 1999.

Dolan, Jay. *The American Catholic Experience: A History from Colonial Times to the Present.* Garden City, N.Y.: Doubleday, 1985.

"The Door Opens on a Holy Year." *Life*, 9 January 1950, 26–29.

Doss, Erika, ed. *Looking at "Life" Magazine.* Washington, D.C.: Smithsonian Institution Press, 2001.

Dulles, John Foster. "A Righteous Faith." *Life*, 28 December 1942, 49–51.

———. "Soviet Foreign Policy, Part I." *Life*, 3 June 1946, 112–122.

———. "Soviet Foreign Policy, Part II" *Life*, 10 June 1946, 119–130.

Dunne, Philip. *Take Two: A Life in Movies and Politics.* New York: Limelight Editions, 1992.

Eastman, Joel W. "From Declining Seaport to Liberty City: Portland during Depression and War." In *Creating Portland: History and Place in Northern New England*, edited by Joseph A. Conforti. Durham: University of New Hampshire Press, 2005.

"An 11-Year-Old-Girl Is Made a Saint." *Life*, 17 July 1950, 107–113.

Ellwood, Robert S. *The Fifties Spiritual Marketplace: American Religion in a Decade of Conflict.* New Brunswick, N.J.: Rutgers University Press, 1997.

Erenberg, Lewis A., and Susan E. Hirsch. *The War in American Culture: Society and Consciousness in World War II.* Chicago: University of Chicago Press, 1996.

"Eye-Intriguing Displays." *Motion Picture Herald*, 22 April 1944, 46.

Eyman, Scott. *Print the Legend: The Life and Times of John Ford.* New York: Simon and Schuster, 1999.

Farber, Manny. "Fathers and Song." *New Republic*, 8 May 1944, 629.

Ferraro, Thomas J. "Boys to Men: 'Angels with Dirty Faces' (1938)." In *Catholics in the Movies*, edited by Colleen McDannell, 59–82. New York: Oxford University Press, 2008.

Fey, Harold E. "Can Catholicism Win America?" *Christian Century*, 29 November 1944 to 17 January 1945.

Fields, Kathleen Riley. "Bishop Fulton J. Sheen: An American Catholic Response to the Twentieth Century." Ph.D. diss., University of Notre Dame; Ann Arbor, Mich.: UMI, 1988.

"Fireside Chat in Reverse." *Catholic World*, December 1938, 260–261.

"First U.S. Troops Land in Greenland to Prepare Main Army and Air Base." *Life*, 18 August 1941, 26.

Fisher, James T. *Dr. America: The Lives of Thomas A. Dooley, 1937–1961*. Amherst: University of Massachusetts Press, 1997.

———. "American Religion since 1945." In *A Companion to Post-1945 America*, edited by Jean-Christophe Agnew and Roy Rosenzweig, 44–63. New York: Blackwell, 2002.

Fisher, James Terrence. *The Catholic Counter-culture in America, 1933–1962*. Chapel Hill: University of North Carolina Press, 1989.

Flanagan, E. J. "The Story behind 'Boys Town.'" *Photoplay*, November 1938, 22–23, 85.

Flanagan, Edward J. "I Meet Spencer Tracy." *Catholic Digest*, November 1938, 39.

Fones-Woolf, Elizabeth. *Selling Free Enterprise: The Business Assault on Labor and Liberalism, 1945–1960*. Urbana: University of Illinois Press, 1994.

Foreman, Joel, ed. *The Other Fifties: Interrogating Midcentury American Icons*. Urbana: University of Illinois Press, 1997.

Fortin, Roger. *Faith and Action: A History of the Catholic Archdiocese of Cincinnati, 1821–1996*. Columbus: Ohio State University Press, 2002.

Franchot, Jenny. *Roads to Rome: The Antebellum Protestant Encounter with Catholicism*. Berkeley: University of California Press, 1994.

Friedman, Lester D. *Unspeakable Images: Ethnicity and the American Cinema*. Urbana: University of Illinois Press, 1991.

"The Gains of Labor." *America*, 2 September 1933, 505–506.

Gallaher, Tag. *John Ford: The Man and His Films*. Berkeley: University of California Press, 1986.

Gallup, George H. *The Gallup Poll: Public Opinion, 1935–1971*, vol. 2, *1949–1958*. New York: Random House, 1972.

Gannon, Mary Margaret. "Dr. Fulton Sheen, Philosopher and Catholic-Hour Celebrity." *Queen's Work* 23 (April 1931): 1.

Gehring, Wes D. *Leo McCarey: From Marx to McCarthy*. Lanham, Md.: Scarecrow Press, 2005.

Gerstle, Gary. "The Working Class Goes to War." In *The War in American Culture: Society and Consciousness during World War II*, edited by Lewis A. Erenberg and Susan E. Hirsch, 105–127. Chicago: University of Chicago Press, 1996.

"Get 'Bernadette' Portraits." *Motion Picture Herald*, 8 April 1944, 42.

"'Getting Tough' with Russia." *Life*, 18 March 1946.

Giddins, Gary. *Bing Crosby: A Pocketful of Dreams—The Early Years, 1903–1940*. Boston: Little, Brown, 2001.

Giles, Paul. *American Catholic Arts and Fiction: Culture, Ideology, Aesthetics*. New York: Cambridge University Press, 1992.

Gleason, Philip. *Speaking of Diversity: Language and Ethnicity in Twentieth-Century America*. Baltimore, Md.: Johns Hopkins University Press, 1992.

———. *Contending with Modernity: Catholic Higher Education in the Twentieth Century*. New York: Oxford University Press, 1995.

"God's Underground." *Life*, 18 April 1949, 34.

"'Going My Way' Heads for New Paramount Record." *Motion Picture Herald*, 8 July 1944, 39.

Goldschmidt, Henry, and Elizabeth McAlister, eds. *Race, Nation, and Religions in the Americas*. New York: Oxford University Press, 2004.

Gordon, Mary. "Father Chuck: A Reading of 'Going My Way' and 'The Bells of St. Mary's', or Why Priests Made Us Crazy." In "Catholic Lives/Contemporary America," special issue, *South Atlantic Quarterly* 93 (Summer 1994): 591–601.

Goulding, Stuart D. "Indictment." *Commonweal*, 1 September 1933, 422–424.

"Governor Roosevelt's Sermon." *America*, 15 October 1932, 31.

Grant, Barry Keith, ed. *John Ford's "Stagecoach."* New York: Cambridge University Press, 2003.

Greene, Graham. "The Assumption of Mary." *Life*, 30 October 1950, 50–58.

———. "The Pope Who Remains a Priest." *Life*, 24 September 1951, 146–162.

Griffith, Robert. "Forging America's Postwar Order: Domestic Politics and Political Economy in the Age of Truman." In *The Truman Presidency*, edited by Michael J. Lacey, 57–88. New York: Cambridge University Press, 1989.

Halsey, William M. *The Survival of American Innocence: Catholicism in an Era of Disillusionment, 1920–1940*. Notre Dame, Ind.: University of Notre Dame Press, 1980.

Harris, Ruth. *Lourdes: Body and Spirit in the Secular Age*. New York: Viking, 1999.

Hartung, Philip T. "Answer to Dead End." *Commonweal*, 23 September 1938, 561.

———. "The Song." *Commonweal*, 11 February 1944, 421.

———. "Your Way Is My Way." *Commonweal*, 28 April 1944, 41.

Harvey, James. *Romantic Comedy in Hollywood from Lubitsch to Sturges*. New York: Knopf, 1987.

Healey, Joseph F. "The Catholic Daily." *Commonweal*, 1 February 1933, 371–372.

Heffron, Edward J. "Ten Years of the 'Catholic Hour.'" *Ecclesiastical Review* 102 (March 1940): 238–249.

Heflen, M. "Professional Catholic Theater." *America*, 5 February 1938, 426.

———. "The Catholic Dramatic Movement." *Commonweal*, 25 February 1938, 497.

Heineman, Kenneth J. *A Catholic New Deal: Religion and Reform in Depression Pittsburgh*. University Park: Pennsylvania State University Press, 1999.

Herberg, Will. *Protestant-Catholic-Jew: An Essay in American Religious Sociology*, rev. ed. Garden City, N.Y.: Anchor Books, 1960.

Herzstein, Robert Edwin. *Henry R. Luce: A Political Portrait of the Man Who Created the American Century*. New York: Charles Scribner's Sons, 1994.

Higham, John. *Strangers in the Land: Patterns of American Nativism, 1860–1925*, 2nd ed. New Brunswick, N.J.: Rutgers University Press, 1988.

Hilmes, Michelle. *Radio Voices: American Broadcasting, 1922–1952*. Minneapolis: University of Minnesota Press, 1997.

Hilmes, Michelle, and Jason Loviglio, eds. *Radio Reader: Essays in the Cultural History of Radio*. New York: Routledge, 2002.

Holland, Jessica. Interview with Andrew Heiskell. Columbia University Libraries Oral History Research Office: Notable New Yorkers, 1987. http://www.columbia .edu/cu/lweb/digital/collections/nny/heiskella/transcripts/heiskella_1_17_802 .html. Accessed 13 December 2006.

Hommel, Alfred W. "The Catholic Press." *Commonweal*, 21 December 1932, 217.

"Honor Pupils Selected on 'Boys Town' Tie-In." *Motion Picture Herald*, 24 December 1938, 57.

Hudnut-Beumler, James. *Looking for God in the Suburbs: The Religion of the American Dream and Its Critics, 1945–1965*. New Brunswick, N.J.: Rutgers University Press, 1994.

Hughes, Emmet John. "The 'Strange, Mute Magic' of Pius XII: The Impact of a Shy, Scholarly Pope." *Life*, 26 December 1955, 158–160.

Hutchinson, Paul. "Does Europe Face Holy War?" *Life*, 23 September 1946, 61–68.

"Ireland: A New Flag Brings Hope to an Old and Pious Land." *Life*, 24 July 1939, 56–63.

"An Italian Family in America." *Life*, 5 October 1953, 135–151.

"Italy's Victory." *Life*, 3 May 1948, 38.

Jessup, John K., ed. *The Ideas of Henry Luce* New York: Atheneum, 1969.

"The Jesuits in America." *Life*, 11 October 1954, 134–148.

Johnson, Mary Ann, ed. *The Many Faces of Hull-House: The Photographs of Wallace Kirkland*. Urbana: University of Illinois Press, 1989.

Kane, Paula. *Separatism and Subculture: Boston Catholicism, 1900–1920*. Chapel Hill: University of North Carolina Press, 1994.

———. "Jews and Catholics Converge: 'The Song of Bernadette' (1943)." In *Catholics in the Movies*, edited by Colleen McDannell, 83–105. New York: Oxford University Press, 2008.

Kass, Robert. "Film and Television." *Catholic World*, May 1952, 142–146.

Kendall, Elizabeth. *The Runaway Bride: Hollywood Romantic Comedy of the 1930s*. New York: Cooper Square Press, 2002.

Kent, Peter C. "The Lonely Cold War of Pope Pius XII." In *Religion and the Cold War*, edited by Dianne Kirby, 67–76. New York: Palgrave Macmillan, 2003.

Keyser, Les, and Barbara Keyser. *Hollywood and the Catholic Church: The Image of Roman Catholicism in American Movies*. Chicago: Loyola University Press, 1984.

Kirby, Dianne, ed. *Religion and the Cold War*. New York: Palgrave Macmillan, 2003.

"Knights of Columbus in 75th Year." *Life*, 27 May 1957, 54–65.

Kozloff, Sarah. "1941: Movies on the Edge of War." In *American Cinema of the 1940s*, edited by Wheeler Winston Dixon, 48–73. New Brunswick, N.J.: Rutgers University Press, 2006.

Kozol, Wendy. *'Life's' America: Family and Nation in Postwar Photojournalism*. Philadelphia: Temple University Press, 1994.

"The Kremlin and the Vatican." *Life*, 14 February 1944, 32.

Lane, Clem. "How to Handle Catholic News." *Commonweal*, 3 November 1933, 12–14.

Lavery, Emmet. "The Catholic Theater New Thought on Old Dream." *America*, 5 December 1936, 197–199.

―――. "The Curtain Goes Up on the Catholic Theater." *America*, 6 March 1937, 508–509.

―――. "The Baby Walks!" *America*, 25 September 1937, 593–594.

―――. "Theatre Dividends." *Commonweal*, 22 October 1937, 591–593.

Leff, Leonard J., and Jerold L. Simmons. *The Dame in the Kimono: Hollywood Censorship and the Production Code*, 2nd ed. Lexington: University of Kentucky Press, 2001.

"Let Catholics Take Warning!" *Commonweal*, 5 April 1933, 617–619.

"Life Goes to a Hero's Homecoming." *Life*, 11 October 1943, 130–135.

"Life Goes to a Party." *Life*, 21 June 1937, 88–92.

Lipsitz, George. "The Meaning of Memory: Family, Class and Ethnicity in Early Network Television." In *Time Passages: Collective Memory and American Popular Culture*. Minneapolis: University of Minnesota Press, 1990.

"'Little Italy' Cloaks Its Healing Saint in Dollars." *Life*, 6 September 1937, 71–72.

Lonergan, William I. "The Key to National Reform." *America*, 19 January 1935, 354.

Lourdeaux, Lee. *Italian and Irish Filmmakers in America: Ford, Capra, Coppola and Scorsese*. Philadelphia: Temple University Press, 1990.

Luce, Henry R. "The American Century." *Life*, 17 February 1941, 61–65.

Lynch, Christopher Owen. *Selling Catholicism: Bishop Sheen and the Power of Television*. Lexington: University Press of Kentucky, 1998.

"A Man of Love Fights Communists in Italy." *Life*, 22 March 1948, 37.

Marie, Rose. "Lourdes in Springtime." *Commonweal*, 39 March 1934, 600–601.

Martin, Pete. "Going His Way." *Saturday Evening Post*, 30 November 1946, 12–13, 64–66, 68–70.

Marty, Martin. *Modern American Religion*, vol. 3, *Under God, Indivisible, 1941–1960*. Chicago: University of Chicago Press, 1996.

Massa, Mark. *Catholics and American Culture: Fulton Sheen, Dorothy Day and the Notre Dame Football Team*. New York: Crossroad Publishing, 1999.

Maxwell, Agnes K. "Advertising Catholic Principles." *Commonweal*, 8 January 1935, 431.

May, Elaine Tyler. *Homeward Bound: American Families in the Cold War Era*. New York: Basic Books, 1988.

May, Grace L. "Finding Faith at Lourdes," pt. 1. *Ave Maria*, 6 June 1931, 705–709.

———. "Finding Faith at Lourdes," pt. 2. *Ave Maria*, 13 June 1931, 745–750.

May, Lary. *Screening Out the Past: The Birth of Mass Culture and the Motion Picture Industry*. Chicago: University of Chicago Press, 1980.

———, ed. *Recasting America: Culture and Politics in the Age of Cold War*. Chicago: University of Chicago Press, 1989.

———. *The Big Tomorrow: Hollywood and the Politics of the American Way*. Chicago: University of Chicago Press, 2000.

Mazur, Eric Michael. "Going My Way?: Crosby and Catholicism on the Road to America." In *"Going My Way": Bing Crosby and American Culture*, edited by Ruth Prigozy and Walter Raubicheck, 17–33. Rochester, N.Y.: University of Rochester Press, 2007.

McAlister, Melanie. *Epic Encounters: Culture, Media and US Interests in the Middle East, 1945–2000*. Berkeley: University of California Press, 2001.

McAllister, Joseph A. "A Haven of the Afflicted." *Ave Maria*, 9 November 1935, 592–596.

McBride, Joseph. *Searching for John Ford: A Life*. New York: St. Martin's Press, 2001.

McCaffrey, Lawrence J. "'Going My Way' and Irish-American Catholicism: Myth and Reality." *New Hibernia Review* 4 (Autumn 2000): 119–217.

McCarey, Leo. "Comedy and a Touch of Cuckoo." *Extension*, November 1944, 5, 34.

McDannell, Colleen. "Catholic Horror: 'The Exorcist' (1973)." In *Catholics in the Movies*, edited by Colleen McDannell, 197–225. New York: Oxford University Press, 2008.

———, ed. *Catholics in the Movies*. New York: Oxford University Press, 2008.

McElvaine, Robert S. *The Great Depression: America, 1929–1941*. New York: Times Books, 1993.

McGowan, Raymond A. "Government and Social Justice." *Catholic Mind*, 8 June 1938, 222–226.

McGrath, Owen A. "Catholic Action's Big Opportunity." *Ecclesiastical Review* 91 (September 1934): 280–287.

McGreevy, John T. *Parish Boundaries: The Catholic Encounter with Race in the Twentieth-Century Urban North*. Chicago: University of Chicago Press, 1996.

———. "Bronx Miracle." *American Quarterly* 52 (September 2000): 405–443.

———. *Catholicism and American Freedom: A History*. New York: W. W. Norton, 2003.

McKeever, Jerome M. "The McCarey Touch: The Life and Films of Leo McCarey."
Ph.D. diss., Case Western Reserve; Ann Arbor, Mich.: UMI, 2000.

McMahan, Leonard A. "This Business of the Movies." *Sign*, January 1939, 331.

McNicholas, John T. "Justice and the Present Crisis." *Catholic Mind*, 22 October
1931, 473–481.

———. "The Episcopal Committee and the Problem of Evil Motion Pictures."
Ecclesiastical Review 91(August 1934): 113–119.

McShane, Joseph M. *Sufficiently Radical: Catholicism, Progressivism and the Bishops'
Program of 1919*. Washington, D.C.: Catholic University of America Press, 1986.

Meagher, Timothy J. "Cops, Priests and the Decline of Irish America, 'True
Confessions' (1981)." In *Catholics in the Movies*, edited by Colleen McDannell,
227–249. New York: Oxford University Press, 2008.

"The Methodists." *Life*, 10 November 1947, 33.

"Mexico: Can a Socialist at Home Be a Good Neighbor Abroad?" *Life*, 11 April 1938,
50–59.

"Microphone Missionary." *Time*, 14 April 1952, 72–79.

"Modern Miracle." *Time*, 8 June 1942, 90.

"Monsignor's Tenth. *Time*, 11 March 1940, 60–61.

Mooney, Edward. "The American Tradition." *Catholic Mind*, 8 June 1938, 215–220.

Mooring, William H. "What McCarey Forgot to Tell." *Extension*, November 1944, 5.

Morgan, David. "The Image of Religion in American 'Life.'" In *Looking at "Life"
Magazine*, edited by Erika Doss, 139–157. Washington, D.C.: Smithsonian
Institution Press, 2001.

Morris, Charles R. *American Catholic: The Saints and Sinners Who Built America's
Most Powerful Church*. New York: Vintage Books, 1997.

Motion Picture Herald, 12 November 1938, 64.

"Movie of the Week: 'Going My Way.'" *Life*, 1 May 1944, 69.

Munby, Jonathan. *Public Enemies, Public Heroes: Screening the Gangster from "Little
Caesar" to "Touch of Evil."* Chicago: University of Chicago Press, 1999.

Mundelein, George. "Catholic Action for Social Justice." *Catholic Mind*, 8 February
1938, 47–49.

Murphy, Eugene P. "The Great Tridium." *America*, 20 April 1935, 33–34.

Murray, Augustine C. "Fiesta in Los Angeles." *Commonweal*, 3 October 1931, 612–613.

Murray, John Courtney. "Special Catholic Challenges." *Life*, 26 December 1955,
144–146.

———. *We Hold These Truths: Catholic Reflections on the American Proposition*.
Kansas City, Mo.: Sheed and Ward, 1988.

Nadel, Alan. *Containment Culture: American Narrative, Postmodernism and the
Atomic Age*. Durham, N.C.: Duke University Press, 1995.

Newcomb, Horace. "Meaningful Difference in 1950s Television." In *The Other Fifties: Interrogating Midcentury American Icons*, edited by Joel Foreman, 103–123. Urbana: University of Illinois Press, 1997.

"The New Deal." *America*, 24 June 1933, 266.

Newman, Larry. "Bishop Sheen and the TV Camera." *Catholic Digest*, May 1952, 115–117.

"Newspictures of the Week." *Life*, 2 May 1938, 17.

Noble, David W. *The End of American History: Democracy, Capitalism and the Metaphor of Two Worlds in Anglo-American Historical Writing, 1880–1980*. Minneapolis: University of Minnesota Press, 1985.

———. *The Death of a Nation: American Culture and the End of Exceptionalism*. Minneapolis: University of Minnesota Press, 2002.

"Nun, President and Poet." *Life*, 10 June 1957 129–132.

"Nuns in a Musical Frolic." *Life*, 6 August 1956, 115–116.

O'Brien, David J. *American Catholics and Social Reform: The New Deal Years*. New York: Oxford University Press, 1968.

O'Donnell, T. Letter to editor. *Commonweal*, 27 July 1934, 330.

O'Neil, William J. "A Planned Theater." *Commonweal*, 18 May 1934, 61–62.

Orsi, Robert Anthony. *The Madonna of 115th Street: Faith and Community in Italian Harlem, 1880–1950*. New Haven, Conn.: Yale University Press, 1985.

———. "'Mildred, is it fun to be a cripple?': The Culture of Suffering in Mid-Twentieth-Century American Catholicism." *South Atlantic Quarterly: Catholic Lives/Contemporary America* 93 (Summer 1994): 547–590.

———. *Thank You St. Jude: Women's Devotions of the Patron Saint of Hopeless Causes*. New Haven, Conn.: Yale University Press, 1996.

"Over the Top." *America*, 16 September 1933, 553–554.

"Parochial High School." *Life*, 19 January 1954, 63–70.

Parsons, Wilfrid. "The Roosevelt Revolution." *America*, 6 January 1934, 322–324.

"Peace of God in Cleveland." *America*, 5 October 1935, 604.

"'People's Bishop' Has a Silver Jubilee." *Life*, 18 May 1953, 63–66.

Petrie, John Clement. "Is Catholicism 'Going My Way'?" *Christian Century*, 4 October 1944, 1132–1134.

"The Picture of the Year: 'David and Bathsheba.'" *Christian Herald*, March 1952, 101.

"Picture of the Year: 'Quo Vadis.'" *Christian Herald*, March 1953, 97.

Pike, James A. "Should a Catholic Be President?" *Life*, 21 December 1959, 78–85.

"Pious Workers Go on a Retreat." *Life*, 2 August 1937, 70–74.

P. J. C. "What the Public Wants." *Ave Maria*, 7 April 1934, 437.

Plate, S. Brent, ed. *Re-viewing the Passion: Mel Gibson's Film and Its Critics*. New York: Palgrave Macmillan, 2004.

"Pluralism—National Menace." *Christian Century*, 13 June 1951, 701–703.

Powers, Murray. "Catholic Publicity." *Commonweal*, 14 September 1934, 461–463.

"The President." *Commonweal*, 15 March 1933, 533–535.

"The President's Album." *Life*, 23 November 1936, 27–28.

"Priest to the Campesinos." *Life*, 14 July 1952, 97–103.

Prigozy, Ruth, and Walter Raubicheck, eds. *Going My Way: Bing Crosby and American Culture*. Rochester, N.Y.: University of Rochester Press, 2007.

Proceedings of the Sixth National Conference: Laymen's Retreat Movement in the United States of America. Chicago, n.d..

Pye, Douglas. "Genre and History: 'Fort Apache' and 'The Man Who Shot Liberty Valence.'" In *The Book of Westerns*, edited by Ian Cameron and Douglas Pye. 111–123. New York: Continuum, 1996.

Ramsaye, Terry. "Bernadette." *Motion Picture Herald*, 29 January 1949, 7.

"Reconversion." *Time*, 22 October 1945, 60.

"Recovery and Reformation." *Commonweal*, 17 November 1933, 57–58.

Reeves, Thomas C. *America's Bishop: The Life and Times of Fulton J. Sheen*. San Francisco: Encounter Books, 2001.

"Religion in Politics." *Commonweal*, 12 October 1932, 545–546.

"Rev. Daniel A. Lord to Succeed Dr. Sheen on 'Catholic Hour' Broadcast." *Catholic Action*, April 1934, 18.

Rotella, Carlo. "Praying for Stones Like This: The 'Godfather' Trilogy (1972, 1974, 1990)." In *Catholics in the Movies*, edited by Colleen McDannell, 177–196. New York: Oxford University Press, 2008.

Rubin, Martin. "Mr. Ford and Mr. Rogers: The Will Rogers Trilogy." *Film Comment* 10 (January–February 1974): 54–57.

Ryan, Cheyney. "Print the Legend: Violence and Recognition in *The Man Who Shot Liberty Valence*." In *Legal Reelism: Movies as Legal Texts*, edited by John Denvir, 23–43. Urbana: University of Illinois Press, 1996.

Ryan, John A. "Economics and Ethics." *Commonweal*, 6 October 1933, 521–523.

———. "Are We on the Right Road?" *Commonweal*, 12 October 1934, 547–549.

———. *The Catholic Teaching on Our Industrial System*. Washington, D.C.: National Council of Catholic Men, 1934.

Schaeffer, George, to Leo McCarey, 30 June 1939. Going My Way Letters and Other Correspondence File, Leo McCarey Collection, American Film Institute, Los Angeles.

Schwarz, Benjamin. "California Cool." *Atlantic Monthly*, March 2008, 87–89.

Sheen, Fulton J. *Manifestations of Christ*. Washington, D.C.: National Council of Catholic Men, 1932.

———. *Hymn of the Conquered*. Washington, D.C.: National Council of Catholic Men, 1933.

———. *The Divine Romance*. New York: D. Appleton-Century, 1940.

———. *Treasure in Clay: The Autobiography of Fulton J. Sheen*. Garden City, N.Y.: Doubleday, 1980.

———. *The Prodigal World*. Washington, D.C.: National Council of Catholic Men, n.d.

Sherry, Michael. *In the Shadow of War: The United State since the 1930s*. New Haven, Conn.: Yale University Press, 1995.

Sherry, Norman. *The Life of Graham Greene*, vol. 2, *1939–1955*. New York, Viking, 1994.

Shohat, Ella. "Ethnicities-in-Relation: Toward a Multicultural Reading of American Cinema." In *Unspeakable Images: Ethnicity and the American Cinema*, edited by Lester D. Friedman, 215–250. Urbana: University of Illinois Press, 1991.

"Showmen Promotions." *Motion Picture Herald*, 1 April 1944, 52.

"Sidewalk Prayers to Governor Save Four out of Six Murderers." *Life*, 18 January 1937, 18.

Silver, Charles. "Leo McCarey: From Marx to McCarthy." *Film Comment* 9 (September–October 1973): 8–11.

Skouras, Spyros P. "Religion and the Movies." *Christian Herald*, June 1952, 71.

Smith, Anthony Burke. "America's Favorite Priest: 'Going My Way' (1944)." In *Catholics in the Movies*, edited by Colleen McDannell, 107–126. New York: Oxford University Press, 2008.

Smith, Margaret. "Laughter, Redemption, Subversion in Eight Films by Leo McCarey." *CineAction* (Summer–Fall 1990): 84–90.

Smith, Terry. "Life-Style Modernity: Making Modern America." In *Looking at "Life" Magazine*, edited by Erika Doss, 25–39. Washington, D.C.: Smithsonian Institution Press, 2001.

Sollors, Werner. *Beyond Ethnicity: Consent and Descent in American Literature*. New York: Oxford University Press, 1986.

"Some Sure-Fire Promotions." *Motion Picture Herald*, 20 May 1944, 64.

Spigel, Lynn. *Make Way for TV: Television and the Family Ideal in Postwar America*. Chicago: University of Chicago Press, 1992.

Starr, Kevin. *The Dream Endures: California Enters the 1940s*. New York: Oxford University Press, 1997.

Steele, Richard W. "The War on Intolerance: The Reformulation of American Nationalism, 1939–1941." *Journal of American Ethnic History* 9 (Fall 1989): 9–35.

Stowell, Peter. *John Ford*. Boston: Twayne Publishers, 1986.

Studlar, Gaylyn. "Sacred Duties, Poetic Passions: John Ford and the Issue of Femininity in the Western." In *John Ford Made Westerns: Filming the Legend in the Sound Era*, edited by Gaylyn Studlar and Matthew Bernstein, 44–74. Bloomington: Indiana University Press, 2001.

———. "'Be a Proud, Glorified Dreg': Class, Gender and Frontier Democracy in 'Stagecoach.'" In *John Ford's "Stagecoach,"* edited by Barry Keith Grant, 132–157. New York: Cambridge University Press, 2003.

Studlar, Gaylyn, and Matthew Bernstein, eds. *John Ford Made Westerns: Filming the Legend in the Sound Era*. Bloomington: Indiana University Press, 2001.

Sullivan, Henry B. "The Catholic Press." *Commonweal*, 22 February 1933, 468.

Swanberg, W. A. *Luce and His Empire*. New York: Scribner, 1972.

Tentler, Leslie Woodcock. *Seasons of Grace: A History of the Archdiocese of Detroit*. Detroit, Mich.: Wayne State University Press, 1990.

"Thanks for Everything." *America*, 21 April 1934, 28.

Time, 1 May 1944, 90.

"Toasts within the Month." *Sign*, March 1937, 453.

"Trappist Monastery." *Life*, 23 May 1949, 84–89.

Treat, Roger L. *Bishop Sheil and the CYO*. New York: Messner, 1951.

U.S. Congress. House of Representatives. Interstate and Foreign Commerce Committee. *Investigation on Radio and Television Programs: Hearing before a Subcommittee of the Committee on Interstate and Foreign Commerce*. 82nd Cong., 2nd sess., 25 September 1952. H.Res. 278, 323–357.

"U.S. Remembers Pearl Harbor Day with Ships and Prayers." *Life*, 21 December 1942, 34–35.

"'Valley' Opens; Plans Set for Other New Films." *Motion Picture Herald*, 6 December 1941, 51.

"Veterans Associations Tied to '69th' Dates." *Motion Picture Herald*, 24 February 1940, 56.

Viera, Mark A. *Sin in Soft Focus: Pre-Code Hollywood*. New York: Harry N. Abrams, 1999.

Walen, Joseph C. "A Ball, a Bat—and God." *Catholic Digest*, March 1937, 72–77.

Wall, Wendy L. *Inventing the "American Way": The Politics of Consensus from the New Deal to the Civil Rights Movement*. New York: Oxford University Press, 2008.

Walsh, Frank. *Sin and Censorship: The Catholic Church and the Motion Picture Industry*. New Haven, Conn.: Yale University Press, 1996.

Ward, Leo R. "Things of Earth at Lourdes." *Ave Maria*, 13 February 1937, 201–203.

Weisenfeld, Judith. *Hollywood Be Thy Name: African American Religion in American Film, 1929–1949*. Berkeley: University of California Press, 2007.

Werfel, Franz. "Writing 'Bernadette.'" *Commonweal*, 29 May 1942, 125–126.

Westbrook, Robert B. "Fighting for the American Family." In *The Power of Culture: Critical Essays in American History*, edited by Richard Wightman Fox and T. J. Jackson Lears, 195–221. Chicago: University of Chicago Press, 1993.

"What Will Happen Next?" *America*, 19 March 1938, 564–565.

Windeatt, Mary Fabyan. "The Catholic Play—Where Is It?" *Commonweal*, 12 March 1937, 557–558.

Winokur, Mark. *American Laughter: Immigrants, Ethnicity and 1930s Hollywood Film Comedy*. New York: St. Martin's Press, 1996.

Wood, Robin. "From Ruggles to Rally; or America, America! The Strange Career of Leo McCarey." *Film International* 5 (May 2007): 30–34.

"Worker's Loss." *Newsweek*, 22 October 1945, 100.

"Young Father Crosby." *Newsweek*, 15 May 1944, 78.

Zawisch, Carla. "The Crowds at Lourdes." *Catholic Digest*, January 1944, 45–48.

INDEX